The Scarlet Letter

A Kaplan SAT Score-Raising Classic

The Scarlet Letter

A Kaplan SAT Score-Raising Classic

By Nathaniel Hawthorne

KAPLAN PUBLISHING

New York · Chicago

This publication is designed to provide accurate and authoritative information in regard to the subject matter covered. It is sold with the understanding that the publisher is not engaged in rendering legal, accounting, or other professional service. If legal advice or other expert assistance is required, the services of a competent professional should be sought.

Editorial Director: Jennifer Farthing
Editor: Caryn Yilmaz
Production Editor: Caitlin Ostrow
Production Artist: John Christensen
Cover Designer: Carly Schnur

© 2006 by Kaplan, Inc.

Published by Kaplan Publishing, a division of Kaplan, Inc.
888 Seventh Ave.
New York, NY 10106

Additional material copyright © 2006 by Kaplan, Inc.

Printed in the United States of America

November 2006
10 9 8 7 6 5 4

ISBN-13: 978-1-4195-4220-6
ISBN-10: 1-4195-4220-6

Library of Congress Cataloging-in-Publication Data is available.

Kaplan Publishing books are available at special quantity discounts to use for sales promotions, employee premiums, or educational purposes. Please call our Special Sales Department to order or for more information at 800-621-9621, ext. 4444, e-mail kaplanpubsales@kaplan.com, or write to Kaplan Publishing, 30 South Wacker Drive, Suite 2500, Chicago, IL 60606-7481.

❧ How To Use This Book ❧

Not only is the classic novel, *The Scarlet Letter*, filled with secrets and revenge—it's also filled with SAT words! Now Kaplan makes it as easy as 1-2-3 for you to learn these vocabulary words as you read the stories.

On the right-hand pages you'll find the story of *The Scarlet Letter* with words **bolded** throughout. These bolded words are frequently found on the SAT. On the left-hand pages, Kaplan defines these SAT words, as well as gives you the part of speech, pronunciation, and synonyms for each word—everything you need to know to improve your vocabulary and to ace the SAT.

Some of the most challenging vocabulary words found in *The Scarlet Letter* aren't likely to appear on the SAT, but we thought you might want to learn those, too. That's why we've <u>underlined</u> them throughout the text and added their definitions to a glossary at the end of the book. After all—you never know where they might pop up next! In this edition you will also find an index of all SAT words at the end of the book.

So what are you waiting for? Start reading!

❧ Table of Contents ❧

DISINCLINED (dihs ihn <u>kliend</u>) *adj.*
unwilling
Synonyms: averse, reluctant

IMPULSE (<u>ihm</u> puhls) *n.*
sudden tendency, inclination
Synonyms: urge, whim

INDULGENT (ihn <u>duhl</u> jehnt) *adj.*
lenient, tolerant
Synonyms: permissive, easygoing, compliant

QUIETUDE (<u>kwie</u> eh tood) *n.*
peace or tranquility
Synonyms: calm, ease, contentment, serenity

INDULGE (ihn <u>duhlj</u>) *v.* **-ing,-ed.**
to give in to a craving or desire
Synonyms: humor, gratify, allow, pamper

DECOROUS (<u>deh</u> kuhr uhs) (deh <u>kohr</u> uhs) *adj.*
proper, tasteful, socially correct
Synonyms: polite, courteous, appropriate

The Custom House

It is a little remarkable that—though **disinclined** to talk over much of myself and my affairs at the fireside, and to my personal friends—an autobiographical **impulse** should twice in my life have taken possession of me, in addressing the public. The first time was three or four years since, when I favored the reader—inexcusably, and for no earthly reason, that either the **indulgent** reader or the intrusive author could imagine—with a description of my way of life in the deep **quietude** of an Old Manse. And now—because, beyond my deserts, I was happy enough to find a listener or two on the former occasion—I again seize the public by the button, and talk of my three years' experience in a Custom House. The example of the famous "P.P., Clerk of this Parish," was never more faithfully followed. The truth seems to be, however, that when he casts his leaves forth upon the wind, the author addresses, not the many who will fling aside his volume, or never take it up, but the few who will understand him, better than most of his schoolmates or lifemates. Some authors, indeed, do far more than this, and **indulge** themselves in such confidential depths of revelation as could fittingly be addressed, only and exclusively, to the one heart and mind of perfect sympathy; as if the printed book, thrown at large on the wide world, were certain to find out the divided segment of the writer's own nature, and complete his circle of existence by bringing him into communion with it. It is scarcely **decorous**, however, to speak at all, even where we speak impersonally. But, as thoughts are frozen and utterance benumbed, unless the speaker stands in some

3

APPREHENSIVE (aa prih <u>hehn</u> sihv) *adj.*
suspicious or fearful of future or unknown evil
Synonyms: concerned, worried, uneasy, uncertain

GENIAL (<u>jeen</u> yuhl) (<u>jee</u> nee uhl) *adj.*
pleasant and friendly; favorable to growth or comfort
Synonyms: nice, amiable; productive, generative

PROPRIETY (pruh <u>prie</u> ih tee) *n.*
the quality of conforming to expected customs and behaviors
Synonyms: appropriateness, correctness, properness

BUSTLING (<u>buh</u> slihng) *adj.*
busy and moving with much activity, energetic
Synonyms: scurrying, scrambling, dashing

MELANCHOLY (<u>mehl</u> uhn kahl ee) *adj.*
sad, depressed
Synonyms: dejected, despondent, woeful, sorrowful

DILAPIDATED (dih <u>laap</u> ih day tihd) *adj.*
in a state of disrepair, shabby
Synonyms: destroyed, ruined, deteriorated, decayed, ramshackle

LANGUID (<u>laang</u> gwihd) *adj.*
lacking energy, indifferent, slow
Synonyms: weak, listless, sluggish

true relation with his audience, it may be pardonable to imagine that a friend, a kind and **apprehensive**, though not the closest friend, is listening to our talk; and then, a native reserve being thawed by this **genial** consciousness, we may prate of the circumstances that lie around us, and even of ourself, but still keep the inmost Me behind its veil. To this extent, and within these limits, an author, methinks, may be autobiographical, without violating either the reader's rights or his own.

It will be seen, likewise, that this Custom House sketch has a certain **propriety**, of a kind always recognized in literature, as explaining how a large portion of the following pages came into my possession, and as offering proofs of the authenticity of a narrative therein contained. This, in fact—a desire to put myself in my true position as editor, or very little more, of the most prolix among the tales that make up my volume—this, and no other, is my true reason for assuming a personal relation with the public. In accomplishing the main purpose, it has appeared allowable, by a few extra touches, to give a faint representation of a mode of life not heretofore described, together with some of the characters that move in it, among whom the author happened to make one.

In my native town of Salem, at the head of what, half a century ago, in the days of old King Derby, was a **bustling** wharf—but which is now burdened with decayed wooden warehouses, and exhibits few or no symptoms of commercial life, except, perhaps, a bark or brig, halfway down its **melancholy** length, discharging hides; or, nearer at hand, a Nova Scotia schooner, pitching out her cargo of firewood—at the head, I say, of this **dilapidated** wharf, which the tide often overflows, and along which, at the base and in the rear of the row of buildings, the track of many **languid** years is seen in a border of unthrifty grass—here, with a view from its

EDIFICE (<u>eh</u> duh fuhs) *n.*
    a large structure
        Synonyms: building, construction, skyscraper

CIVIL (<u>sih</u> vuhl) *adj.*
    involving the public or government; polite
        Synonyms: communal; courteous

DESCEND (dih <u>sehnd</u>) (dee <u>sehnd</u>) *v.* **-ing,-ed.**
    to pass from a higher place to a lower place
        Synonyms: fall, dismount, gravitate

INFIRMITY (ihn <u>fuhr</u> mih tee) *n.*
    weakness; disease, ailment
        Synonyms: frailty; illness, affliction

TRUCULENCY (<u>truh</u> kyuh lehn see) *n.*
    fierce aggressiveness
        Synonyms: ferocity, cruelty, viciousness

MULTITUDINOUS (muhl tih <u>too</u> dih nihs) *adj.*
    many, numerous
        Synonyms: myriad, countless

front windows adown this not very enlivening prospect, and thence across the harbor, stands a spacious **edifice** of brick. From the loftiest point of its roof, during precisely three and a half hours of each <u>forenoon</u>, floats or droops, in breeze or calm, the banner of the republic; but with the thirteen stripes turned vertically, instead of horizontally, and thus indicating that a **civil**, and not a military post of Uncle Sam's government is here established. Its front is ornamented with a <u>portico</u> of half a dozen wooden pillars, supporting a balcony, beneath which a flight of wide granite steps **descends** towards the street. Over the entrance hovers an enormous specimen of the American eagle, with outspread wings, a shield before her breast, and, if I recollect aright, a bunch of intermingled thunderbolts and barbed arrows in each claw. With the customary **infirmity** of temper that characterizes this unhappy fowl, she appears, by the fierceness of her beak and eye, and the general **truculency** of her attitude, to threaten mischief to the inoffensive community; and especially to warn all citizens, careful of their safety, against intruding on the premises which she overshadows with her wings. Nevertheless, <u>vixenly</u> as she looks, many people are seeking, at this very moment, to shelter themselves under the wing of the federal eagle; imagining, I presume, that her bosom has all the softness and snugness of an eiderdown pillow. But she has no great tenderness, even in her best of moods, and, sooner or later—oftener soon than late—is apt to fling off her nestlings, with a scratch of her claw, a dab of her beak, or a <u>rankling</u> wound from her barbed arrows.

The pavement round about the above-described **edifice**—which we may as well name at once as the Custom House of the port—has grass enough growing in its chinks to show that it has not, of late days, been worn by any **multitudinous** resort of business. In some

IMPERCEPTIBLY (ihn puhr <u>sehp</u> tih blee) *adv.*
    in a manner which is unable to be seen or perceived
        Synonyms: unnoticeably, insignificantly, invisibly,
        faintly

TARNISHED (<u>tahr</u> nihshd) *adj.*
    corroded, discolored; discredited, disgraced
        Synonyms: stained, blemished; dishonored,
        defected

SOMBRE or SOMBER (<u>sahm</u> buhr) *adj.*
    melancholy, dismal, dark and gloomy
        Synonyms: serious, grave, mournful, lugubrious,
        funereal

INCOMMODITY (ihn kuh <u>mah</u> dih tee) *n.*
    an inconvenience or disadvantage
        Synonyms: burden, obstacle

MIMIC (<u>mih</u> mihk) *adj.*
    imitation
        Synonym: mock

months of the year, however, there often chances a <u>forenoon</u> when affairs move onward with a livelier tread. Such occasions might remind the elderly citizen of that period before the last war with England, when Salem was a port by itself; not scorned, as she is now, by her own merchants and ship-owners, who permit her wharves to crumble to ruin, while their ventures go to swell, needlessly and **imperceptibly**, the mighty flood of commerce at New York or Boston. On some such morning, when three or four vessels happen to have arrived at once—usually from Africa or South America—or to be on the verge of their departure thitherward, there is a sound of frequent feet, passing briskly up and down the granite steps. Here, before his own wife has greeted him, you may greet the sea-flushed shipmaster, just in port, with his vessel's papers under his arm, in a **tarnished** tin box. Here, too, comes his owner, cheerful or **sombre**, gracious or in the sulks, accordingly as his scheme of the now accomplished voyage has been realized in merchandise that will readily be turned to gold, or has buried him under a bulk of **incommodities** such as nobody will care to rid him of. Here, likewise—the germ of the wrinkle-browed, grizzly-bearded, care-worn merchant—we have the smart young clerk, who gets the taste of traffic as a wolf-cub does of blood, and already sends adventures in his master's ships, when he had better be sailing **mimic** boats upon a mill-pond. Another figure in the scene is the outward-bound sailor in quest of a protection; or the recently arrived one, pale and feeble, seeking a passport to the hospital. Nor must we forget the captains of the rusty little <u>schooners</u> that bring firewood from the British provinces; a rough-looking set of tarpaulins, without the alertness of the Yankee aspect, but contributing an item of no slight importance to our decaying trade.

SAT Vocabulary

ASCEND (uh <u>sehnd</u>) *v.* **-ing,-ed.**
   to rise to another level or climb; to move upward
     Synonyms: elevate, escalate, mount; hoist, lift

DISCERN (dihs <u>uhrn</u>) *v.* **-ing,-ed.**
   to perceive or recognize something
     Synonyms: descry, observe, glimpse, distinguish

VENERABLE (<u>veh</u> nehr uh buhl) *adj.*
   respected because of age
     Synonyms: distinguished, elderly

SUBSISTENCE (suhb <u>sihst</u> ihnts) *n.*
   the necessities of life, the resources of survival
     Synonyms: nourishment, sustenance, provisions

DILAPIDATED (dih <u>laap</u> ih day tihd) *adj.*
   in a state of disrepair, shabby
     Synonyms: destroyed, ruined, deteriorated,
     decayed, ramshackle

SLOVENLINESS (<u>slah</u> vuhn lee nehs) *n.*
   lack of cleanliness, untidiness
     Synonyms: negligence, sloppiness, unkemptness

SANCTUARY (<u>saank</u> choo eh ree) *n.*
   haven, retreat
     Synonyms: refuge, asylum, shelter

VOLUMINOUS (vuh <u>loo</u> mih nuhs) *adj.*
   very large in size or number, having great volume
     Synonyms: copious, extensive, massive, abundant

Cluster all these individuals together, as they some-times were, with other miscellaneous ones to diversify the group, and, for the time being, it made the Custom House a stirring scene. More frequently, however, on **ascending** the steps, you would **discern**—in the entry, if it were summer time, or in their appropriate rooms, if win-try or <u>inclement</u> weather—a row of **venerable** figures, sitting in old-fashioned chairs, which were tipped on their hind legs back against the wall. Oftentimes they were asleep, but occasionally might be heard talking together, in voices between speech and a snore, and with that lack of energy that distinguishes the occupants of almshouses, and all other human beings who depend for **subsistence** on charity, on monopolized labor, or any-thing else, but their own independent exertions. These old gentlemen—seated, like Matthew, at the receipt of cus-tom, but not very liable to be summoned thence, like him, for <u>apostolic</u> errands—were Custom House officers.

Furthermore, on the left hand as you enter the front door, is a certain room or office about fifteen feet square, and of a lofty height; with two of its arched win-dows commanding a view of the aforesaid **dilapidated** wharf, and the third looking across a narrow lane, and along a portion of Derby Street. All three give glimpses of the shops of grocers, block-makers, slop-sellers, and ship-chandlers; around the doors of which are generally to be seen, laughing and gossiping, clusters of old salts, and such other wharf-rats as haunt the <u>Wapping</u> of a seaport. The room itself is cob-webbed and dingy with old paint; its floor is strewn with gray sand, in a fashion that has elsewhere fallen into long disuse; and it is easy to conclude, from the general **slovenliness** of the place, that this is a **sanctuary** into which womankind, with her tools of magic, the broom and mop, has very infrequent access. In the way of furniture, there is a stove with a **voluminous** funnel; an old pine desk with a three-legged

11

INFIRM (ihn <u>fuhrm</u>) *adj.*
weak; diseased, ailing
Synonyms: frail; ill, afflicted

SCORE (skohr) *n.*
1. twenty; a very large number
Synonyms: many, multitude
2. a notch or scratch, made to keep tally
Synonyms: furrow, scrape, groove

ASCEND (uh <u>sehnd</u>) *v.* **-ing,-ed.**
to rise to another level or climb; to move upward
Synonyms: elevate, escalate, mount; hoist, lift

MEDIUM (<u>mee</u> dee uhm) *n.*
a substance or object that is used to transmit or
accomplish something
Synonyms: means, instrument, vehicle, mechanism

EDIFICE (<u>eh</u> duh fuhs) *n.*
a large structure
Synonyms: building, construction, skyscraper

HONORED (<u>ah</u> nuhrd) *adj.*
praised, glorified, deserving of tribute
Synonyms: revered, venerated, respected

SENTIMENTAL (sehn tuh <u>mehn</u> tuhl) *adj.*
relating to a romantic or nostalgic feeling, prompted
by feeling
Synonyms: emotional, passionate, affectionate

INVARIABLY (ihn <u>vaa</u> ree uh blee) *adv.*
without change, constantly
Synonyms: always, repeatedly, perpetually

stool beside it; two or three wooden-bottom chairs, exceedingly decrepit and **infirm**; and—not to forget the library—on some shelves, a **score** or two of volumes of the Acts of Congress and a bulky Digest of the Revenue Laws. A tin pipe **ascends** through the ceiling, and forms a **medium** of vocal communication with other parts of the **edifice**. And here, some six months ago, pacing from corner to corner, or lounging on the long-legged stool, with his elbow on the desk, and his eyes wandering up and down the columns of the morning newspaper, you might have recognized, **honored** reader, the same individual who welcomed you into his cheery little study, where the sunshine glimmered so pleasantly through the willow branches, on the western side of the Old Manse. But now, should you go thither to seek him, you would inquire in vain for the <u>Locofoco Surveyor</u>. The <u>besom</u> of reform has swept him out of office; and a worthier successor wears his dignity, and pockets his <u>emoluments</u>.

This old town of Salem—my native place, though I have dwelt much away from it, both in boyhood and maturer years—possesses, or did possess, a hold on my affections, the force of which I have never realized, during my seasons of actual residence here. Indeed, so far as its physical aspect is concerned, with its flat, unvaried surface, covered chiefly with wooden houses, few or none of which pretend to architectural beauty—its irregularity, which is neither picturesque nor quaint, but only tame—its long and lazy street lounging wearisomely through the whole extent of the peninsula, with gallows Hill and New Guinea at one end, and a view of the almshouse at the other—such being the features of my native town, it would be quite as reasonable to form a **sentimental** attachment to a disarranged checkerboard. And yet, though **invariably** happiest elsewhere, there is within me a feeling for old Salem, which, in lack

SENTIMENT (<u>sehn</u> tuh muhnt) *n.*
an attitude, thought, or judgment prompted by feeling
Synonym: emotion

EMIGRANT (<u>eh</u> mih graant) *n.*
a person from another country or land
Synonym: foreigner

DESCENDANT (dih <u>sehn</u> dehnt) *n.*
an offspring or heir
Synonyms: child, kin, progeny

INDUCE (ih <u>doos</u>) (ihn <u>dyoos</u>) *v.* **-ing,-ed.**
to bring about; to persuade
Synonyms: cause; convince, prevail

PROGENITOR (proh <u>jeh</u> nih tuhr) *n.*
a direct ancestor
Synonyms: forerunner, predecessor, forefather

of a better phrase, I must be content to call affection. The **sentiment** is probably assignable to the deep and aged roots which my family has struck into the soil. It is now nearly two centuries and a quarter since the original Briton, the earliest **emigrant** of my name, made his appearance in the wild and forest-bordered settlement, which has since become a city. And here his **descendants** have been born and died, and have mingled their earthy substance with the soil, until no small portion of it must necessarily be akin to the mortal frame wherewith, for a little while, I walk the streets. In part, therefore, the attachment which I speak of is the mere sensuous sympathy of dust for dust. Few of my countrymen can know what it is; nor, as frequent transplantation is perhaps better for the stock, need they consider it desirable to know.

But the **sentiment** has likewise its moral quality. The figure of that first ancestor, invested by family tradition with a dim and dusky grandeur, was present to my boyish imagination, as far back as I can remember. It still haunts me, and **induces** a sort of home-feeling with the past, which I scarcely claim in reference to the present phase of the town. I seem to have a stronger claim to a residence here on account of this grave, bearded, sable-cloaked and steeple-crowned **progenitor**, who came so early, with his Bible and his sword, and trode the unworn street with such a stately port, and made so large a figure, as a man of war and peace, a stronger claim than for myself, whose name is seldom heard and my face hardly known. He was a soldier, legislator, judge; he was a ruler in the Church; he had all the Puritanic traits, both good and evil. He was likewise a bitter persecutor, as witness the Quakers, who have remembered him in their histories, and relate an incident of his hard severity toward a woman of their sect, which will last longer, it is to be feared, than any record

MARTYRDOM (<u>mahr</u> tuhr duhm) *n.*
death or intense suffering experienced due to one's beliefs
Synonyms: sacrifice, anguish

RETAIN (rih <u>tayn</u>) *v.* **-ing,-ed.**
to hold, keep possession of
Synonyms: withhold, reserve

REPENT (rih <u>pehnt</u>) *v.* **-ing,-ed.**
to regret a past action
Synonyms: rue, atone, apologize

INCUR (ihn <u>kuhr</u>) *v.* **-ring,-red.**
to acquire or meet with, usually something negative or harmful; to become liable
Synonyms: get, obtain, endure, sustain; oblige, owe

UNPROSPEROUS (uhn <u>prah</u> spuhr uhs) *adj.*
unsuccessful
Synonyms: weak, needy, disadvantaged, poor

RETRIBUTION (reh trih <u>byoo</u> shuhn) *n.*
something which is justly deserved, such as repayment or punishment
Synonyms: vengeance, payback, compensation

VENERABLE (<u>veh</u> nehr uh buhl) *adj.*
respected because of age
Synonyms: distinguished, elderly

LAUDABLE (<u>law</u> duh buhl) *adj.*
deserving of praise
Synonyms: commendable, admirable, splendid, meritorious, exemplary

DEGENERATE (dih <u>jehn</u> uhr iht) *adj.*
having low morals and an inferior intellect
Synonyms: corrupt, depraved, debased, shameful

of his better deeds, although these were many. His son, too, inherited the persecuting spirit, and made himself so conspicuous in the **martyrdom** of the witches, that their blood may fairly be said to have left a stain upon him. So deep a stain, indeed, that his old dry bones, in the Charter Street burial-ground, must still **retain** it, if they have not crumbled utterly to dust! I know not whether these ancestors of mine bethought themselves to **repent**, and ask pardon of Heaven for their cruelties; or whether they are now groaning under the heavy consequences of them, in another state of being. At all events, I, the present writer, as their representative, hereby take shame upon myself for their sakes, and pray that any curse **incurred** by them—as I have heard, and as the dreary and **unprosperous** condition of the race, for many a long year back, would argue to exist—may be now and henceforth removed.

Doubtless, however, either of these stern and black-browed <u>Puritans</u> would have thought it quite a sufficient **retribution** for his sins, that, after so long a lapse of years, the old trunk of the family tree, with so much **venerable** moss upon it, should have borne, as its topmost bough, an idler like myself. No aim, that I have ever cherished, would they recognize as **laudable**; no success of mine—if my life, beyond its domestic scope, had ever been brightened by success—would they deem otherwise than worthless, if not positively disgraceful. "What is he?" murmurs one gray shadow of my forefathers to the other. "A writer of story-books! What kind of a business in life—what mode of glorifying God, or being serviceable to mankind in his day and generation—may that be? Why, the **degenerate** fellow might as well have been a fiddler!" Such are the compliments <u>bandied</u> between my great-grandsires and myself, across the gulf of time! And yet, let them scorn me as

SUBSIST (suhb <u>sihst</u>) *v.* **-ing,-ed.**
to have existence; to have or acquire the necessities
of life, to nourish oneself
Synonyms: live, survive, endure, inhabit

TEMPESTUOUS (tehm <u>pehs</u> tyoo uhs) *adj.*
stormy, raging, furious
Synonyms: tumultuous, blustery, inclement,
turbulent, torrential

TENACITY (tih <u>naa</u> sih tee) *n.*
stubbornness, diligence, determination
Synonyms: persistence, strength, inflexibility

SENTIMENT (<u>sehn</u> tuh muhnt) *n.*
an attitude, thought, or judgment prompted by feeling
Synonym: emotion

they will, strong traits of their nature have intertwined themselves with mine.

Planted deep in the town's earliest infancy and childhood, by these two earnest and energetic men, the race has ever since **subsisted** here; always, too, in respectability; never, so far as I have known, disgraced by a single unworthy member; but seldom or never, on the other hand, after the first two generations, performing any memorable deed, or so much as putting forward a claim to public notice. Gradually, they have sunk almost out of sight; as old houses, here and there about the streets, get covered halfway to the eaves by the accumulation of new soil. From father to son, for above a hundred years, they followed the sea; a gray-headed shipmaster, in each generation, retiring from the quarter-deck to the homestead, while a boy of fourteen took the hereditary place before the mast, confronting the salt spray and the gale, which had blustered against his sire and grandsire. The boy, also, in due time, passed from the forecastle to the cabin, spent a **tempestuous** manhood, and returned from his world-wanderings, to grow old, and die, and mingle his dust with the natal earth. This long connection of a family with one spot, as its place of birth and burial, creates a kindred between the human being and the locality, quite independent of any charm in the scenery or moral circumstances that surround him. It is not love, but instinct. The new inhabitant—who came himself from a foreign land, or whose father or grandfather came—has little claim to be called a Salemite; he has no conception of the oysterlike **tenacity** with which an old settler, over whom his third century is creeping, clings to the spot where his successive generations have been imbedded. It is no matter that the place is joyless for him; that he is weary of the old wooden houses, the mud and dust, the dead level of site and **sentiment**, the chill east wind, and the chillest of social atmospheres—all these, and

SENTIMENT (<u>sehn</u> tuh muhnt) *n.*
  an attitude, thought, or judgment prompted by feeling
    Synonym: emotion

INDOLENT (<u>ihn</u> duh luhnt) *adj.*
  habitually lazy and easygoing, idle
    Synonyms: slothful, languid, lethargic, sluggish

EDIFICE (<u>eh</u> duh fuhs) *n.*
  a large structure
    Synonyms: building, construction, skyscraper

INEVITABLE (ihn <u>ehv</u> ih tuh buhl) *adj.*
  certain, unavoidable
    Synonyms: inescapable, sure, predictable

ASCEND (uh <u>sehnd</u>) *v.* **-ing,-ed.**
  to rise to another level or climb; to move upward
    Synonyms: elevate, escalate, mount; hoist, lift

CIVIL (<u>sih</u> vuhl) *adj.*
  involving the public or government; polite
    Synonyms: communal; courteous

PATRIARCHAL (pay tree <u>ahr</u> kuhl) *adj.*
  relating to the qualities of an old, well-respected
  man, often the head of a family or a high member of
  a church
    Synonyms: dignified, experienced, reverenced

whatever faults besides he may see or imagine, are nothing to the purpose. The spell survives, and just as powerfully as if the natal spot were an earthly paradise. So has it been in my case. I felt it almost as a destiny to make Salem my home; so that the mould of features and cast of character which had all along been familiar here—ever, as one representative of the race lay down in his grave, another assuming, as it were, his sentry-march along the main street—might still in my little day be seen and recognized in the old town. Nevertheless, this very **sentiment** is an evidence that the connection, which has become an unhealthy one, should at last be severed. Human nature will not flourish, any more than a potato, if it be planted and replanted, for too long a series of generations, in the same worn-out soil. My children have had other birthplaces, and, so far as their fortunes may be within my control, shall strike their roots into unaccustomed earth.

On emerging from the Old Manse, it was chiefly this strange, **indolent**, unjoyous attachment for my native town, that brought me to fill a place in Uncle Sam's brick **edifice**, when I might as well, or better, have gone somewhere else. My doom was on me. It was not the first time, nor the second, that I had gone away—as it seemed, permanently—but yet returned, like the bad half-penny; or as if Salem were for me the **inevitable** centre of the universe. So, one fine morning, I **ascended** the flight of granite steps, with the President's commission in my pocket, and was introduced to the corps of gentlemen who were to aid me in my weighty responsibility, as chief executive officer of the Custom House.

I doubt greatly—or, rather, I do not doubt at all—whether any public functionary of the United States, either in the **civil** or military line, has ever had such a **patriarchal** body of veterans under his orders as myself. The whereabouts of the Oldest Inhabitant was at once settled when I looked at them. For upwards of twenty

EPOCH (<u>eh</u> pihk) *n.*
a specific time in history; a particular day or time
    Synonyms: period, era, generation; date

VICISSITUDE (vih <u>sih</u> sih tood) *n.*
change or variation, ups and downs
    Synonyms: mutability, inconstancy, wavering

LIBERALITY (lihb uh <u>raa</u> lih tee) *n.*
tolerance, broad-mindedness; generosity, lavishness
    Synonyms: progressiveness, permissiveness;
    munificence

TEMPESTUOUS (tehm <u>pehs</u> tyoo uhs) *adj.*
stormy, raging, furious
    Synonyms: tumultuous, blustery, inclement,
    turbulent, torrential

INFIRMITY (ihn <u>fuhr</u> mih tee) *n.*
weakness; disease, ailment
    Synonyms: frailty; illness, affliction

TALISMAN (<u>taa</u> lihs mehn) *n.*
a magical object that is believed to bring protection
or supernatural powers to its keeper
    Synonyms: lucky charm, amulet, idol

TORPID (<u>tohr</u> pihd) *adj.*
dormant; lethargic, unable to move
    Synonyms: hibernating, inactive, inert; apathetic,
    sluggish

VENERABLE (<u>veh</u> nehr uh buhl) *adj.*
respected because of age
    Synonyms: distinguished, elderly

ARDUOUS (<u>ahr</u> jyoo uhs) (<u>aar</u> dyoo uhs) *adj.*
extremely difficult, laborious
    Synonyms: burdensome, onerous, hard, toilsome

years before this **epoch**, the independent position of the Collector had kept the Salem Custom House out of the whirlpool of political **vicissitude**, which makes the tenure of office generally so fragile. A soldier—New England's most distinguished soldier—stood firmly on the pedestal of his gallant services; and, himself secure in the wise **liberality** of the successive administrations through which he had held office, he had been the safety of his subordinates in many an hour of danger and heartquake. General Miller was radically conservative; a man over whose kindly nature habit had no slight influence, attaching himself strongly to familiar faces, and with difficulty moved to change, even when change might have brought unquestionable improvement. Thus, on taking charge of my department, I found few but aged men. They were ancient sea-captains, for the most part, who, after being tossed on every sea, and standing up sturdily against life's **tempestuous** blast, had finally drifted into this quiet nook; where, with little to disturb them, except the periodical terrors of a presidential election, they one and all acquired a new lease of existence. Though by no means less liable than their fellow-men to age and **infirmity**, they had evidently some **talisman** or other that kept death at bay. Two or three of their number, as I was assured, being <u>gouty</u> and rheumatic, or perhaps bedridden, never dreamed of making their appearance at the Custom House during a large part of the year; but, after a **torpid** winter, would creep out into the warm sunshine of May or June, go lazily about what they termed duty, and, at their own leisure and convenience, betake themselves to bed again. I must plead guilty to the charge of abbreviating the official breath of more than one of these **venerable** servants of the republic. They were allowed, on my representation, to rest from their **arduous** labors, and soon afterwards—as if their sole principle of life had

ZEAL (zeel) *n.*
passion or devotion to a cause
Synonyms: fanaticism, enthusiasm

VERILY (<u>veh</u> rih lee) *adv.*
truly, with accuracy and confidence
Synonyms: truthfully, reliably, assuredly

PIOUS (<u>pie</u> uhs) *adj.*
dedicated, devout; extremely religious
Synonyms: observant, reverent; sanctimonious

CONSOLATION (kahn suh <u>lay</u> shuhn) *n.*
something providing comfort or solace for a loss or hardship
Synonym: condolence

REPENTANCE (rih <u>pehn</u> tehnts) *n.*
sorrow expressed for sins or offenses, penitence
Synonyms: remorse, contrition, apology

VENERABLE (<u>veh</u> nehr uh buhl) *adj.*
respected because of age
Synonyms: distinguished, elderly

INFIRMITY (ihn <u>fuhr</u> mih tee) *n.*
weakness; disease, ailment
Synonyms: frailty; illness, affliction

DISCERN (dihs <u>uhrn</u>) *v.* **-ing,-ed.**
to perceive or recognize something
Synonyms: descry, observe, glimpse, distinguish

FURROWED (<u>fuhr</u> rohd) *adj.*
having wrinkles or grooves; rugged
Synonyms: crinkled, ridged, creased; weathered, worn

been **zeal** for their country's service, as I **verily** believe it was—withdrew to a better world. It is a **pious consolation** to me, that, through my interference, a sufficient space was allowed them for **repentance** of the evil and corrupt practices into which, as a matter of course, every Custom House officer must be supposed to fall. Neither the front nor the back entrance of the Custom House opens on the road to Paradise.

The greater part of my officers were <u>Whigs</u>. It was well for their **venerable** brotherhood that the new Surveyor was not a politician, and though a faithful Democrat in principle, neither received nor held his office with any reference to political services. Had it been otherwise—had an active politician been put into this influential post, to assume the easy task of making head against a <u>Whig</u> Collector, whose **infirmities** withheld him from the personal administration of his office—hardly a man of the old corps would have drawn the breath of official life, within a month after the exterminating angel had come up the Custom House steps. According to the received code in such matters, it would have been nothing short of duty, in a politician, to bring every one of those white heads under the axe of the guillotine. It was plain enough to **discern** that the old fellows dreaded some such discourtesy at my hands. It pained, and at the same time amused me, to behold the terrors that attended my advent; to see a **furrowed** cheek, weather-beaten by half a century of storm, turn ashy pale at the glance of so harmless an individual as myself; to detect, as one or another addressed me, the tremor of a voice, which, in long-past days, had been wont to bellow through a speaking-trumpet, hoarsely enough to frighten <u>Boreas</u> himself to silence. They knew, these excellent old persons, that, by all established rule—and, as regarded some of them, weighed by their own lack of efficiency for business—they ought to have given place

ORTHODOX (<u>ohr</u> thuh dahks) *adj.*
  conservative, accepted, traditional
    Synonyms: conventional, standard, customary

DISCREDIT (dihs <u>kreh</u> diht) *n.*
  damage to one's reputation
    Synonyms: shame, disrepute, humiliation

DETRIMENT (<u>deht</u> ruh mehnt) *n.*
  disadvantage, something that causes harm or injury
    Synonyms: loss, impairment, disservice

INCUMBENCY (ihn <u>kuhm</u> buhn see) *n.*
  the term of holding a specified office, often political
    Synonyms: tenure, position

LOITER (<u>loy</u> tuhr) *v.* **-ing,-ed.**
  to stand around idly
    Synonyms: linger, delay, dawdle

SAGACIOUSLY (suh <u>gay</u> shuhs lee) *adv.*
  shrewdly, intelligently
    Synonyms: astutely, perspicaciously, wisely

OBTUSENESS (uhb <u>toos</u> nehs) *n.*
  insensitivity, stupidity; dullness
    Synonyms: slowness, ignorance; bluntness

VIGILANCE (<u>vih</u> juh lehnts) *n.*
  attentiveness, watchfulness
    Synonyms: alertness, awareness, care, diligence

ALACRITY (uh <u>laak</u> crih tee) *n.*
  speed; cheerful willingness, eagerness
    Synonyms: dispatch, celerity, briskness;
    enthusiasm, fervor

NEGLIGENCE (<u>nehg</u> lih jehnts) *n.*
  carelessness, inattention
    Synonyms: indifference, casualness, disinterest

EULOGIUM (yoo <u>loh</u> jee uhm) *n.*
  high praise, often in a public speech
    Synonyms: tribute, commendation, panegyric,
    salute

ZEAL (zeel) *n.*
  passion or devotion to a cause
    Synonyms: fanaticism, enthusiasm

to younger men, more **orthodox** in politics, and altogether fitter than themselves to serve our common Uncle. I knew it too, but could never quite find in my heart to act upon the knowledge. Much and deservedly to my own **discredit**, therefore, and considerably to the **detriment** of my official conscience, they continued, during my **incumbency**, to creep about the wharves, and **loiter** up and down the Custom House steps. They spent a good deal of time, also, asleep in their accustomed corners, with their chairs tilted back against the wall; awaking, however, once or twice in a <u>forenoon</u>, to bore one another with the several thousandth repetition of old sea-stories, and mouldy jokes, that had grown to be passwords and countersigns among them.

The discovery was soon made, I imagine, that the new Surveyor had no great harm in him. So, with lightsome hearts, and the happy consciousness of being usefully employed—in their own behalf, at least, if not for our beloved country—these good old gentlemen went through the various formalities of office **sagaciously**, under their spectacles, did they peep into the holds of vessels! Mighty was their fuss about little matters, and marvellous, sometimes, the **obtuseness** that allowed greater ones to slip between their fingers! Whenever such a mischance occurred—when a wagonload of valuable merchandise had been smuggled ashore, at noonday, perhaps, and directly beneath their unsuspicious noses—nothing could exceed the **vigilance** and **alacrity** with which they proceeded to lock, and double-lock, and secure with tape and sealing-wax, all the avenues of the delinquent vessel. Instead of a reprimand for their previous **negligence**, the case seemed rather to require an **eulogium** on their praiseworthy caution, after the mischief had happened; a grateful recognition of the promptitude of their **zeal**, the moment that there was no longer any remedy.

PATERNAL (puh <u>tuhr</u> nuhl) *adj.*
fatherly, related to the characteristics of fatherhood;
inherited from the father
Synonyms: parental; hereditary

SENTIMENT (<u>sehn</u> tuh muhnt) *n.*
an attitude, thought, or judgment prompted by feeling
Synonym: emotion

FERVENT (<u>fuhr</u> vehnt) *adj.*
passionate, intense, zealous
Synonyms: vehement, eager, enthusiastic, avid

GENIAL (<u>jeen</u> yuhl) (<u>jee</u> nee uhl) *adj.*
pleasant and friendly; favorable to growth or comfort
Synonyms: nice, amiable; productive, generative

TORPID (<u>tohr</u> pihd) *adj.*
lethargic, unable to move; dormant
Synonyms: apathetic, sluggish; hibernating,
inactive, inert

MIRTH (muhrth) *n.*
frivolity, gaiety, laughter
Synonyms: merriment, jollity, hilarity, glee

IMPART (ihm <u>pahrt</u>) *v.* **-ing,-ed.**
to give or share, to pass on
Synonyms: bestow, contribute, reveal, convey

INVARIABLY (ihn <u>vaa</u> ree uh blee) *adv.*
without change, constantly
Synonyms: always, repeatedly, perpetually

TENEMENT (<u>teh</u> nuh muhnt) *n.*
a place for dwelling or human habitation
Synonyms: rental, apartment, residence

Unless people are more than commonly disagreeable, it is my foolish habit to contract a kindness for them. The better part of my companion's character, if it has a better part, is that which usually comes uppermost in my regard, and forms the type whereby I recognize the man. As most of these old Custom House officers had good traits, and as my position in reference to them, being **paternal** and protective, was favorable to the growth of friendly **sentiments**, I soon grew to like them all. It was pleasant, in the summer <u>forenoons</u>, when the **fervent** heat, that almost liquefied the rest of the human family, merely communicated a **genial** warmth to their half-**torpid** systems. It was pleasant to hear them chatting in the back entry, a row of them all tipped against the wall, as usual; while the frozen witticisms of past generations were thawed out, and came bubbling with laughter from their lips. Externally, the jollity of aged men has much in common with the **mirth** of children; the intellect, any more than a deep sense of humor, has little to do with the matter; it is, with both, a gleam that plays upon the surface, and **imparts** a sunny and cheery aspect alike to the green branch, and gray, mouldering trunk. In one case, however, it is real sunshine; in the other, it more resembles the <u>phosphorescent</u> glow of decaying wood.

It would be sad injustice, the reader must understand, to represent all my excellent old friends as in their <u>dotage</u>. In the first place, my <u>coadjutors</u> were not **invariably** old; there were men among them in their strength and prime, of marked ability and energy, and altogether superior to the sluggish and dependent mode of life on which their evil stars had cast them. Then, moreover, the white locks of age were sometimes found to be the thatch of an intellectual **tenement** in good repair. But, as respects the majority of my corps of veterans, there will be no wrong done, if I characterize

PATRIARCH (<u>pay</u> tree ahrk) *n.*
an old well-respected man, often the head of a
family; a high member or head of a church
Synonyms: elder, leader; bishop, dignitary

SCORE (skohr) *n.*
1. twenty; a very large number
Synonyms: many, multitude
2. a notch or scratch, made to keep tally
Synonyms: furrow, scrape, groove

FLORID (<u>flohr</u> ihd) (<u>flahr</u> ihd) *adj.*
ruddy, flushed; gaudy, extremely ornate
Synonyms: rosy, reddish; flamboyant,
ostentatious, loud, garish

VIGOROUS (<u>vih</u> guhr uhs) *adj.*
having great physical or mental energy
Synonyms: strong, powerful, intense

CONTRIVANCE (kuhn <u>triev</u> ehnts) *n.*
an invention; the act of creating art or an artistic
creation
Synonyms: concoction, scheme; design, project

INFIRMITY (ihn <u>fuhr</u> mih tee) *n.*
weakness; disease, ailment
Synonyms: frailty; illness, affliction

PERPETUALLY (puhr <u>peht</u> chyoo uh lee) *adv.*
endlessly, always
Synonyms: continuously, constantly, eternally,
perennially

TREMULOUS (<u>treh</u> myoo luhs) *adj.*
trembling, quivering; fearful, timid
Synonyms: shaking, palsied; timorous, anxious

them generally as a set of wearisome old souls, who had gathered nothing worth preservation from their varied experience of life. They seemed to have flung away all the golden grain of practical wisdom, which they had enjoyed so many opportunities of harvesting, and most carefully to have stored their memories with the husks. They spoke with far more interest and <u>unction</u> of their morning's breakfast, or yesterday's, today's or tomorrow's dinner, than of the shipwreck of forty or fifty years ago, and all the world's wonders which they had witnessed with their youthful eyes.

The father of the Custom House—the **patriarch**, not only of this little squad of officials, but, I am bold to say, of the respectable body of tide-waiters all over the United States—was a certain permanent Inspector. He might truly be termed a legitimate son of the revenue system, dyed in the wool, or, rather, born in the purple; since his sire, a Revolutionary colonel, and formerly collector of the port, had created an office for him, and appointed him to fill it, at a period of the early ages which few living men can now remember. This Inspector, when I first knew him, was a man of four-**score** years, or thereabouts, and certainly one of the most wonderful specimens of wintergreen that you would be likely to discover in a lifetime's search. With his **florid** cheek, his compact figure, smartly arrayed in a bright-buttoned blue coat, his brisk and **vigorous** step, and his hale and hearty aspect, altogether he seemed—not young, indeed—but a kind of new **contrivance** of Mother Nature in the shape of man, whom age and **infirmity** had no business to touch. His voice and laugh, which **perpetually** reechoed through the Custom House, had nothing of the **tremulous** quaver and cackle of an old man's utterance; they came strutting out of his lungs, like the crow of a cock, or the blast of a <u>clarion</u>. Looking at him merely as an animal—and there was

APPREHENSION (aa prih <u>hehn</u> shuhn) *n.*
suspicion or fear of future or unknown evil; the act
of perceiving or comprehending; a legal seizure
Synonyms: concern, worry; understanding; capture

MODERATE (<u>mah</u> duhr iht) *adj.*
average, reasonable
Synonyms: mediocre, temperate

TRIFLING (<u>trie</u> flihng) *adj.*
minor, of slight worth or little importance
Synonyms: trivial, insignificant

INEVITABLY (ihn <u>ehv</u> ih tuh blee) *adv.*
certainly, unavoidably
Synonyms: inescapably, surely, predictably

IMBUE (ihm <u>byoo</u>) *v.* **-ing,-ed.**
to infuse; to dye, wet
Synonyms: permeate; moisten

TINGE (tihnj) *n.*
a slight shade of color, stain, odor, or taste
Synonyms: hint, hue, tincture, tone, wash

REMINISCENCE (reh muh <u>nihs</u> ehnts) *n.*
remembrance of past events
Synonyms: memory, recollection, recall

PATRIARCHAL (pay tree <u>ahr</u> kuhl) *adj.*
relating to the qualities of an old, well-respected
man, often the head of a family or a high member of
a church
Synonyms: dignified, experienced, reverenced

DELUSIVE (duh <u>loo</u> sihv) *adj.*
deceptive, imaginary
Synonyms: misleading, false

IMPALPABLE (ihm <u>paalp</u> uh buhl) *adj.*
unreal, intangible
Synonyms: imperceptible, tenuous, unsubstantial

very little else to look at—he was a most satisfactory object, from the thorough healthfulness and wholesomeness of his system, and his capacity, at that extreme age, to enjoy all, or nearly all, the delights which he had ever aimed at, or conceived of. The careless security of his life in the Custom House, on a regular income, and with but slight and infrequent **apprehensions** of removal, had no doubt contributed to make time pass lightly over him. The original and more potent causes, however, lay in the rare perfection of his animal nature, the **moderate** proportion of intellect, and the very **trifling** admixture of moral and spiritual ingredients; these latter qualities, indeed, being in barely enough measure to keep the old gentleman from walking on all-fours. He possessed no power of thought, no depth of feeling, no troublesome sensibilities; nothing, in short, but a few commonplace instincts, which, aided by the cheerful temper that grew **inevitably** out of his physical well-being, did duty very respectably, and to general acceptance, in lieu of a heart. He had been the husband of three wives, all long since dead; the father of twenty children, most of whom, at every age of childhood or maturity, had likewise returned to dust. Here, one would suppose, might have been sorrow enough to **imbue** the sunniest disposition, through and through, with a sable **tinge**. Not so with our old Inspector! One brief sigh sufficed to carry off the entire burden of these dismal **reminiscences**. The next moment, he was as ready for sport as any <u>unbreeched</u> infant; far readier than the Collector's junior clerk, who, at nineteen years, was much the elder and graver man of the two.

I used to watch and study this **patriarchal** personage with, I think, livelier curiosity, than any other form of humanity there presented to my notice. He was, in truth, a rare phenomenon; so perfect, in one point of view; so shallow, so **delusive**, so **impalpable**, such an absolute

IMMUNITY (ih <u>myoo</u> nih tee) *n.*
protection from harm or disease; exemption
Synonyms: resistance, unsusceptibility; liberty, invulnerability

ENDOWMENT (ehn <u>dow</u> mehnt) (ihn <u>dow</u> mehnt) *n.*
a gift; talent
Synonyms: grant, benefit; ability, aptitude

INGENUITY (ihn jeh <u>noo</u> ih tee) *n.*
cleverness
Synonyms: inventiveness, imagination, creativity

REMINISCENCE (reh muh <u>nihs</u> ehnts) *n.*
remembrance of past events
Synonyms: memory, recollection, recall

SAVOR (<u>say</u> vuhr) *n.*
a distinctive taste or smell
Synonyms: flavor, pungency, piquancy, succulence

nonentity, in every other. My conclusion was that he had no soul, no heart, no mind; nothing, as I have already said, but instincts; and yet, withal, so cunningly had the few materials of his character been put together, that there was no painful perception of deficiency, but, on my part, an entire contentment with what I found in him. It might be difficult—and it was so—to conceive how he should exist hereafter, so earthy and sensuous did he seem; but surely his existence here, admitting that it was to terminate with his last breath, had been not unkindly given; with no higher moral responsibilities than the beasts of the field, but with a larger scope of enjoyment than theirs, and with all their blessed **immunity** from the dreariness and duskiness of age.

One point, in which he had vastly the advantage over his four-footed brethren, was his ability to recollect the good dinners which it had made no small portion of the happiness of his life to eat. His gourmandism was a highly agreeable trait; and to hear him talk of roast meat was as appetizing as a pickle or an oyster. As he possessed no higher attribute, and neither sacrificed nor vitiated any spiritual **endowment** by devoting all his energies and **ingenuities** to subserve the delight and profit of his maw, it always pleased and satisfied me to hear him expatiate on fish, poultry, and butcher's meat, and the most eligible methods of preparing them for the table. His **reminiscences** of good cheer, however ancient the date of the actual banquet, seemed to bring the **savor** of pig or turkey under one's very nostrils. There were flavors on his palate, that had lingered there not less than sixty or seventy years, and were still apparently as fresh as that of the mutton-chop which he had just devoured for his breakfast. I have heard him smack his lips over dinners, every guest at which, except himself, had long been food for worms. It was marvellous to observe how the ghosts of bygone meals were

RETRIBUTION (reh trih <u>byoo</u> shuhn) *n.*
something which is justly deserved, such as
repayment or punishment
  Synonyms: vengeance, payback, compensation

SUBSEQUENT (<u>suhb</u> suh kwehnt) *adj.*
following in time or order
  Synonyms: succeeding, next, after

INVETERATELY (ihn <u>veht</u> uhr iht lee) *adv.*
in a long-standing and deeply rooted manner
  Synonyms: habitually, chronically

DETRIMENT (<u>deht</u> ruh mehnt) *n.*
disadvantage, something that causes harm or injury
  Synonyms: loss, impairment, disservice

SUBSEQUENTLY (<u>suhb</u> suh kwehnt lee) *adv.*
in time or order, in succession, behind
  Synonyms: next, afterward

continually rising up before him; not in anger or **retribution**, but as if grateful for his former appreciation and seeking to reduplicate an endless series of enjoyment, at once shadowy and sensual. A tenderloin of beef, a hindquarter of veal, a sparerib of pork, a particular chicken, or a remarkably praiseworthy turkey, which had perhaps adorned his board in the days of the elder Adams, would be remembered; while all the **subsequent** experience of our race, and all the events that brightened or darkened his individual career, had gone over him with as little permanent effect as the passing breeze. The chief tragic event of the old man's life, so far as I could judge, was his mishap with a certain goose which lived and died some twenty or forty years ago; a goose of most promising figure, but which, at table, proved so **inveterately** tough that the carving knife would make no impression on its carcass, and it could only be divided with an axe and handsaw.

But it is time to quit this sketch; on which, however, I should be glad to dwell at considerably more length, because of all men whom I have ever known, this individual was fittest to be a Custom House officer. Most persons, owing to causes which I may not have space to hint at, suffer moral **detriment** from this peculiar mode of life. The old Inspector was incapable of it, and, were he to continue in office to the end of time, would be as good as he was then, and sit down to dinner with just as good an appetite.

There is one likeness, without which my gallery of Custom House portraits would be strangely incomplete; but which my comparatively few opportunities for observation enable me to sketch only in the merest outline. It is that of the Collector, our gallant old General, who, after his brilliant military service, **subsequently** to which he had ruled over a wild Western territory, had come hither, twenty years before, to spend the decline of

HONORABLE (<u>ah</u> nuhr uh buhl) *adj.*
illustrious, praiseworthy, deserving
Synonyms: respectable, dignified, noble

SCORE (skohr) *n.*
1. twenty; a very large number
Synonyms: many, multitude
2. a notch or scratch, made to keep tally
Synonyms: furrow, scrape, groove

INFIRMITY (ihn <u>fuhr</u> mih tee) *n.*
weakness; disease, ailment
Synonyms: frailty; illness, affliction

MARTIAL (<u>mahr</u> shuhl) *adj.*
warlike, pertaining to the military
Synonyms: soldierly, combative

ASCEND (uh <u>sehnd</u>) *v.* **-ing,-ed.**
to rise to another level or climb; to move upward
Synonyms: elevate, escalate, mount; hoist, lift

SERENITY (suh <u>reh</u> nuh tee) *n.*
calm, peacefulness
Synonyms: tranquility, equanimity, composure,
contentment

COUNTENANCE (<u>kown</u> tuh nuhns) *n.*
appearance, facial expression
Synonyms: face, features, visage

REPOSE (rih <u>pohz</u>) *n.*
a state of peace or tranquility; relaxation, leisure
Synonyms: calmness, serenity; rest, ease, idleness

MEDIUM (<u>mee</u> dee uhm) *n.*
a substance or object that is used to transmit or
accomplish something
Synonyms: means, instrument, vehicle, mechanism

QUIETUDE (<u>kwie</u> eh tood) *n.*
peace or tranquility
Synonyms: calm, ease, contentment, serenity

his varied and **honorable** life. The brave soldier had already numbered, nearly or quite, his three-**score** years and ten, and was pursuing the remainder of his earthly march, burdened with **infirmities** which even the **martial** music of his own spirit-stirring recollections could do little towards lightening. The step was palsied now that he had been foremost in the charge. It was only with the assistance of a servant, and by leaning his hand heavily on the iron balustrade, that he could slowly and painfully **ascend** the Custom House steps, and, with a toilsome progress across the floor, attain his customary chair beside the fireplace. There he used to sit, gazing with a somewhat dim **serenity** of aspect at the figures that came and went; amid the rustle of papers, the administering of oaths, the discussion of business, and the casual talk of the office; all which sounds and circumstances seemed but indistinctly to impress his senses, and hardly to make their way into his inner sphere of contemplation. His **countenance**, in this **repose**, was mild and kindly. If his notice was sought, an expression of courtesy and interest gleamed out upon his features; proving that there was light within him, and that it was only the outward **medium** of the intellectual lamp that obstructed the rays in their passage. The closer you penetrated to the substance of his mind, the sounder it appeared. When no longer called upon to speak, or listen, either of which operations cost him an evident effort, his face would briefly subside into its former not uncheerful **quietude**. It was not painful to behold this look; for, though dim, it had not the imbecility of decaying age. The framework of his nature, originally strong and massive, was not yet crumbled into ruin.

To observe and define his character, however, under such disadvantages, was as difficult a task as to trace out and build up anew, in imagination, an old fortress,

BIPED (<u>bie</u> pehd) *n.*
   a two-footed animal, often refers to humans
      Synonym: upright creature

DISCERN (dihs <u>uhrn</u>) *v.* **-ing,-ed.**
   to perceive or recognize something
      Synonyms: descry, observe, glimpse, distinguish

IMPULSE (<u>ihm</u> puhls) *n.*
   sudden tendency, inclination
      Synonyms: urge, whim

PERVADE (puhr <u>vayd</u>) *v.* **-ing,-ed.**
   to become diffused throughout every part of
      Synonyms: permeate, spread, fill, transfuse

EXTINCT (ihk <u>stingkt</u>) *adj.*
   dead; no longer active
      Synonyms: exterminated, eradicated, annihilated,
      eliminated, destroyed; defunct

REPOSE (rih <u>pohz</u>) *n.*
   a state of peace or tranquility; relaxation, leisure
      Synonyms: calmness, serenity; rest, ease, idleness

INFIRMITY (ihn <u>fuhr</u> mih tee) *n.*
   weakness; disease, ailment
      Synonyms: frailty; illness, affliction

DEMEANOR (dih <u>meen</u> uhr) *n.*
   one's behavior or conduct
      Synonyms: attitude, disposition, manner, presence

like Ticonderoga, from a view of its gray and broken ruins. Here and there, perchance, the walls may remain almost complete, but elsewhere may be only a shapeless mound, <u>cumbrous</u> with its very strength, and over-grown, through long years of peace and neglect, with grass and alien weeds.

Nevertheless, looking at the old warrior with affection—for, slight as was the communication between us, my feeling towards him, like that of all **bipeds** and quadrupeds who knew him, might not improperly be termed so—I could **discern** the main points of his portrait. It was marked with the noble and heroic qualities which showed it to be not by a mere accident, but of good right, that he had won a distinguished name. His spirit could never, I conceive, have been characterized by an uneasy activity; it must, at any period of his life, have required an **impulse** to set him in motion; but, once stirred up, with obstacles to overcome and an adequate object to be attained, it was not in the man to give out or fail. The heat that had formerly **pervaded** his nature, and which was not yet **extinct**, was never of the kind that flashes and flickers in a blaze; but, rather, a deep, red glow, as of iron in a furnace. Weight, solidity, firmness; this was the expression of his **repose**, even in such decay as had crept untimely over him, at the period of which I speak. But I could imagine, even then, that under some excitement which should go deeply into his consciousness—roused by a trumpet peal loud enough to awaken all of his energies that were not dead, but only slumbering—he was yet capable of flinging off his **infirmities** like a sick man's gown, dropping the staff of age to seize a battle-sword, and starting up once more a warrior. And, in so intense a moment, his **demeanor** would have still been calm. Such an exhibition, however, was but to be pictured in fancy; not to be anticipated, nor desired. What I saw in him—as evidently as the

SAT Vocabulary

PONDEROUS (<u>pahn</u> duhr uhs) *adj.*
  weighty, heavy, large
    Synonyms: hefty, massive, cumbersome, unwieldy

OBSTINACY (<u>ahb</u> stih nuh see) *n.*
  stubbornness
    Synonyms: bullheadedness, pertinacity

INTEGRITY (ihn <u>tehg</u> rih tee) *n.*
  decency, honesty, wholeness
    Synonyms: honor, probity, rectitude, virtue

ENDOWMENT (ehn <u>dow</u> mehnt) (ihn <u>dow</u> mehnt) *n.*
  a gift; talent
    Synonyms: grant, benefit; ability, aptitude

UNMALLEABLE (uhn <u>maa</u> lee uh buhl) *adj.*
  difficult to work with or form into shape
    Synonyms: inflexible, unyielding, rigid

BENEVOLENCE (buh <u>neh</u> vuh luhnts) *n.*
  kindness, compassion
    Synonyms: charity, altruism, generosity

ACTUATE (<u>aak</u> chuh wayt) (<u>aak</u> shuh wayt) *v.* **-ing,-ed.**
  to move into action; to put into mechanical action
    Synonyms: stimulate, motivate, inspire; activate

POLEMICAL (puh <u>leh</u> mih kuhl) *adj.*
  controversial, argumentative
    Synonyms: quarrelsome, contentious

PHILANTHROPIST (fihl <u>aan</u> throh pihst) *n.*
  someone who donates time or money to benefit
  humankind
    Synonyms: altruist, humanitarian, do-gooder

IMPART (ihm <u>pahrt</u>) *v.* **-ing,-ed.** *(See page 28.)*

INNATE (ih <u>nayt</u>) (<u>ihn</u> ayt) *adj.*
  natural, inborn
    Synonyms: congenital, inherent, intrinsic

OBSCURE (uhb <u>skyoor</u>) *v.* **-ing,-ed.**
  to make dim or unclear
    Synonyms: hide, conceal, blur, veil

EVANESCENT (eh vuh <u>nehs</u> uhnt) *adj.*
  momentary, tendency toward vanishing
    Synonyms: transient, ephemeral, fleeting, fugitive

indestructible ramparts of Old Ticonderoga already cited as the most appropriate simile—were the features of stubborn and **ponderous** endurance, which might well have amounted to **obstinacy** in his earlier days; of **integrity**, that, like most of his other **endowments**, lay in a somewhat heavy mass, and was just as **unmalleable** and unmanageable as a ton of iron ore; and of **benevolence**, which, fiercely as he led the bayonets on at Chippewa or Fort Erie, I take to be of quite as genuine a stamp as what **actuates** any or all of the **polemical philanthropists** of the age. He had slain men with his own hand for aught I know—certainly they had fallen, like blades of grass at the sweep of the <u>scythe</u>, before the charge to which his spirit **imparted** its triumphant energy, but, be that as it might, there was never in his heart so much cruelty as would have brushed the down off a butterfly's wing. I have not known the man, to whose **innate** kindliness I would more confidently make an appeal.

Many characteristics—and those, too, which contribute not the least forcibly to **impart** resemblance in a sketch—must have vanished, or been **obscured**, before I met the General. All merely graceful attributes are usually the most **evanescent**; nor does Nature adorn the human ruin with blossoms of new beauty that have their roots and proper nutriment only in the chinks and crevices of decay, as she sows wallflowers over the ruined fortress of Ticonderoga. Still, even in respect of grace and beauty, there were points well worth noting. A ray of humor, now and then, would make its way through the veil of dim obstruction, and glimmer pleasantly upon our faces. A trait of native elegance, seldom seen in the masculine character after childhood or early youth, was shown in the General's fondness for the sight and fragrance of flowers. An old soldier might be supposed to prize only the bloody laurel on his brow; but

FLORAL (<u>flohr</u> uhl) *adj.*
relating to flowering plants
Synonyms: botanical, verdant, herbal

COUNTENANCE (<u>kown</u> tuh nuhns) *n.*
appearance, facial expression
Synonyms: face, features, visage

TUMULT (<u>tuh</u> muhlt) *n.*
state of confusion, agitation
Synonyms: disturbance, turmoil, din, commotion

UNCOUTH (uhn <u>kooth</u>) *adj.*
lacking in refinement, awkward and uncultivated in
appearance or manner
Synonyms: crude, clumsy, ungraceful

BUSTLE (<u>buh</u> suhl) *n.*
busy and energetic activity
Synonyms: chaos, commotion, hubbub

SUSTAIN (suh <u>stayn</u>) *v.* **-ing,-ed.**
to support, uphold; endure, undergo
Synonyms: maintain, prop, encourage; withstand

STALWART (<u>stahl</u> wuhrt) *adj.*
stout, physically sturdy and strong; resolute
Synonyms: husky, muscular; steadfast, tenacious

PERIL (<u>pehr</u> ihl) *n.*
danger
Synonyms: trouble, hazard, harm

VALOR (<u>vaa</u> luhr) *n.*
bravery, courage
Synonyms: heroism, intrepidity, gallantry, valiance

here was one who seemed to have a young girl's appreciation of the **floral** tribe.

There, beside the fireplace, the brave old General used to sit; while the Surveyor—though seldom, when it could be avoided, taking upon himself the difficult task of engaging him in conversation—was fond of standing at a distance, and watching his quiet and almost slumberous **countenance**. He seemed away from us, although we saw him but a few yards off; remote, though we passed close beside his chair; unattainable, though we might have stretched forth our hands and touched his own. It might be that he lived a more real life within his thoughts than amid the unappropriate environment of the Collector's office. The evolutions of the parade; the **tumult** of the battle; the flourish of old, heroic music, heard thirty years before—such scenes and sounds, perhaps, were all alive before his intellectual sense. Meanwhile, the merchants and shipmasters, the spruce clerks and **uncouth** sailors, entered and departed; the **bustle** of this commercial and Custom House life kept up its little murmur round about him; and neither with the men nor their affairs did the General appear to **sustain** the most distant relation. He was as much out of place as an old sword—now rusty, but which had flashed once in the battle's front, and showed still a bright gleam along its blade—would have been, among the inkstands, paper-folders, and mahogany rulers on the Deputy Collector's desk.

There was one thing that much aided me in renewing and re-creating the **stalwart** soldier of the Niagara frontier—the man of true and simple energy. It was the recollection of those memorable words of his—"I'll try, Sir!"—spoken on the very verge of a desperate and heroic enterprise, and breathing the soul and spirit of New England hardihood, comprehending all **perils,** and encountering all. If, in our country, **valor** were rewarded

ACUTE (uh <u>kyoot</u>) *adj.*
   clever, shrewd; sharp, pointed, severe
      Synonyms: ingenious, keen; intense, fierce

FACULTY (<u>faa</u> kuhl tee) *n.*
   the ability to act or do
      Synonyms: aptitude, capability, sense, skill

INTERLOPER (<u>ihn</u> tuhr loh puhr) *n.*
   a meddler, a person who interferes in others' affairs
      Synonyms: intruder, tresspasser

IDEAL (ie <u>deel</u>) *n.*
   an example of perfection or excellence
      Synonyms: model, exemplar, standard, paragon

DEXTERITY (dehk <u>stayr</u> ih tee) *n.*
   physical or mental skill, ability
      Synonyms: aptitude, adroitness, proficiency

INEVITABLE (ihn <u>ehv</u> ih tuh buhl) *adj.*
   certain, unavoidable
      Synonyms: inescapable, sure, predictable

DRAW *v.* **-ing, drew, drawn.**
   1. to attract; to pull, drag
      Synonyms: lure, entice; haul, tow, lug
   2. to move steadily
      Synonyms: proceed, continue, progress

CONDESCENSION (kahn dih <u>sehn</u> shuhn) *n.*
   an attitude of superiority
      Synonyms: patronization, smugness

FORBEARANCE (fohr <u>bayr</u> uhnts) *n.*
   patience, restraint, leniency
      Synonyms: resignation, tolerance

by heraldic honor, this phrase—which it seems so easy to speak, but which only he, with such a task of danger and glory before him, has ever spoken—would be the best and fittest of all mottoes for the General's shield of arms.

It contributes greatly towards a man's moral and intellectual health, to be brought into habits of companionship with individuals unlike himself, who care little for his pursuits, and whose sphere and abilities he must go out of himself to appreciate. The accidents of my life have often afforded me this advantage, but never with more fulness and variety than during my continuance in office. There was one man, especially, the observation of whose character gave me a new idea of talent. His gifts were emphatically those of a man of business; prompt, **acute**, clear-minded; with an eye that saw through all perplexities, and a **faculty** of arrangement that made them vanish, as by the waving of an enchanter's wand. Bred up from boyhood in the Custom House, it was his proper field of activity; and the many intricacies of business, so harassing to the **interloper**, presented themselves before him with the regularity of a perfectly comprehended system. In my contemplation, he stood as the **ideal** of his class. He was, indeed, the Custom House in himself, or, at all events, the mainspring that kept its variously revolving wheels in motion; for, in an institution like this, where its officers are appointed to subserve their own profit and convenience, and seldom with a leading reference to their fitness for the duty to be performed, they must perforce seek elsewhere the **dexterity** which is not in them. Thus, by an **inevitable** necessity, as a magnet attracts steel-filings, so did our man of business **draw** to himself the difficulties which everybody met with. With an easy **condescension**, and kind **forbearance** towards our stupidity—which, to his order of mind, must have seemed little short of crime—would he forthwith, by the merest

ESOTERIC (eh suh <u>tehr</u> ihk) *adj.*
understood by or designed for only a few; relating to a small circle of people
Synonyms: mysterious, arcane, occult, recondite; limited

INTEGRITY (ihn <u>tehg</u> rih tee) *n.*
decency, honesty, wholeness
Synonyms: honor, probity, rectitude, virtue

ADAPTED (uh <u>daap</u> tihd) *adj.*
adjusted, changed, fit
Synonyms: accustomed, altered, conformed

PROVIDENCE (<u>prah</u> vih dehnts) *n.*
divine control and direction by God; preparation and foresight
Synonyms: fate, destiny, good luck; prudence, precaution

IMPRACTICABLE (ihm <u>praak</u> tih kuh buhl) *adj.*
incapable of being performed by the means employed; impassable
Synonyms: imprudent, impossible; blocked

INDULGE (ihn <u>duhlj</u>) *v.* **-ing,-ed.**
to give in to a craving or desire
Synonyms: humor, gratify, allow, pamper

RELIC (<u>rehl</u> ihk) *n.*
an object or idea that is special because of its connection to the past; remains
Synonyms: memento, treasure, token; trace

FASTIDIOUS (faa <u>stihd</u> ee uhs) *adj.*
carefully attentive or overattentive to details
Synonyms: meticulous, precise

IMBUE (ihm <u>byoo</u>) *v.* **-ing,-ed.**
to infuse; to dye, wet
Synonyms: permeate; moisten

SENTIMENT (<u>sehn</u> tuh muhnt) *n.*
an attitude, thought, or judgment prompted by feeling
Synonym: emotion

FACULTY (<u>faa</u> kuhl tee) *n.* *(See page 46.)*

touch of his finger, make the incomprehensible as clear as daylight. The merchants valued him not less than we, his **esoteric** friends. His **integrity** was perfect; it was a law of nature with him, rather than a choice or a principle; nor can it be otherwise than the main condition of an intellect so remarkably clear and accurate as his, to be honest and regular in the administration of affairs. A stain on his conscience, as to anything that came within the range of his vocation, would trouble such a man very much in the same way, though to a far greater degree, than an error in the balance of an account, or an ink-blot on the fair page of a book of record. Here, in a word—and it is a rare instance in my life—I had met with a person thoroughly **adapted** to the situation which he held.

Such were some of the people with whom I now found myself connected. I took it in good part, at the hands of **Providence**, that I was thrown into a position so little akin to my past habits, and set myself seriously to gather from it whatever profit was to be had. After my fellowship of toil and **impracticable** schemes with the dreamy brethren of Brook Farm; after living for three years within the subtile influence of an intellect like Emerson's; after those wild, free days on the Assabeth, **indulging** fantastic speculations beside our fire of fallen boughs with Ellery Channing; after talking with Thoreau about pine-trees and Indian **relics** in his hermitage at Walden; after growing **fastidious** by sympathy with the classic refinement of Hillard's culture; after becoming **imbued** with poetic **sentiment** at Longfellow's hearth-stone—it was time, at length, that I should exercise other **faculties** of my nature, and nourish myself with food for which I had hitherto had little appetite. Even the old Inspector was desirable, as a change of diet, to a man who had known Alcott. I looked upon it as an evidence, in some measure, of a

FACULTY (<u>faa</u> kuhl tee) *n.*
the ability to act or do
Synonyms: aptitude, capability, sense, skill

SUSPEND (suh <u>spehnd</u>) *v.* **-ing,-ed.**
to delay, interrupt; to dangle, hang
Synonyms: defer, cease, disrupt, halt, discontinue;
swing

INANIMATE (ihn <u>aan</u> ih miht) *adj.*
not active or alive, lacking energy
Synonyms: dead, lifeless, dull, soulless

IMPUNITY (ihm <u>pyoo</u> nih tee) *n.*
freedom from punishment or harm
Synonyms: exemption, immunity, liberty

TRANSITORY (<u>traan</u> sih tohr ee) *adj.*
short-lived, existing only briefly
Synonyms: transient, ephemeral, fleeting, fugitive,
momentary

PROPHETIC (pruh <u>feh</u> tihk) *adj.*
relating to the ability to foretell events
Synonyms: intuitive, clairvoyant, predictive

PRESUME (prih <u>zoom</u>) *v.* **-ing,-ed.**
to assume or believe something without proof; to dare
Synonyms: take for granted; venture

system naturally well balanced, and lacking no essential part of a thorough organization, that, with such associates to remember, I could mingle at once with men of altogether different qualities and never murmur at the change.

Literature, its exertions and objects, were now of little moment in my regard. I cared not, at this period, for books; they were apart from me. Nature—except it were human nature—the nature that is developed in earth and sky, was, in one sense, hidden from me; and all the imaginative delight, wherewith it had been spiritualized, passed away out of my mind. A gift, a **faculty** if it had not departed, was **suspended** and **inanimate** within me. There would have been something sad, unutterably dreary, in all this, had I not been conscious that it lay at my own option to recall whatever was valuable in the past. It might be true, indeed, that this was a life which could not with **impunity** be lived too long; else it might make me permanently other than I had been without transforming me into any shape which it would be worth my while to take. But I never considered it as other than a **transitory** life. There was always a **prophetic** instinct, a low whisper in my ear, that, within no long period, and whenever a new change of custom should be essential to my good, a change would come.

Meanwhile, there I was, a Surveyor of the Revenue, and, so far as I have been able to understand, as good a Surveyor as need be. A man of thought, fancy, and sensibility (had he ten times the Surveyor's proportion of those qualities) may, at any time, be a man of affairs, if he will only choose to give himself the trouble. My fellow-officers, and the merchants and sea-captains with whom my official duties brought me into any manner of connection, viewed me in no other light, and probably knew me in no other character. None of them, I **presume**, had ever read a page of my inditing, or would

51

DEVOID (dih <u>voyd</u>) *adj.*
   being without, lacking
      Synonyms: destitute, empty, vacant, null, bare

REBUKE (ree <u>byook</u>) *n.*
   a reprimand, scolding, punishment
      Synonyms: admonition, reproof, reproach

COMMODITY (kuh <u>mah</u> dih tee) *n.*
   a useful item, a convenience
      Synonyms: benefit, advantage

have cared a fig the more for me if they had read them all; nor would it have mended the matter, in the least, had those same unprofitable pages been written with a pen like that of <u>Burns</u> or of Chaucer, each of whom was a Custom House officer in his day, as well as I. It is a good lesson—though it may often be a hard one—for a man who has dreamed of literary fame, and of making for himself a rank among the world's dignitaries by such means, to step aside out of the narrow circle in which his claims are recognized, and to find how utterly **devoid** of significance, beyond that circle, is all that he achieves, and all he aims at. I know not that I especially needed the lesson, either in the way of warning or **rebuke**; but, at any rate, I learned it thoroughly; nor, it gives me pleasure to reflect, did the truth, as it came home to my perception, ever cost me a pang, or require to be thrown off in a sigh. In the way of literary talk, it is true, the Naval Officer—an excellent fellow, who came into office with me and went out only a little later—would often engage me in a discussion about one or the other of his favorite topics, Napoleon or Shakespeare. The Collector's junior clerk, too—a young gentleman who, it was whispered, occasionally covered a sheet of Uncle Sam's letter-paper with what (at the distance of a few yards) looked very much like poetry—used now and then to speak to me of books, as matters with which I might possibly be conversant. This was my all of lettered <u>intercourse</u>; and it was quite sufficient for my necessities.

No longer seeking nor caring that my name should be blazoned abroad on title-pages, I smiled to think that it had now another kind of vogue. The Custom House marker imprinted it, with a stencil and black paint, on pepper-bags, and baskets of anatto, and cigar boxes, and bales of all kinds of dutiable merchandise, in testimony that these **commodities** had paid the <u>impost</u>, and

PROPRIETY (pruh <u>prie</u> ih tee) *n.*
the quality of conforming to expected customs and
behaviors
Synonyms: appropriateness, correctness,
properness

EDIFICE (<u>eh</u> duh fuhs) *n.*
a large structure
Synonyms: building, construction, skyscraper

ADAPTED (uh <u>daap</u> tihd) *adj.*
adjusted, changed, fit
Synonyms: accustomed, altered, conformed

SUBSEQUENT (<u>suhb</u> suh kwehnt) *adj.*
following in time or order
Synonyms: succeeding, next, after

PROSPERITY (prah <u>speh</u> ruh tee) *n.*
wealth or success
Synonyms: affluence, abundance, opulence

EFFUSION (ih <u>fyoo</u> shuhn) *n.*
expression of emotion without restraint
Synonyms: profusion, overflow, outburst

OBLIVION (oh <u>blih</u> vee uhn) *n.*
the state of being forgotten; lack of awareness
Synonyms: nothingness, nowhere, nonexistence;
mindlessness, forgetfulness, indifference

gone regularly through the office. Borne on such queer vehicle of fame, a knowledge of my existence, so far as a name conveys it, was carried where it had never been before, and, I hope, will never go again.

But the past was not dead. Once in a great while, the thoughts, that had seemed so vital and so active, yet had been put to rest so quietly, revived again. One of the most remarkable occasions, when the habit of bygone days awoke in me, was that which brings it within the law of literary **propriety** to offer the public the sketch which I am now writing.

In the second story of the Custom House there is a large room, in which the brick-work and naked rafters have never been covered with panelling and plaster. The **edifice**—originally projected on a scale **adapted** to the old commercial enterprise of the port, and with an idea of **subsequent prosperity** destined never to be realized—contains far more space than its occupants know what to do with. This airy hall, therefore, over the Collector's apartments, remains unfinished to this day, and, in spite of the aged cobwebs that <u>festoon</u> its dusky beams, appears still to await the labor of the carpenter and mason. At one end of the room, in a recess, were a number of barrels, piled one upon another, containing bundles of official documents. Large quantities of similar rubbish lay <u>lumbering</u> the floor. It was sorrowful to think how many days and weeks and months and years of toil had been wasted on these musty papers, which were now only an <u>encumbrance</u> on earth, and were hidden away in this forgotten corner, never more to be glanced at by human eyes. But, then, what reams of other manuscripts—filled not with the dullness of official formalities, but with the thought of inventive brains and the rich **effusion** of deep hearts—had gone equally to **oblivion**; and that, moreover, without serving a purpose in their day, as these heaped-up papers had,

MAGNATE (<u>maag</u> nayt) (<u>maag</u> niht) *n.*
   a powerful or influential person
      Synonyms: potentate, tycoon, nabob, dignitary,
      luminary

OBSCURE (uhb <u>skyoor</u>) *adj.*
   not well known; dim, unclear
      Synonyms: remote, minor; dark, faint

POSTERIOR (pah <u>stih</u> ree ohr) *adj.*
   after; located behind or to the rear of
      Synonyms: subsequent, following; caudal, dorsal,
      aft, hindmost

DEARTH (duhrth) *n.*
   lack, scarcity, insufficiency
      Synonyms: absence, shortage

FOUNDER (<u>fown</u> duhr) *v.* **-ing,-ed.**
   sink, to fall helplessly
      Synonyms: immerse, plunge

DECIPHERABLE (dih <u>sie</u> fuhr uh buhl) *adj.*
   easily readable; understandable
      Synonyms: legible, clear, lucid; comprehensible

and—saddest of all—without purchasing for their writers the comfortable livelihood which the clerks of the Custom House had gained by these worthless scratchings of the pen! Yet not altogether worthless, perhaps, as materials of local history. Here, no doubt, statistics of the former commerce of Salem might be discovered, and memorials of her princely merchants, old <u>King Derby</u>, old Billy Gray, old Simon Forrester, and many another **magnate** in his day whose powdered head, however, was scarcely in the tomb, before his mountain pile of wealth began to dwindle. The founders of the greater part of the families which now compose the aristocracy of Salem might here be traced, from the petty and **obscure** beginnings of their traffic, at periods generally much **posterior** to the Revolution, upward to what their children look upon as long-established rank.

Prior to the Revolution, there is a **dearth** of records; the earlier documents and archives of the Custom House having, probably, been carried off to Halifax, when all the King's officials accompanied the British army in its flight from Boston. It has often been a matter of regret with me; for, going back, perhaps to the days of the <u>Protectorate</u>, those papers must have contained many references to forgotten or remembered men, and to antique customs, which would have affected me with the same pleasure as when I used to pick up Indian arrowheads in the field near the Old Manse.

But one idle and rainy day, it was my fortune to make a discovery of some little interest. Poking and burrowing into the heaped-up rubbish in the corner; unfolding one and another document, and reading the names of vessels that had long ago **foundered** at sea or rotted at the wharves, and those of merchants never heard of now on 'Change, nor very readily **decipherable** on their mossy tombstones; glancing at such matters with the

BESTOW (bih <u>stoh</u>) *v.* **-ing,-ed.**
  to apply or devote time or effort; to give as a gift
    Synonyms: allocate, dedicate; endow, confer, present

SUBSTANTIAL (suhb <u>staan</u> shuhl) *adj.*
  having substance; large in size or amount
    Synonyms: important, significant; ample, hearty,
    strong

SCORE (skohr) *n.*
  1. twenty; a very large number
    Synonyms: many, multitude
  2. a notch or scratch, made to keep tally
    Synonyms: furrow, scrape, groove

EDIFICE (<u>eh</u> duh fuhs) *n.*
  a large structure
    Synonyms: building, construction, skyscraper

VENERABLE (<u>veh</u> nehr uh buhl) *adj.*
  respected because of age
    Synonyms: distinguished, elderly

saddened, weary, half-reluctant interest which we **bestow** on the corpse of dead activity—and exerting my fancy, sluggish with little use, to raise up from these dry bones an image of the old town's brighter aspect, when India was a new region, and only Salem knew the way thither—I chanced to lay my hand on a small package, carefully done up in a piece of ancient yellow parchment. This envelope had the air of an official record of some period long past, when clerks engrossed their stiff and formal <u>chirography</u> on more **substantial** materials than at present. There was something about it that quickened an instinctive curiosity, and made me undo the faded red tape that tied up the package, with the sense that a treasure would here be brought to light. Unbending the rigid folds of the parchment cover I found it to be a commission, under the hand and seal of Governor Shirley, in favor of one Jonathan Pue, as Surveyor of his Majesty's Customs for the port of Salem, in the Province of Massachusetts Bay. I remembered to have read (probably in Felt's <u>Annals</u>) a notice of the decease of Mr. Surveyor Pue, about four-**score** years ago; and likewise, in a newspaper of recent times, an account of the digging up of his remains in the little graveyard of St. Peter's Church, during the renewal of that **edifice**. Nothing, if I rightly call to mind, was left of my respected predecessor, save an imperfect skeleton, and some fragments of apparel, and a wig of majestic frizzle; which, unlike the head that it once adorned, was in very satisfactory preservation. But, on examining the papers which the parchment commission served to envelop, I found more traces of Mr. Pue's mental part, and the internal operations of his head, than the frizzled wig had contained of the **venerable** skull itself.

They were documents, in short, not official, but of a private nature, or at least written in his private capacity, and apparently with his own hand. I could account for

ANTIQUARIAN (aan tih <u>kwayr</u> ee ihn) *n.*
an expert on antiques
Synonyms: collector, historian

VENERATION (veh nehr <u>ay</u> shuhn) *n.*
adoration, honor, respect
Synonyms: homage, reverence, deference, esteem

IMPEL (ihm <u>pehl</u>) *v.* **-ling,-led.**
to urge forward as if driven by a strong moral pressure
Synonyms: push, prompt, incite, instigate

PIOUS (<u>pie</u> uhs) *adj.*
dedicated, devout; extremely religious
Synonyms: observant, reverent; sanctimonious

INCLINE (ihn <u>klien</u>) *v.* **-ing,-ed.**
to have a specific tendency, to be predisposed
Synonyms: lean toward, influence, impel, prefer

DISPOSITION (dihs puh <u>zih</u> shuhn) *n.*
1. an act of removing or disposing of something
Synonyms: riddance, transfer, placement, conclusion
2. mood or temperament
Synonyms: behavior, tendency, inclination, nature

DRAW *v.* **-ing, drew, drawn.**
1. to attract; to pull, drag
Synonyms: lure, entice; haul, tow, lug
2. to move steadily
Synonyms: proceed, continue, progress

DEFACED (dih <u>faysd</u>) *adj.*
damaged, marred, vandalized
Synonyms: spoiled, impaired, disfigured

their being included in the heap of Custom House lumber only by the fact that Mr. Pue's death had happened suddenly; and that these papers, which he probably kept in his official desk, had never come to the knowledge of his heirs, or were supposed to relate to the business of the revenue. On the transfer of the archives to Halifax, this package, proving to be of no public concern, was left behind, and had remained ever since unopened.

The ancient Surveyor—being little molested, I suppose, at that early day, with business pertaining to his office—seems to have devoted some of his many leisure hours to researches as a local **antiquarian**, and other inquisitions of a similar nature. These supplied material for petty activity to a mind that would otherwise have been eaten up with rust. A portion of his facts, by the by, did me good service in the preparation of the article entitled "MAIN STREET," included in the present third volume of this edition. The remainder may perhaps be applied to purposes equally valuable hereafter; or not impossibly may be worked up, so far as they go, into a regular history of Salem, should my **veneration** for the natal soil ever **impel** me to so **pious** a task. Meanwhile, they shall be at the command of any gentleman, **inclined**, and competent, to take the unprofitable labor off my hands. As a final **disposition**, I contemplate depositing them with the Essex Historical Society.

But the object that most **drew** my attention, in the mysterious package, was a certain affair of fine red cloth, much worn and faded. There were traces about it of gold embroidery, which, however, was greatly frayed and **defaced**; so that none, or very little, of the glitter was left. It had been wrought, as was easy to perceive, with wonderful skill of needlework; and the stitch (as I am assured by ladies conversant with such mysteries) gives evidence of a now forgotten art, not to be recovered even by the process of picking out the threads. This

SACRILEGIOUS (saa kruh <u>lihj</u> uhs) *adj.*
relating to the violation of something, someone, or someplace sacred
Synonyms: blasphemous, irreverent, ungodly

EVANESCENT (eh vuh <u>nehs</u> uhnt) *adj.*
momentary, tendency toward vanishing
Synonyms: transient, ephemeral, fleeting, fugitive

SUBTLY (<u>suh</u> tuh lee) (<u>suh</u> tlee) *adv.*
in a manner that is hard to detect or describe
Synonyms: elusively, delicately, tactfully, slightly

COGITATE (<u>kah</u> jih tayt) *v.* **-ing,-ed.**
to ponder or think carefully
Synonyms: reflect, consider, deliberate

CONTRIVE (kuhn <u>triev</u>) *v.* **-ing,-ed.**
to form in an artistic manner; to devise, plan, or manage
Synonyms: create, design; concoct, scheme

rag of scarlet cloth—for time and wear and a **sacrilegious** moth had reduced it to little other than a rag—on careful examination, assumed the shape of a letter. It was the capital letter A. By an accurate measurement, each limb proved to be precisely three inches and a quarter in length. It had been intended, there could be no doubt, as an ornamental article of dress; but how it was to be worn, or what rank, honor, and dignity, in by-past times, were signified by it, was a riddle which (so **evanescent** are the fashions of the world in these particulars) I saw little hope of solving. And yet it strangely interested me. My eyes fastened themselves upon the old scarlet letter, and would not be turned aside. Certainly, there was some deep meaning in it, most worthy of interpretation, and which, as it were, streamed forth from the mystic symbol, **subtly** communicating itself to my sensibilities, but evading the analysis of my mind.

While thus perplexed—and **cogitating**, among other hypotheses, whether the letter might not have been one of those decorations which the white men used to **contrive**, in order to take the eyes of Indians—I happened to place it on my breast. It seemed to me—the reader may smile, but must not doubt my word—it seemed to me, then, that I experienced a sensation not altogether physical, yet almost so, as of burning heat; and as if the letter were not of red cloth, but red-hot iron. I shuddered, and involuntarily let it fall upon the floor.

In the absorbing contemplation of the scarlet letter, I had hitherto neglected to examine a small roll of dingy paper, around which it had been twisted. This I now opened, and had the satisfaction to find, recorded by the old Surveyor's pen, a reasonably complete explanation of the whole affair. There were several foolscap sheets, containing many particulars respecting the life and conversation of one Hester Prynne, who appeared

SOLEMN (<u>sah</u> luhm) *adj.*
deeply serious, somberly impressive
Synonyms: dignified, earnest, ceremonial

PROPENSITY (pruh <u>pehn</u> suh tee) *n.*
inclination, tendency
Synonyms: predilection, bias, penchant

INEVITABLY (ihn <u>ehv</u> ih tuh blee) *adv.*
certainly, unavoidably
Synonyms: inescapably, surely, predictably

REVERENCE (<u>reh</u> vuhr ehnts) *n.*
deep respect, awe
Synonyms: veneration, adoration, admiration

PRY (prie) *v.* **-ing,-ied.**
to look closely at; to meddle; force open
Synonyms: probe; snoop, nose, spy; lever

SINGULAR (<u>sihn</u> gyuh luhr) *adj.*
uncommon, peculiar
Synonyms: unusual, odd, rare, unique, individual

RELIC (<u>rehl</u> ihk) *n.*
an object or idea that is special because of its
connection to the past; remains
Synonyms: memento, treasure, token; trace

INDUCE (ih <u>doos</u>) (ihn <u>dyoos</u>) *v.* **-ing,-ed.**
to persuade; bring about
Synonyms: convince, prevail; cause

AFFIRM (uh <u>fihrm</u>) *v.* **-ing,-ed.**
to state positively, to assert as valid or confirmed
Synonyms: declare, avow, maintain

INVARIABLY (ihn <u>vaa</u> ree uh blee) *adv.*
without change, constantly
Synonyms: always, repeatedly, perpetually

to have been rather a noteworthy personage in the view of our ancestors. She had flourished during the period between the early days of Massachusetts and the close of the seventeenth century. Aged persons, alive in the time of Mr. Surveyor Pue, and from whose oral testimony he had made up his narrative, remembered her, in their youth, as a very old, but not decrepit woman, of a stately and **solemn** aspect. It had been her habit, from an almost immemorial date, to go about the country as a kind of voluntary nurse, and doing whatever miscellaneous good she might; taking upon herself, likewise, to give advice in all matters, especially those of the heart; by which means, as a person of such **propensities inevitably** must, she gained from many people the **reverence** due to an angel, but I should imagine, was looked upon by others as an intruder and a nuisance. **Prying** further into the manuscript, I found the record of other doings and sufferings of this **singular** woman, for most of which the reader is referred to the story entitled "The Scarlet Letter"; and it should be borne carefully in mind, that the main facts of that story are authorized and authenticated by the document of Mr. Surveyor Pue. The original papers, together with the scarlet letter itself—a most curious **relic**—are still in my possession, and shall be freely exhibited to whomsoever, **induced** by the great interest of the narrative, may desire a sight of them. I must not be understood as **affirming**, that, in the dressing up of the tale, and imagining the motives and modes of passion that influenced the characters who figure in it, I have **invariably** confined myself within the limits of the old Surveyor's half a dozen sheets of <u>foolscap</u>. On the contrary, I have allowed myself, as to such points, nearly or altogether as much license as if the facts had been entirely of my own invention. What I contend for is the authenticity of the outline.

This incident recalled my mind, in some degree, to its

OBSCURELY (uhb <u>skyoor</u> lee) *adv.*
dimly, unclearly
Synonyms: faintly, remotely

IMPART (ihm <u>pahrt</u>) *v.* **-ing,-ed.**
to give or share, to pass on
Synonyms: bestow, contribute, reveal, convey

EXHORT (ihg <u>zohrt</u>) *v.* **-ing,-ed.**
to urge or incite by strong appeals
Synonyms: press, prod, provoke, convince, inspire

FILIAL (<u>fihl</u> ee uhl) *adj.*
relating to a sequence of generations or family
connection, particularly that of a child and parent
Synonym: familial

REVERENCE (<u>reh</u> vuhr ehnts) *n.*
deep respect, awe
Synonyms: veneration, adoration, admiration

IMPOSING (ihm <u>poh</u> zihng) *adj.*
impressive in size or appearance
Synonyms: magisterial, commanding, grand, striking

BESTOW (bih <u>stoh</u>) *v.* **-ing,-ed.**
to apply or devote time or effort; to give as a gift
Synonyms: allocate, dedicate; endow, confer, present

TRAVERSE (truh <u>vuhrs</u>) (traa <u>vuhrs</u>) *v.* **-ing,-ed.**
to travel across, to move laterally
Synonyms: cross, pass through, tread, span,
intersect

old track. There seemed to be here the groundwork of a tale. It impressed me as if the ancient Surveyor, in his garb of a hundred years gone by, and wearing his immortal wig—which was buried with him, but did not perish in the grave—had met me in the deserted chamber of the Custom House. In his port was the dignity of one who had borne his Majesty's commission, and who was therefore illuminated by a ray of the splendor that shone so dazzlingly about the throne. How unlike, alas, the hang-dog look of a republican official, who, as the servant of the people, feels himself less than the least, and below the lowest, of his masters. With his own ghostly hand, the **obscurely** seen but majestic figure had **imparted** to me the scarlet symbol, and the little roll of explanatory manuscript. With his own ghostly voice he had **exhorted** me, on the sacred consideration of my **filial** duty and **reverence** towards him—who might reasonably regard himself as my official ancestor—to bring his mouldy and moth-eaten <u>lucubrations</u> before the public. "Do this," said the ghost of Mr. Surveyor Pue, emphatically nodding the head that looked so **imposing** within its memorable wig. "Do this and the profit shall be all your own! You will shortly need it; for it is not in your days as it was in mine, when a man's office was a life-lease, and oftentimes an heirloom. But, I charge you, in this matter of old Mistress Prynne, give to your predecessor's memory the credit which will be rightfully its due!" And I said to the ghost of Mr. Surveyor Pue, "I will!"

On Hester Prynne's story, therefore, I **bestowed** much thought. It was the subject of my meditations for many an hour, while pacing to and fro across my room, or **traversing**, with a hundred-fold repetition, the long extent from the front-door of the Custom House to the side-entrance, and back again. Great were the weariness and annoyance of the old Inspector and the Weighers and Gaugers, whose slumbers were disturbed by the

INDEFATIGABLE (ihn dih <u>faat</u> ih guh buhl) *adj.*
  incapable of being tired
    Synonyms: unflagging, weariless, inexhaustible

ADAPTED (uh <u>daap</u> tihd) *adj.*
  adjusted, changed, fit
    Synonyms: accustomed, altered, conformed

TARNISHED (<u>tahr</u> nihshd) *adj.*
  corroded, discolored; discredited, disgraced
    Synonyms: stained, blemished; dishonored,
    defected

MALLEABLE (<u>maa</u> lee uh buhl) *adj.*
  easy to work with or form into shape
    Synonyms: flexible, yielding, pliable, adaptable

KINDLE (<u>kihn</u> duhl) *v.* **-ing,-ed.**
  to excite or inspire; to set fire to or ignite
    Synonyms: arouse, awaken; light, spark

SENTIMENT (<u>sehn</u> tuh muhnt) *n.*
  an attitude, thought, or judgment prompted by feeling
    Synonym: emotion

RETAIN (rih <u>tayn</u>) *v.* **-ing,-ed.**
  to hold, keep possession of
    Synonyms: withhold, reserve

CONTEMPTUOUS (kuhn <u>tehmp</u> choo uhs) *adj.*
  scornful
    Synonyms: derisive, disdainful, supercilious

PITTANCE (<u>pih</u> tuhnts) *n.*
  a small portion, amount, or wage
    Synonyms: trace, trifle, paltry sum, scrap

TORPID (<u>tohr</u> pihd) *adj.*
  dormant; lethargic, unable to move
    Synonyms: hibernating, inactive, inert; apathetic,
    sluggish

INVIGORATING (ihn <u>vih</u> guh ray tihng) *adj.*
  able to make lively and energetic
    Synonyms: stimulating, strengthening, revitalizing

unmercifully lengthened tramp of my passing and returning footsteps. Remembering their own former habits, they used to say that the Surveyor was walking the quarter-deck. They probably fancied that my sole object—and, indeed, the sole object for which a sane man could ever put himself into voluntary motion—was, to get an appetite for dinner. And to say the truth, an appetite, sharpened by the east wind that generally blew along the passage, was the only valuable result of so much **indefatigable** exercise. So little **adapted** is the atmosphere of a Custom House to the delicate harvest of fancy and sensibility, that, had I remained there through ten presidencies yet to come, I doubt whether the tale of "The Scarlet Letter" would ever have been brought before the public eye. My imagination was a **tarnished** mirror. It would not reflect, or only with miserable dimness, the figures with which I did my best to people it. The characters of the narrative would not be warmed and rendered **malleable** by any heat that I could **kindle** at my intellectual forge. They would take neither the glow of passion nor the tenderness of **sentiment**, but **retained** all the rigidity of dead corpses, and stared me in the face with a fixed and ghastly grin of **contemptuous** defiance. "What have you to do with us?" that expression seemed to say. "The little power you might once have possessed over the tribe of unrealities is gone! You have bartered it for a **pittance** of the public gold. Go, then, and earn your wages!" In short, the almost **torpid** creatures of my own fancy twitted me with imbecility, and not without fair occasion.

It was not merely during the three hours and a half which Uncle Sam claimed as his share of my daily life, this wretched numbness held possession of me. It went with me on my sea-shore walks, and rambles into the country, whenever—which was seldom and reluctantly—I bestirred myself to seek that **invigorating**

TORPOR (<u>tohr</u> puhr) *n.*
   physical or mental inactivity, dormancy
      Synonyms: apathy, hibernation, immobility

FACULTY (<u>faa</u> kuhl tee) *n.*
   the ability to act or do
      Synonyms: aptitude, capability, sense, skill

MINUTELY (mie <u>noot</u> lee) (mih <u>noot</u> lee) *adv.*
   precisely, in a detailed manner
      Synonyms: attentively, critically

MEDIUM (<u>mee</u> dee uhm) *n.*
   a substance or object that is used to transmit or
   accomplish something
      Synonyms: means, instrument, vehicle, mechanism

ILLUSIVE (ih <u>loo</u> sihv) *adj.*
   unreal, deceptive
      Synonyms: chimerical, imaginary, fantastic

SUSTAIN (suh <u>stayn</u>) *v.* **-ing,-ed.**
   to support, uphold; endure, undergo
      Synonyms: maintain, prop, encourage; withstand

TRIFLING (<u>trie</u> flihng) *adj.*
   minor, of slight worth or little importance
      Synonyms: trivial, insignificant

IMBUE (ihm <u>byoo</u>) *v.* **-ing,-ed.**
   to infuse; to dye, wet
      Synonyms: permeate; moisten

charm of Nature, which used to give me such freshness and activity of thought, the moment that I stepped across the threshold of the Old Manse. The same **torpor**, as regarded the capacity for intellectual effort, accompanied me home, and weighed upon me in the chamber which I most absurdly termed my study. Nor did it quit me, when, late at night, I sat in the deserted parlor, lighted only by the glimmering coal-fire and the moon, striving to picture forth imaginary scenes, which, the next day, might flow out on the brightening page in many-hued description.

If the imaginative **faculty** refused to act at such an hour, it might well be deemed a hopeless case. Moonlight, in a familiar room, falling so white upon the carpet, and showing all its figures so distinctly—making every object so **minutely** visible, yet so unlike a morning or noontide visibility—is a **medium** most suitable for a romance-writer to get acquainted with his **illusive** guests. There is the little domestic scenery of the well-known apartment; the chairs with each its separate individuality; the centre-table, **sustaining** a work-basket, a volume or two, and an extinguished lamp; the sofa; the bookcase; the picture on the wall—all these details, so completely seen, are so spiritualized by the unusual light, that they seem to lose their actual substance, and become things of intellect. Nothing is too small or too **trifling** to undergo this change, and acquire dignity thereby. A child's shoe; the doll, seated in her little wicker carriage; the hobby-horse—whatever, in a word, has been used or played with, during the day, is now invested with a quality of strangeness and remoteness, though still almost as vividly present as by daylight. Thus, therefore, the floor of our familiar room has become a neutral territory, somewhere between the real world and fairy-land, where the actual and the Imaginary may meet, and each **imbue** itself with

71

TINGE (tihnj) *n.*
a slight shade of color, stain, odor, or taste
Synonyms: hint, hue, tincture, tone, wash

RUDDINESS (<u>ruh</u> dee nehs) *n.*
a healthy redness or rosy complexion
Synonyms: flush, coloring, freshness, pinkness

AVAIL (uh <u>vayl</u>) *n.*
use or advantage
Synonyms: help, benefit, service

SUSCEPTIBILITY (suh sehp tuh <u>bihl</u> ih tee) *n.*
vulnerability, defenselessness
Synonyms: sensitivity, exposure, risk

FACULTY (<u>faa</u> kuhl tee) *n.*
the ability to act or do
Synonyms: aptitude, capability, sense, skill

INEFFICACIOUS (ihn eff uh <u>kay</u> shuhs) *adj.*
ineffective, inefficient
Synonyms: useless, worthless

the nature of the other. Ghosts might enter here without affrighting us. It would be too much in keeping with the scene to excite surprise, were we to look about us and discover a form beloved, but gone hence, now sitting quietly in a streak of this magic moonshine, with an aspect that would make us doubt whether it had returned from afar, or had never once stirred from our fireside.

The somewhat dim coal-fire has an essential influence in producing the effect which I would describe. It throws its unobtrusive **tinge** throughout the room, with a faint **ruddiness** upon the walls and ceiling, and a reflected gleam from the polish of the furniture. This warmer light mingles itself with the cold spirituality of the moonbeams, and communicates, as it were, a heart and sensibilities of human tenderness to the forms which fancy summons up. It converts them from snow-images into men and women. Glancing at the looking-glass, we behold—deep within its haunted verge—the smouldering glow of the half-extinguished anthracite, the white moonbeams on the floor, and a repetition of all the gleam and shadow of the picture, with one remove further from the actual, and nearer to the imaginative. Then, at such an hour, and with this scene before him, if a man, sitting all alone, cannot dream strange things and make them look like truth, he need never try to write romances.

But, for myself, during the whole of my Custom House experience, moonlight and sunshine, and the glow of firelight, were just alike in my regard; and neither of them was of one <u>whit</u> more **avail** than the twinkle of a tallow-candle. An entire class of **susceptibilities**, and a gift connected with them—of no great richness or value, but the best I had—was gone from me.

It is my belief, however, that, had I attempted a different order of composition, my **faculties** would not have been found so pointless and **inefficacious**. I might,

SAT Vocabulary

IMPALPABLE (ihm <u>paalp</u> uh buhl) *adj.*
unreal, intangible
Synonyms: imperceptible, tenuous, unsubstantial

DIFFUSE (dih <u>fyooz</u>) *v.* **-ing,-ed.**
to spread out widely
Synonyms: scatter, disperse

OPAQUE (oh <u>payk</u>) *adj.*
difficult to understand; impervious to light
Synonyms: obscure, dense; impenetrable

RESOLUTELY (reh suh <u>loot</u> lee) *adv.*
with determination; with a clear purpose
Synonyms: firmly, unwaveringly; intently

FATHOM (<u>faath</u> uhm) *v.* **-ing,-ed.**
to understand fully, to gauge; to measure the depth of
Synonyms: comprehend; sound

TRANSCRIBE (traan <u>skrieb</u>) *v.* **-ing,-ed.**
to write or type a copy of spoken material
Synonyms: transfer, record, reproduce

for instance, have contented myself with writing out the narratives of a veteran shipmaster, one of the Inspectors, whom I should be most ungrateful not to mention, since scarcely a day passed that he did not stir me to laughter and admiration by his marvellous gifts as a story-teller. Could I have preserved the picturesque force of his style, and the humorous coloring which nature taught him how to throw over his descriptions, the result, I honestly believe, would have been something new in literature. Or I might readily have found a more serious task. It was a folly, with the materiality of this daily life pressing so intrusively upon me, to attempt to fling myself back into another age; or to insist on creating the semblance of a world out of airy matter, when, at every moment, the **impalpable** beauty of my soap-bubble was broken by the rude contact of some actual circumstance. The wiser effort would have been to **diffuse** thought and imagination through the **opaque** substance of today, and thus to make it a bright transparency; to spiritualize the burden that began to weigh so heavily; to seek, **resolutely**, the true and indestructible value that lay hidden in the petty and wearisome incidents, and ordinary characters, with which I was now conversant. The fault was mine. The page of life that was spread out before me seemed dull and commonplace, only because I had not **fathomed** its deeper import. A better book than I shall ever write was there; leaf after leaf presenting itself to me, just as it was written out by the reality of the flitting hour, and vanishing as fast as written, only because my brain wanted the insight and my hand the cunning to **transcribe** it. At some future day, it may be, I shall remember a few scattered fragments and broken paragraphs, and write them down, and find the letters turn to gold upon the page.

These perceptions have come too late. At the instant,

VOLATILE (<u>vahl</u> iht uhl) (<u>vahl</u> ih tiel) *adj.*
   able to evaporate easily at normal temperatures;
   varying, inconstant
      Synonyms: vaporizable; changeable, fickle

RESIDUUM (ree <u>zih</u> joo uhm) *n.*
   remainder, leftover, remnant
      Synonyms: rest, balance, dregs

ENERVATING (<u>ehn</u> uhr vay tihng) *adj.*
   weakening, exhausting
      Synonyms: depleting, debilitating, draining

I was only conscious that what would have been a pleasure once was now a hopeless toil. There was no occasion to make much moan about this state of affairs. I had ceased to be a writer of tolerably poor tales and essays, and had become a tolerably good Surveyor of the Customs. That was all. But, nevertheless, it is anything but agreeable to be haunted by a suspicion that one's intellect is dwindling away; or exhaling, without your consciousness, like ether out of a phial; so that, at every glance, you find a smaller and less **volatile residuum**. Of the fact there could be no doubt; and, examining myself and others, I was led to conclusions, in reference to the effect of public office on the character, not very favorable to the mode of life in question. In some other form, perhaps, I may hereafter develop these effects. Suffice it here to say, that a Custom House officer, of long continuance, can hardly be a very praiseworthy or respectable personage, for many reasons; one of them, the tenure by which he holds his situation, and another, the very nature of his business, which—though, I trust, an honest one—is of such a sort that he does not share in the united effort of mankind.

An effect—which I believe to be observable, more or less, in every individual who has occupied the position—is, that, while he leans on the mighty arm of the Republic, his own proper strength departs from him. He loses, in an extent proportioned to the weakness or force of his original nature, the capability of self-support. If he possess an unusual share of native energy, or the **enervating** magic of place do not operate too long upon him, his forfeited powers may be redeemable. The ejected officer—fortunate in the unkindly shove that sends him forth <u>betimes</u> to struggle amid a struggling world—may return to himself and become all that he has ever been. But this seldom happens. He usually keeps his ground just long enough for his own ruin, and

SINEW (<u>sihn</u> yoo) *n.*
a tendon of the body
Synonyms: cord, ligament

TOTTER (<u>tah</u> tuhr) *v.* **-ing,-ed.**
to stand with much unsteadiness
Synonyms: wobble, sway, reel, stagger

INFIRMITY (ihn <u>fuhr</u> mih tee) *n.*
weakness; disease, ailment
Synonyms: frailty; illness, affliction

PERVADING (puhr <u>vay</u> dihng) *adj.*
diffused throughout every part of
Synonyms: permeating, spreading, filling,
transfusing

SINGULAR (<u>sihn</u> gyuh luhr) *adj.*
uncommon, peculiar
Synonyms: unusual, odd, rare, unique, individual

is then thrust out, with **sinews** all unstrung, to **totter** along the difficult footpath of life as he best may. Conscious of his own **infirmity**—that his tempered steel and elasticity are lost—he forever afterwards looks wistfully about him in quest of support external to himself. His **pervading** and continual hope—a hallucination, which, in the face of all discouragement, and making light of impossibilities, haunts him while he lives, and, I fancy, like the convulsive throes of the cholera, torments him for a brief space after death—is that finally, and in no long time, by some happy coincidence of circumstances, he shall be restored to office. This faith, more than anything else, steals the pith and availability out of whatever enterprise he may dream of undertaking. Why should he toil and moil, and be at so much trouble to pick himself up out of the mud, when, in a little while hence, the strong arm of his Uncle will raise and support him? Why should he work for his living here, or go to dig gold in California, when he is so soon to be made happy, at monthly intervals, with a little pile of glittering coin out of his Uncle's pocket? It is sadly curious to observe how slight a taste of office suffices to infect a poor fellow with this **singular** disease. Uncle Sam's gold—meaning no disrespect to the worthy old gentleman—has, in this respect, a quality of enchantment like that of the Devil's wages. Whoever touches it should look well to himself, or he may find the bargain to go hard against him, involving, if not his soul, yet many of its better attributes; its sturdy force, its courage and constancy, its truth, its self-reliance, and all that gives the emphasis to manly character.

Here was a fine prospect in the distance! Not that the Surveyor brought the lesson home to himself, or admitted that he could be so utterly undone, either by continuance in office, or ejectment. Yet my reflections were not the most comfortable. I began to grow

SAT Vocabulary

MELANCHOLY (<u>mehl</u> uhn kahl ee) *adj.*
  sad, depressed
  Synonyms: dejected, despondent, woeful, sorrowful
PRY (prie) *v.* **-ing,-ied.**
  to look closely at; to meddle; force open
  Synonyms: probe; snoop, nose, spy; lever
DETRIMENT (<u>deht</u> ruh mehnt) *n.*
  something that causes harm or injury, disadvantage
  Synonyms: loss, impairment, disservice
ACCRUE (uh <u>kroo</u>) *v.* **-ing,-ed.**
  to accumulate, grow by additions
  Synonyms: augment, enlarge, expand
APPREHENSION (aa prih <u>hehn</u> shuhn) *n.*
  suspicion or fear of future or unknown evil; the act
  of perceiving or comprehending; a legal seizure
  Synonyms: concern, worry; understanding; capture
TEDIOUS (<u>tee</u> dee uhs) *adj.*
  tiresome because of length or dullness; very slow
  Synonyms: wearisome, boring; dragging
VENERABLE (<u>veh</u> nehr uh buhl) *adj.*
  respected because of age
  Synonyms: distinguished, elderly
FACULTY (<u>faa</u> kuhl tee) *n.*
  the ability to act or do
  Synonyms: aptitude, capability, sense, skill
PROVIDENCE (<u>prah</u> vih dehnts) *n.*
  divine control and direction by God; preparation
  and foresight
  Synonyms: fate, destiny, good luck; prudence,
  precaution
INCUMBENT (ihn <u>kuhm</u> buhnt) *n.*
  a person holding a specified office, often political
  Synonyms: officeholder, occupant, resider
SINGULARLY (<u>sihn</u> gyuh luhr lee) *adv.*
  uncommonly, peculiarly
  Synonyms: unusually, oddly, rarely, uniquely

melancholy and restless, continually **prying** into my mind, to discover which of its poor properties were gone, and what degree of **detriment** had already **accrued** to the remainder. I endeavored to calculate how much longer I could stay in the Custom House, and yet go forth a man. To confess the truth, it was my greatest **apprehension**—as it would never be a measure of policy to turn out so quiet an individual as myself, and it being hardly in the nature of a public officer to resign—it was my chief trouble, therefore, that I was likely to grow gray and decrepit in the Surveyorship, and become much such another animal as the old Inspector. Might it not, in the **tedious** lapse of official life that lay before me, finally be with me as it was with this **venerable** friend—to make the dinner-hour the nucleus of the day, and to spend the rest of it as an old dog spends it, asleep in the sunshine or in the shade? A dreary look-forward this, for a man who felt it to be the best definition of happiness to live throughout the whole range of his **faculties** and sensibilities! But, all this while, I was giving myself very unnecessary alarm. **Providence** had meditated better things for me than I could possibly imagine for myself.

A remarkable event of the third year of my Surveyorship—to adopt the tone of "P. P."—was the election of General Taylor to the Presidency. It is essential, in order to a complete estimate of the advantages of official life, to view the **incumbent** at the incoming of a hostile administration. His position is then one of the most **singularly** irksome, and, in every contingency, disagreeable, that a wretched mortal can possibly occupy; with seldom an alternative of good, on either hand, although what presents itself to him as the worst event may very probably be the best. But it is a strange experience, to a man of pride and sensibility, to know that his interests are within the control of individuals who neither love nor understand him, and by whom, since one

OBLIGE (uh <u>bliej</u>) *v.* **-ing,-ed.**
to be obligated, to require or force someone to obey
Synonyms: compel, constrain, bind

METAPHOR (<u>meht</u> uh fohr) (<u>meht</u> uh fuhr) *n.*
figure of speech comparing two different things
Synonyms: analogy, symbol, allegory

MALICE (<u>maal</u> ihs) *n.*
animosity, spite, hatred
Synonyms: malevolence, cruelty, hostility

IGNOMINIOUSLY (ihg nuh <u>mih</u> nee uhs lee) *adv.*
disgracefully and dishonorably
Synonyms: despicably, shamefully, hatefully

PARTISAN (<u>pahr</u> tih zaan) *n.*
a devoted, or even militant, supporter of someone or
something
Synonyms: zealot, enthusiast, follower

PERIL (<u>pehr</u> ihl) *n.*
danger
Synonyms: trouble, hazard, harm

ADVERSITY (aad <u>vuhr</u> sih tee) *n.*
hardship
Synonyms: suffering, distress, tribulation

ACUTELY (uh <u>kyoot</u> lee) *adv.*
sharply, severely
Synonyms: intensely, extremely

PREDILECTION (preh dih <u>lehk</u> shuhn) *n.*
preference, liking
Synonyms: bias, leaning, partiality, penchant,
proclivity

or the other must needs happen, he would rather be injured than **obliged**. Strange, too, for one who has kept his calmness throughout the contest, to observe the bloodthirstiness that is developed in the hour of triumph, and to be conscious that he is himself among its objects! There are few uglier traits of human nature than this tendency—which I now witnessed in men no worse than their neighbors—to grow cruel, merely because they possessed the power of inflicting harm. If the guillotine, as applied to office holders, were a literal fact instead of one of the most apt of **metaphors**, it is my sincere belief that the active members of the victorious party were sufficiently excited to have chopped off all our heads, and have thanked Heaven for the opportunity! It appears to me—who have been a calm and curious observer, as well in victory as defeat—that this fierce and bitter spirit of **malice** and revenge has never distinguished the many triumphs of my own party as it now did that of the Whigs. The Democrats take the offices, as a general rule, because they need them, and because the practice of many years has made it the law of political warfare, which, unless a different system be proclaimed, it were weakness and cowardice to murmur at. But the long habit of victory has made them generous. They know how to spare, when they see occasion; and when they strike, the axe may be sharp, indeed, but its edge is seldom poisoned with ill will; nor is it their custom **ignominiously** to kick the head which they have just struck off.

In short, unpleasant as was my predicament, at best, I saw much reason to congratulate myself that I was on the losing side, rather than the triumphant one. If, heretofore, I had been none of the warmest of **partisans**, I began now, at this season of **peril** and **adversity**, to be pretty **acutely** sensible with which party my **predilections** lay; nor was it without something like regret and shame,

RETAIN (rih <u>tayn</u>) *v.* **-ing,-ed.**
to hold, keep possession of
Synonyms: withhold, reserve

INCLINE (ihn <u>klien</u>) *v.* **-ing,-ed.**
to have a specific tendency, to be predisposed
Synonyms: lean toward, influence, impel, prefer

CONSOLATION (kahn suh <u>lay</u> shuhn) *n.*
something providing comfort or solace for a loss or hardship
Synonym: condolence

CONSOLATORY (<u>kahn</u> suh luh tohr ee) *adj.*
providing comfort or solace for a loss or hardship
Synonym: cheering, soothing, warming, reassuring

REQUISITE (<u>reh</u> kwih ziht) *adj.*
essential, necessary
Synonyms: required, indispensable

IMPULSE (<u>ihm</u> puhls) *n.*
sudden tendency, inclination
Synonyms: urge, whim

DIVERGE (<u>die</u> vuhrj) (dih <u>vuhrj</u>) *v.* **-ing,-ed.**
to separate, to move in different directions from a particular point
Synonyms: deviate, radiate, depart, branch

that, according to a reasonable calculation of chances, I saw my own prospect of **retaining** office to be better than those of my Democratic brethren. But who can see an inch into futurity beyond his nose? My own head was the first that fell!

The moment when a man's head drops off is seldom or never, I am **inclined** to think, precisely the most agreeable of his life. Nevertheless, like the greater part of our misfortunes, even so serious a contingency brings its remedy and **consolation** with it, if the sufferer will but make the best, rather than the worst, of the accident which has befallen him. In my particular case, the **consolatory** topics were close at hand, and, indeed, had suggested themselves to my meditations a considerable time before it was **requisite** to use them. In view of my previous weariness of office and vague thoughts of resignation, my fortune somewhat resembled that of a person who should entertain an idea of committing suicide, and, altogether beyond his hopes, meet with the good hap to be murdered. In the Custom House, as before in the Old Manse, I had spent three years; a term long enough to rest a weary brain; long enough to break off old intellectual habits and make room for new ones; long enough, and too long, to have lived in an unnatural state, doing what was really of no advantage nor delight to any human being, and withholding myself from toil that would, at least, have stilled an unquiet **impulse** in me. Then, moreover, as regarded his unceremonious ejectment, the late Surveyor was not altogether ill-pleased to be recognized by the Whigs as an enemy; since his inactivity in political affairs—his tendency to roam, at will, in that broad and quiet field where all mankind may meet, rather than confine himself to those narrow paths where brethren of the same household must **diverge** from one another—had sometimes made it questionable with his brother Democrats whether he

MARTYRDOM (<u>mahr</u> tuhr duhm) *n.*
death or intense suffering experienced due to one's beliefs
Synonyms: sacrifice, anguish

DECOROUS (<u>deh</u> kuhr uhs) (deh <u>kohr</u> uhs) *adj.*
proper, tasteful, socially correct
Synonyms: polite, courteous, appropriate

FORLORN (fohr <u>lohrn</u>) *adj.*
hopeless, despairing; dreary, deserted; unhappy
Synonyms: dejected, despondent; desolate; downcast, depressed

SUBSIST (suhb <u>sihst</u>) *v.* **-ing,-ed.**
to have existence; to have or acquire the necessities of life, to nourish oneself
Synonyms: live, survive, endure, inhabit

COMPEL (kuhm <u>pehl</u>) *v.* **-ling,-led.**
to urge or force
Synonyms: coerce, oblige, constrain

REQUISITE (<u>reh</u> kwih ziht) *adj.*
essential, necessary
Synonyms: required, indispensable

SOMBRE or SOMBER (<u>sahm</u> buhr) *adj.*
melancholy, dismal, dark and gloomy
Synonyms: serious, grave, mournful, lugubrious, funereal

GENIAL (<u>jeen</u> yuhl) (<u>jee</u> nee uhl) *adj.*
pleasant and friendly; favorable to growth or comfort
Synonyms: nice, amiable; productive, generative

was a friend. Now, after he had won the crown of **martyrdom** (though with no longer a head to wear it on), the point might be looked upon as settled. Finally, little heroic as he was, it seemed more **decorous** to be overthrown in the downfall of the party with which he had been content to stand, than to remain a **forlorn** survivor, when so many worthier men were falling; and, at last, after **subsisting** for four years on the mercy of a hostile administration, to be **compelled** then to define his position anew, and claim the yet more humiliating mercy of a friendly one.

Meanwhile the press had taken up my affair, and kept me, for a week or two, <u>careering</u> through the public prints, in my decapitated state, like Irving's Headless Horseman; ghastly and grim, and longing to be buried, as a politically dead man ought. So much for my figurative self. The real human being, all this time with his head safely on his shoulders, had brought himself to the comfortable conclusion that everything was for the best; and, making an investment in ink, paper, and steel-pens, had opened his long-disused writing desk, and was again a literary man.

Now it was that the <u>lucubrations</u> of my ancient predecessor, Mr. Surveyor Pue, came into play. Rusty through long idleness, some little space was **requisite** before my intellectual machinery could be brought to work upon the tale, with an effect in any degree satisfactory. Even yet, though my thoughts were ultimately much absorbed in the task, it wears, to my eye, a stern and **sombre** aspect; too much ungladdened by **genial** sunshine; too little relieved by the tender and familiar influences which soften almost every scene of nature and real life, and, undoubtedly, should soften every picture of them. This uncaptivating effect is perhaps due to the period of hardly accomplished revolution, and still seething turmoil, in which the story shaped itself. It is

NOVELTY (<u>nah</u> vuhl tee) *n.*
something new and original
Synonyms: surprise, change, innovation

METAPHOR (<u>meht</u> uh fohr) (<u>meht</u> uh fuhr) *n.*
figure of speech comparing two different things
Synonyms: analogy, symbol, allegory

VENERABLE (<u>veh</u> nehr uh buhl) *adj.*
respected because of age
Synonyms: distinguished, elderly

APPELLATION (aa puhl <u>ay</u> shuhn) *n.*
a title or name
Synonyms: denomination, designation, moniker, tag

no indication, however, of a lack of cheerfulness in the writer's mind; for he was happier, while straying through the gloom of these sunless fantasies, than at any time since he had quitted the Old Manse. Some of the briefer articles, which contribute to make up the volume, have likewise been written since my involuntary withdrawal from the toils and honors of public life, and the remainder are gleaned from annuals and magazines, of such antique date that they have gone round the circle, and come back to **novelty** again. Keeping up the **metaphor** of the political guillotine, the whole may be considered as the <u>POSTHUMOUS</u> PAPERS OF A DECAPITATED SURVEYOR; and the sketch which I am now bringing to a close, if too autobiographical for a modest person to publish in his lifetime, will readily be excused in a gentleman who writes from beyond the grave. Peace be with all the world! My blessing on my friends! My forgiveness to my enemies! For I am in the realm of quiet!

The life of the Custom House lies like a dream behind me. The old Inspector—who, by the by, I regret to say, was overthrown and killed by a horse, some time ago; else he would certainly have lived forever—he, and all those other **venerable** personages who sat with him at the receipt of custom, are but shadows in my view; white-headed and wrinkled images which my fancy used to sport with, and has now flung aside forever. The merchants—Pingree, Phillips, Shepard, Upton, Kimball, Bertram, Hunt—these, and many other names, which had such a classic familiarity for my ear six months ago—these men of traffic, who seemed to occupy so important a position in the world—how little time has it required to disconnect me from them all, not merely in act, but recollection! It is with an effort that I recall the figures and **appellations** of these few. Soon, likewise, my old native town will loom upon me through the haze of

BROOD *v.* **-ing,-ed.**
1. to hang over in a threatening manner
   Synonyms: loom, hover
2. to think about in a gloomy or serious way
   Synonyms: ponder, worry, obsess

GENIAL (<u>jeen</u> yuhl) (<u>jee</u> nee uhl) *adj.*
favorable to growth or comfort; pleasant and friendly
   Synonyms: productive, generative; nice, amiable

ANTIQUARY (<u>aan</u> tih kwayr ee) *n.*
an expert on antiques
   Synonyms: collector, historian

memory, a mist **brooding** over and around it; as if it were no portion of the real earth, but an overgrown village in cloud-land, with only imaginary inhabitants to people its wooden houses, and walk its homely lanes, and the unpicturesque <u>prolixity</u> of its main street. Henceforth it ceases to be a reality of my life. I am a citizen of somewhere else. My good townspeople will not much regret me; for—though it has been as dear an object as any, in my literary efforts, to be of some importance in their eyes and to win myself a pleasant memory in this abode and burial-place of so many of my forefathers—there has never been, for me, the **genial** atmosphere which a literary man requires in order to ripen the best harvest of his mind. I shall do better amongst other faces; and these familiar ones, it need hardly be said, will do just as well without me.

It may be, however—oh, transporting and triumphant thought—that the great-grandchildren of the present race may sometimes think kindly of the scribbler of bygone days, when the **antiquary** of days to come, among the sites memorable in the town's history, shall point out the locality of <u>THE TOWN PUMP</u>.

EDIFICE (<u>eh</u> duh fuhs) *n.*
a large structure
Synonyms: building, construction, skyscraper

UTOPIA (yoo <u>toh</u> pee uh) *n.*
perfect place
Synonyms: paradise, Eden, heaven, cloudland

INVARIABLY (ihn <u>vaa</u> ree uh blee) *adv.*
without change, constantly
Synonyms: always, repeatedly, perpetually

SUBSEQUENTLY (<u>suhb</u> suh kwehnt lee) *adv.*
in time or order, in succession, behind
Synonyms: next, afterward

CONGREGATED (<u>kahn</u> gruh gay tihd) *adj.*
crowded, assembled together
Synonyms: grouped, gathered

PONDEROUS (<u>pahn</u> duhr uhs) *adj.*
weighty, heavy, large
Synonyms: hefty, massive, cumbersome, unwieldy

CONGENIAL (kuhn <u>jee</u> nee uhl) (kuhn <u>jeen</u> yuhl) *adj.*
naturally suited; similar in tastes and habits; having
a pleasant disposition
Synonyms: favorable, agreeable; compatible,
harmonious; amiable, personable

The Prison-Door

Chapter 1

A throng of bearded men, in sad-colored garments, and gray, steeple-crowned hats, intermixed with women, some wearing hoods and others bareheaded, was assembled in front of a wooden **edifice**, the door of which was heavily timbered with oak, and studded with iron spikes.

The founders of a new colony, whatever **utopia** of human virtue and happiness they might originally project, have **invariably** recognized it among their earliest practical necessities to allot a portion of the virgin soil as a cemetery, and another portion as the site of a prison. In accordance with this rule, it may safely be assumed that the forefathers of Boston had built the first prison-house somewhere in the vicinity of Cornhill, almost as seasonably as they marked out the first burial ground, on Isaac Johnson's lot and round about his grave, which **subsequently** became the nucleus of all the **congregated** sepulchres in the old churchyard of King's Chapel. Certain it is, that, some fifteen or twenty years after the settlement of the town, the wooden jail was already marked with weather-stains and other indications of age which gave a yet darker aspect to its beetle-browed and gloomy front. The rust on the **ponderous** iron-work of its oaken door looked more antique than anything else in the New World. Like all that pertains to crime, it seemed never to have known a youthful era. Before this ugly **edifice**, and between it and the wheel-track of the street, was a grass-plot, much overgrown with burdock, pigweed, apple-peru, and such unsightly vegetation, which evidently found something **congenial** in the soil that had so early borne the

CIVILIZED (<u>sih</u> vuhl iezd) *adj.*
  relating to human lifestyle as opposed to the wild,
  humane; politely sophisticated, cultured
    Synonyms: refined, cultivated; courteous,
    pleasant, affable

INAUSPICIOUS (ihn aw <u>spih</u> shuhs) *adj.*
  having unfavorable prospects, unfortunate
    Synonyms: negative, unlucky, ominous, threatening

black flower of **civilized** society, a prison. But, on one side of the portal, and rooted almost at the threshold, was a wild rose-bush, covered, in this month of June, with its delicate gems, which might be imagined to offer their fragrance and fragile beauty to the prisoner as he went in, and to the condemned criminal, as he came forth to his doom, in token that the deep heart of Nature could pity and be kind to him.

This rose-bush, by a strange chance, has been kept alive in history; but whether it had merely survived out of the stern old wilderness, so long after the fall of the gigantic pines and oaks that originally over-shadowed it—or whether, as there is fair authority for believing, it had sprung up under the footsteps of the sainted Ann Hutchinson, as she entered the prison-door—we shall not take upon us to determine. Finding it so directly on the threshold of our narrative, which is now about to issue from that **inauspicious** portal, we could hardly do otherwise than pluck one of its flowers, and present it to the reader. It may serve, let us hope, to symbolize some sweet moral blossom, that may be found along the track, or relieve the darkening close of a tale of human frailty and sorrow.

PHYSIOGNOMY (fih zee <u>ahg</u> nuh mee) *n.*
characteristic facial features; the art of judging one's character from facial features
Synonyms: visage, expression; divination

AUGUR (<u>aw</u> guhr) *v.* **-ing,-ed.**
to foretell or predict from omens and signs
Synonyms: portend, read, prophesy, forecast

EXECUTION (ehk sih <u>kyoo</u> shuhn) *n.*
1. the act of putting to death
Synonyms: killing, suicide, murder
2. the act of performing or carrying out a task
Synonyms: accomplishment, achievement

SENTIMENT (<u>sehn</u> tuh muhnt) *n.*
an attitude, thought, or judgment prompted by feeling
Synonym: emotion

INDUBITABLY (ihn <u>doo</u> bih tuh blee) *adv.*
unquestionably, undoubtedly
Synonyms: certainly, apparently, unassailably

CIVIL (<u>sih</u> vuhl) *adj.*
involving the public or government; polite
Synonyms: communal; courteous

MAGISTRATE (<u>maa</u> juh strayt) *n.*
an official who can administrate laws
Synonyms: judge, arbiter, authority, marshal

SOLEMNITY (suh <u>lehm</u> nih tee) *n.*
dignified seriousness
Synonyms: ceremoniousness, formality

DEMEANOR (dih <u>meen</u> uhr) *n.*
one's behavior or conduct
Synonyms: attitude, disposition, manner, presence

VENERABLE (<u>veh</u> nehr uh buhl) *adj.*
respected because of age
Synonyms: distinguished, elderly

The Market-Place
Chapter 2

The grass-plot before the jail, in Prison Lane, on a certain summer morning, not less than two centuries ago, was occupied by a pretty large number of the inhabitants of Boston, all with their eyes intently fastened on the iron-clamped oaken door. Amongst any other population, or at a later period in the history of New England, the grim rigidity that petrified the bearded **physiognomies** of these good people would have **augured** some awful business in hand. It could have betokened nothing short of the anticipated **execution** of some noted culprit, on whom the sentence of a legal tribunal had but confirmed the verdict of public **sentiment**. But, in that early severity of the Puritan character, an inference of this kind could not so **indubitably** be drawn. It might be that a sluggish bond-servant, or an undutiful child, whom his parents had given over to the **civil** authority, was to be corrected at the whipping-post. It might be that an Antinomian, a Quaker, or other heterodox religionist was to be scourged out of the town, or an idle and vagrant Indian, whom the white man's fire-water had made riotous about the streets, was to be driven with stripes into the shadow of the forest. It might be, too, that a witch, like old Mistress Hibbins, the bitter-tempered widow of the **magistrate**, was to die upon the gallows. In either case, there was very much the same **solemnity** of **demeanor** on the part of the spectators; as befitted a people amongst whom religion and law were almost identical, and in whose character both were so thoroughly interfused, that the mildest and the severest acts of public discipline were alike made **venerable** and awful. Meager, indeed,

Theocracy

97

TRANSGRESSOR (traans <u>greh</u> suhr) *n.*
  violator; a trespasser
    Synonyms: sinner, offender; overstepper

INFAMY (<u>ihn</u> fuh mee) *n.*
  reputation for bad deeds
    Synonyms: disgrace, dishonor, shame

IMPROPRIETY (ihm pruh <u>prie</u> ih tee) *n.*
  the quality of not conforming to expected customs
  and behaviors, improperness
    Synonyms: inappropriateness, incorrectness,
    indecency

RESTRAIN (rih <u>strayn</u>) *v.* **-ing,-ed.**
  to control, repress, restrict, hold back
    Synonyms: hamper, bridle, curb, check

UNSUBSTANTIAL (uhn suhb <u>staan</u> shuhl) *adj.*
  small in size or amount; weak, lacking substance
    Synonyms: slight, puny, thin; feeble, infirm

EXECUTION (ehk sih <u>kyoo</u> shuhn) *n.*
  1. the act of putting to death
    Synonyms: killing, suicide, murder
  2. the act of performing or carrying out a task
    Synonyms: accomplishment, achievement

DESCENDANT (dih <u>sehn</u> dehnt) *n.*
  an offspring or heir
    Synonyms: child, kin, progeny

RUDDY (<u>ruh</u> dee) *adj.*
  healthily reddish or rosy
    Synonyms: flushed, sanguine, fresh, pinkish

ROTUNDITY (roh <u>tuhn</u> dih tee) *n.*
  fullness of sound; roundness in shape, fatness
    Synonyms: resonance, strength, vibrance;
    corpulence, obesity

and cold was the sympathy that a **transgressor** might look for from such by-standers at the scaffold. On the other hand, a penalty, which, in our days, would infer a degree of mocking **infamy** and ridicule, might then be invested with almost as stern a dignity as the punishment of death itself.

It was a circumstance to be noted, on the summer morning when our story begins its course, that the women, of whom there were several in the crowd, appeared to take a peculiar interest in whatever penal infliction might be expected to ensue. The age had not so much refinement, that any sense of **impropriety restrained** the wearers of petticoat and farthingale from stepping forth into the public ways, and wedging their not **unsubstantial** persons, if occasion were, into the throng nearest to the scaffold at an **execution**. Morally, as well as materially, there was a coarser fiber in those wives and maidens of old English birth and breeding, than in their fair **descendants**, separated from them by a series of six or seven generations; for, throughout that chain of ancestry, every successive mother has transmitted to her child a fainter bloom, a more delicate and briefer beauty, and a slighter physical frame, if not a character of less force and solidity, than her own. The women who were now standing about the prison-door stood within less than half a century of the period when the man-like Elizabeth had been the not altogether unsuitable representative of the sex. They were her countrywomen; and the beef and ale of their native land, with a moral diet not a whit more refined, entered largely into their composition. The bright morning sun, therefore, shone on broad shoulders and well-developed busts and on round and **ruddy** cheeks, that had ripened in the far-off island, and had hardly yet grown paler or thinner in the atmosphere of New England. There was, moreover, a boldness and **rotundity** of speech among

99

PURPORT (puhr <u>pohrt</u>) *n.*
intention, purpose
Synonyms: importance, meaning

MALEFACTRESS (maal uh <u>faak</u> trehs) *n.*
a female evil-doer, culprit
Synonyms: criminal, offender, felon

MAGISTRATE (<u>maa</u> juh strayt) *n.*
an official who can administrate laws
Synonyms: judge, arbiter, authority, marshal

GRIEVOUSLY (<u>gree</u> vuhs lee) *adv.*
in a serious and distressing manner
Synonyms: gravely, mournfully, dolefully

CONGREGATION (kahn gruh <u>gay</u> shuhn) *n.*
an assembly, a crowd of people (often in a church)
Synonyms: group, gathering, fold, multitude

WINCE (wihns) *v.* **-ing,-ed.**
to flinch, to shrink away from pain or fear
Synonyms: cringe, recoil, grimace, cower

WARRANT (<u>wahr</u> ihnt) *v.* **-ing,-ed.**
to guarantee; to give a good reason for
Synonyms: endorse, promise, attest; justify

HEATHENISH (<u>hee</u> thuhn ihsh) *adj.*
pagan, uncivilized and irreligious
Synonyms: idolatrous, polytheistic, unbelieving

INTERPOSE (ihn tuhr <u>pohz</u>) *v.* **-ing,-ed.**
to interject or interrupt; to come between
Synonyms: encroach, butt in, intrude; interfere,
divide, meddle

CONSTITUTE (kahn stih <u>toot</u>) *v.* **-ing,-ed.**
1. to designate or charge with a specific task
Synonyms: appoint, name
2. to be the parts or components of something,
to compose; to equal
Synonyms: comprise, form, make up; amount to

these matrons, as most of them seemed to be, that would startle us at the present day, whether in respect to its **purport** or its volume of tone.

"Goodwives," said a hard-featured dame of fifty, "I'll tell ye a piece of my mind. It would be greatly for the public behoof, if we women, being of mature age and church-members in good repute, should have the handling of such **malefactresses** as this Hester Prynne. What think ye, gossips? If the hussy stood up for judgment before us five, that are now here in a knot together, would she come off with such a sentence as the worshipful **magistrates** have awarded? Marry, I trow not!"

"People say," said another, "that the Reverend Master Dimmesdale, her godly pastor, takes it very **grievously** to heart that such a scandal should have come upon his **congregation**."

"The **magistrates** are God-fearing gentlemen, but merciful overmuch—that is a truth," added a third autumnal matron. "At the very least, they should have put the brand of a hot iron on Hester Prynne's forehead. Madam Hester would have **winced** at that, I **warrant** me. But she—the naughty baggage—little will she care what they put upon the bodice of her gown! Why, look you, she may cover it with a brooch, or suchlike **heathenish** adornment, and so walk the streets as brave as ever!"

"Ah, but," **interposed**, more softly, a young wife, holding a child by the hand, "let her cover the mark as she will, the pang of it will be always in her heart."

"What do we talk of marks and brands, whether on the bodice of her gown, or the flesh of her forehead?" cried another female, the ugliest as well as the most pitiless of these self-**constituted** judges. "This woman has brought shame upon us all, and ought to die. Is there not law for it? Truly there is, both in the Scripture and the statute-book. Then let the **magistrates**, who have

DRAW *v.* **-ing, drew, drawn.**
   1. to pull, drag; to attract
     Synonyms: haul, tow, lug; lure, entice
   2. to move steadily
     Synonyms: proceed, continue, progress

REPEL (rih <u>pehl</u>) *v.* **-ling,-led.**
   to rebuff, repulse; disgust, offend
     Synonyms: reject, spurn, parry; nauseate, revolt

IMPULSE (<u>ihm</u> puhls) *n.*
   sudden tendency, inclination
     Synonyms: urge, whim

HAUGHTY (<u>haw</u> tee) (<u>hah</u> tee) *adj.*
   arrogant and condescending
     Synonyms: proud, disdainful, supercilious,
     scornful

made it of no effect, thank themselves if their own wives and daughters go astray!"

"Mercy on us, goodwife," exclaimed a man in the crowd, "is there no virtue in woman, save what springs from a wholesome fear of the gallows? That is the hardest word yet! Hush, now, gossips, for the lock is turning in the prison door, and here comes Mistress Prynne herself."

The door of the jail being flung open from within, there appeared, in the first place, like a black shadow emerging into the sunshine, the grim and grisly presence of the town-beadle, with a sword by his side, and his staff of office in his hand. This personage prefigured and represented in his aspect the whole dismal severity of the Puritanic code of law, which it was his business to administer in its final and closest application to the offender. Stretching forth the official staff in his left hand, he laid his right upon the shoulder of a young woman, whom he thus **drew** forward; until, on the threshold of the prison-door, she **repelled** him, by an action marked with natural dignity and force of character, and stepped into the open air, as if by her own free will. She bore in her arms a child, a baby of some three months old, who winked and turned aside its little face from the too vivid light of day; because its existence, heretofore, had brought it acquainted only with the gray twilight of a dungeon, or other darksome apartment of the prison.

When the young woman—the mother of this child—stood fully revealed before the crowd, it seemed to be her first **impulse** to clasp the infant closely to her bosom; not so much by an **impulse** of motherly affection, as that she might thereby conceal a certain token, which was wrought or fastened into her dress. In a moment, however, wisely judging that one token of her shame would but poorly serve to hide another, she took the baby on her arm, and, with a burning blush, and yet a **haughty**

ABASHED (uh <u>baashd</u>) *adj.*
embarrassed
Synonyms: disconcerted, self-conscious, uneasy

LUXURIANCE (luhg <u>zhoor</u> ee ehnts) *n.*
elegance, lavishness
Synonyms: richness, abundance, profusion

SUMPTUARY (<u>suhmp</u> choo ayr ee) *adj.*
relating to laws that control personal behaviors
Synonyms: regulatory, limiting

Hester's inner beauty = strength

EVANESCENT (eh vuh <u>nehs</u> uhnt) *adj.*
momentary, tendency toward vanishing
Synonyms: transient, ephemeral, fleeting, fugitive

OBSCURED (uhb <u>skyoord</u>) *adj.*
hidden
Synonyms: concealed, blurred, veiled

IGNOMINY (<u>ihg</u> nuh mih nee) *n.*
disgrace and dishonor
Synonyms: degradation, debasement

DRAW *v.* **-ing, drew, drawn.**
1. to attract; to pull, drag
Synonyms: lure, entice; haul, tow, lug
2. to move steadily
Synonyms: proceed, continue, progress

smile, and a glance that would not be **abashed**, looked around at her townspeople and neighbors. On the breast of her gown, in fine red cloth surrounded with an elaborate embroidery and fantastic flourishes of gold thread, appeared the letter A. It was so artistically done, and with so much fertility and gorgeous **luxuriance** of fancy, that it had all the effect of a last and fitting decoration to the apparel which she wore; and which was of a splendor in accordance with the taste of the age, but greatly beyond what was allowed by the **sumptuary** regulations of the colony.

The young woman was tall, with a figure of perfect elegance on a large scale. She had dark and abundant hair, so glossy that it threw off the sunshine with a gleam, and a face which, besides being beautiful from regularity of feature and richness of complexion, had the impressiveness belonging to a marked brow and deep black eyes. She was ladylike, too, after the manner of the feminine gentility of those days; characterized by a certain state and dignity, rather than by the delicate, **evanescent**, and indescribable grace, which is now recognized as its indication. And never had Hester Prynne appeared more lady-like, in the antique interpretation of the term, than as she issued from the prison. Those who had before known her, and had expected to behold her dimmed and **obscured** by a disastrous cloud, were astonished, and even startled, to perceive how her beauty shone out, and made a halo of the misfortune and **ignominy** in which she was enveloped. It may be true, that, to a sensitive observer, there was something exquisitely painful in it. Her attire, which, indeed, she had wrought for the occasion, in prison, and had modelled much after her own fancy, seemed to express the attitude of her spirit, the desperate recklessness of her mood, by its wild and picturesque peculiarity. But the point which **drew** all eyes and, as it were, transfigured

BRAZEN (<u>bray</u> zihn) *adj.*
shameless, defiant
Synonyms: brash, audacious, forward

CONTRIVE (kuhn <u>triev</u>) *v.* **-ing,-ed.**
to form in an artistic manner; to devise, plan, or manage
Synonyms: create, design; concoct, scheme

MAGISTRATE (<u>maa</u> juh strayt) *n.*
an official who can administrate laws
Synonyms: judge, arbiter, authority, marshal

VISAGED (<u>vih</u> zihjd) *adj.*
having a facial appearance (*in context, usually paired with a descriptive word*)
Synonyms: seeming, looking

DAINTY (<u>dayn</u> tee) *adj.*
delicate, sweet
Synonyms: fine, graceful

BESTOW (bih <u>stoh</u>) *v.* **-ing,-ed.**
to give as a gift; to apply or devote time or effort
Synonyms: endow, confer, present; allocate, dedicate

INIQUITY (ih <u>nihk</u> wih tee) *n.*
sin, evil act
Synonyms: immorality, injustice, wickedness, vice

the wearer—so that both men and women, who had been familiarly acquainted with Hester Prynne, were now impressed as if they beheld her for the first time—was that SCARLET LETTER, so fantastically embroidered and illuminated upon her bosom. It had the effect of a spell, taking her out of the ordinary relations with humanity, and enclosing her in a sphere by herself.

"She hath good skill at her needle, that's certain," remarked one of her female spectators, "but did ever a woman, before this **brazen** hussy, **contrive** such a way of showing it! Why, gossips, what is it but to laugh in the faces of our godly **magistrates**, and make a pride out of what they, worthy gentlemen, meant for a punishment?"

"It were well," muttered the most iron-**visaged** of the old dames, "if we stripped Madam Hester's rich gown off her **dainty** shoulders; and as for the red letter, which she hath stitched so curiously, I'll **bestow** a rag of mine own rheumatic flannel, to make a fitter one!"

"O, peace, neighbors, peace!" whispered their youngest companion. "Do not let her hear you! Not a stitch in that embroidered letter, but she has felt it in her heart."

The grim beadle now made a gesture with his staff.

"Make way, good people, make way, in the King's name!" cried he. "Open a passage; and, I promise ye, Mistress Prynne shall be set where man, woman, and child may have a fair sight of her brave apparel, from this time till an hour past meridian. A blessing on the righteous Colony of the Massachusetts, where **iniquity** is dragged out into the sunshine! Come along, Madam Hester, and show your scarlet letter in the market-place!"

A lane was forthwith opened through the crowd of spectators. Preceded by the beadle, and attended by an irregular procession of stern-browed men and unkindly **visaged** women, Hester Prynne set forth towards the

IGNOMINIOUS (ihg nuh <u>mih</u> nee uhs) *adj.*
 disgraceful and dishonorable
  Synonyms: despicable, degrading, debasing

HAUGHTY (<u>haw</u> tee) (<u>hah</u> tee) *adj.*
 arrogant and condescending
  Synonyms: proud, disdainful, supercilious,
  scornful

DEMEANOR (dih <u>meen</u> uhr) *n.*
 one's behavior or conduct
  Synonyms: attitude, disposition, manner, presence

SPURN (spuhrn) *v.* **-ing,-ed.**
 to reject or refuse contemptuously, scorn
  Synonyms: disdain, snub, ostracize, ignore, cut

PROVISION (pruh <u>vih</u> zhuhn) *n.*
 a stipulation; a stock of needed materials or supplies
  Synonyms: rule, qualification; equipment,
  necessities

SERENE (suh <u>reen</u>) *adj.*
 calm, peaceful
  Synonyms: tranquil, composed, content, placid

CONSTITUTE (kahn stih <u>toot</u>) *v.* **-ing,-ed.**
 1. to be the parts or components of something,
 to compose; to equal
  Synonyms: comprise, form, make up; amount to
 2. to designate or charge with a specific task
  Synonyms: appoint, name

IDEAL (ie <u>deel</u>) *n.*
 a perfect or excellent example
  Synonyms: model, exemplar, standard, paragon

IGNOMINY (<u>ihg</u> nuh mih nee) *n.*
 disgrace and dishonor
  Synonyms: degradation, debasement

MANIFEST (<u>maan</u> uh fehst) *adj.*
 evidently obvious
  Synonyms: apparent, distinct, prominent, glaring

CONTRIVANCE (kuhn <u>triev</u> ehnts) *n.*
 the act of creating art or an artistic creation; an
 invention
  Synonyms: design, project; concoction, scheme

place appointed for her punishment. A crowd of eager and curious school-boys, understanding little of the matter in hand, except that it gave them a half-holiday, ran before her progress, turning their heads continually to stare into her face, and at the winking baby in her arms, and at the **ignominious** letter on her breast. It was no great distance, in those days, from the prison door to the market-place. Measured by the prisoner's experience, however, it might be reckoned a journey of some length; for, **haughty** as her **demeanor** was, she perchance underwent an agony from every footstep of those that thronged to see her, as if her heart had been flung into the street for them all to **spurn** and trample upon. In our nature, however, there is a **provision**, alike marvellous and merciful, that the sufferer should never know the intensity of what he endures by its present torture, but chiefly by the pang that rankles after it. With almost a **serene** deportment, therefore, Hester Prynne passed through this portion of her ordeal, and came to a sort of scaffold, at the western extremity of the market-place. It stood nearly beneath the eaves of Boston's earliest church, and appeared to be a fixture there.

In fact, this scaffold **constituted** a portion of a penal machine, which now, for two or three generations past, has been merely historical and traditionary among us, but was held, in the old time, to be as effectual an agent, in the promotion of good citizenship, as ever was the guillotine among the terrorists of France. It was, in short, the platform of the pillory; and above it rose the framework of that instrument of discipline, so fashioned as to confine the human head in its tight grasp, and thus hold it up to the public gaze. The very **ideal** of **ignominy** was embodied and made **manifest** in this **contrivance** of wood and iron. There can be no outrage, methinks, against our common nature—whatever be the delinquencies of the individual—no outrage more

FLAGRANT (<u>flay</u> gruhnt) *adj.*
    outrageous, conspicuous
      Synonyms: glaring, blatant

ASCEND (uh <u>sehnd</u>) *v.* **-ing,-ed.**
    to rise to another level or climb; to move upward
      Synonyms: elevate, escalate, mount; hoist, lift

MULTITUDE (<u>muhl</u> tuh tood) *n.*
    a crowd; the state of being many, a great number
      Synonyms: throng; mass, myriad

MIEN (meen) *n.*
    characteristics expressive of attitude or personality
      Synonyms: manner, demeanor, expression, style

ILLUSTRIOUS (ih <u>luhs</u> tree uhs) *adj.*
    famous, renowned
      Synonyms: celebrated, eminent, famed, notable

VIE *v.* **vying,-ied.**
    to compete, contend
      Synonyms: strive, rival, emulate

TAINT (taynt) *n.*
    a moral flaw; a smear or stain
      Synonyms: fault, shame, corruption;
      contamination, blemish, pollution

DISPOSITION (dihs puh <u>zih</u> shuhn) *n.*
    1. a habitual tendency, an inclination
      Synonyms: willingness, propensity
    2. mood or temperament
      Synonyms: behavior, nature

flagrant than to forbid the culprit to hide his face for shame; as it was the essence of this punishment to do. In Hester Prynne's instance, however, as not unfrequently in other cases, her sentence bore, that she should stand a certain time upon the platform but without undergoing that gripe about the neck and confinement of the head, the proneness to which was the most devilish characteristic of this ugly engine. Knowing well her part, she **ascended** a flight of wooden steps, and was thus displayed to the surrounding **multitude**, at about the height of a man's shoulders above the street.

Had there been a <u>Papist</u> among the crowd of <u>Puritans</u>, he might have seen in this beautiful woman, so picturesque in her attire and **mien**, and with the infant at her bosom, an object to remind him of the image of divine Maternity, which so many **illustrious** painters have **vied** with one another to represent; something which should remind him, indeed, but only by contrast, of that sacred image of sinless motherhood, whose infant was to redeem the world. Here, there was the **taint** of deepest sin in the most sacred quality of human life, working such effect, that the world was only the darker for this woman's beauty, and the more lost for the infant that she had borne.

The scene was not without a mixture of awe, such as must always invest the spectacle of guilt and shame in a fellow-creature, before society shall have grown corrupt enough to smile, instead of shuddering, at it. The witnesses of Hester Prynne's disgrace had not yet passed beyond their simplicity. They were stern enough to look upon her death, had that been the sentence, without a murmur at its severity, but had none of the heartlessness of another social state, which would find only a theme for jest in an exhibition like the present. Even had there been a **disposition** to turn the matter into ridicule, it must have been repressed and overpowered by the

SOLEMN (<u>sah</u> luhm) *adj.*
    deeply serious, somberly impressive
        Synonyms: dignified, earnest, ceremonial
CONSTITUTE (kahn stih <u>toot</u>) *v.* **-ing,-ed.**
    1. to be the parts or components of something,
    to compose; to equal
        Synonyms: comprise, form, make up; amount to
    2. to designate or charge with a specific task
        Synonyms: appoint, name
REVERENCE (<u>reh</u> vuhr ehnts) *n.*
    deep respect, awe
        Synonyms: veneration, adoration, admiration
SOMBRE or SOMBER (<u>sahm</u> buhr) *adj.* *(See page 86.)*
SUSTAIN (suh <u>stayn</u>) *v.* **-ing,-ed.**
    to support, uphold; endure, undergo
        Synonyms: maintain, prop, encourage; withstand
IMPULSIVE (ihm <u>puhl</u> sihv) *adj.*
    sudden, spontaneous
        Synonyms: whimsical, unprompted, involuntary
VENOMOUS (<u>vehn</u> uh muhs) *adj.*
    malicious or spiteful; poisonous
        Synonyms: harmful; noxious, deadly
CONTUMELY (kahn <u>too</u> muh lee) *n.*
    harsh language or treatment arising from haughtiness
        Synonynms: rudeness, arrogance
COUNTENANCE (<u>kown</u> tuh nuhns) *n.*
    appearance, facial expression
        Synonyms: face, features, visage
MULTITUDE (<u>muhl</u> tuh tood) *n.* *(See page 110.)*
DISDAINFUL (dihs <u>dayn</u> fuhl) *adj.*
    contemptuous, scornful
        Synonyms: insulting, arrogant, haughty
PRETERNATURALLY (pree tuhr <u>naach</u> uh ruh lee) *adv.*
    in an extraordinary or unnatural manner
        Synonyms: abnormally, mysteriously, oddly,
        unearthly

solemn presence of men no less dignified than the Governor, and several of his counsellors, a judge, a general, and the ministers of the town; all of whom sat or stood in a balcony of the meeting-house, looking down upon the platform. When such personages could **constitute** a part of the spectacle, without risking the majesty or **reverence** of rank and office, it was safely to be inferred that the infliction of a legal sentence would have an earnest and effectual meaning. Accordingly, the crowd was **sombre** and grave. The unhappy culprit **sustained** herself as best a woman might, under the heavy weight of a thousand unrelenting eyes, all fastened upon her, and concentrated at her bosom. It was almost intolerable to be borne. Of an **impulsive** and passionate nature, she had fortified herself to encounter the stings and **venomous** stabs of public **contumely**, wreaking itself in every variety of insult; but there was a quality so much more terrible in the **solemn** mood of the popular mind, that she longed rather to behold all those rigid **countenances** contorted with scornful merriment, and herself the object. Had a roar of laughter burst from the **multitude**—each man, each woman, each little shrill-voiced child, contributing their individual parts— Hester Prynne might have repaid them all with a bitter and **disdainful** smile. But, under the leaden infliction which it was her doom to endure, she felt, at moments, as if she must needs shriek out with the full power of her lungs and cast herself from the scaffold down upon the ground, or else go mad at once.

Yet there were intervals when the whole scene, in which she was the most conspicuous object, seemed to vanish from her eyes, or, at least, glimmered indistinctly before them, like a mass of imperfectly shaped and spectral images. Her mind, and especially her memory, was **preternaturally** active, and kept bringing up other scenes than this roughly hewn street of a little town, on

REMINISCENCE (reh muh <u>nihs</u> ehnts) *n.*
remembrance of past events
Synonyms: memory, recollection, recall

TRIFLING (<u>trie</u> flihng) *adj.*
minor, of slight worth or little importance
Synonyms: trivial, insignificant

SUBSEQUENT (<u>suhb</u> suh kwehnt) *adj.*
following in time or order
Synonyms: succeeding, next, after

EMINENCE (<u>ehm</u> uh nuhnts) *n.*
1. a prominent place, something which projects outward
Synonyms: elevation, summit, peak
2. a position of distinction or superiority
Synonyms: prominence, importance

PATERNAL (puh <u>tuhr</u> nuhl) *adj.*
inherited from or belonging to one's father; fatherly,
related to the characteristics of fatherhood
Synonyms: hereditary; parental

RETAIN (rih <u>tayn</u>) *v.* **-ing,-ed.**
to hold, keep possession of
Synonyms: withhold, reserve

IMPEDIMENT (ihm <u>pehd</u> uh muhnt) *n.*
barrier, obstacle; speech disorder
Synonyms: obstruction, hindrance, block, hurdle

REMONSTRANCE (reh <u>mahn</u> strehnts) *n.*
the presentation and urging of reasons in opposition,
protestation
Synonyms: objection, complaint, expostulation

COUNTENANCE (<u>kown</u> tuh nuhns) *n.*
appearance, facial expression
Synonyms: face, features, visage

VISAGE (<u>vih</u> sihj) *n.*
the appearance of a person or place, face
Synonyms: expression, look, style, manner

PORE (pohr) *v.* **-ing,-ed.**
to study closely or meditatively
Synonyms: gaze, ponder

PONDEROUS (<u>pahn</u> duhr uhs) *adj.*
weighty, heavy, large
Synonyms: hefty, massive, cumbersome, unwieldy

the edge of the Western wilderness; other faces than were lowering upon her from beneath the brims of those steeple-crowned hats. **Reminiscences**, the most **trifling** and immaterial, passages of infancy and schooldays, sports, childish quarrels, and the little domestic traits of her maiden years, came swarming back upon her, intermingled with recollections of whatever was gravest in her **subsequent** life; one picture precisely as vivid as another; as if all were of similar importance, or all alike a play. Possibly it was an instinctive device of her spirit, to relieve itself, by the exhibition of these phantasmagoric forms, from the cruel weight and hardness of the reality.

Be that as it might, the scaffold of the pillory was a point of view that revealed to Hester Prynne the entire track along which she had been treading since her happy infancy. Standing on that miserable **eminence**, she saw again her native village, in Old England, and her **paternal** home; a decayed house of gray stone, with a poverty-stricken aspect, but **retaining** a half-obliterated shield of arms over the portal, in token of antique gentility. She saw her father's face, with its bald brow and reverend white beard, that flowed over the old-fashioned Elizabethan ruff; her mother's, too, with the look of heedful and anxious love which it always wore in her remembrance, and which, even since her death, had so often laid the **impediment** of a gentle **remonstrance** in her daughter's pathway. She saw her own face, glowing with girlish beauty, and illuminating all the interior of the dusky mirror in which she had been wont to gaze at it. There she beheld another **countenance**, of a man well stricken in years, a pale, thin, scholar-like **visage**, with eyes dim and bleared by the lamplight that had served them to **pore** over many **ponderous** books. Yet those same bleared optics had a strange, penetrating power, when it was their owner's purpose to read the human

CLOISTER (<u>kloy</u> stuhr) *n.*
a small secluded space
Synonyms: cell, alcove, recess, stall, den

DEFORMED (dih <u>fohrmd</u>) *adj.*
disfigured, spoiled
Synonyms: contorted, twisted, marred, misshapen

TRIFLE (<u>trie</u> fuhl) *n.*
a slight degree or small amount; something of slight
worth or little importance
Synonyms: bit, speck, fraction, trace, dash;
triviality, novelty, trinket, bit

EDIFICE (<u>eh</u> duh fuhs) *n.*
a large structure
Synonyms: building, construction, skyscraper

soul. This figure of the study and the **cloister**, as Hester Prynne's womanly fancy failed not to recall, was slightly **deformed**, with the left shoulder a **trifle** higher than the right. Next rose before her, in memory's picture-gallery, the intricate and narrow thoroughfares, the tall, gray houses, the huge cathedrals, and the public **edifices**, ancient in date and quaint in architecture, of a Continental city; where a new life had awaited her, still in connection with the misshapen scholar; a new life, but feeding itself on time-worn materials, like a tuft of green moss on a crumbling wall. Lastly, in lieu of these shifting scenes, came back the rude market-place of the <u>Puritan</u> settlement, with all the townspeople assembled and levelling their stern regards at Hester Prynne—yes, at herself—who stood on the scaffold of the <u>pillory</u>, an infant on her arm, and the letter A, in scarlet, fantastically embroidered with gold thread, upon her bosom!

Could it be true? She clutched the child so fiercely to her breast that it sent forth a cry; she turned her eyes downward at the scarlet letter, and even touched it with her finger, to assure herself that the infant and the shame were real. Yes—these were her realities—all else had vanished!

DISCERN (dihs <u>uhrn</u>) *v.* **-ing,-ed.**
  to perceive or recognize something
  Synonyms: descry, observe, glimpse, distinguish
SUSTAIN (suh <u>stayn</u>) *v.* **-ing,-ed.**
  to support, uphold; endure, undergo
  Synonyms: maintain, prop, encourage; withstand
DISARRAY (dihs uh <u>ray</u>) *n.*
  clutter, disorder
  Synonyms: chaos, confusion, muddle, jumble,
  disorganization
CIVILIZED (<u>sih</u> vuhl iezd) *adj.*
  relating to human lifestyle as opposed to the wild,
  humane; politely sophisticated, cultured
  Synonyms: refined, cultivated; courteous,
  pleasant, affable
FURROWED (<u>fuhr</u> rohd) *adj.*
  having wrinkles or grooves; rugged
  Synonyms: crinkled, ridged, creased; weathered,
  worn
VISAGE (<u>vih</u> sihj) *n.*
  the appearance of a person or place, face
  Synonyms: expression, look, style, manner
MANIFEST (<u>maan</u> uh fehst) *adj.*
  evidently obvious
  Synonyms: apparent, distinct, prominent, glaring
HETEROGENEOUS (heh tuh ruh <u>jee</u> nee uhs) *adj.*
  composed of unlike parts, different, diverse
  Synonyms: miscellaneous, mixed, varied, motley,
  assorted
ABATE (uh <u>bayt</u>) *v.* **-ing,-ed.**
  to decrease, reduce
  Synonyms: dwindle, ebb, recede, flag, wane
DEFORMITY (dih <u>fohr</u> mih tee) *n.*
  disfigurement
  Synonyms: malformation, disproportion

The Recognition
Chapter 3

From this intense consciousness of being the object of severe and universal observation, the wearer of the scarlet letter was at length relieved, by **discerning** on the outskirts of the crowd, a figure which irresistibly took possession of her thoughts. An Indian, in his native garb, was standing there; but the red men were not so infrequent visitors of the English settlements, that one of them would have attracted any notice from Hester Prynne at such a time; much less would he have excluded all other objects and ideas from her mind. By the Indian's side, and evidently **sustaining** a companionship with him, stood a white man, clad in a strange **disarray** of **civilized** and savage costume.

He was small in stature, with a **furrowed visage**, which, as yet, could hardly be termed aged. There was a remarkable intelligence in his features, as of a person who had so cultivated his mental part that it could not fail to mould the physical to itself, and become **manifest** by unmistakable tokens. Although, by a seemingly careless arrangement of his **heterogeneous** garb, he had endeavored to conceal or **abate** the peculiarity, it was sufficiently evident to Hester Prynne that one of this man's shoulders rose higher than the other. Again, at the first instant of perceiving that thin **visage**, and the slight **deformity** of the figure, she pressed her infant to her bosom with so convulsive a force that the poor babe uttered another cry of pain. But the mother did not seem to hear it.

At his arrival in the market-place, and some time before she saw him, the stranger had bent his eyes on Hester Prynne. It was carelessly, at first, like a man

KEEN *adj.*
intellectually sharp, perceptive; having a sharp edge
Synonyms: acute, quick, canny; pointed, razorlike

IMPERCEPTIBLE (ihn puhr <u>sehp</u> tih buhl) *adj.*
unable to be seen or perceived
Synonyms: unnoticeable, insignificant, invisible, faint

GRIEVOUS (<u>gree</u> vuhs) *adj.*
causing grief and sorrow, serious and distressing
Synonyms: grave, dire, mournful, dolorous

HEATHEN-FOLK (<u>hee</u> thuhn fohk) *n.*
pagans, uncivilized and irreligious people
Synonyms: idolaters, polytheists, unbelievers

chiefly accustomed to look inward, and to whom external matters are of little value and import, unless they bear relation to something within his mind. Very soon, however, his look became **keen** and penetrative. A writhing horror twisted itself across his features, like a snake gliding swiftly over them, and making one little pause, with all its wreathed intervolutions in open sight. His face darkened with some powerful emotion, which, nevertheless, he so instantaneously controlled by an effort of his will, that, save at a single moment, its expression might have passed for calmness. After a brief space, the convulsion grew almost **imperceptible**, and finally subsided into the depths of his nature. When he found the eyes of Hester Prynne fastened on his own, and saw that she appeared to recognize him, he slowly and calmly raised his finger, made a gesture with it in the air, and laid it on his lips.

Then, touching the shoulder of a townsman who stood next to him, he addressed him in a formal and courteous manner.

"I pray you, good Sir," said he, "who is this woman? And wherefore is she here set up to public shame?"

"You must needs be a stranger in this region, friend," answered the townsman, looking curiously at the questioner and his savage companion, "else you would surely have heard of Mistress Hester Prynne, and her evil doings. She hath raised a great scandal, I promise you, in godly Master Dimmesdale's church."

"You say truly," replied the other. "I am a stranger, and have been a wanderer, sorely against my will. I have met with **grievous** mishaps by sea and land, and have been long held in bonds among the **heathen-folk**, to the southward; and am now brought hither by this Indian, to be redeemed out of my captivity. Will it please you, therefore, to tell me of Hester Prynne's—have I her

SOJOURN (<u>soh</u> juhrn) (soh <u>juhrn</u>) *n.*
  visit, stay
    Synonyms: residency, stop, tenancy

INIQUITY (ih <u>nihk</u> wih tee) *n.*
  sin, evil act
    Synonyms: immorality, injustice, wickedness, vice

EXPOUND (ihk <u>spownd</u>) *v.* **-ing,-ed.**
  to explain or describe in detail
    Synonyms: elucidate, elaborate, explicate

MAGISTRATE (<u>maa</u> juh strayt) *n.*
  an official who can administrate laws
    Synonyms: judge, arbiter, authority, marshal

name rightly?—of this woman's offences, and what has brought her to yonder scaffold?"

"Truly, friend; and methinks it must gladden your heart, after your troubles and **sojourn** in the wilderness," said the townsman, "to find yourself, at length, in a land where **iniquity** is searched out, and punished in the sight of rulers and people, as here in our godly New England. Yonder woman, Sir, you must know, was the wife of a certain learned man, English by birth, but who had long dwelt in Amsterdam, whence, some good time agone, he was minded to cross over and cast in his lot with us of the Massachusetts. To this purpose, he sent his wife before him, remaining himself to look after some necessary affairs. Marry, good Sir, in some two years, or less, that the woman has been a dweller here in Boston, no tidings have come of this learned gentleman, Master Prynne; and his young wife, look you, being left to her own misguidance—"

"Ah!—aha!—I conceive you," said the stranger, with a bitter smile. "So learned a man as you speak of should have learned this too in his books. And who, by your favor, Sir, may be the father of yonder babe—it is some three or four months old, I should judge—which Mistress Prynne is holding in her arms?"

"Of a truth, friend, that matter remaineth a riddle; and the Daniel who shall **expound** it is yet a-wanting," answered the townsman. "Madam Hester absolutely refuseth to speak, and the **magistrates** have laid their heads together in vain. Peradventure the guilty one stands looking on at this sad spectacle, unknown of man, and forgetting that God sees him."

"The learned man," observed the stranger, with another smile, "should come himself, to look into the mystery."

"It behooves him well, if he be still in life," responded the townsman. "Now, good Sir, our Massachusetts

MAGISTRACY (<u>maa</u> juh struh see) *n.*
a group of officials who can administrate laws
Synonyms: administration, authority, jurisdiction

IGNOMINIOUS (ihg nuh <u>mih</u> nee uhs) *adj.*
disgraceful and dishonorable
Synonyms: despicable, degrading, debasing

INIQUITY (ih <u>nihk</u> wih tee) *n.*
sin, evil act
Synonyms: immorality, injustice, wickedness, vice

INFAMY (<u>ihn</u> fuh mee) *n.*
reputation for bad deeds
Synonyms: disgrace, dishonor, shame

DRAW *v.* **-ing, drew, drawn.**
1. to attract; to pull, drag
Synonyms: lure, entice; haul, tow, lug
2. to move steadily
Synonyms: proceed, continue, progress

magistracy, bethinking themselves that this woman is youthful and fair, and doubtless was strongly tempted to her fall—and that, moreover, as is most likely, her husband may be at the bottom of the sea—they have not been bold to put in force the extremity of our righteous law against her. The penalty thereof is death. But in their great mercy and tenderness of heart, they have doomed Mistress Prynne to stand only a space of three hours on the platform of the <u>pillory</u>, and then and thereafter, for the remainder of her natural life, to wear a mark of shame upon her bosom."

"A wise sentence!" remarked the stranger, gravely bowing his head. "Thus she will be a living sermon against sin, until the **ignominious** letter be engraved upon her tombstone. It irks me, nevertheless, that the partner of her **iniquity** should not, at least, stand on the scaffold by her side. But he will be known! He will be known! He will be known!"

He bowed courteously to the communicative townsman, and, whispering a few words to his Indian attendant, they both made their way through the crowd.

While this passed, Hester Prynne had been standing on her pedestal, still with a fixed gaze towards the stranger; so fixed a gaze, that, at moments of intense absorption, all other objects in the visible world seemed to vanish, leaving only him and her. Such an interview, perhaps, would have been more terrible than even to meet him as she now did, with the hot, midday sun burning down upon her face, and lighting up its shame; with the scarlet token of **infamy** on her breast; with the sin-born infant in her arms; with a whole people, **drawn** forth as to a festival, staring at the features that should have been seen only in the quiet gleam of the fireside, in the happy shadow of a home, or beneath a matronly veil, at church. Dreadful as it was, she was conscious of a shelter in the presence of these thousand witnesses. It

SOLEMN (<u>sah</u> luhm) *adj.*
deeply serious, somberly impressive
Synonyms: dignified, earnest, ceremonial

AUDIBLE (<u>aw</u> dih buhl) *adj.*
capable of being heard
Synonyms: detectable, perceptible

MULTITUDE (<u>muhl</u> tuh tood) *n.*
a crowd; the state of being many, a great number
Synonyms: throng; mass, myriad

MAGISTRACY (<u>maa</u> juh struh see) *n.*
a group of officials who can administrate laws
Synonyms: administration, authority, jurisdiction

IMPULSE (<u>ihm</u> puhls) *n.*
sudden tendency, inclination
Synonyms: urge, whim

SOMBRE or SOMBER (<u>sahm</u> buhr) *adj.*
melancholy, dismal, dark and gloomy
Synonyms: serious, grave, mournful, lugubrious,
funereal

SAGACITY (suh <u>gaa</u> sih tee) *n.*
shrewdness, intelligence
Synonyms: perspicacity, wisdom, knowledge

EMINENT (<u>ehm</u> uh nuhnt) *adj.*
celebrated, distinguished, outstanding, towering
Synonyms: noted, famous, prominent, important,
illustrious

MIEN (meen) *n.*
characteristics expressive of attitude or personality
Synonyms: manner, demeanor, expression, style

was better to stand thus, with so many <u>betwixt</u> him and her, than to greet him, face to face, they two alone. She fled for refuge, as it were, to the public exposure, and dreaded the moment when its protection should be withdrawn from her. Involved in these thoughts, she scarcely heard a voice behind her, until it had repeated her name more than once, in a loud and **solemn** tone, **audible** to the whole **multitude**.

"Hearken unto me, Hester Prynne!" said the voice.

It has already been noticed that directly over the platform on which Hester Prynne stood was a kind of balcony, or open gallery, appended to the meetinghouse. It was the place whence proclamations were wont to be made, amidst assemblage of the **magistracy**, with all the ceremonial that attended such public observances in those days. Here, to witness the scene which we are describing, sat Governor Bellingham himself, with four sergeants about his chair, bearing <u>halberds</u>, as a guard of honor. He wore a dark feather in his hat, a border of embroidery on his cloak, and a black velvet tunic beneath; a gentleman advanced in years, with a hard experience written in his wrinkles. He was not ill fitted to be the head and representative of a community, which owed its origin and progress, and its present state of development, not to the **impulses** of youth, but to the stern and tempered energies of manhood and the **sombre sagacity** of age; accomplishing so much, precisely because it imagined and hoped so little. The other **eminent** characters, by whom the chief ruler was surrounded, were distinguished by a dignity of **mien**, belonging to a period when the forms of authority were felt to possess the sacredness of divine institutions. They were, doubtless, good men, just and sage. But, out of the whole human family, it would not have been easy to select the same number of wise and virtuous persons, who should be less capable of sitting in judgment on an

SAGE (sayj) *n.*
a very wise person
Synonyms: scholar, genius, intellectual

MULTITUDE (muhl tuh tood) *n.*
a crowd; the state of being many, a great number
Synonyms: throng; mass, myriad

GENIAL (jeen yuhl) (jee nee uhl) *adj.*
pleasant and friendly; favorable to growth or comfort
Synonyms: nice, amiable; productive, generative

UNADULTERATED (uhn uh duhl tuhr ay tihd) *adj.*
pure, undiluted
Synonyms: complete, natural, full, unconditional

MEDDLE (meh duhl) *v.* **-ing,-ed.**
to interfere in others' affairs, to impose
Synonyms: tamper, encroach

VILENESS (viel nehs) *n.*
wretchedness, offensiveness
Synonyms: wickedness, nastiness, repulsiveness

PREVAIL (prih vayl) *v.* **-ing,-ed.**
to overcome; to succeed lastingly
Synonyms: dominate, triumph; persist, endure

OBSTINACY (ahb stih nuh see) *n.*
stubbornness
Synonyms: bullheadedness, pertinacity

erring woman's heart, and disentangling its mesh of good and evil, than the **sages** of rigid aspect towards whom Hester Prynne now turned her face. She seemed conscious, indeed, that whatever sympathy she might expect lay in the larger and warmer heart of the **multitude**; for, as she lifted her eyes towards the balcony, the unhappy woman grew pale and trembled. The voice which had called her attention was that of the reverend and famous John Wilson, the eldest clergyman of Boston, a great scholar, like most of his contemporaries in the profession, and withal a man of kind and **genial** spirit. This last attribute, however, had been less carefully developed than his intellectual gifts, and was, in truth, rather a matter of shame than self-congratulation with him. There he stood, with a border of grizzled locks beneath his skull-cap; while his gray eyes, accustomed to the shaded light of his study, were winking, like those of Hester's infant, in the **unadulterated** sunshine. He looked like the darkly engraved portraits which we see prefixed to old volumes of sermons; and had no more right than one of those portraits would have to step forth, as he now did, and **meddle** with a question of human guilt, passion, and anguish.

"Hester Prynne," said the clergyman, "I have striven with my young brother here, under whose preaching of the word you have been privileged to sit"—here Mr. Wilson laid his hand on the shoulder of a pale young man beside him—"I have sought, I say, to persuade this godly youth, that he should deal with you, here in the face of Heaven, and before these wise and upright rulers, and in hearing of all the people, as touching the **vileness** and blackness of your sin. Knowing your natural temper better than I, he could the better judge what arguments to use, whether of tenderness or terror, such as might **prevail** over your hardness and **obstinacy**; insomuch that you should no longer hide the name of him

GRIEVOUS (<u>gree</u> vuhs) *adj. (See page 120.)*

MULTITUDE (<u>muhl</u> tuh tood) *n. (See page 128.)*

PURPORT (puhr <u>pohrt</u>) *n.*
intention, purpose
Synonyms: importance, meaning

EXHORT (ihg <u>zohrt</u>) *v.* **-ing,-ed.**
to urge or incite by strong appeals
Synonyms: press, prod, provoke, convince, inspire

REPENTANCE (rih <u>pehn</u> tehnts) *n.*
sorrow expressed for sins or offenses, penitence
Synonyms: remorse, contrition, apology

DRAW *v.* **-ing, drew, drawn.** *(See page 124.)*

ELOQUENCE (<u>eh</u> luh kwuhns) *n.*
persuasive and effective speech
Synonyms: expressiveness, fluency

FERVOR (<u>fuhr</u> vuhr) *n.*
passion, intensity, zeal
Synonyms: vehemence, eagerness, enthusiasm

EMINENCE (<u>ehm</u> uh nuhnts) *n.*
1. a position of distinction or superiority
Synonyms: prominence, importance
2. a prominent place, something which projects outward or upward
Synonyms: elevation, summit, peak

MELANCHOLY (<u>mehl</u> uhn kahl ee) *adj.*
sad, depressed
Synonyms: dejected, despondent, woeful, sorrowful

TREMULOUS (<u>treh</u> myoo luhs) *adj.*
trembling, quivering; fearful, timid
Synonyms: shaking, palsied; timorous, anxious

SELF-RESTRAINT (sehlf rih <u>straynt</u>) *n.*
control over one's own emotions and actions
Synonyms: temperateness, repression

APPREHENSIVE (aa prih <u>hehn</u> sihv) *adj.*
suspicious or fearful of future or unknown evil
Synonyms: concerned, worried, uneasy, uncertain

SECLUSION (sih <u>cloo</u> zhuhn) *n.*
isolation, detachment
Synonyms: separation, privacy, solitude

who tempted you to this **grievous** fall. But he opposes to me (with a young man's over-softness, albeit wise beyond his years) that it were wronging the very nature of woman to force her to lay open her heart's secrets in such broad daylight, and in the presence of so great a **multitude**. Truly, as I sought to convince him, the shame lay in the commission of the sin, and not in the showing of it forth. What say you to it, once again, Brother Dimmesdale? Must it be thou, or I, that shall deal with this poor sinner's soul?"

There was a murmur among the dignified and reverend occupants of the balcony; and Governor Bellingham gave expression to its **purport**, speaking in an authoritative voice, although tempered with respect towards the youthful clergyman whom he addressed.

"Good Master Dimmesdale," said he, "the responsibility of this woman's soul lies greatly with you. It behooves you, therefore, to **exhort** her to **repentance**, and to confession, as a proof and consequence thereof."

The directness of this appeal **drew** the eyes of the whole crowd upon the Reverend Mr. Dimmesdale; a young clergyman who had come from one of the great English universities, bringing all the learning of the age into our wild forest-land. His **eloquence** and religious **fervor** had already given the earnest of high **eminence** in his profession. He was a person of very striking aspect, with a white, lofty, and impending brow, large, brown, **melancholy** eyes, and a mouth which, unless when he forcibly compressed it, was apt to be **tremulous**, expressing both nervous sensibility and a vast power of **self-restraint**. Notwithstanding his high native gifts and scholar-like attainments, there was an air about this young minister—an **apprehensive**, a startled, a half-frightened look—as of a being who felt himself quite astray and at a loss in the pathway of human existence, and could only be at ease in some **seclusion** of his own.

TREMULOUS (<u>treh</u> myoo luhs) *adj.*
trembling, quivering; fearful, timid
Synonyms: shaking, palsied; timorous, anxious

EXHORT (ihg <u>zohrt</u>) *v.* **-ing,-ed.**
to urge or incite by strong appeals
Synonyms: press, prod, provoke, convince, inspire

STEADFASTLY (<u>stehd</u> faast lee) *adv.*
with persistence; without wavering, loyally
Synonyms: relentlessly, faithfully, constantly,
staunchly

COMPEL (kuhm <u>pehl</u>) *v.* **-ling,-led.**
to urge or force
Synonyms: coerce, oblige, constrain

HYPOCRISY (hih <u>pah</u> krih see) *n.*
the practice of claiming beliefs or virtues that one
doesn't really possess
Synonyms: fraud, falseness, fakeness, lip service

IGNOMINY (<u>ihg</u> nuh mih nee) *n.*
disgrace and dishonor
Synonyms: degradation, debasement

Therefore, so far as his duties would permit, he trod in the shadowy by-paths, and thus kept himself simple and childlike, coming forth, when occasion was, with a freshness, and fragrance, and dewy purity of thought, which, as many people said, affected them like the speech of an angel.

Such was the young man whom the Reverend Mr. Wilson and the Governor had introduced so openly to the public notice, bidding him speak, in the hearing of all men, to that mystery of a woman's soul, so sacred even in its pollution. The trying nature of his position drove the blood from his cheek, and made his lips **tremulous**.

"Speak to the woman, my brother," said Mr. Wilson. "It is of moment to her soul, and therefore, as the worshipful Governor says, momentous to thine own, in whose charge hers is. **Exhort** her to confess the truth!"

The Reverend Mr. Dimmesdale bent his head, in silent prayer, as it seemed, and then came forward.

"Hester Prynne," said he, leaning over the balcony, and looking down **steadfastly** into her eyes, "thou hearest what this good man says, and seest the accountability under which I labor. If thou feelest it to be for thy soul's peace, and that thy earthly punishment will thereby be made more effectual to salvation, I charge thee to speak out the name of thy fellow-sinner and fellow-sufferer! Be not silent from any mistaken pity and tenderness for him; for, believe me, Hester, though he were to step down from a high place, and stand there beside thee, on thy pedestal of shame, yet better were it so, than to hide a guilty heart through life. What can thy silence do for him, except it tempt him—yea, **compel** him, as it were—to add **hypocrisy** to sin? Heaven hath granted thee an open **ignominy**, that thereby thou mayest work out an open triumph over the evil within thee, and the sorrow without. Take heed how

TREMULOUSLY (<u>treh</u> myoo luhs lee) *adv.*
in a trembling, quivering manner; fearfully, timidly
Synonyms: unsteadily, weakly; timorously, anxiously

MANIFEST (<u>maan</u> uh fehst) *v.* **-ing,-ed.**
to make evident or certain by display
Synonyms: exhibit, showcase, expose

PURPORT (puhr <u>pohrt</u>) *n.*
intention, purpose
Synonyms: importance, meaning

PLAINTIVE (<u>playn</u> tihv) *adj.*
sad, lamenting
Synonyms: mournful, melancholy

DRAW *v.* **-ing, drew, drawn.**
1. to pull, drag; to attract
Synonyms: haul, tow, lug; lure, entice
2. to move steadily
Synonyms: proceed, continue, progress

INEVITABLE (ihn <u>ehv</u> ih tuh buhl) *adj.*
certain, unavoidable
Synonyms: inescapable, sure, predictable

COMPEL (kuhm <u>pehl</u>) *v.* **-ling,-led.**
to urge or force
Synonyms: coerce, oblige, constrain

ASCEND (uh <u>sehnd</u>) *v.* **-ing,-ed.**
to rise to another level or climb; to move upward
Synonyms: elevate, escalate, mount; hoist, lift

TRANSGRESS (traans <u>grehs</u>) *v.* **-ing,-ed.**
to trespass; to violate a law or command
Synonyms: overstep; sin, disobey, offend

REPENTANCE (rih <u>pehn</u> tehnts) *n.*
sorrow expressed for sins or offenses, penitence
Synonyms: remorse, contrition, apology

AVAIL (uh <u>vayl</u>) *v.* **-ing,-ed.**
to result in; to be of use or advantage to; to make use of
Synonyms: transpire, eventuate; help, serve, benefit; employ

thou deniest to him—who, perchance, hath not the courage to grasp it for himself—the bitter, but wholesome, cup that is now presented to thy lips!"

The young pastor's voice was **tremulously** sweet, rich, deep, and broken. The feeling that it so evidently **manifested**, rather than the direct **purport** of the words, caused it to vibrate within all hearts, and brought the listeners into one accord of sympathy. Even the poor baby at Hester's bosom, was affected by the same influence; for it directed its hitherto vacant gaze towards Mr. Dimmesdale, and held up its little arms, with a half-pleased, half-**plaintive** murmur. So powerful seemed the minister's appeal that the people could not believe but that Hester Prynne would speak out the guilty name; or else that the guilty one himself, in whatever high or lowly place he stood, would be **drawn** forth by an inward and **inevitable** necessity, and **compelled** to **ascend** the scaffold. Hester shook her head.

"Woman, **transgress** not beyond the limits of Heaven's mercy!" cried the Reverend Mr. Wilson, more harshly than before. "That little babe hath been gifted with a voice, to second and confirm the counsel which thou hast heard. Speak out the name! That, and thy **repentance**, may **avail** to take the scarlet letter off thy breast."

"Never!" replied Hester Prynne, looking not at Mr. Wilson, but into the deep and troubled eyes of the younger clergyman. "It is too deeply branded. Ye cannot take it off. And would that I might endure his agony, as well as mine!"

"Speak, woman!" said another voice, coldly and sternly, proceeding from the crowd about the scaffold. "Speak; and give your child a father!"

"I will not speak!" answered Hester, turning pale as death, but responding to this voice, which she too surely

DRAW *v.* **-ing, drew, drawn.** *(See page 134.)*

RESPIRATION (reh spuhr <u>ay</u> shuhn) *n.*
breath
Synonyms: inhalation, exhalation

DISCERN (dihs <u>uhrn</u>) *v.* **-ing,-ed.** *(See page 118.)*

IMPRACTICABLE (ihm <u>praak</u> tih kuh buhl) *adj.*
(See page 48.)

MULTITUDE (<u>muhl</u> tuh tood) *n.* *(See page 128.)*

DISCOURSE (<u>dihs</u> kohrs) *n.*
a formal, orderly, and extended expression of thought;
the verbal exchange of ideas
Synonyms: dialogue, conversation; speech

IGNOMINIOUS (ihg nuh <u>mih</u> nee uhs) *adj.* *(See pg. 124.)*

DERIVE (dih <u>riev</u>) *v.* **-ing,-ed.**
to receive from a source, to originate
Synonyms: infer, descend, deduce, come (from)

INFERNAL (ihn <u>fuhr</u> nuhl) *adj.*
relating to the dead or hell; devilish
Synonyms: damned, accursed; fiendish, awful, malicious

INDIFFERENCE (ihn <u>dihf</u> ruhnts) *n.*
lack of caring
Synonyms: detachment, disinterest, apathy

TEMPERAMENT (<u>tehm</u> puhr uh mehnt) *n.*
an attitude, a manner of behaving
Synonyms: disposition, mood, mentality

FACULTY (<u>faa</u> kuhl tee) *n.* *(See page 80.)*

REMORSELESSLY (rih <u>mohrs</u> lehs lee) *adv.*
without feelings of distress or guilt
Synonyms: mercilessly, unyieldingly, shamelessly

UNAVAILINGLY (uhn uh <u>vayl</u> ihng lee) *adv.*
of no use or advantage
Synonyms: futilely, ineffectually, worthlessly

DEMEANOR (dih <u>meen</u> uhr) *n.* *(See page 108.)*

LURID (<u>loor</u> ihd) *adj.*
glowing; harshly shocking, revolting
Synonyms: fiery; ghastly, garish, gruesome, grisly,
macabre

recognized. "And my child must seek a heavenly Father; she shall never know an earthly one!"

"She will not speak," murmured Mr. Dimmesdale, who, leaning over the balcony, with his hand upon his heart, had awaited the result of his appeal. He now **drew** back, with a long **respiration**. "Wondrous strength and generosity of a woman's heart! She will not speak!"

Discerning the **impracticable** state of the poor culprit's mind, the elder clergyman, who had carefully prepared himself for the occasion, addressed to the **multitude** a **discourse** on sin, in all its branches, but with continual reference to the **ignominious** letter. So forcibly did he dwell upon this symbol, for the hour or more during which his periods were rolling over the people's heads, that it assumed new terrors in their imagination, and seemed to **derive** its scarlet hue from the flames of the **infernal** pit. Hester Prynne, meanwhile, kept her place upon the pedestal of shame, with glazed eyes, and an air of weary **indifference**. She had borne, that morning, all that nature could endure; and as her **temperament** was not of the order that escapes from too intense suffering by a swoon, her spirit could only shelter itself beneath a stony crust of insensibility, while the **faculties** of animal life remained entire. In this state, the voice of the preacher thundered **remorselessly**, but **unavailingly**, upon her ears. The infant, during the latter portion of her ordeal, pierced the air with its wailings and screams; she strove to hush it, mechanically, but seemed scarcely to sympathize with its trouble. With the same hard **demeanor**, she was led back to prison, and vanished from the public gaze within its iron-clamped portal. It was whispered, by those who peered after her, that the scarlet letter threw a **lurid** gleam along the dark passage-way of the interior.

PERPETRATE (<u>puhr</u> puh trayt) *v.* **-ing,-ed.**
   to bring about, to carry out
      Synonyms: inflict, commit, wreak

QUELL (kwehl) *v.* **-ing,-ed.**
   to subdue; to crush
      Synonyms: suppress, pacify, quiet; quash, stifle

REBUKE (ree <u>byook</u>) *n.*
   a reprimand, scolding, punishment
      Synonyms: admonition, reproof, reproach

SUSTENANCE (<u>suh</u> steh nehns) *n.*
   means of living, source of nourishment
      Synonyms: food, provisions, necessities

PERVADE (puhr <u>vayd</u>) *v.* **-ing,-ed.**
   to become diffused throughout every part of
      Synonyms: permeate, spread, fill, transfuse

SINGULAR (<u>sihn</u> gyuh luhr) *adj.*
   uncommon, peculiar
      Synonyms: unusual, odd, rare, unique, individual

DISPOSE (dih <u>spohz</u>) *v.* **-ing,-ed.**
   to put in place, to settle; to incline or give a tendency
   to; to get rid of
      Synonyms: organize, position; determine,
      motivate; discard

MAGISTRATE (<u>maa</u> juh strayt) *n.*
   an official who can administrate laws
      Synonyms: judge, arbiter, authority, marshal

The Interview
Chapter 4

After her return to the prison, Hester Prynne was found to be in a state of nervous excitement that demanded constant watchfulness, lest she should **perpetrate** violence on herself, or do some half-frenzied mischief to the poor babe. As night approached, it proving impossible to **quell** her <u>insubordination</u> by **rebuke** or threats of punishment, Master Brackett, the jailer, thought fit to introduce a physician. He described him as a man of skill in all Christian modes of physical science, and likewise familiar with whatever the savage people could teach, in respect to medicinal herbs and roots that grew in the forest. To say the truth, there was much need of professional assistance, not merely for Hester herself, but still more urgently for the child, who, drawing its **sustenance** from the maternal bosom, seemed to have drunk in with it all the turmoil, the anguish and despair, which **pervaded** the mother's system. It now writhed in convulsions of pain, and was a forcible type, in its little frame, of the moral agony which Hester Prynne had borne throughout the day.

Closely following the jailer into the dismal apartment appeared that individual, of **singular** aspect, whose presence in the crowd had been of such deep interest to the wearer of the scarlet letter. He was lodged in the prison, not as suspected of any offence, but as the most convenient and suitable mode of **disposing** of him, until the **magistrates** should have conferred with the Indian <u>sagamores</u> respecting his ransom. His name was announced as Roger Chillingworth. The jailer, after ushering him into the room, remained a moment, marvelling at the comparative quiet that followed his

AMENABLE (uh <u>mehn</u> uh buhl) *adj.*
  agreeable, cooperative
    Synonyms: compliant, receptive
VERILY (<u>veh</u> rih lee) *adv.*
  truly, with accuracy and confidence
    Synonyms: truthfully, reliably, assuredly
QUIETUDE (<u>kwie</u> eh tood) *n.*
  peace or tranquility
    Synonyms: calm, ease, contentment, serenity
DEMEANOR (dih <u>meen</u> uhr) *n.*
  one's behavior or conduct
    Synonyms: attitude, disposition, manner, presence
INTIMATE (<u>ihn</u> tuh mayt) *v.* **-ing,-ed.**
  to hint or suggest obscurely
    Synonyms: implicate, allude, insinuate
PEREMPTORY (puhr <u>ehmp</u> tuh ree) *adj.*
  absolute and final; commanding
    Synonyms: conclusive, decisive; self-assured,
    dominating
ALCHEMY (<u>aal</u> kuh mee) *n.*
  medieval chemical philosophy aimed at trying to
  change metal into gold, cure all diseases, and
  lengthen human life
    Synonyms: hermeticism, magic, pseudo-science
SOJOURN (<u>soh</u> juhrn) (soh <u>juhrn</u>) *n.*
  visit, stay
    Synonyms: residency, stop, tenancy
REPEL (rih <u>pehl</u>) *v.* **-ling,-led.**
  to rebuff, repulse; disgust, offend
    Synonyms: reject, spurn, parry; nauseate, revolt
APPREHENSION (aa prih <u>hehn</u> shuhn) *n.*
  suspicion or fear of future or unknown evil; the act
  of perceiving or comprehending; a legal seizure
    Synonyms: concern, worry; understanding; capture

entrance; for Hester Prynne had immediately become as still as death, although the child continued to moan.

"Prithee, friend, leave me alone with my patient," said the practitioner. "Trust me, good jailer, you shall briefly have peace in your house; and, I promise you, Mistress Prynne shall hereafter be more **amenable** to just authority than you may have found her heretofore."

"Nay, if your worship can accomplish that," answered Master Brackett, "I shall own you for a man of skill indeed! **Verily**, the woman hath been like a possessed one; and there lacks little, that I should take in hand to drive Satan out of her with stripes."

The stranger had entered the room with the characteristic **quietude** of the profession to which he announced himself as belonging. Nor did his **demeanor** change when the withdrawal of the prison-keeper left him face to face with the woman, whose absorbed notice of him, in the crowd, had **intimated** so close a relation between himself and her. His first care was given to the child; whose cries, indeed, as she lay writhing on the trundle-bed, made it of **peremptory** necessity to postpone all other business to the task of soothing her. He examined the infant carefully, and then proceeded to unclasp a leathern case, which he took from beneath his dress. It appeared to contain medical preparations, one of which he mingled with a cup of water.

"My old studies in **alchemy**," observed he, "and my **sojourn**, for above a year past, among a people well versed in the kindly properties of simples, have made a better physician of me than many that claim the medical degree. Here, woman! The child is yours—she is none of mine—neither will she recognize my voice or aspect as a father's. Administer this draught, therefore, with thine own hand."

Hester **repelled** the offered medicine, at the same time gazing with strongly marked **apprehension** into his face.

AVENGE (uh <u>vehnj</u>) *v.* **-ing,-ed.**
  to retaliate or take revenge for an injury or crime
    Synonyms: punish, vindicate

EFFICACY (<u>eff</u> uh kuh see) *n.*
  effectiveness, efficiency
    Synonym: potency

PROFOUND (pruh <u>fownd</u>) (proh <u>fownd</u>) *adj.*
  deep; having intellectual depth
    Synonyms: bottomless; serious, thorough, weighty

BESTOW (bih <u>stoh</u>) *v.* **-ing,-ed.**
  to apply or devote time or effort; to give as a gift
    Synonyms: allocate, dedicate; endow, confer, present

SCRUTINY (<u>skroot</u> nee) *n.*
  careful observation
    Synonyms: examination, study, surveillance

REQUITAL (rih <u>kwie</u> tuhl) *n.*
  repayment, compensation
    Synonyms: reciprocation, reimbursement

TEMPESTUOUS (tehm <u>pehs</u> tyoo uhs) *adj.*
  stormy, raging, furious
    Synonyms: tumultuous, blustery, inclement,
      turbulent, torrential

"Wouldst thou **avenge** thyself on the innocent babe?" whispered she.

"Foolish woman!" responded the physician, half coldly, half soothingly. "What should ail me, to harm this misbegotten and miserable babe? The medicine is potent for good; and were it my child—yea, mine own, as well as thine—I could do no better for it."

As she still hesitated, being, in fact, in no reasonable state of mind, he took the infant in his arms, and himself administered the draught. It soon proved its **efficacy**, and redeemed the leech's pledge. The moans of the little patient subsided; its convulsive tossings gradually ceased; and, in a few moments, as is the custom of young children after relief from pain, it sank into a **profound** and dewy slumber. The physician, as he had a fair right to be termed, next **bestowed** his attention on the mother. With calm and intent **scrutiny**, he felt her pulse, looked into her eyes—a gaze that made her heart shrink and shudder, because so familiar, and yet so strange and cold—and, finally, satisfied with his investigation, proceeded to mingle another draught.

"I know not <u>Lethe</u> nor <u>Nepenthe</u>," remarked he, "but I have learned many new secrets in the wilderness, and here is one of them—a recipe that an Indian taught me, in **requital** of some lessons of my own, that were as old as <u>Paracelsus</u>. Drink it! It may be less soothing than a sinless conscience. That I cannot give thee. But it will calm the swell and heaving of thy passion, like oil thrown on the waves of a **tempestuous** sea."

He presented the cup to Hester, who received it with a slow, earnest look into his face; not precisely a look of fear, yet full of doubt and questioning, as to what his purposes might be. She looked also at her slumbering child.

"I have thought of death," said she—"have wished for it—would even have prayed for it, were it fit that such as I should pray for anything. Yet, if death be in

VENGEANCE (<u>vehn</u> juhns) *n.*
 punishment inflicted in retaliation; vehemence
  Synonyms: revenge, repayment; wrath

PERIL (<u>pehr</u> ihl) *n.*
 danger
  Synonyms: trouble, hazard, harm

EXPOSTULATION (ihk spahs chuh <u>lay</u> shuhn) *n.*
 an expression of opposition; reasoning
  Synonyms: argument, dissuasion, remonstration;
  assertion

DRAW *v.* **-ing, drew, drawn.**
  1. to pull, drag; to attract
   Synonyms: haul, tow, lug; lure, entice
  2. to move steadily
   Synonyms: proceed, continue, progress

IMPEL (ihm <u>pehl</u>) *v.* **-ling,-led.**
 to urge forward as if driven by a strong moral pressure
  Synonyms: push, prompt, incite, instigate

ASCEND (uh <u>sehnd</u>) *v.* **-ing,-ed.**
 to rise to another level or climb; to move upward
  Synonyms: elevate, escalate, mount; hoist, lift

INFAMY (<u>ihn</u> fuh mee) *n.*
 reputation for bad deeds
  Synonyms: disgrace, dishonor, shame

this cup, I bid thee think again, ere thou beholdest me quaff it. See! It is even now at my lips."

"Drink, then," replied he, still with the same cold composure. "Dost thou know me so little, Hester Prynne? Are my purposes wont to be so shallow? Even if I imagine a scheme of **vengeance**, what could I do better for my object than to let thee live—than to give thee medicines against all harm and **peril** of life—so that this burning shame may still blaze upon thy bosom?" As he spoke, he laid his long forefinger on the scarlet letter, which forthwith seemed to scorch into Hester's breast, as if it had been red-hot. He noticed her involuntary gesture, and smiled. "Live, therefore, and bear about thy doom with thee, in the eyes of men and women—in the eyes of him whom thou didst call thy husband—in the eyes of yonder child! And, that thou mayest live, take off this draught." *Live w/ the guilt*

Without further **expostulation** or delay, Hester Prynne drained the cup, and, at the motion of the man of skill, seated herself on the bed where the child was sleeping; while he **drew** the only chair which the room afforded, and took his own seat beside her. She could not but tremble at these preparations; for she felt that—having now done all that humanity, or principle, or, if so it were, a refined cruelty, **impelled** him to do, for the relief of physical suffering—he was next to treat with her as the man whom she had most deeply and irreparably injured.

"Hester," said he, "I ask not wherefore, nor how, thou hast fallen into the pit, or say, rather, thou hast **ascended** to the pedestal of **infamy** on which I found thee. The reason is not far to seek. It was my folly, and thy weakness. I—a man of thought—the bookworm of great libraries—a man already in decay, having given my best years to feed the hungry dream of knowledge— what had I to do with youth and beauty like thine own!

DEFORMITY (dih <u>fohr</u> mih tee) *n.*
disfigurement
Synonyms: malformation, disproportion

SAGE (sayj) *n.*
a very wise person
Synonyms: scholar, genius, intellectual

IGNOMINY (<u>ihg</u> nuh mih nee) *n.*
disgrace and dishonor
Synonyms: degradation, debasement

FEIGN (fayn) *v.* **-ing,-ed.**
to pretend or fake
Synonyms: imitate, fabricate, bluff, simulate

EPOCH (<u>eh</u> pihk) *n.*
a particular day or time; a specific time in history
Synonyms: date; period, era, generation

KINDLE (<u>kihn</u> duhl) *v.* **-ing,-ed.**
to set fire to or ignite; to excite or inspire
Synonyms: light, spark; arouse, awaken

SOMBRE or SOMBER (<u>sahm</u> buhr) *adj.*
melancholy, dismal, dark and gloomy
Synonyms: serious, grave, mournful, lugubrious,
funereal

DRAW *v.* **-ing, drew, drawn.**
1. to pull, drag; to attract
Synonyms: haul, tow, lug; lure, entice
2. to move steadily
Synonyms: proceed, continue, progress

VENGEANCE (<u>vehn</u> juhns) *n.*
punishment inflicted in retaliation; vehemence
Synonyms: revenge, repayment; wrath

Misshapen from my birth-hour, how could I delude myself with the idea that intellectual gifts might veil physical **deformity** in a young girl's fantasy! Men call me wise. If **sages** were ever wise in their own behoof, I might have foreseen all this. I might have known that, as I came out of the vast and dismal forest and entered this settlement of Christian men, the very first object to meet my eyes would be thyself, Hester Prynne, standing up, a statue of **ignominy**, before the people. Nay, from the moment when we came down the old church steps together, a married pair, I might have beheld the balefire of that scarlet letter blazing at the end of our path!"

"Thou knowest," said Hester—for, depressed as she was, she could not endure this last quiet stab at the token of her shame—"thou knowest that I was frank with thee. I felt no love, nor **feigned** any."

"True," replied he. "It was my folly! I have said it. But, up to that **epoch** of my life, I had lived in vain. The world had been so cheerless! My heart was a habitation large enough for many guests, but lonely and chill, and without a household fire. I longed to **kindle** one! It seemed not so wild a dream—old as I was, and **sombre** as I was, and misshapen as I was—that the simple bliss, which is scattered far and wide for all mankind to gather up, might yet be mine. And so, Hester, I **drew** thee into my heart, into its innermost chamber, and sought to warm thee by the warmth which thy presence made there!"

"I have greatly wronged thee," murmured Hester.

"We have wronged each other," answered he. "Mine was the first wrong, when I betrayed thy budding youth into a false and unnatural relation with my decay. Therefore, as a man who has not thought and philosophized in vain, I seek no **vengeance**, plot no evil against thee. Between thee and me, the scale hangs fairly

147

PRYING (<u>prie</u> ihng) *adj.*
intrusively nosy, curious
Synonyms: snooping, spying, eavesdropping,
probing

MULTITUDE (<u>muhl</u> tuh tood) *n.*
a crowd; the state of being many, a great number
Synonyms: throng; mass, myriad

MAGISTRATE (<u>maa</u> juh strayt) *n.*
an official who can administrate laws
Synonyms: judge, arbiter, authority, marshal

INQUEST (<u>ihn</u> kwehst) *n.*
investigation; court or legal proceeding
Synonyms: inquiry, probe, examination; trial

ALCHEMY (<u>aal</u> kuh mee) *n.*
medieval chemical philosophy aimed at trying to
change metal into gold, cure all diseases, and
lengthen human life
Synonyms: hermeticism, magic, pseudo-science

INFAMY (<u>ihn</u> fuh mee) *n.*
reputation for bad deeds
Synonyms: disgrace, dishonor, shame

RETRIBUTION (reh trih <u>byoo</u> shuhn) *n.*
something which is justly deserved, such as
repayment or punishment
Synonyms: vengeance, payback, compensation

CONTRIVE (kuhn <u>triev</u>) *v.* **-ing,-ed.**
to devise, plan, or manage; to form in an
artistic manner
Synonyms: concoct, scheme; create, design

balanced. But, Hester, the man lives who has wronged us both! Who is he?"

"Ask me not!" replied Hester Prynne, looking firmly into his face. "That thou shalt never know!"

"Never, sayest thou?" rejoined he, with a smile of dark and self-relying intelligence. "Never know him! Believe me, Hester, there are few things—whether in the outward world, or, to a certain depth, in the invisible sphere of thought—few things hidden from the man who devotes himself earnestly and unreservedly to the solution of a mystery. Thou mayest cover up thy secret from the **prying multitude**. Thou mayest conceal it, too, from the ministers and **magistrates**, even as thou didst this day, when they sought to wrench the name out of thy heart, and give thee a partner on thy pedestal. But, as for me, I come to the **inquest** with other senses than they possess. I shall seek this man as I have sought truth in books; as I have sought gold in **alchemy**. There is a sympathy that will make me conscious of him. I shall see him tremble. I shall feel myself shudder, suddenly and unaware. Sooner or later, he must be mine!"

The eyes of the wrinkled scholar glowed so intensely upon her, that Hester Prynne clasped her hands over her heart, dreading lest he should read the secret there at once.

"Thou wilt not reveal his name? Not the less he is mine," resumed he, with a look of confidence, as if destiny were at one with him. "He bears no letter of **infamy** wrought into his garment, as thou dost; but I shall read it on his heart. Yet fear not for him! Think not that I shall interfere with Heaven's own method of **retribution**, or, to my own loss, betray him to the gripe of human law. Neither do thou imagine that I shall **contrive** aught against his life; no, nor against his fame, if, as I judge, he be a man of fair repute. Let him live! Let him hide himself in outward honor, if he may! Not the less he shall be mine!"

APPALL (uh <u>pahl</u>) *v.* **-ing,-ed.**
    to overcome with shock or dismay
        Synonyms: horrify, astound, petrify

ENJOIN (ehn <u>joyn</u>) *v.* **-ing,-ed.**
    to urge, order, command; forbid or prohibit, as by
  judicial order
        Synonyms: direct, instruct; proscribe

"Thy acts are like mercy," said Hester, bewildered and **appalled**. "But thy words interpret thee as a terror!"

"One thing, thou that wast my wife, I would **enjoin** upon thee," continued the scholar. "Thou hast kept the secret of thy paramour. Keep, likewise, mine! There are none in this land that know me. Breathe not, to any human soul, that thou didst ever call me husband! Here, on this wild outskirt of the earth, I shall pitch my tent; for, elsewhere a wanderer, and isolated from human interests, I find here a woman, a man, a child, amongst whom and myself there exist the closest ligaments. No matter whether of love or hate; no matter whether of right or wrong! Thou and thine, Hester Prynne, belong to me. My home is where thou art, and where he is. But betray me not!"

"Wherefore dost thou desire it?" inquired Hester, shrinking, she hardly knew why, from this secret bond. "Why not announce thyself openly, and cast me off at once?"

"It may be," he replied, "because I will not encounter the dishonor that besmirches the husband of a faithless woman. It may be for other reasons. Enough, it is my purpose to live and die unknown. Let, therefore, thy husband be to the world as one already dead, and of whom no tidings shall ever come. Recognize me not, by word, by sign, by look! Breathe not the secret, above all, to the man thou wottest of. Shouldst thou fail me in this, beware! His fame, his position, his life, will be in my hands. Beware!"

"I will keep thy secret, as I have his," said Hester.

"Swear it!" rejoined he.

And she took the oath.

"And now, Mistress Prynne," said old Roger Chillingworth, as he was hereafter to be named, "I leave thee alone; alone with thy infant, and the scarlet letter! How is it, Hester? Doth thy sentence bind thee to wear

151

the token in thy sleep? Art thou not afraid of nightmares and hideous dreams?"

"Why dost thou smile so at me?" inquired Hester, troubled at the expression of his eyes. "Art thou like the Black Man that haunts the forest round about us? Hast thou enticed me into a bond that will prove the ruin of my soul?"

"Not thy soul," he answered, with another smile. "No, not thine!"

MORBID (<u>mohr</u> bihd) *adj.*
1. abnormally terrible and gloomy; gruesome
   Synonyms: dismal, dreary; grisly, macabre
2. having an unhealthy mentality; relating to disease
   Synonyms: unwholesome; pathological

INFAMY (<u>ihn</u> fuh mee) *n.*
reputation for bad deeds
   Synonyms: disgrace, dishonor, shame

LURID (<u>loor</u> ihd) *adj.*
harshly shocking, revolting; glowing
   Synonyms: ghastly, garish, gruesome, grisly,
   macabre; fiery

VIGOR (<u>vih</u> guhr) *n.*
physical or mental energy
   Synonyms: strength, vitality, power, capability

IGNOMINY (<u>ihg</u> nuh mih nee) *n.*
disgrace and dishonor
   Synonyms: degradation, debasement

SUSTAIN (suh <u>stayn</u>) *v.* **-ing,-ed.**
endure, undergo; to support, uphold
   Synonyms: withstand; maintain, prop, encourage

GRIEVOUS (<u>gree</u> vuhs) *adj.*
causing grief and sorrow, serious and distressing
   Synonyms: grave, dire, mournful, dolorous

Hester at Her Needle
Chapter 5

Hester Prynne's term of confinement was now at an end. Her prison door was thrown open and she came forth into the sunshine, which, falling on all alike, seemed, to her sick and **morbid** heart, as if meant for no other purpose than to reveal the scarlet letter on her breast. Perhaps there was a more real torture in her first unattended footsteps from the threshold of the prison than even in the procession and spectacle that have been described, where she was made the common **infamy** at which all mankind was summoned to point its finger. Then, she was supported by an unnatural tension of the nerves and by all the combative energy of her character, which enabled her to convert the scene into a kind of **lurid** triumph. It was, moreover, a separate and insulated event, to occur but once in her lifetime, and to meet which, therefore, reckless of economy, she might call up the vital strength that would have sufficed for many quiet years. The very law that condemned her—a giant of stern features, but with **vigor** to support, as well as to annihilate, in his iron arm—had held her up through the terrible ordeal of her **ignominy**. But now, with this unattended walk from her prison-door, began the daily custom; and she must either **sustain** and carry it forward by the ordinary resources of her nature, or sink beneath it. She could no longer borrow from the future to help her through the present grief. Tomorrow would bring its own trial with it; so would the next day, and so would the next; each its own trial, and yet the very same that was now so unutterably **grievous** to be borne. The days of the far-off future would toil onward; still with the same burden for her to take up, and bear

HONORABLE (<u>ah</u> nuhr uh buhl) *adj.*
praiseworthy, deserving, illustrious
Synonyms: respectable, dignified, noble

INFAMY (<u>ihn</u> fuh mee) *n.*
reputation for bad deeds
Synonyms: disgrace, dishonor, shame

OBSCURE (uhb <u>skyoor</u>) *adj.*
not well known; dim, unclear
Synonyms: remote, minor; dark, faint

INSCRUTABLE (ihn <u>skroo</u> tuh buhl) *adj.*
impossible to see or understand fully
Synonyms: mysterious, impenetrable, cryptic, enigmatic

INEVITABLE (ihn <u>ehv</u> ih tuh buhl) *adj.*
certain, unavoidable
Synonyms: inescapable, sure, predictable

INVARIABLY (ihn <u>vaa</u> ree uh blee) *adv.*
without change, constantly
Synonyms: always, repeatedly, perpetually

COMPEL (kuhm <u>pehl</u>) *v.* **-ling,-led.**
to urge or force
Synonyms: coerce, oblige, constrain

TINGE (tihnj) *n.*
a slight shade of color, stain, odor, or taste
Synonyms: hint, hue, tincture, tone, wash

IGNOMINY (<u>ihg</u> nuh mih nee) *n.*
disgrace and dishonor
Synonyms: degradation, debasement

along with her, but never to fling down; for the accumulating days and added years would pile up their misery upon the heap of shame. Throughout them all, giving up her individuality, she would become the general symbol at which the preacher and moralist might point, and in which they might <u>vivify</u> and embody their images of woman's frailty and sinful passion. Thus the young and pure would be taught to look at her, with the scarlet letter flaming on her breast—at her, the child of **honorable** parents—at her, the mother of a babe, that would hereafter be a woman—at her, who had once been innocent—as the figure, the body, the reality of sin. And over her grave, the **infamy** that she must carry thither would be her only monument.

It may seem marvellous, that, with the world before her—kept by no restrictive clause of her condemnation within the limits of the <u>Puritan</u> settlement, so remote and so **obscure**—free to return to her birthplace, or to any other European land, and there hide her character and identity under a new exterior, as completely as if emerging into another state of being—and having also the passes of the dark, **inscrutable** forest open to her, where the wildness of her nature might assimilate itself with a people whose customs and life were alien from the law that had condemned her—it may seem marvellous, that this woman should still call that place her home, where, and where only, she must needs be the type of shame. But there is a fatality, a feeling so irresistible and **inevitable** that it has the force of doom, which almost **invariably compels** human beings to linger around and haunt, ghostlike, the spot where some great and marked event has given the color to their lifetime; and still the more irresistibly, the darker the **tinge** that saddens it. Her sin, her **ignominy**, were the roots which she had struck into the soil. It was as if a new birth, with stronger assimilations than the first, had converted

UNCONGENIAL (uhn kuhn <u>jee</u> nee uhl) *adj.*
unsuitable
Synonyms: unfavorable, disagreeable, incompatible
unpleasurable

GALL (gahl) *v.* **-ing,-ed.**
to make sore from abrasion; to exasperate and
irritate
Synonyms: chafe, scar; irk, vex

RETRIBUTION (reh trih <u>byoo</u> shuhn) *n.*
something which is justly deserved, such as
repayment or punishment
Synonyms: vengeance, payback, compensation

COMPEL (kuhm <u>pehl</u>) *v.* **-ling,-led.**
to urge or force
Synonyms: coerce, oblige, constrain

PURGE (puhrj) *v.* **-ing,-ed.**
to cleanse or free from impurities
Synonyms: purify, eliminate, rid

MARTYRDOM (<u>mahr</u> tuhr duhm) *n.*
death or intense suffering experienced due to one's
beliefs
Synonyms: sacrifice, anguish

the forest-land, still so **uncongenial** to every other pilgrim and wanderer, into Hester Prynne's wild and dreary but life-long home. All other scenes of earth—even that village of rural England, where happy infancy and stainless maidenhood seemed yet to be in her mother's keeping, like garments put off long ago—were foreign to her, in comparison. The chain that bound her here was of iron links, and **galling** to her inmost soul, but could never be broken.

It might be, too—doubtless it was so, although she hid the secret from herself, and grew pale whenever it struggled out of her heart, like a serpent from its hole—it might be that another feeling kept her within the scene and pathway that had been so fatal. There dwelt, there trod the feet of one with whom she deemed herself connected in a union, that, unrecognized on earth, would bring them together before the bar of final judgment, and make that their marriage-altar, for a joint futurity of endless **retribution**. Over and over again, the tempter of souls had thrust this idea upon Hester's contemplation, and laughed at the passionate and desperate joy with which she seized, and then strove to cast it from her. She barely looked the idea in the face, and hastened to bar it in its dungeon. What she **compelled** herself to believe—what, finally, she reasoned upon as her motive for continuing a resident of New England—was half a truth, and half a self-delusion. Here, she said to herself, had been the scene of her guilt, and here should be the scene of her earthly punishment; and so, perchance, the torture of her daily shame would at length **purge** her soul, and work out another purity than that which she had lost; more saint-like, because the result of **martyrdom**.

Hester Prynne, therefore, did not flee. On the outskirts of town, within the verge of the peninsula, but not in close vicinity to any other habitation, there was a small thatched cottage. It had been built by an earlier

EMIGRANT (<u>eh</u> mih graant) *n.*
a person from another country or land
Synonym: foreigner

MAGISTRATE (<u>maa</u> juh strayt) *n.*
an official who can administrate laws
Synonyms: judge, arbiter, authority, marshal

DISCERN (dihs <u>uhrn</u>) *v.* **-ing,-ed.**
to perceive or recognize something
Synonyms: descry, observe, glimpse, distinguish

INCUR (ihn <u>kuhr</u>) *v.* **-ring,-red.**
to acquire or meet with, usually something negative
or harmful; to become liable
Synonyms: get, obtain, endure, sustain; oblige, owe

AVAIL (uh <u>vayl</u>) *v.* **-ing,-ed.**
to make use of or to be of use or advantage to;
to result in
Synonyms: employ, help, serve, benefit; transpire,
eventuate

INGENUITY (ihn jeh <u>noo</u> ih tee) *n.*
cleverness
Synonyms: inventiveness, imagination, creativity

settler, and abandoned because the soil about it was too sterile for cultivation, while its comparative remoteness put it out of the sphere of that social activity which already marked the habits of the **emigrants**. It stood on the shore, looking across a basin of the sea at the forest-covered hills, toward the west. A clump of scrubby trees, such as alone grew on the peninsula, did not so much conceal the cottage from view, as seem to denote that there was some object which would have been, or at least ought to be, concealed. In this little, lonesome dwelling, with some slender means that she possessed, and by the license of the **magistrates**, who still kept an inquisitorial watch over her, Hester established herself, with her infant child. A mystic shadow of suspicion immediately attached itself to the spot. Children, too young to comprehend wherefore this woman should be shut out from the sphere of human charities, would creep <u>nigh</u> enough to behold her plying her needle at the cottage-window, or standing in the doorway, or laboring in her little garden, or coming forth along the pathway that led downward; and, **discerning** the scarlet letter on her breast, would scamper off with a strange, contagious fear.

Lonely as was Hester's situation, and without a friend on earth who dared to show himself, she, however, **incurred** ever, no risk of want. She possessed an art that sufficed, even in a land that afforded comparatively little scope for its exercise, to supply food for her thriving infant and herself. It was the art—then, as now, almost the only one within a woman's grasp—of needle-work. She bore on her breast, in the curiously embroidered letter, a specimen of her delicate and imaginative skill, of which the dames of a court might gladly have **availed** themselves, to add the richer and more spiritual adornment of human **ingenuity** to their fabrics of silk and gold. Here, indeed, in the sable simplicity that

PROGENITOR (proh <u>jeh</u> nih tuhr) *n.*
a direct ancestor
Synonyms: forerunner, predecessor, forefather

MAGISTRATE (<u>maa</u> juh strayt) *n.*
an official who can administrate laws
Synonyms: judge, arbiter, authority, marshal

MANIFEST (<u>maan</u> uh fehst) *v.* **-ing,-ed.**
to make evident or certain by display
Synonyms: exhibit, showcase, expose

SOMBRE or SOMBER (<u>sahm</u> buhr) *adj.*
melancholy, dismal, dark and gloomy
Synonyms: serious, grave, mournful, lugubrious,
funereal

SUMPTUARY (<u>suhmp</u> choo ayr ee) *adj.*
relating to laws that control personal behaviors
Synonyms: regulatory, limiting

PLEBEIAN (<u>plee</u> bee uhn) *adj.*
low-class, crude, vulgar
Synonyms: unrefined, coarse, common

MORBID (<u>mohr</u> bihd) *adj.*
1. having an unhealthy mentality; relating to disease
Synonyms: unwholesome; pathological
2. abnormally terrible and gloomy; gruesome
Synonyms: dismal, dreary; grisly, macabre

INTANGIBLE (ihn <u>taan</u> juh buhl) *adj.*
not perceptible to the touch, not material
Synonyms: impalpable, imponderable, illusory,
abstract

BESTOW (bih <u>stoh</u>) *v.* **-ing,-ed.**
to give as a gift; to apply or devote time or effort
Synonyms: endow, confer, present; allocate, dedicate

REQUITE (rih <u>kwiet</u>) *v.* **-ing,-ed.**
to return or repay
Synonyms: reciprocate, avenge, compensate,
reimburse

162

generally characterized the <u>Puritanic</u> modes of dress, there might be an infrequent call for the finer productions of her handiwork. Yet the taste of the age, demanding whatever was elaborate in compositions of this kind, did not fail to extend its influence over our stern **progenitors**, who had cast behind them so many fashions which it might seem harder to dispense with. Public ceremonies, such as ordinations, the installation of **magistrates**, and all that could give majesty to the forms in which a new government **manifested** itself to the people, were, as a matter of policy, marked by a stately and well-conducted ceremonial and a **sombre**, but yet a studied magnificence. Deep <u>ruffs</u>, painfully wrought bands and gorgeously embroidered gloves, were all deemed necessary to the official state of men assuming the reins of power; and were readily allowed to individuals dignified by rank or wealth, even while **sumptuary** laws forbade these and similar extravagances to the **plebeian** order. In the array of funerals, too—whether for the apparel of the dead body, or to typify, by manifold emblematic devices of sable cloth and snowy lawn, the sorrow of the survivors—there was a frequent and characteristic demand for such labor as Hester Prynne could supply. Baby-linen—for babies then wore robes of state—afforded still another possibility of toil and <u>emolument</u>.

By degrees, nor very slowly, her handiwork became what would now be termed the fashion. Whether from commiseration for a woman of so miserable a destiny; or from the **morbid** curiosity that gives a fictitious value even to common or worthless things; or by whatever other **intangible** circumstance was then, as now, sufficient to **bestow**, on some persons, what others might seek in vain; or because Hester really filled a gap which must otherwise have remained vacant; it is certain that she had ready and fairly **requited** employment for as many hours

VIGOR (<u>vih</u> guhr) *n.*
  physical or mental energy
    Synonyms: strength, vitality, power, capability

SUBSISTENCE (suhb <u>sihst</u> ihnts) *n.*
  the necessities of life, the resources of survival
    Synonyms: nourishment, sustenance, provisions

ASCETIC (uh <u>seh</u> tihk) *adj.*
  self-denying, abstinent, austere
    Synonyms: continent, temperate, abstemious

SOMBRE or SOMBER (<u>sahm</u> buhr) *adj.*
  melancholy, dismal, dark and gloomy
    Synonyms: serious, grave, mournful, lugubrious,
    funereal

INGENUITY (ihn jeh <u>noo</u> ih tee) *n.*
  cleverness
    Synonyms: inventiveness, imagination, creativity

BESTOW (bih <u>stoh</u>) *v.* **-ing,-ed.**
  to give as a gift; to apply or devote time or effort
    Synonyms: endow, confer, present; allocate, dedicate

SUPERFLUOUS (soo <u>puhr</u> floo uhs) *adj.*
  extra, more than necessary
    Synonyms: excess, spare, surplus

PENANCE (<u>peh</u> nihns) *n.*
  voluntary suffering to repent for a wrong
    Synonyms: atonement, reparation, chastening,
    reconciliation

as she saw fit to occupy with her needle. Vanity, it may be, chose to mortify itself, by putting on, for ceremonials of <u>pomp</u> and state, the garments that had been wrought by her sinful hands. Her needlework was seen on the <u>ruff</u> of the Governor; military men wore it on their scarfs, and the minister on his band; it decked the baby's little cap; it was shut up to be mildewed and moulder away, in the coffins of the dead. But it is not recorded that, in a single instance, her skill was called in aid to embroider the white veil which was to cover the pure blushes of a bride. The exception indicated the ever-relentless **vigor** with which society frowned upon her sin.

Hester sought not to acquire anything beyond a **subsistence**, of the plainest and most **ascetic** description, for herself, and a simple abundance for her child. Her own dress was of the coarsest materials and the most **sombre** hue; with only that one ornament—the scarlet letter—which it was her doom to wear. The child's attire, on the other hand, was distinguished by a fanciful, or, we might rather say, a fantastic **ingenuity**, which served, indeed, to heighten the airy charm that early began to develop itself in the little girl, but which appeared to have also a deeper meaning. We may speak further of it hereafter. Except for that small expenditure in the decoration of her infant, Hester **bestowed** all her **superfluous** means in charity, on wretches less miserable than herself, and who not unfrequently insulted the hand that fed them. Much of the time which she might readily have applied to the better efforts of her art, she employed in making coarse garments for the poor. It is probable that there was an idea of **penance** in this mode of occupation, and that she offered up a real sacrifice of enjoyment, in devoting so many hours to such rude handiwork. She had in her nature a rich, voluptuous, Oriental characteristic—a taste for the gorgeously beautiful, which, save in the exquisite productions of her

SAT Vocabulary

DERIVE (dih <u>riev</u>) *v.* **-ing,-ed.**
to receive from a source, to originate
Synonyms: infer, descend, deduce, come (from)

MORBID (<u>mohr</u> bihd) *adj.*
1. having an unhealthy mentality; relating to disease
Synonyms: unwholesome; pathological
2. abnormally terrible and gloomy; gruesome
Synonyms: dismal, dreary; grisly, macabre

MEDDLE (<u>meh</u> duhl) *v.* **-ing,-ed.**
to interfere in others' affairs, to impose
Synonyms: tamper, encroach

STEADFAST (<u>stehd</u> faast) *adj.*
unwavering, loyal
Synonyms: faithful, true, constant, fast, staunch

PENITENCE (<u>peh</u> nih tehnts) *n.*
sorrow expressed for sins or offenses, repentance
Synonyms: remorse, contrition, apology

BANISH (<u>baan</u> ish) *v.* **-ing,-ed.**
to expel from a group; to force to leave, exile
Synonyms: ostracize, shun; deport, extradite

MANIFEST (<u>maan</u> uh fehst) *v.* **-ing,-ed.**
to make evident or certain by display
Synonyms: exhibit, showcase, expose

REPUGNANCE (rih <u>puhg</u> nehnts) *n.*
strong dislike, distaste, or antagonism; an instance of
contradiction or inconsistency
Synonyms: repulsion, aversion; incompatibility

RETAIN (rih <u>tayn</u>) *v.* **-ing,-ed.**
to hold, keep possession of
Synonyms: withhold, reserve

needle, found nothing else in all the possibilities of her life to exercise itself upon. Women **derive** a pleasure, incomprehensible to the other sex, from the delicate toil of the needle. To Hester Prynne it might have been a mode of expressing, and therefore soothing, the passion of her life. Like all other joys, she rejected it as sin. This **morbid meddling** of conscience with an immaterial matter <u>betokened</u>, it is to be feared, no genuine and **steadfast penitence**, but something doubtful, something that might be deeply wrong, beneath.

In this manner, Hester Prynne came to have a part to perform in the world. With her native energy of character, and rare capacity, it could not entirely cast her off, although it had set a mark upon her, more intolerable to a woman's heart than that which branded the brow of Cain. In all her <u>intercourse</u> with society, however, there was nothing that made her feel as if she belonged to it. Every gesture, every word, and even the silence of those with whom she came in contact, implied, and often expressed, that she was **banished**, and as much alone as if she inhabited another sphere, or communicated with the common nature by other organs and senses than the rest of human kind. She stood apart from moral interests, yet close beside them, like a ghost that revisits the familiar fireside and can no longer make itself seen or felt; no more smile with the household joy, nor mourn with the kindred sorrow; or, should it succeed in **manifesting** its forbidden sympathy, awakening only terror and horrible **repugnance**. These emotions, in fact, and its bitterest scorn besides, seemed to be the sole portion that she **retained** in the universal heart. It was not an age of delicacy; and her position, although she understood it well, and was in little danger of forgetting it, was often brought before her vivid self-perception, like a new anguish, by the rudest touch upon the tenderest spot. The poor, as we have already

REVILE (rih <u>vie</u> uhl) *v.* **-ing,-ed.**
to criticize with harsh language, verbally abuse
Synonyms: vituperate, scold, assail, upbraid, berate

SUCCOR (<u>suh</u> kuhr) *v.* **-ing,-ed.**
to give or offer relief
Synonyms: aid, help, support

DISTILL (dihs <u>tihl</u>) *v.* **-ing,-ed.**
to evaporate and collect a liquid by condensing it as a
means of purification; to extract the essential parts
Synonyms: vaporize, precipitate; clarify, separate

ALCHEMY (<u>aal</u> kuh mee) *n.* *(See page 148.)*

MALICE (<u>maal</u> ihs) *n.*
animosity, spite, hatred
Synonyms: malevolence, cruelty, hostility

TRIFLE (<u>trie</u> fuhl) *n.* *(See page 116.)*

MARTYR (<u>mahr</u> tuhr) *n.*
a person who suffers or dies for his or her beliefs
Synonyms: saint, hero

ASPIRATION (aa spuhr <u>ay</u> shuhn) *n.*
a great hope or goal
Synonyms: intention, purpose, expectation

INNUMERABLE (ih <u>noo</u> muhr uh buhl) *adj.*
too many to be counted
Synonyms: incalculable, immeasurable, infinite,
inestimable

CONTRIVE (kuhn <u>triev</u>) *v.* **-ing,-ed.** *(See page 148.)*

EXHORTATION (ihg zohr <u>tay</u> shuhn) *n.*
a persuasive verbal attempt to urge people to take
action
Synonyms: incitement, inspiration, warning

DISCOURSE (<u>dihs</u> kohrs) *n.* *(See page 136.)*

PURPORT (puhr <u>pohrt</u>) *n.*
intention, purpose
Synonyms: importance, meaning

DIFFUSION (dih <u>fyoo</u> zhuhn) *n.*
the act of spreading
Synonyms: scattering, dispersion, dissipation

said, whom she sought out to be the objects of her bounty, often **reviled** the hand that was stretched forth to **succor** them. Dames of elevated rank, likewise, whose doors she entered in the way of her occupation, were accustomed to **distill** drops of bitterness into her heart; sometimes through that **alchemy** of quiet **malice**, by which women can concoct a subtile poison from ordinary **trifles**; and sometimes, also, by a coarser expression, that fell upon the sufferer's defenseless breast like a rough blow upon an ulcerated wound. Hester had schooled herself long and well; she never responded to these attacks, save by a flush of crimson that rose irrepressibly over the pale cheek, and again subsided into the depths of her bosom. She was patient—a **martyr**, indeed—but she forebore to pray for her enemies, lest, in spite of her forgiving **aspirations**, the words of the blessing should stubbornly twist themselves into a curse.

Continually, and in a thousand other ways, did she feel the **innumerable** throbs of anguish that had been so cunningly **contrived** for her by the undying, the ever-active sentence of the <u>Puritan</u> tribunal. Clergymen paused in the street to address words of **exhortation** that brought a crowd, with its mingled grin and frown, around the poor, sinful woman. If she entered a church, trusting to share the Sabbath smile of the Universal Father, it was often her mishap to find herself the text of the **discourse**. She grew to have a dread of children; for they had <u>imbibed</u> from their parents a vague idea of something horrible in this dreary woman, gliding silently through the town, with never any companion but one only child. Therefore, first allowing her to pass, they pursued her at a distance with shrill cries, and the utterance of a word that had no distinct **purport** to their own minds, but was none the less terrible to her, as proceeding from lips that babbled it unconsciously. It seemed to argue so wide a **diffusion** of her shame, that

CALLOUS (<u>kaa</u> luhs) *adj.*
   insensitive, thick-skinned
      Synonyms: impervious, stony, unmoved, unfeeling

IGNOMINIOUS (ihg nuh <u>mih</u> nee uhs) *adj.*
   disgraceful and dishonorable
      Synonyms: despicable, degrading, debasing

ENDOW (ehn <u>dow</u>) *v.* **-ing,-ed.**
   to provide with something naturally or freely; to
   furnish with an income or grant
      Synonyms: grant, donate, bestow; empower,
      support

all nature knew of it; it could have caused her no deeper pang, had the leaves of the trees whispered the dark story among themselves—had the summer breeze murmured about it—had the wintry blast shrieked it aloud! Another peculiar torture was felt in the gaze of a new eye. When strangers looked curiously at the scarlet letter—and none ever failed to do so—they branded it afresh into Hester's soul; so that oftentimes, she could scarcely refrain, yet always did refrain, from covering the symbol with her hand. But then, again, an accustomed eye had likewise its own anguish to inflict. Its cool stare of familiarity was intolerable. From first to last, in short, Hester Prynne had always this dreadful agony in feeling a human eye upon the token; the spot never grew **callous**; it seemed, on the contrary, to grow more sensitive with daily torture.

But sometimes, once in many days, or perchance in many months, she felt an eye—a human eye—upon the **ignominious** brand, that seemed to give a momentary relief, as if half of her agony were shared. The next instant, back it all rushed again, with still a deeper throb of pain; for, in that brief interval, she had sinned anew. Had Hester sinned alone?

Her imagination was somehow affected, and, had she been of a softer moral and intellectual fibre, would have been still more so, by the strange and solitary anguish of her life. Walking to and fro, with those lonely footsteps in the little world with which she was outwardly connected, it now and then appeared to Hester—if altogether fancy, it was nevertheless too potent to be resisted—she felt or fancied, then, that the scarlet letter had **endowed** her with a new sense. She shuddered to believe, yet could not help believing, that it gave her a sympathetic knowledge of the hidden sin in other hearts. She was terror-stricken by the revelations that were thus made. What were they? Could they be other than the

INSIDIOUS (ihn <u>sihd</u> ee uhs) *adj.*
  treacherous, devious
    Synonyms: deceitful, perfidious
INTIMATION (ihn tuh <u>may</u> shuhn) *n.*
  suggestion, clue
    Synonyms: implication, allusion, insinuation
OBSCURE (uhb <u>skyoor</u>) *adj. (See page 156.)*
LOATHSOME (<u>lohth</u> suhm) *adj.*
  abhorrent, hateful
    Synonyms: offensive, disgusting
IRREVERENT (ih <u>rehv</u> uhr uhnt) *adj.*
  disrespectful, gently or humorously mocking
    Synonyms: impious, iconoclastic, satirical
INOPPORTUNENESS (ihn ah pohr <u>toon</u> nehs) *n.*
  inappropriateness, unfavorableness
    Synonyms: inconvenience, untimeliness
INFAMY (<u>ihn</u> fuh mee) *n. (See page 156.)*
VENERABLE (<u>veh</u> nehr uh buhl) *adj. (See page 96.)*
MAGISTRATE (<u>maa</u> juh strayt) *n. (See page 162.)*
PIETY (<u>pie</u> eh tee) *n.*
  devoutness
    Synonyms: devotion, reverence
REVERENCE (<u>reh</u> vuhr ehnts) *n. (See page 112.)*
SANCTIFIED (<u>saank</u> tih fied) *adj.*
  pious; holy, sacred
    Synonyms: self-righteous; consecrated, divine
AVERT (uh <u>vuhrt</u>) *v.* **-ing,-ed.**
  to turn away; avoid
    Synonyms: deflect, parry; deter, forestall, preclude
SULLY (<u>suh</u> lee) *v.* **-ing,-ied.**
  to soil, stain, tarnish, taint
    Synonyms: mar, defile
TALISMAN (<u>taa</u> lihs mehn) *n. (See page 22.)*
REVERE (rih <u>veer</u>) *v.* **-ing,-ed.**
  to worship, regard with awe
    Synonyms: venerate, adore, idolize, admire

insidious whispers of the bad angel, who would have persuaded the struggling woman, as yet only half his victim, that the outward guise of purity was but a lie, and that, if truth were everywhere to be shown, a scarlet letter would blaze forth on many a bosom besides Hester Prynne's? Or, must she receive those **intimations**—so **obscure**, yet so distinct—as truth? In all her miserable experience, there was nothing else so awful and so **loathsome** as this sense. It perplexed as well as shocked her, by the **irreverent inopportuneness** of the occasions that brought it into vivid action. Sometimes the red **infamy** upon her breast would give a sympathetic throb, as she passed near a **venerable** minister or **magistrate**, the model of **piety** and justice, to whom that age of antique **reverence** looked up, as to a mortal man in fellowship with angels. "What evil thing is at hand?" would Hester say to herself. Lifting her reluctant eyes, there would be nothing human within the scope of view, save the form of this earthly saint! Again, a mystic sisterhood would <u>contumaciously</u> assert itself as she met the **sanctified** frown of some matron, who, according to the rumor of all tongues, had kept cold snow within her bosom throughout life. That unsunned snow in the matron's bosom, and the burning shame on Hester Prynne's—what had the two in common? Or, once more, the electric thrill would give her warning—"Behold, Hester, here is a companion!"—and, looking up, she would detect the eyes of a young maiden glancing at the scarlet letter, shyly and aside, and quickly **averted** with a faint, chill crimson in her cheeks; as if her purity were somewhat **sullied** by that momentary glance. O Fiend, whose **talisman** was that fatal symbol, wouldst thou leave nothing, whether in youth or age, for this poor sinner to **revere**? Such loss of faith is ever one of the saddest results of sin. Be it accepted as a proof that all was not corrupt in this poor victim of her own frailty, and man's

AVER (uh <u>vuhr</u>) *v.* **-ring,-red.**
    to declare to be true, affirm
        Synonyms: assert, attest

TINGE (tihnj) *v.* **-ing,-ed.**
    to color with a slight shade, stain, odor, or taste; to
    affect or modify in character
        Synonyms: dye, imbue, hue, tint; tarnish, sully, mar

INFERNAL (ihn <u>fuhr</u> nuhl) *adj.*
    relating to the dead or hell; devilish
        Synonyms: damned, accursed; fiendish, awful,
        malicious

INCREDULITY (ihn kreh <u>doo</u> lih tee) *n.*
    skepticism, doubt
        Synonyms: disbelief, suspicion

INCLINE (ihn <u>klien</u>) *v.* **-ing,-ed.**
    to have a specific tendency, to be predisposed
        Synonyms: lean toward, influence, impel, prefer

hard law, that Hester Prynne yet struggled to believe that no fellow-mortal was guilty like herself.

The vulgar, who, in those dreary old times, were always contributing a grotesque horror to what interested their imaginations, had a story about the scarlet letter which we might readily work up into a terrific legend. They **averred**, that the symbol was not mere scarlet cloth, **tinged** in an earthly dye-pot, but was red-hot with **infernal** fire, and could be seen glowing all alight, whenever Hester Prynne walked abroad in the night-time. And we must needs say, it seared Hester's bosom so deeply, that perhaps there was more truth in the rumor than our modern **incredulity** may be **inclined** to admit.

INSCRUTABLE (ihn <u>skroo</u> tuh buhl) *adj.*
impossible to see or understand fully
Synonyms: mysterious, impenetrable, cryptic, enigmatic

PROVIDENCE (<u>prah</u> vih dehnts) *n.*
divine control and direction by God; preparation and foresight
Synonyms: fate, destiny, good luck; prudence, precaution

LUXURIANCE (luhg <u>zhoor</u> ee ehnts) *n.*
abundance; elegance, lavishness
Synonyms: excess, overload, profusion; richness

EFFICACY (<u>eff</u> uh kuh see) *n.*
effectiveness, efficiency
Synonym: potency

DISHONORED (dihs <u>ah</u> nuhrd) *adj.*
shamed, undeserving of praise
Synonyms: disgraced, discredited, disrespected

DESCENT (dih <u>sehnt</u>) (dee <u>sehnt</u>) *n.*
1. one's ancestry
Synonyms: heredity, lineage
2. the passing from a higher place to a lower place; a decline
Synonyms: lowering, dismount, gravitation; slope

APPREHENSION (aa prih <u>hehn</u> shuhn) *n.*
suspicion or fear of future or unknown evil; the act of perceiving or comprehending; a legal seizure
Synonyms: concern, worry; understanding; capture

VIGOR (<u>vih</u> guhr) *n.*
physical or mental energy
Synonyms: strength, vitality, power, capability

DEXTERITY (dehk <u>stayr</u> ih tee) *n.*
physical or mental skill, ability
Synonyms: aptitude, adroitness, proficiency

Pearl
Chapter 6

We have as yet hardly spoken of the infant; that little creature, whose innocent life had sprung, by the **inscrutable** decree of **Providence**, a lovely and immortal flower, out of the rank **luxuriance** of a guilty passion. How strange it seemed to the sad woman, as she watched the growth and the beauty that became every day more brilliant, and the intelligence that threw its quivering sunshine over the tiny features of this child! Her Pearl—for so had Hester called her; not as a name expressive of her aspect, which had nothing of the calm, white, unimpassioned lustre that would be indicated by the comparison. But she named the infant "Pearl," as being of great price—purchased with all she had—her mother's only treasure! How strange, indeed! Man had marked this woman's sin by a scarlet letter, which had such potent and disastrous **efficacy** that no human sympathy could reach her, save it were sinful like herself. God, as a direct consequence of the sin which man thus punished, had given her a lovely child, whose place was on that same **dishonored** bosom, to connect her parent forever with the race and **descent** of mortals, and to be finally a blessed soul in Heaven! Yet these thoughts affected Hester Prynne less with hope than **apprehension**. She knew that her deed had been evil; she could have no faith, therefore, that its result would be for good. Day after day, she looked fearfully into the child's expanding nature, ever dreading to detect some dark and wild peculiarity, that should correspond with the guiltiness to which she owed her being.

Certainly, there was no physical defect. By its perfect shape, its **vigor**, and its natural **dexterity** in the use of all

INVARIABLY (ihn <u>vaa</u> ree uh blee) *adv.*
without change, constantly
Synonyms: always, repeatedly, perpetually

RUSTIC (<u>ruh</u> stihk) *adj.*
simple and unsophisticated; typical of country life
Synonyms: unrefined, crude; bucolic, pastoral

MORBID (<u>mohr</u> bihd) *adj.*
1. having an unhealthy mentality; relating to disease
   Synonyms: unwholesome; pathological
2. abnormally terrible and gloomy; gruesome
   Synonyms: dismal, dreary; grisly, macabre

PROCURE (proh <u>kyoor</u>) *v.* **-ing,-ed.**
to obtain
Synonyms: acquire, secure, get, gain

FACULTY (<u>faa</u> kuhl tee) *n.*
the ability to act or do
Synonyms: aptitude, capability, sense, skill

IMBUE (ihm <u>byoo</u>) *v.* **-ing,-ed.**
to infuse; to dye, wet
Synonyms: permeate; moisten

MUTABILITY (myoo tuh <u>bihl</u> uh tee) *n.*
changeability, inconsistency
Synonym: impermanence

ADAPTATION (uh daap <u>tay</u> shuhn) *n.*
suitability; adjustment, transformation
Synonyms: preparedness, fit; accomodation

AMENABLE (uh <u>mehn</u> uh buhl) *adj.*
agreeable, cooperative
Synonyms: compliant, receptive

its untried limbs, the infant was worthy to have been brought forth in Eden; worthy to have been left there, to be the plaything of the angels, after the world's first parents were driven out. The child had a native grace which does not **invariably** coexist with faultless beauty; its attire, however simple, always impressed the beholder as if it were the very garb that precisely became it best. But little Pearl was not clad in **rustic** weeds. Her mother, with a **morbid** purpose, that may be better understood hereafter, had bought the richest tissues that could be **procured**, and allowed her imaginative **faculty** its full play in the arrangement and decoration of the dresses which the child wore, before the public eye. So magnificent was the small figure when thus arrayed, and such was the splendor of Pearl's own proper beauty, shining through the gorgeous robes which might have extinguished a paler loveliness, that there was an absolute circle of radiance around her on the darksome cottage floor. And yet a russet gown, torn and soiled with the child's rude play, made a picture of her just as perfect. Pearl's aspect was **imbued** with a spell of infinite variety; in this one child there were many children, comprehending the full scope between the wild-flower prettiness of a peasant-baby, and the pomp, in little, of an infant princess. Throughout all, however, there was a trait of passion, a certain depth of hue, which she never lost; and if, in any of her changes, she had grown fainter or paler, she would have ceased to be herself—it would have been no longer Pearl.

This outward **mutability** indicated, and did not more than fairly express, the various properties of her inner life. Her nature appeared to possess depth, too, as well as variety; but—or else Hester's fears deceived her—it lacked reference and **adaptation** to the world into which she was born. The child could not be made **amenable** to rules. In giving her existence, a great law had been bro-

MEDIUM (<u>mee</u> dee uhm) *n.*
a substance or object that is used to transmit or
accomplish something
Synonyms: means, instrument, vehicle, mechanism

UNTEMPERED (uhn <u>tehm</u> puhrd) *adj.*
unrestrained, unreasonable; extreme
Synonyms: uncontrolled; excessive, exorbitant

EPOCH (<u>eh</u> pihk) *n. (See page 22.)*

PERPETUATE (puhr <u>peht</u> chyoo ayt) *v.* **-ing,-ed.**
to be or make endless or eternal
Synonyms: continue, live on, preserve, sustain

DESPONDENCY (dih <u>spahn</u> duhn see) *n.*
discouragement, dejection
Synonyms: sadness, depression, desolation

BROOD *v.* **-ing,-ed.**
1. to think about in a gloomy or serious way
Synonyms: ponder, worry, obsess
2. to hang over in a threatening manner
Synonyms: loom, hover

DISPOSITION (dihs puh <u>zih</u> shuhn) *n.*
1. mood or temperament
Synonyms: behavior, nature
2. a habitual tendency, an inclination
Synonyms: willingness, propensity

PROLIFIC (proh <u>lih</u> fihk) *adj.*
productive, generative; fertile
Synonyms: teeming, bountiful; fecund, fruitful

REBUKE (ree <u>byook</u>) *n.*
a reprimand, scolding, punishment
Synonyms: admonition, reproof, reproach

ENJOIN (ehn <u>joyn</u>) *v.* **-ing,-ed.**
to urge or command; to forbid or prohibit, as by
judicial order
Synonyms: direct, instruct; proscribe

REGIMEN (<u>reh</u> juh mihn) *n.*
a systematic plan, a government rule
Synonyms: control, procedure, course

IMPOSE (ihm <u>pohz</u>) *v.* **-ing,-ed.**
to inflict, force upon
Synonyms: dictate, decree, demand, ordain

ken; and the result was a being whose elements were perhaps beautiful and brilliant, but all in disorder; or with an order peculiar to themselves, amidst which the point of variety and arrangement was difficult or impossible to be discovered. Hester could only account for the child's character—and even then most vaguely and imperfectly—by recalling what she herself had been, during that momentous period while Pearl was <u>imbibing</u> her soul from the spiritual world, and her bodily frame from its material of earth. The mother's impassioned state had been the **medium** through which were transmitted to the unborn infant the rays of its moral life; and, however white and clear originally, they had taken the deep stains of crimson and gold, the fiery lustre, the black shadow, and the **untempered** light of the intervening substance. Above all, the warfare of Hester's spirit, at that **epoch**, was **perpetuated** in Pearl. She could recognize her wild, desperate, defiant mood, the flightiness of her temper, and even some of the very cloud-shapes of gloom and **despondency** that had **brooded** in her heart. They were now illuminated by the morning radiance of a young child's **disposition**, but, later in the day of earthly existence, might be **prolific** of the storm and whirlwind.

The discipline of the family, in those days, was of a far more rigid kind than now. The frown, the harsh **rebuke**, the frequent application of the rod, **enjoined** by Scriptural authority, were used, not merely in the way of punishment for actual offences, but as a wholesome **regimen** for the growth and promotion of all childish virtues. Hester Prynne, nevertheless, the lonely mother of this one child, ran little risk of erring on the side of undue severity. Mindful, however, of her own errors and misfortunes, she early sought to **impose** a tender but strict control over the infant immortality that was committed to her charge. But the task was beyond her skill.

SAT Vocabulary

COMPEL (kuhm pehl) *v.* **-ling,-led.**
to urge or force
Synonyms: coerce, oblige, constrain
IMPULSE (ihm puhls) *n.*
sudden tendency, inclination
Synonyms: urge, whim
COMPULSION (kuhm puhl shuhn) *n.*
an irresistible urge, an impulsive act
Synonyms: drive, obsession, necessity, preoccupation
RESTRAINT (rih straynt) *n.*
control, repression, restriction; a rule or limitation
Synonyms: confinement; barrier, order, rein
CAPRICE (kuh prees) *n.*
an impulsive change of mind, fickleness
Synonym: whim
PERVERSE (puhr vuhrs) *adj.*
1. having the tendency to oppose or contradict
Synonyms: contrary, improper, obstinate
2. immoral, mean
Synonyms: corrupted, disobedient, depraved
MALICIOUS (muh lihsh uhs) *adj.*
having feelings of spite and hatred
Synonyms: malevolent, cruel, rancorous, hostile
INTANGIBILITY (ihn taan juh bihl ih tee) *n.*
the quality of being imperceptible, illusory
Synonyms: impalpability, elusiveness, invisibility,
abstraction
CONSTRAIN (kuhn strayn) *v.* **-ing,-ed.**
to force, impel; restrain
Synonyms: prompt, urge; restrict, control,
calculate
INVARIABLY (ihn vaa ree uh blee) *adv.*
without change, constantly
Synonyms: always, repeatedly, perpetually
DELUSIVE (duh loo sihv) *adj.*
imaginary, deceptive
Synonyms: misleading, false

After testing both smiles and frowns, and proving that neither mode of treatment possessed any calculable influence, Hester was ultimately **compelled** to stand aside, and permit the child to be swayed by her own **impulses**. Physical **compulsion** or **restraint** was effectual, of course, while it lasted. As to any other kind of discipline, whether addressed to her mind or heart, little Pearl might or might not be within its reach, in accordance with the **caprice** that ruled the moment. Her mother, while Pearl was yet an infant, grew acquainted with a certain peculiar look, that warned her when it would be labor thrown away to insist, persuade, or plead. It was a look so intelligent, yet inexplicable, so **perverse**, sometimes so **malicious**, but generally accompanied by a wild flow of spirits, that Hester could not help questioning, at such moments, whether Pearl was a human child. She seemed rather an airy <u>sprite</u>, which, after playing its fantastic sports for a little while upon the cottage floor, would flit away with a mocking smile. Whenever that look appeared in her wild, bright, deeply-black eyes, it invested her with a strange remoteness and **intangibility**; it was as if she were hovering in the air and might vanish, like a glimmering light that comes we know not whence, and goes we know not whither. Beholding it, Hester was **constrained** to rush towards the child to pursue the little elf in the flight which she **invariably** began, to snatch her to her bosom, with a close pressure and earnest kisses,—not so much from overflowing love, as to assure herself that Pearl was flesh and blood, and not utterly **delusive**. But Pearl's laugh, when she was caught, though full of merriment and music, made her mother more doubtful than before.

Heart-smitten at this bewildering and baffling spell that so often came between herself and her sole treasure, whom she had bought so dear and who was all her world, Hester sometimes burst into passionate tears.

BROOD *v.* **-ing,-ed.**
1. to think about in a gloomy or serious way
   Synonyms: ponder, worry, obsess
2. to hang over in a threatening manner
   Synonyms: loom, hover

EVOKE (ih <u>vohk</u>) *v.* **-ing,-ed.**
to summon or call forth, to inspire memories, to produce a reaction
   Synonyms: conjure, educe, elicit, arouse

CONJURATION (kahn juhr <u>ay</u> shuhn) *n.*
a summoning of a devil or spirit by invocation; a magic trick or effect; the process of bringing to mind
   Synonyms: materialization; spell, charm; recollection

PLACIDITY (plaa <u>sih</u> dih tee) *n.*
calmness
   Synonyms: tranquility, serenity, complacency

PERVERSE (puhr <u>vuhrs</u>) *adj.*
1. having the tendency to oppose or contradict
   Synonyms: contrary, improper, obstinate
2. immoral, disobedient
   Synonyms: corrupted, mean, depraved

UPROAR (<u>uhp</u> rohr) *n.*
a situation of loud and confusing excitement
   Synonyms: noise, hubbub, commotion

SPORTIVE (<u>spohr</u> tihv) *adj.*
frolicsome, playful
   Synonyms: frisky, merry, lively

Then, perhaps—for there was no foreseeing how it might affect her—Pearl would frown, and clench her little fist, and harden her small features into a stern, unsympathizing look of discontent. Not seldom, she would laugh anew, and louder than before, like a thing incapable and unintelligent of human sorrow. Or—but this more rarely happened—she would be convulsed with a rage of grief, and sob out her love for her mother in broken words, and seem intent on proving that she had a heart, by breaking it. Yet Hester was hardly safe in confiding herself to that gusty tenderness; it passed as suddenly as it came. **Brooding** over all these matters, the mother felt like one who has **evoked** a spirit, but, by some irregularity in the process of **conjuration**, has failed to win the master-word that should control this new and incomprehensible intelligence. Her only real comfort was when the child lay in the **placidity** of sleep. Then she was sure of her, and tasted hours of quiet, sad, delicious happiness; until—perhaps with that **perverse** expression glimmering from beneath her opening lids— little Pearl awoke!

How soon—with what strange rapidity, indeed—did Pearl arrive at an age that was capable of social inter-course, beyond the mother's ever-ready smile and nonsense-words! And then what a happiness would it have been, could Hester Prynne have heard her clear, birdlike voice mingling with the **uproar** of other childish voices, and have distinguished and unravelled her own darling's tones, amid all the entangled outcry of a group of **sportive** children! But this could never be. Pearl was a born outcast of the infantile world. An imp of evil, emblem and product of sin, she had no right among christened infants. Nothing was more remarkable than the instinct, as it seemed, with which the child comprehended her loneliness; the destiny that had drawn an inviolable circle round about her; the whole peculiarity,

WRATH (raath) *n.*
anger, rage
Synonyms: fury, ire, resentment, indignation

INCOHERENT (ihn koh <u>hihr</u> uhnt) *adj.*
unable to think or express one's thoughts in a clear
or orderly manner; lacking cohesion or connection
Synonyms: unintelligible; disordered, incohesive

ANATHEMA (uh <u>naath</u> uh muh) *n.*
curse; something shunned or disliked
Synonyms: ban; execration, aversion, horror,
abomination

REVILE (rih <u>vie</u> uhl) *v.* **-ing,-ed.**
to criticize with harsh language, verbally abuse
Synonyms: vituperate, scold, assail, upbraid, berate

SENTIMENT (<u>sehn</u> tuh muhnt) *n.*
an attitude, thought, or judgment prompted by feeling
Synonym: emotion

REQUITE (rih <u>kwiet</u>) *v.* **-ing,-ed.**
to return or repay
Synonyms: reciprocate, avenge, compensate,
reimburse

CAPRICE (kuh <u>prees</u>) *n.*
an impulsive change of mind, fickleness
Synonym: whim

THWART (thwahrt) *v.* **-ing,-ed.**
to frustrate; to block or prevent from happening
Synonyms: hinder, baffle; oppose, defeat, foil, balk

MANIFESTATION (maan uh fehs <u>tay</u> shuhn) *n.*
a clear appearance or display
Synonyms: expression, exhibition, indication

APPALL (uh <u>pahl</u>) *v.* **-ing,-ed.**
to overcome with shock or dismay
Synonyms: horrify, astound, petrify

DISCERN (dihs <u>uhrn</u>) *v.* **-ing,-ed.**
to perceive or recognize something
Synonyms: descry, observe, glimpse, distinguish

in short, of her position in respect to other children. Never, since her release from prison, had Hester met the public gaze without her. In all her walks about the town, Pearl, too, was there; first as the babe in arms, and afterwards as the little girl, small companion of her mother, holding a forefinger with her whole grasp, and tripping along at the rate of three or four footsteps to one of Hester's. She saw the children of the settlement, on the grassy margin of the street, or at the domestic thresholds, <u>disporting</u> themselves in such grim fashions as the <u>Puritanic</u> nurture would permit; playing at going to church, perchance; or at scourging <u>Quakers</u>; or taking scalps in a sham-fight with the Indians; or scaring one another with freaks of imitative witchcraft. Pearl saw, and gazed intently, but never sought to make acquaintance. If spoken to, she would not speak again. If the children gathered about her, as they sometimes did, Pearl would grow positively terrible in her puny **wrath**, snatching up stones to fling at them, with shrill, **incoherent** exclamations, that made her mother tremble because they had so much the sound of a witch's **anathemas** in some unknown tongue.

The truth was that the little <u>Puritans</u>, being of the most intolerant brood that ever lived, had got a vague idea of something outlandish, unearthly, or at variance with ordinary fashions, in the mother and child; and therefore scorned them in their hearts, and not unfrequently **reviled** them with their tongues. Pearl felt the **sentiment**, and **requited** it with the bitterest hatred that can be supposed to <u>rankle</u> in a childish bosom. These outbreaks of a fierce temper had a kind of value, and even comfort, for her mother; because there was at least an intelligible earnestness in the mood, instead of the fitful **caprice** that so often **thwarted** her in the child's **manifestations**. It **appalled** her, nevertheless, to **discern** here, again, a shadowy reflection of the evil that had

ENMITY (<u>ehn</u> muh tee) *n.*
  hostility, antagonism, ill-will
    Synonyms: animosity, antipathy, rancor, animus
SECLUSION (sih <u>cloo</u> zhuhn) *n.*
  isolation, detachment
    Synonyms: separation, privacy, solitude
PERPETUATE (puhr <u>peht</u> chyoo ayt) *v.* **-ing,-ed.**
  to be or make endless or eternal
    Synonyms: continue, live on, preserve, sustain
KINDLE (<u>kihn</u> duhl) *v.* **-ing,-ed.**
  to set fire to or ignite; to excite or inspire
    Synonyms: light, spark; arouse, awaken
ADAPTED (uh <u>daap</u> tihd) *adj.*
  adjusted, changed, fit
    Synonyms: accustomed, altered, conformed
MULTITUDE (<u>muhl</u> tuh tood) *n.*
  the state of being many, a great number; a crowd
    Synonyms: mass, myriad; throng
SOLEMN (<u>sah</u> luhm) *adj.*
  somberly impressive, deeply serious
    Synonyms: dignified, earnest, ceremonial
MELANCHOLY (<u>mehl</u> uhn kahl ee) *adj.*
  sad, depressed
    Synonyms: dejected, despondent, woeful, sorrowful
PRETERNATURAL (pree tuhr <u>naach</u> uh ruhl) *adj.*
  extraordinary or unnatural
    Synonyms: abnormal, mysterious, odd, unearthly
SPORTIVENESS (<u>spohr</u> tihv nehs) *n.*
  playfulness, happy amusement
    Synonyms: friskiness, merriment, liveliness
FACULTY (<u>faa</u> kuhl tee) *n.*
  the ability to act or do
    Synonyms: aptitude, capability, sense, skill
DEARTH (duhrth) *n.*
  lack, scarcity, insufficiency
    Synonyms: absence, shortage

existed in herself. All this **enmity** and passion had Pearl inherited, by <u>inalienable</u> right, out of Hester's heart. Mother and daughter stood together in the same circle of **seclusion** from human society; and in the nature of the child seemed to be **perpetuated** those unquiet elements that had distracted Hester Prynne before Pearl's birth, but had since begun to be soothed away by the softening influences of maternity.

At home, within and around her mother's cottage, Pearl wanted not a wide and various circle of acquaintance. The spell of life went forth from her ever-creative spirit, and communicated itself to a thousand objects, as a torch **kindles** a flame wherever it may be applied. The unlikeliest materials—a stick, a bunch of rags, a flower—were the puppets of Pearl's witchcraft, and, without undergoing any outward change, became spiritually **adapted** to whatever drama occupied the stage of her inner world. Her one baby-voice served a **multitude** of imaginary personages, old and young, to talk withal. The pine-trees, aged, black, and **solemn**, and flinging groans and other **melancholy** utterances on the breeze, needed little transformation to figure as <u>Puritan</u> elders; the ugliest weeds of the garden were their children, whom Pearl smote down and uprooted, most unmercifully. It was wonderful, the vast variety of forms into which she threw her intellect, with no continuity, indeed, but darting up and dancing, always in a state of **preternatural** activity—soon sinking down, as if exhausted by so rapid and feverish a tide of life—and succeeded by other shapes of a similar wild energy. It was like nothing so much as the <u>phantasmagoric</u> play of the northern lights. In the mere exercise of the fancy, however, and the **sportiveness** of a growing mind, there might be little more than was observable in other children of bright **faculties**; except as Pearl, in the **dearth** of human playmates, was thrown more upon the visionary

SINGULARITY (sihn gyuh <u>layr</u> ih tee) *n.*
uncommonness, peculiarity
Synonyms: difference, oddity, rarity, uniqueness,
individuality

ADVERSE (<u>aad</u> vuhrs) (aad <u>vuhrs</u>) *adj.*
unfavorable, causing hardship; opposing
Synonyms: unfortunate, distressing; contrary

EJACULATION (ih <u>jaak</u> yuh lay shuhn) *n.*
a sudden exclamation
Synonyms: chatter, vociferation, expletive

throng which she created. The **singularity** lay in the hostile feelings with which the child regarded all these offspring of her own heart and mind. She never created a friend, but seemed always to be sowing broadcast the dragon's teeth, whence sprung a harvest of armed enemies, against whom she rushed to battle. It was inexpressibly sad—then what depth of sorrow to a mother, who felt in her own heart the cause—to observe, in one so young, this constant recognition of an **adverse** world, and so fierce a training of the energies that were to make good her cause in the contest that must ensue.

Gazing at Pearl, Hester Prynne often dropped her work upon her knees, and cried out with an agony which she would <u>fain</u> have hidden, but which made utterance for itself, <u>betwixt</u> speech and a groan, "O Father in Heaven—if Thou art still my Father—what is this being which I have brought into the world!" And Pearl, overhearing the **ejaculation**, or aware, through some more subtle channel, of those throbs of anguish, would turn her vivid and beautiful little face upon her mother, smile with <u>sprite</u>-like intelligence, and resume her play.

One peculiarity of the child's deportment remains yet to be told. The very first thing which she had noticed in her life, was—what?—not the mother's smile, responding to it, as other babies do, by that faint, embryo smile of the little mouth, remembered so doubtfully afterwards, and with such fond discussion whether it were indeed a smile. By no means! But that first object of which Pearl seemed to become aware was—shall we say it?—the scarlet letter on Hester's bosom! One day, as her mother stooped over the cradle, the infant's eyes had been caught by the glimmering of the gold embroidery about the letter; and, putting up her little hand, she grasped at it, smiling, not doubtfully, but with a decided

EPOCH (<u>eh</u> pihk) *n.*
a particular day or time; a specific time in history
Synonyms: date; period, era, generation

SOLITUDE (<u>sahl</u> ih tood) *n.*
social isolation; time spent alone
Synonyms: seclusion, withdrawal, retirement;
loneliness

MALICE (<u>maal</u> ihs) *n.*
animosity, spite, hatred
Synonyms: malevolence, cruelty, hostility

gleam, that gave her face the look of a much older child. Then, gasping for breath, did Hester Prynne clutch the fatal token, instinctively endeavoring to tear it away; so infinite was the torture inflicted by the intelligent touch of Pearl's baby-hand. Again, as if her mother's agonized gesture were meant only to make sport for her, did little Pearl look into her eyes, and smile! From that **epoch**, except when the child was asleep, Hester had never felt a moment's safety; not a moment's calm enjoyment of her. Weeks, it is true, would sometimes elapse, during which Pearl's gaze might never once be fixed upon the scarlet letter; but then, again, it would come at unawares, like the stroke of sudden death, and always with that peculiar smile, and odd expression of the eyes.

Once, this freakish, elvish cast came into the child's eyes, while Hester was looking at her own image in them, as mothers are fond of doing; and, suddenly—for women in **solitude**, and with troubled hearts, are pestered with unaccountable delusions—she fancied that she beheld, not her own miniature portrait, but another face, in the small black mirror of Pearl's eye. It was a face, fiendlike, full of smiling **malice**, yet bearing the semblance of features that she had known full well, though seldom with a smile, and never with **malice** in them. It was as if an evil spirit possessed the child, and had just then peeped forth in mockery. Many a time afterwards had Hester been tortured, though less vividly, by the same illusion.

In the afternoon of a certain summer's day, after Pearl grew big enough to run about, she amused herself with gathering handfuls of wild-flowers and flinging them, one by one, at her mother's bosom, dancing up and down like a little elf whenever she hit the scarlet letter. Hester's first motion had been to cover her bosom with her clasped hands. But, whether from pride or

PENANCE (<u>peh</u> nihns) *n.*
voluntary suffering to repent for a wrong
Synonyms: atonement, reparation, chastening, reconciliation

IMPULSE (<u>ihm</u> puhls) *n.*
sudden tendency, inclination
Synonyms: urge, whim

INVARIABLY (ihn <u>vaa</u> ree uh blee) *adv.*
without change, constantly
Synonyms: always, repeatedly, perpetually

BALM (bahm) *n.*
a soothing, healing influence or substance
Synonyms: succor, comfort, palliative, anodyne, salve

GESTICULATION (jeh stih kyuh <u>lay</u> shuhn) *n.*
the act of making gestures; a particularly expressive gesture
Synonyms: motion, indication; signal, expression

SPORTIVE (<u>spohr</u> tihv) *adj.*
frolicsome, playful
Synonyms: frisky, merry, lively

resignation, or a feeling that her **penance** might best be wrought out by this unutterable pain, she resisted the **impulse**, and sat erect, pale as death, looking sadly into little Pearl's wild eyes. Still came the battery of flowers, almost **invariably** hitting the mark, and covering the mother's breast with hurts for which she could find no **balm** in this world, nor knew how to seek it in another. At last, her shot being all expended, the child stood still and gazed at Hester with that little, laughing image of a fiend peeping out—or, whether it peeped or no, her mother so imagined it—from the unsearchable abyss of her black eyes.

"Child, what art thou?" cried the mother.

"O, I am your little Pearl!" answered the child.

But, while she said it, Pearl laughed, and began to dance up and down, with the humorsome **gesticulation** of a little imp, whose next freak might be to fly up the chimney.

"Art thou my child, in very truth?" asked Hester.

Nor did she put the question altogether idly, but, for the moment, with a portion of genuine earnestness; for such was Pearl's wonderful intelligence, that her mother half doubted whether she were not acquainted with the secret spell of her existence, and might not now reveal herself.

"Yes, I am little Pearl!" repeated the child, continuing her antics.

"Thou art not my child! Thou art no Pearl of mine!" said the mother, half playfully; for it was often the case that a **sportive impulse** came over her, in the midst of her deepest suffering. "Tell me, then, what thou art, and who sent thee hither?"

"Tell me, Mother!" said the child seriously, coming up to Hester, and pressing herself close to her knees. "Do thou tell me!"

ACUTENESS (uh <u>kyoot</u> nehs) *n.*
  intelligence, keen wit; sharpness, severity
    Synonyms: genius, cleverness; intensity

SUPPRESS (suh <u>prehs</u>) *v.* **-ing,-ed.**
  to hold back, restrain
    Synonyms: subdue, stifle, muffle, quell, curb

RESOLVE (rih <u>sahlv</u>) *v.* **-ing,-ed.**
  to determine or to make a firm decision about
    Synonyms: solve, decide, clear up

QUERY (<u>kweh</u> ree) *n.*
  question
    Synonyms: inquiry, interrogation

LABYRINTH (<u>laab</u> uh rihnth) *n.*
  maze
    Synonyms: entanglement, mesh, web

PATERNITY (puh <u>tuhr</u> nih tee) *n.*
  fatherhood; descent from father's ancestors
    Synonyms: siring, begetting; origin

INAUSPICIOUS (ihn aw <u>spih</u> shuhs) *adj.*
  having unfavorable prospects, unfortunate
    Synonyms: negative, unlucky, ominous, threatening

"Thy Heavenly Father sent thee!" answered Hester Prynne.

But she said it with a hesitation that did not escape the **acuteness** of the child. Whether moved only by her ordinary freakishness, or because an evil spirit prompted her, she put up her small forefinger, and touched the scarlet letter.

"He did not send me!" cried she, positively. "I have no Heavenly Father!"

"Hush, Pearl, hush! Thou must not talk so!" answered the mother, **suppressing** a groan. "He sent us all into this world. He sent even me, thy mother. Then, much more, thee! Or, if not, thou strange and elfish child, whence didst thou come?"

"Tell me! Tell me!" repeated Pearl, no longer seriously, but laughing, and capering about the floor. "It is thou that must tell me!"

But Hester could not **resolve** the **query**, being herself in a dismal **labyrinth** of doubt. She remembered— betwixt a smile and a shudder—the talk of the neighboring townspeople; who, seeking vainly elsewhere for the child's **paternity**, and observing some of her odd attributes, had given out that poor little Pearl was a demon offspring; such as, ever since old catholic times, had occasionally been seen on earth, through the agency of their mother's sin, and to promote some foul and wicked purpose. Luther, according to the scandal of his monkish enemies, was a brat of that hellish breed; nor was Pearl the only child to whom this **inauspicious** origin was assigned, among the New England Puritans.

DESCEND (dih <u>sehnd</u>) (dee <u>sehnd</u>) *v.* **-ing,-ed.**
to pass from a higher place to a lower place
Synonyms: fall, dismount, gravitate

HONORABLE (<u>ah</u> nuhr uh buhl) *adj.*
illustrious, praiseworthy, deserving
Synonyms: respectable, dignified, noble

MAGISTRACY (<u>maa</u> juh struh see) *n.*
a group of officials who can administrate laws
Synonyms: administration, authority, jurisdiction

IMPEL (ihm <u>pehl</u>) *v.* **-ling,-led.**
to urge forward as if driven by a strong moral pressure
Synonyms: push, prompt, incite, instigate

SINGULAR (<u>sihn</u> gyuh luhr) *adj.*
uncommon, peculiar
Synonyms: unusual, odd, rare, unique, individual

LUDICROUS (<u>loo</u> dih kruhs) *adj.*
laughable, ridiculous
Synonyms: hilarious, absurd, foolish, silly,
preposterous

The Governor's Hall
Chapter 7

Hester Prynne went one day to the mansion of Governor Bellingham, with a pair of gloves, which she had fringed and embroidered to his order, and which were to be worn on some great occasion of state; for, though the chances of a popular election had caused this former ruler to **descend** a step or two from the highest rank, he still held an **honorable** and influential place among the colonial **magistracy**.

Another and far more important reason than the delivery of a pair of embroidered gloves **impelled** Hester, at this time, to seek an interview with a personage of so much power and activity in the affairs of the settlement. It had reached her ears, that there was a design on the part of some of the leading inhabitants, cherishing the more rigid order of principles in religion and government, to deprive her of her child. On the supposition that Pearl, as already hinted, was of demon origin, these good people not unreasonably argued that a Christian interest in the mother's soul required them to remove such a stumbling-block from her path. If the child, on the other hand, were really capable of moral and religious growth, and possessed the elements of ultimate salvation, then, surely, it would enjoy all the fairer prospect of these advantages by being transferred to wiser and better guardianship than Hester Prynne's. Among those who promoted the design, Governor Bellingham was said to be one of the most busy. It may appear **singular**, and indeed not a little **ludicrous**, that an affair of this kind, which, in later days, would have been referred to no higher jurisdiction than that of the selectmen of the town, should then have been a question

EMINENCE (<u>ehm</u> uh nuhnts) *n.*
   1. a position of distinction or superiority
   Synonyms: prominence, importance
   2. a prominent place, something which projects outward or upward
   Synonyms: elevation, summit, peak

EPOCH (<u>eh</u> pihk) *n.*
   a specific time in history; a particular day or time
   Synonyms: period, era, generation; date

PRISTINE (prih <u>steen</u>) *adj.*
   untouched, uncorrupted
   Synonyms: pure, clean

INTRINSIC (ihn <u>trihn</u> zihk) (ihn <u>trihn</u> sihk) *adj.*
   inherent, internal
   Synonyms: fundamental, essential, innate

CAPRICE (kuh <u>prees</u>) *n.*
   an impulsive change of mind, fickleness
   Synonym: whim

IMPERIOUS (ihm <u>pihr</u> ee uhs) *adj.*
   domineering, overbearing, arrogantly self-assured
   Synonyms: despotic, authoritarian

LUXURIANT (luhg <u>zhoor</u> ee ehnt) *adj.*
   elegant, lavish
   Synonyms: rich, abundant, profuse

CONTRIVE (kuhn <u>triev</u>) *v.* **-ing,-ed.**
   to form in an artistic manner; to devise, plan, or manage
   Synonyms: create, design; concoct, scheme

publicly discussed, and on which statesmen of **eminence** took sides. At that **epoch** of **pristine** simplicity, however, matters of even slighter public interest, and of far less **intrinsic** weight, than the welfare of Hester and her child, were strangely mixed up with the deliberations of legislators and acts of state. The period was hardly, if at all, earlier than that of our story, when a dispute concerning the right of property in a pig not only caused a fierce and bitter contest in the legislative body of the colony, but resulted in an important modification of the framework itself of the legislature.

Full of concern, therefore—but so conscious of her own right that it seemed scarcely an unequal match between the public, on the one side, and a lonely woman, backed by the sympathies of nature, on the other—Hester Prynne set forth from her solitary cottage. Little Pearl, of course, was her companion. She was now of an age to run lightly along by her mother's side, and, constantly in motion, from morn till sunset, could have accomplished a much longer journey than that before her. Often, nevertheless, more from **caprice** than necessity, she demanded to be taken up in arms; but was soon as **imperious** to be set down again, and frisked onward before Hester on the grassy pathway, with many a harmless trip and tumble. We have spoken of Pearl's rich and **luxuriant** beauty; a beauty that shone with deep and vivid tints; a bright complexion, eyes possessing intensity both of depth and glow, and hair already of a deep, glossy brown, and which, in after years, would be nearly akin to black. There was fire in her and throughout her; she seemed the unpremeditated offshoot of a passionate moment. Her mother, in **contriving** the child's garb, had allowed the gorgeous tendencies of her imagination their full play; arraying her in a crimson velvet tunic of a peculiar cut, abundantly embroidered with fantasies and flourishes of

WAN (wahn) *adj.*
  sickly pale
    Synonyms: ashen, pallid
PALLID (<u>paa</u> lihd) *adj.*
  lacking color or liveliness
    Synonyms: pale, wan, ashen
ADAPTED (uh <u>daap</u> tihd) *adj.*
  adjusted, changed, fit
    Synonyms: accustomed, altered, conformed
INEVITABLY (ihn <u>ehv</u> ih tuh blee) *adv.*
  certainly, unavoidably
    Synonyms: inescapably, surely, predictably
ENDOW (ehn <u>dow</u>) *v.* **-ing,-ed.** *(See page 170.)*
IGNOMINY (<u>ihg</u> nuh mih nee) *n.* *(See page 156.)*
LAVISH (<u>laa</u> vihsh) *v.* **-ing,-ed.**
  to shower with abundance or extravagance; to waste
  or spend excessively
    Synonyms: cram, overflow, saturate, teem; squander
MORBID (<u>mohr</u> bihd) *adj.* *(See page 178.)*
INGENUITY (ihn jeh <u>noo</u> ih tee) *n.*
  cleverness
    Synonyms: inventiveness, imagination, creativity
ANALOGY (uh <u>naal</u> uh jee) *n.*
  a relation or likeness, parallelism
    Synonyms: correlation, comparison, similarity
CONTRIVE (kuhn <u>triev</u>) *v.* **-ing,-ed.** *(See page 200.)*
SOMBRE (<u>sahm</u> buhr) *adj.* *(See page 164.)*
VERILY (<u>veh</u> rih lee) *adv.*
  truly, with accuracy and confidence
    Synonyms: truthfully, reliably, assuredly
DAUNTLESS (<u>dawnt</u> lehs) *adj.*
  fearless, unintimidated
    Synonyms: brave, courageous, unafraid
PESTILENCE (<u>peh</u> stihl ehnts) *n.*
  epidemic, plague, illness
    Synonyms: contagion, scourge, sickness, disease
HALF-FLEDGED (haaf flehjd) *adj.*
  immature, juvenile, inexperienced
    Synonyms: unprepared, untrained

gold thread. So much strength of coloring, which must have given a **wan** and **pallid** aspect to cheeks of a fainter bloom, was admirably **adapted** to Pearl's beauty and made her the very brightest little jet of flame that ever danced upon the earth.

But it was a remarkable attribute of this garb, and, indeed, of the child's whole appearance, that it irresistibly and **inevitably** reminded the beholder of the token which Hester Prynne was doomed to wear upon her bosom. It was the scarlet letter in another form; the scarlet letter **endowed** with life! The mother herself—as if the red **ignominy** were so deeply scorched into her brain that all her conceptions assumed its form—had carefully wrought out the similitude; **lavishing** many hours of **morbid ingenuity** to create an **analogy** between the object of her affection and the emblem of her guilt and torture. But, in truth, Pearl was the one, as well as the other; and only in consequence of that identity had Hester **contrived** so perfectly to represent the scarlet letter in her appearance.

As the two wayfarers came within the precincts of the town, the children of the Puritans looked up from their play—or what passed for play with those **sombre** little urchins—and spoke gravely one to another:

"Behold, **verily**, there is the woman of the scarlet letter; and, of a truth, moreover, there is the likeness of the scarlet letter running along by her side! Come, therefore, and let us fling mud at them!"

But Pearl, who was a **dauntless** child, after frowning, stamping her foot, and shaking her little hand with a variety of threatening gestures, suddenly made a rush at the knot of her enemies, and put them all to flight. She resembled, in her fierce pursuit of them, an infant **pestilence**—the scarlet fever, or some such **half-fledged** angel of judgment—whose mission was to punish the sins of the rising generation. She screamed and shouted,

MELANCHOLY (<u>mehl</u> uhn kahl ee) *adj.*
sad, depressed
Synonyms: dejected, despondent, woeful, sorrowful

EDIFICE (<u>eh</u> duh fuhs) *n.*
a large structure
Synonyms: building, construction, skyscraper

IMPERATIVELY (ihm <u>pehr</u> uh tihv lee) *adv.*
immediately, essentially, in an urgent manner
Synonyms: peremptorily, critically

too, with a terrific volume of sound which, doubtless, caused the hearts of the fugitives to quake within them. The victory accomplished, Pearl returned quietly to her mother, and looked up, smiling, into her face.

Without further adventure, they reached the dwelling of Governor Bellingham. This was a large wooden house, built in a fashion of which there are specimens still extant in the streets of our elder towns; now moss-grown, crumbling to decay, and **melancholy** at heart with the many sorrowful or joyful occurrences, remembered or forgotten, that have happened, and passed away, within their dusky chambers. Then, however, there was the freshness of the passing year on its exterior, and the cheerfulness, gleaming forth from the sunny windows, of a human habitation, into which death had never entered. It had, indeed, a very cheery aspect; the walls being overspread with a kind of stucco, in which fragments of broken glass were plentifully intermixed; so that, when the sunshine fell aslant-wise over the front of the **edifice**, it glittered and sparkled as if diamonds had been flung against it by the double handful. The brilliancy might have befitted Aladdin's palace rather than the mansion of a grave old <u>Puritan</u> ruler. It was further decorated with strange and seemingly <u>cabalistic</u> figures and diagrams, suitable to the quaint taste of the age, which had been drawn in the stucco when newly laid on, and had now grown hard and durable, for the admiration of after times.

Pearl, looking at this bright wonder of a house, began to caper and dance, and **imperatively** required that the whole breadth of sunshine should be stripped off its front, and given her to play with.

"<u>No</u>, my little Pearl!" said her mother. "<u>Thou must gather thine own sunshine. I have none to give thee!</u>"

They approached the door, which was of an arched form, and flanked on each side by a narrow tower or

EDIFICE (<u>eh</u> duh fuhs) *n.*
a large structure
Synonyms: building, construction, skyscraper

COMMODITY (kuh <u>mah</u> dih tee) *n.*
a useful item, a convenience
Synonyms: benefit, advantage

HONORABLE (<u>ah</u> nuhr uh buhl) *adj.*
illustrious, praiseworthy, deserving
Synonyms: respectable, dignified, noble

MEDIUM (<u>mee</u> dee uhm) *n.*
a substance or object that is used to transmit or
accomplish something
Synonyms: means, instrument, vehicle, mechanism

projection of the **edifice**, in both of which were lattice windows, with wooden shutters to close over them at need. Lifting the iron hammer that hung at the portal, Hester Prynne gave a summons, which was answered by one of the Governor's bond-servants; a free-born Englishman, but now a seven years' slave. During that term he was to be the property of his master, and as much a **commodity** of bargain and sale as an ox, or a joint-stool. The serf wore the blue coat, which was the customary garb of serving-men at that period, and long before, in the old hereditary halls of England.

"Is the worshipful Governor Bellingham within?" inquired Hester.

"Yea, forsooth," replied the bond-servant, staring with wide-open eyes at the scarlet letter, which, being a newcomer in the country, he had never before seen. "Yea, his **honorable** worship is within. But he hath a godly minister or two with him, and likewise a leech. Ye may not see his worship now."

"Nevertheless, I will enter," answered Hester Prynne, and the bond-servant, perhaps judging from the decision of her air, and the glittering symbol on her bosom that she was a great lady in the land, offered no opposition.

So the mother and little Pearl were admitted into the hall of entrance. With many variations, suggested by the nature of his building-materials, diversity of climate, and a different mode of social life, Governor Bellingham had planned his new habitation after the residences of gentlemen of fair estate in his native land. Here, then, was a wide and reasonably lofty hall, extending through the whole depth of the house, and forming a **medium** of general communication, more or less directly, with all the other apartments. At one extremity, this spacious room was lighted by the windows of the two towers, which formed a small recess on

TOME (tohm) *n.*
a book, usually large and academic
Synonyms: volume, codex

SUBSTANTIAL (suhb staan shuhl) *adj.*
having substance; large in size or amount
Synonyms: important, significant; ample, hearty, strong

PONDEROUS (pahn duhr uhs) *adj.*
weighty, heavy, large
Synonyms: hefty, massive, cumbersome, unwieldy

PATERNAL (puh tuhr nuhl) *adj.*
inherited from the father; fatherly, related to the characteristics of fatherhood
Synonyms: hereditary; parental

SENTIMENT (sehn tuh muhnt) *n.*
an attitude, thought, or judgment prompted by feeling
Synonym: emotion

INVARIABLY (ihn vaa ree uh blee) *adv.*
without change, constantly
Synonyms: always, repeatedly, perpetually

SUSPEND (suh spehnd) *v.* **-ing,-ed.**
to dangle, hang; to delay, interrupt
Synonyms: swing; defer, cease, disrupt, halt, discontinue

RELIC (rehl ihk) *n.*
an object or idea that is special because of its connection to the past; remains
Synonyms: memento, treasure, token; trace

either side of the portal. At the other end, though partly muffled by a curtain, it was more powerfully illuminated by one of those embowed hall-windows which we read of in old books, and which was provided with a deep and cushioned seat. Here, on the cushion, lay a folio **tome**, probably of the Chronicles of England, or other such **substantial** literature; even as, in our own days, we scatter gilded volumes on the centre-table, to be turned over by the casual guest. The furniture of the hall consisted of some **ponderous** chairs, the backs of which were elaborately carved with wreaths of oaken flowers; and likewise a table in the same taste; the whole being of the Elizabethan age, or perhaps earlier, and heirlooms, transferred hither from the Governor's **paternal** home. On the table—in token that the **sentiment** of old English hospitality had not been left behind—stood a large pewter tankard, at the bottom of which, had Hester or Pearl peeped into it, they might have seen the frothy remnant of a recent draught of ale.

On the wall hung a row of portraits, representing the forefathers of the Bellingham lineage, some with armor on their breasts, and others with stately <u>ruffs</u> and robes of peace. All were characterized by the sternness and severity which old portraits so **invariably** put on; as if they were the ghosts, rather than the pictures, of departed worthies, and were gazing with harsh and intolerant criticism at the pursuits and enjoyments of living men.

At about the centre of the oaken panels, that lined the hall was **suspended** a suit of mail, not, like the pictures, an ancestral **relic**, but of the most modern date; for it had been manufactured by a skilful armorer in London the same year in which Governor Bellingham came over to New England. There was a steel headpiece, a <u>cuirass</u>, a <u>gorget</u>, and <u>greaves</u>, with a pair of gauntlets and a sword hanging beneath; all, and especially the

BURNISH (<u>buhr</u> nihsh) *v.* **-ing,-ed.**
to polish, make smooth and bright
Synonyms: shine, buff

SOLEMN (<u>sah</u> luhm) *adj.*
somberly impressive, deeply serious
Synonyms: dignified, earnest, ceremonial

REGIMENT (<u>reh</u> jih muhnt) *n.*
a military unit
Synonyms: legion, division, group

EXIGENCE (<u>ehk</u> suh juhnts) *n.*
a demand or requirement
Synonyms: emergency, necessity, crisis, urgency

PHYSIOGNOMY (fih zee <u>ahg</u> nuh mee) *n.*
characteristic facial features; the art of judging one's
character from facial features
Synonyms: visage, expression; divination

DRAW *v.* **-ing, drew, drawn.**
1. to pull, drag; to attract
Synonyms: haul, tow, lug; lure, entice
2. to move steadily
Synonyms: proceed, continue, progress

helmet and breastplate, so highly **burnished** as to glow with white radiance, and scatter an illumination everywhere about upon the floor. This bright <u>panoply</u> was not meant for mere idle show, but had been worn by the Governor on many a **solemn** muster and training field, and had glittered, moreover, at the head of a **regiment** in the Pequod war. For, though bred a lawyer, and accustomed to speak of Bacon, Coke, Noye, and Finch as his professional associates, the **exigences** of this new country had transformed Governor Bellingham into a soldier as well as a statesman and ruler.

Little Pearl—who was as greatly pleased with the gleaming armor as she had been with the glittering <u>frontispiece</u> of the house—spent some time looking into the polished mirror of the breastplate.

"Mother," cried she, "I see you here. Look! Look!"

Hester looked, by way of humoring the child; and she saw that, owing to the peculiar effect of this convex mirror, the scarlet letter was represented in exaggerated and gigantic proportions, so as to be greatly the most prominent feature of her appearance. In truth, she seemed absolutely hidden behind it. Pearl pointed upward, also, at a similar picture in the headpiece, smiling at her mother, with the elfish intelligence that was so familiar an expression on her small **physiognomy**. That look of naughty merriment was likewise reflected in the mirror, with so much breadth and intensity of effect, that it made Hester Prynne feel as if it could not be the image of her own child, but of an imp who was seeking to mould itself into Pearl's shape.

"Come along, Pearl," said she, **drawing** her away. "Come and look into this fair garden. It may be we shall see flowers there; more beautiful ones than we find in the woods."

Pearl, accordingly, ran to the bow-window at the farther end of the hall, and looked along the vista of a

RELINQUISH (rih <u>lihn</u> kwihsh) *v.* **-ing,-ed.**
to renounce or surrender something
Synonyms: yield, resign, abandon, cede, waive

PERPETUATE (puhr <u>peht</u> chyoo ayt) *v.* **-ing,-ed.**
to be or make endless or eternal
Synonyms: continue, live on, preserve, sustain

SUBSISTENCE (suhb <u>sihst</u> ihnts) *n.*
the necessities of life, the resources of survival
Synonyms: nourishment, sustenance, provisions

DESCENDANT (dih <u>sehn</u> dehnt) *n.*
an offspring or heir
Synonyms: child, kin, progeny

PACIFY (<u>paa</u> suh fie) *v.* **-ing,-ied.**
to restore calm, bring peace
Synonyms: mollify, conciliate, appease, placate

DISPOSITION (dihs puh <u>zih</u> shuhn) *n.*
1. mood or temperament
Synonyms: behavior, nature
2. a habitual tendency, an inclination
Synonyms: willingness, propensity

garden-walk, carpeted with closely shaven grass and bordered with some rude and immature attempt at shrubbery. But the proprietor appeared already to have **relinquished**, as hopeless, the effort to **perpetuate** on this side of the Atlantic, in a hard soil and amid the close struggle for **subsistence**, the native English taste for ornamental gardening. Cabbages grew in plain sight; and a pumpkin-vine, rooted at some distance, had run across the intervening space, and deposited one of its gigantic products directly beneath the hall-window; as if to warn the Governor that this great lump of vegetable gold was as rich an ornament as New England earth would offer him. There were a few rose-bushes, however, and a number of apple-trees, probably the **descendants** of those planted by the Reverend Mr. Blackstone, the first settler of the peninsula, that half-mythological personage, who rides through our early annals, seated on the back of a bull.

Pearl, seeing the rose-bushes, began to cry for a red rose, and would not be **pacified**.

"Hush, child, hush!" said her mother earnestly. "Do not cry, dear little Pearl! I hear voices in the garden. The Governor is coming, and gentlemen along with him!"

In fact, adown the vista of the garden avenue a number of persons were seen approaching towards the house. Pearl, in utter scorn of her mother's attempt to quiet her, gave an eldritch scream and then became silent; not from any notion of obedience, but because the quick and mobile curiosity of her **disposition** was excited by the appearance of these new personages.

ANTIQUATED (<u>aan</u> tih kway tihd) *adj.*
outdated, obsolete
Synonyms: archaic, old-fashioned

UNFEIGNEDLY (uhn <u>fay</u> nihd lee) *adv.*
with sincerity, truly
Synonym: genuinely

LUXURY (<u>luhg</u> zhoor ee) *n.*
something done or had purely for enjoyment
Synonyms: comfort, indulgence, splendor, frill

CREED (kreed) *n.*
a statement of belief or principle
Synonyms: tenet, credo, doctrine, dogma, precept

VENERABLE (<u>veh</u> nehr uh buhl) *adj.*
respected because of age
Synonyms: distinguished, elderly

COMPEL (kuhm <u>pehl</u>) *v.* **-ling,-led.**
to urge or force
Synonyms: coerce, oblige, constrain

TRANSGRESSION (traans <u>greh</u> shuhn) *n.*
a violation or trespass of a law or command
Synonyms: overstep, sin, offense

The Elf-Child and the Minister

Chapter 8

Governor Bellingham, in a loose gown and easy cap—such as elderly gentlemen loved to <u>endue</u> themselves with, in their domestic privacy—walked foremost, and appeared to be showing off his estate, and <u>expatiating</u> on his projected improvements. The wide circumference of an elaborate <u>ruff</u> beneath his gray beard, in the **antiquated** fashion of King James's reign, caused his head to look not a little like that of John the Baptist in a charger. The impression made by his aspect, so rigid and severe, and frost-bitten with more than autumnal age, was hardly in keeping with the appliances of worldly enjoyment wherewith he had evidently done his utmost to surround himself. But it is an error to suppose that our grave forefathers—though accustomed to speak and think of human existence as a state merely of trial and warfare, and though **unfeignedly** prepared to sacrifice goods and life at the <u>behest</u> of duty—made it a matter of conscience to reject such means of comfort, or even **luxury**, as lay fairly within their grasp. This **creed** was never taught, for instance, by the **venerable** pastor, John Wilson, whose beard, white as a snow-drift, was seen over Governor Bellingham's shoulder; while its wearer suggested that pears and peaches might yet be naturalized in the New England climate, and that purple grapes might possibly be **compelled** to flourish against the sunny garden-wall. The old clergyman, nurtured at the rich bosom of the English Church, had a long-established and legitimate taste for all good and comfortable things; and however stern he might show himself in the pulpit or in his public <u>reproof</u> of such **transgressions** as that of Hester

GENIAL (<u>jeen</u> yuhl) (<u>jee</u> nee uhl) *adj.*
   pleasant and friendly; favorable to growth or comfort
      Synonyms: nice, amiable; productive, generative

BENEVOLENCE (buh <u>neh</u> vuh luhnts) *n.*
   kindness, compassion
      Synonyms: charity, altruism, generosity

ASCEND (uh <u>sehnd</u>) *v.* **-ing,-ed.**
   to rise to another level or climb; to move upward
      Synonyms: elevate, escalate, mount; hoist, lift

APPARITION (aa puh <u>rih</u> shuhn) *n.*
   a ghostly figure; an unexpected or unusual sight or
   appearance
      Synonyms: spirit, specter; illusion

Prynne, still, the **genial benevolence** of his private life had won him warmer affection than was accorded to any of his professional contemporaries.

Behind the Governor and Mr. Wilson came two other guests; one, the Reverend Arthur Dimmesdale, whom the reader may remember as having taken a brief and reluctant part in the scene of Hester Prynne's disgrace; and, in close companionship with him, old Roger Chillingworth, a person of great skill in physic, who, for two or three years past, had been settled in the town. It was understood that this learned man was the physician as well as friend of the young minister, whose health had severely suffered, of late, by his too unreserved self-sacrifice to the labors and duties of the pastoral relation.

The Governor, in advance of his visitors, **ascended** one or two steps, and, throwing open the leaves of the great hall-window, found himself close to little Pearl. The shadow of the curtain fell on Hester Prynne, and partially concealed her.

"What have we here?" said Governor Bellingham, looking with surprise at the scarlet little figure before him. "I profess, I have never seen the like, since my days of vanity, in old King James's time, when I was wont to esteem it a high favor to be admitted to a court mask! There used to be a swarm of these small **apparitions**, in holiday time; and we called them children of the Lord of Misrule. But how got such a guest into my hall?"

"Ay, indeed!" cried good old Mr. Wilson. "What little bird of scarlet plumage may this be? Methinks I have seen just such figures, when the sun has been shining through a richly painted window, and tracing out the golden and crimson images across the floor. But that was in the old land. Prithee, young one, who art thou, and what has ailed thy mother to bedizen thee in this strange fashion? Art thou a Christian child—ha? Dost

RELIC (<u>rehl</u> ihk) *n.*
    remains; an object or idea that is special because of
    its connection to the past
        Synonyms: trace; memento, treasure, token

SOBERLY (<u>soh</u> buhr lee) *adv.*
    in a simple and controlled manner; seriously; not in
    a drunken manner
        Synonyms: plainly, sedately; gravely; dryly

know thy catechism? Or art thou one of those naughty elfs or fairies, whom we thought to have left behind us, with other **relics** of Papistry, in merry old England?"

"I am Mother's child," answered the scarlet vision, "and my name is Pearl!"

"Pearl? Ruby, rather—or Coral—or Red Rose, at the very least, judging from thy hue!" responded the old minister, putting forth his hand in a vain attempt to pat little Pearl on the cheek. "But where is this mother of thine? Ah! I see," he added; and, turning to Governor Bellingham, whispered, "This is the selfsame child of whom we have held speech together; and behold here the unhappy woman, Hester Prynne, her mother!"

"Sayest thou so?" cried the Governor. "Nay, we might have judged that such a child's mother must needs be a scarlet woman, and a worthy type of her of Babylon! But she comes at a good time; and we will look into this matter forthwith."

Governor Bellingham stepped through the window into the hall, followed by his three guests.

"Hester Prynne," said he, fixing his naturally stern regard on the wearer of the scarlet letter, "there hath been much question concerning thee, of late. The point hath been weightily discussed, whether we, that are of authority and influence, do well discharge our consciences by trusting an immortal soul, such as there is in yonder child, to the guidance of one who hath stumbled and fallen, amid the pitfalls of this world. Speak thou, the child's own mother! Were it not, thinkest thou, for thy little one's temporal and eternal welfare, that she be taken out of thy charge, and clad **soberly**, and disciplined strictly, and instructed in the truths of heaven and earth? What canst thou do for the child, in this kind?"

"I can teach my little Pearl what I have learned from

MAGISTRATE (<u>maa</u> juh strayt) *n.*
an official who can administrate laws
Synonyms: judge, arbiter, authority, marshal

DRAW *v.* **-ing, drew, drawn.**
1. to pull, drag; to attract
Synonyms: haul, tow, lug; lure, entice
2. to move steadily
Synonyms: proceed, continue, progress

SOLEMNITY (suh <u>lehm</u> nih tee) *n.*
dignified seriousness
Synonyms: ceremoniousness, formality

PIOUS (<u>pie</u> uhs) *adj.*
extremely religious; dedicated, devout
Synonyms: sanctimonious; reverent, observant

this!" answered Hester Prynne, laying her finger on the red token.

"Woman, it is thy badge of shame!" replied the stern **magistrate**. "It is because of the stain which that letter indicates, that we would transfer thy child to other hands."

"Nevertheless," said the mother, calmly, though growing more pale, "this badge hath taught me—it daily teaches me—it is teaching me at this moment—lessons whereof my child may be the wiser and better, albeit they can profit nothing to myself."

"We will judge warily," said Bellingham, "and look well what we are about to do. Good Master Wilson, I pray you, examine this Pearl—since that is her name—and see whether she hath had such Christian nurture as befits a child of her age."

The old minister seated himself in an arm-chair, and made an effort to **draw** Pearl betwixt his knees. But the child, unaccustomed to the touch or familiarity of any but her mother, escaped through the open window, and stood on the upper step looking like a wild tropical bird, of rich plumage, ready to take flight into the upper air. Mr. Wilson, not a little astonished at this outbreak—for he was a grandfatherly sort of personage, and usually a vast favorite with children—essayed, however, to proceed with the examination.

"Pearl," said he, with great **solemnity**, "thou must take heed to instruction, that so, in due season, thou mayest wear in thy bosom the pearl of great price. Canst thou tell me, my child, who made thee?"

Now Pearl knew well enough who made her; for Hester Prynne, the daughter of a **pious** home, very soon after her talk with the child about her Heavenly Father, had begun to inform her of those truths which the human spirit, at whatever stage of immaturity, imbibes with such eager interest. Pearl, therefore, so large were

PERVERSITY (puhr <u>vuhr</u> sih tee) *n.*
deliberate misbehavior
Synonyms: disobedience, defiance, opposition

INOPPORTUNE (ihn ah pohr <u>toon</u>) *adj.*
inappropriate or unfavorable
Synonym: inconvenient

IMPEL (ihm <u>pehl</u>) *v.* **-ling,-led.**
to urge forward as if driven by a strong moral pressure
Synonyms: push, prompt, incite, instigate

AMISS (uh <u>mihs</u>) *adv.*
improperly, mistakenly; in a defective way
Synonyms: astray, awry; faultily

CONSTRAIN (kuhn <u>strayn</u>) *v.* **-ing,-ed.**
to force, impel; restrain
Synonyms: prompt, urge; restrict, control, calculate

DEPRAVITY (dih <u>praav</u> ih tee) *n.*
sinfulness, moral corruption
Synonyms: decadence, debauchery, degradation

the attainments of her three years' lifetime, could have borne a fair examination in the New England Primer, or the first column of the Westminster Catechism although unacquainted with the outward form of either of those celebrated works. But that **perversity** which all children have more or less of, and of which little Pearl had a tenfold portion, now, at the most **inopportune** moment, took thorough possession of her, and closed her lips, or **impelled** her to speak words **amiss**. After putting her fingers in her mouth, with many ungracious refusals to answer good Mr. Wilson's questions, the child finally announced that she had not been made at all, but had been plucked by her mother off the bush of wild roses that grew by the prison-door.

This fantasy was probably suggested by the near proximity of the Governor's red roses, as Pearl stood outside of the window, together with her recollection of the prison rose-bush, which she had passed in coming hither.

Old Roger Chillingworth, with a smile on his face, whispered something in the young clergyman's ear. Hester Prynne looked at the man of skill, and even then, with her fate hanging in the balance, was startled to perceive what a change had come over his features—how much uglier they were—how his dark complexion seemed to have grown duskier, and his figure more misshapen—since the days when she had familiarly known him. She met his eyes for an instant, but was immediately **constrained** to give all her attention to the scene now going forward.

"This is awful!" cried the Governor, slowly recovering from the astonishment into which Pearl's response had thrown him. "Here is a child of three years old, and she cannot tell who made her! Without question, she is equally in the dark as to her soul, its present **depravity**,

DRAW *v.* **-ing, drew, drawn.**
  1. to pull, drag; to attract
     Synonyms: haul, tow, lug; lure, entice
  2. to move steadily
     Synonyms: proceed, continue, progress

MAGISTRATE (<u>maa</u> juh strayt) *n.*
an official who can administrate laws
     Synonyms: judge, arbiter, authority, marshal

INDEFEASIBLE (ihn dih <u>fee</u> zuh buhl) *adj.*
not able to be voided or undone
     Synonyms: decisive, permanent

REQUITAL (rih <u>kwie</u> tuhl) *n.*
repayment, compensation
     Synonyms: reciprocation, reimbursement

ENDOW (ehn <u>dow</u>) *v.* **-ing,-ed.**
to provide with something naturally or freely; to
furnish with an income or grant
     Synonyms: empower, support; grant, donate,
     bestow

RETRIBUTION (reh trih <u>byoo</u> shuhn) *n.*
something which is justly deserved, such as
repayment or punishment
     Synonyms: vengeance, payback, compensation

IMPULSE (<u>ihm</u> puhls) *n.*
sudden tendency, inclination
     Synonyms: urge, whim

SINGULAR (<u>sihn</u> gyuh luhr) *adj.*
uncommon, peculiar
     Synonyms: unusual, odd, rare, unique, individual

PROVOKE (proh <u>vohk</u>) *v.* **-ing,-ed.**
to cause a response, e.g., anger or disagreement
     Synonyms: aggravate, stimulate, vex, incite

and future destiny! Methinks, gentlemen, we need inquire no further."

Hester caught hold of Pearl, and **drew** her forcibly into her arms, confronting the old Puritan **magistrate** with almost a fierce expression. Alone in the world, cast off by it, and with this sole treasure to keep her heart alive, she felt that she possessed **indefeasible** rights against the world, and was ready to defend them to the death.

"God gave me the child!" cried she. "He gave her in **requital** of all things else, which ye had taken from me. She is my happiness! She is my torture, none the less! Pearl keeps me here in life! Pearl punishes me too! See ye not, she is the scarlet letter, only capable of being loved, and so **endowed** with a million-fold the power of **retribution** for my sin? Ye shall not take her! I will die first!"

"My poor woman," said the not unkind old minister, "the child shall be well cared for—far better than thou canst do it."

"God gave her into my keeping," repeated Hester Prynne, raising her voice almost to a shriek. "I will not give her up!" And here, by a sudden **impulse**, she turned to the young clergyman, Mr. Dimmesdale, at whom, up to this moment, she had seemed hardly so much as once to direct her eyes. "Speak thou for me!" cried she. "Thou wast my pastor, and hadst charge of my soul, and knowest me better than these men can. I will not lose the child! Speak for me! Thou knowest—for thou hast sympathies which these men lack—thou knowest what is in my heart, and what are a mother's rights, and how much the stronger they are when that mother has but her child and the scarlet letter! Look thou to it! I will not lose the child! Look to it!"

At this wild and **singular** appeal, which indicated that Hester Prynne's situation had **provoked** her to little less than madness, the young minister at once came forward, pale, and holding his hand over his heart,

TEMPERAMENT (<u>tehm</u> puhr uh mehnt) *n.*
  an attitude, a manner of behaving
    Synonyms: disposition, mood, mentality

AGITATION (aa gih <u>tay</u> shuhn) *n.*
  uneasiness; commotion, excitement
    Synonyms: restlessness, anxiety; disturbance

EMACIATED (ih <u>may</u> shee ay tihd) *adj.*
  very thin due to hunger or disease, feeble
    Synonyms: bony, gaunt, haggard, skeletal

IGNOMINY (<u>ihg</u> nuh mih nee) *n.*
  disgrace and dishonor
    Synonyms: degradation, debasement

MELANCHOLY (<u>mehl</u> uhn kahl ee) *adj.*
  sad, depressed
    Synonyms: dejected, despondent, woeful, sorrowful

TREMULOUS (<u>treh</u> myoo luhs) *adj.*
  trembling, quivering; fearful, timid
    Synonyms: shaking, palsied; timorous, anxious

UNHALLOWED (un <u>haa</u> lohd) *adj.*
  unholy, immoral
    Synonyms: irreligious, desecrated

RETRIBUTION (reh trih <u>byoo</u> shuhn) *n.*
  something which is justly deserved, such as
  repayment or punishment
    Synonyms: vengeance, payback, compensation

as was his custom whenever his peculiarly nervous **temperament** was thrown into **agitation**. He looked now more careworn and **emaciated** than as we described him at the scene of Hester's public **ignominy**; and whether it were his failing health, or whatever the cause might be, his large dark eyes had a world of pain in their troubled and **melancholy** depth.

["There is truth in what she says," began the minister, with a voice sweet, **tremulous**, but powerful, insomuch that the hall reechoed, and the hollow armor rang with it. "Truth in what Hester says, and in the feeling which inspires her! God gave her the child, and gave her, too, an instinctive knowledge of its nature and requirements—both seemingly so peculiar—which no other mortal being can possess. And, moreover, is there not a quality of awful sacredness in the relation between this mother and this child?"]

"Ay—how is that, good Master Dimmesdale?" interrupted the Governor. "Make that plain, I pray you!"

"It must be even so," resumed the minister. "For, if we deem it otherwise, do we not thereby say that the Heavenly Father, the Creator of all flesh, hath lightly recognized a deed of sin, and made of no account the distinction between **unhallowed** lust and holy love? This child of its father's guilt and its mother's shame hath come from the hand of God, to work in many ways upon her heart, who pleads so earnestly, and with such bitterness of spirit, the right to keep her. It was meant for a blessing, for the one blessing of her life! It was meant, doubtless, as the mother herself hath told us, for a **retribution** too; a torture to be felt at many an unthought-of moment; a pang, a sting, an ever-recurring agony, in the midst of a troubled joy! Hath she not expressed this thought in the garb of the poor child, so forcibly reminding us of that red symbol which sears her bosom?"

SOLEMN (<u>sah</u> luhm) *adj.*
somberly impressive, deeply serious
Synonyms: dignified, earnest, ceremonial

BOON *n.*
a blessing, something to be thankful for
Synonyms: windfall, favor, treasure, benefit

PROVIDENCE (<u>prah</u> vih dehnts) *n.*
divine control and direction by God; preparation
and foresight
Synonyms: fate, destiny, good luck; prudence,
precaution

MAGISTRATE (<u>maa</u> juh strayt) *n.*
an official who can administrate laws
Synonyms: judge, arbiter, authority, marshal

ADDUCE (uh <u>doos</u>) (uh <u>dyoos</u>) *v.* **-ing,-ed.**
to cite as proof; to lead to
Synonyms: allege, propose, urge, promote; further

"Well said, again!" cried good Mr. Wilson. "I feared the woman had no better thought than to make a mountebank of her child!"

"Oh, not so—not so!" continued Mr. Dimmesdale. "She recognizes, believe me, the **solemn** miracle which God hath wrought, in the existence of that child. And may she feel, too—what, methinks, is the very truth—that this **boon** was meant, above all things else, to keep the mother's soul alive, and to preserve her from blacker depths of sin into which Satan might else have sought to plunge her! Therefore it is good for this poor, sinful woman that she hath an infant immortality, a being capable of eternal joy or sorrow, confided to her care—to be trained up by her to righteousness—to remind her, at every moment, of her fall—but yet to teach her, as it were by the Creator's sacred pledge, that, if she bring the child to Heaven, the child also will bring its parent thither! Herein is the sinful mother happier than the sinful father. For Hester Prynne's sake, then, and no less for the poor child's sake, let us leave them as **Providence** hath seen fit to place them!"

"You speak, my friend, with a strange earnestness," said old Roger Chillingworth, smiling at him.

"And there is a weighty import in what my young brother hath spoken," added the Reverend Mr. Wilson. "What say you, worshipful Master Bellingham? Hath he not pleaded well for the poor woman?"

"Indeed hath he," answered the **magistrate**, "and hath **adduced** such arguments that we will even leave the matter as it now stands, so long, at least, as there shall be no further scandal in the woman. Care must be had, nevertheless, to put the child to due and stated examination in the catechism, at thy hands or Master Dimmesdale's. Moreover, at a proper season, the tithing-men must take heed that she go both to school and to meeting."

The young minister, on ceasing to speak, had

TREMULOUS (<u>treh</u> myoo luhs) *adj.*
trembling, quivering; fearful, timid
Synonyms: shaking, palsied; timorous, anxious

VEHEMENCE (<u>vee</u> huh muhnts) *n.*
strength, urgency
Synonyms: fervor, intensity, ferocity, passion, ardor

SENTIMENT (<u>sehn</u> tuh muhnt) *n.*
an attitude, thought, or judgment prompted by feeling
Synonym: emotion

PROFANE (proh <u>fayn</u>) *adj.*
contrary to religion, sacrilegious; impure
Synonyms: secular; blasphemous, vulgar, coarse

PROVIDENCE (<u>prah</u> vih dehnts) *n.*
divine control and direction by God; preparation
and foresight
Synonyms: fate, destiny, good luck; prudence,
precaution

withdrawn a few steps from the group, and stood with his face partially concealed in the heavy folds of the window-curtains; while the shadow of his figure, which the sunlight cast upon the floor, was **tremulous** with the **vehemence** of his appeal. Pearl, that wild and flighty little elf, stole softly towards him, and taking his hand in the grasp of both of her own, laid her cheek against it; a caress so tender, and withal so unobtrusive, that her mother, who was looking on, asked herself, "Is that my Pearl?" Yet she knew that there was love in the child's heart, although it mostly revealed itself in passion, and hardly twice in her lifetime had been softened by such gentleness as now. The minister—for, save the long-sought regards of woman, nothing is sweeter than these marks of childish preference, accorded spontaneously by a spiritual instinct, and therefore seeming to imply in us something truly worthy to be loved—the minister looked round, laid his hand on the child's head, hesitated an instant, and then kissed her brow. Little Pearl's unwonted mood of **sentiment** lasted no longer; she laughed, and went capering down the hall, so airily, that old Mr. Wilson raised a question whether even her tiptoes touched the floor.

"The little baggage hath witchcraft in her, I profess," said he to Mr. Dimmesdale. "She needs no old woman's broomstick to fly withal!"

"A strange child!" remarked old Roger Chillingworth. "It is easy to see the mother's part in her. Would it be beyond a philosopher's research, think ye, gentlemen, to analyze that child's nature, and, from its make and mould, to give a shrewd guess at the father?"

"Nay; it would be sinful, in such a question, to follow the clue of **profane** philosophy," said Mr. Wilson. "Better to fast and pray upon it; and still better, it may be, to leave the mystery as we find it, unless **Providence** reveal it of its own accord. Thereby, every good

DESCEND (dih <u>sehnd</u>) (dee <u>sehnd</u>) *v.* **-ing,-ed.**
to pass from a higher place to a lower place
Synonyms: fall, dismount, gravitate

AVER (uh <u>vuhr</u>) *v.* **-ring,-red.**
to declare to be true, affirm
Synonyms: assert, attest

EXECUTE (ehk sih <u>kyoot</u>) *v.* **-ing,-ed.**
1. to put to death
Synonyms: kill, murder
2. to perform or carry out a task
Synonyms: accomplish, achieve

PHYSIOGNOMY (fih zee <u>ahg</u> nuh mee) *n.*
characteristic facial features; the art of judging one's character from facial features
Synonyms: visage, expression; divination

COMELY (<u>kuhm</u> lee) *adj.*
physically graceful and beautiful
Synonyms: attractive, becoming, pretty

DRAW *v.* **-ing, drew, drawn.**
1. to pull, drag; to attract
Synonyms: haul, tow, lug; lure, entice
2. to move steadily
Synonyms: proceed, continue, progress

Christian man hath a title to show a father's kindness towards the poor, deserted babe."

The affair being so satisfactorily concluded, Hester Prynne, with Pearl, departed from the house. As they **descended** the steps, it is **averred** that the lattice of a chamber-window was thrown open, and forth into the sunny day was thrust the face of Mistress Hibbins, Governor Bellingham's bitter-tempered sister, and the same who, a few years later, was **executed** as a witch.

"Hist, hist!" said she, while her ill-omened **physiognomy** seemed to cast a shadow over the cheerful newness of the house. "Wilt thou go with us tonight? There will be a merry company in the forest; and I wellnigh promised the Black Man that **comely** Hester Prynne should make one."

"Make my excuse to him, so please you!" answered Hester, with a triumphant smile. "I must tarry at home, and keep watch over my little Pearl. Had they taken her from me, I would willingly have gone with thee into the forest, and signed my name in the Black Man's book too, and that with mine own blood!"

"We shall have thee there anon!" said the witch-lady, frowning, as she **drew** back her head.

But here—if we suppose this interview betwixt Mistress Hibbins and Hester Prynne to be authentic, and not a parable—was already an illustration of the young minister's argument against sundering the relation of a fallen mother to the offspring of her frailty. Even thus early had the child saved her from Satan's snare.

APPELLATION (aa puhl <u>ay</u> shuhn) *n.*
a title or name
Synonyms: denomination, designation, moniker, tag

RESOLVE (rih <u>sahlv</u>) *v.* **-ing,-ed.**
to determine or to make a firm decision about
Synonyms: solve, decide, clear up

IGNOMINIOUS (ihg nuh <u>mih</u> nee uhs) *adj.*
disgraceful and dishonorable
Synonyms: despicable, degrading, debasing

PERILOUS (<u>pehr</u> uh luhs) *adj.*
full of danger
Synonyms: risky, hazardous, unsafe

INFAMY (<u>ihn</u> fuh mee) *n.*
reputation for bad deeds
Synonyms: disgrace, dishonor, shame

VINDICATE (<u>vihn</u> dih kayt) *v.* **-ing,-ed.**
to clear of blame; support a claim
Synonyms: justify, acquit, exonerate, exculpate

The Leech
Chapter 9

Under the **appellation** of Roger Chillingworth, the reader will remember, was hidden another name, which its former wearer had **resolved** should never more be spoken. It has been related how, in the crowd that witnessed Hester Prynne's **ignominious** exposure, stood a man, elderly, travel-worn, who, just emerging from the **perilous** wilderness, beheld the woman, in whom he hoped to find embodied the warmth and cheerfulness of home, set up as a type of sin before the people. Her matronly fame was trodden under all men's feet. **Infamy** was babbling around her in the public market-place. For her kindred, should the tidings ever reach them, and for the companions of her unspotted life, there remained nothing but the contagion of her dishonor—which would not fail to be distributed in strict accordance and proportion with the intimacy and sacredness of their previous relationship. Then why—since the choice was with himself—should the individual, whose connection with the fallen woman had been the most intimate and sacred of them all, come forward to **vindicate** his claim to an inheritance so little desirable? He **resolved** not to be <u>pilloried</u> beside her on her pedestal of shame. Unknown to all but Hester Prynne, and possessing the lock and key of her silence, he chose to withdraw his name from the roll of mankind, and, as regarded his former ties and interests, to vanish out of life as completely as if he indeed lay at the bottom of the ocean, whither rumor had long ago consigned him. This purpose once effected, new interests would immediately spring up, and likewise a new purpose; dark, it is true, if

FACULTY (faa kuhl tee) *n.*
the ability to act or do
Synonyms: aptitude, capability, sense, skill

RESOLVE (rih sahlv) *n.*
determination, a firm decision
Synonyms: dedication, perseverance, willpower

ZEAL (zeel) *n.*
passion or devotion to a cause
Synonyms: fanaticism, enthusiasm

EMIGRANT (eh mih graant) *n.*
a person from another country or land
Synonym: foreigner

PIETY (pie eh tee) *n.*
devoutness
Synonyms: devotion, reverence

MANIFEST (maan uh fehst) *v.* **-ing,-ed.**
to make evident or certain by display
Synonyms: exhibit, showcase, expose

PONDEROUS (pahn duhr uhs) *adj.*
weighty, heavy, large
Synonyms: hefty, massive, cumbersome, unwieldy

IMPOSING (ihm poh zihng) *adj.*
impressive in size or appearance
Synonyms: magisterial, commanding, grand, striking

MULTITUDE (muhl tuh tood) *n.*
the state of being many, a great number; a crowd
Synonyms: mass, myriad; throng

HETEROGENEOUS (heh tuh ruh jee nee uhs) *adj.*
composed of unlike parts, different, diverse
Synonyms: miscellaneous, mixed, varied, motley

ELIXIR (ih lihk suhr) *n.*
a substance capable of sustaining life indefinitely, a
medicinal concoction
Synonyms: cure-all, magic potion; solution,
remedy

not guilty, but of force enough to engage the full strength of his **faculties**.

In pursuance of this **resolve**, he took up his residence in the <u>Puritan</u> town as Roger Chillingworth, without other introduction than the learning and intelligence of which he possessed more than a common measure. As his studies, at a previous period of his life, had made him extensively acquainted with the medical science of the day, it was as a physician that he presented himself, and as such was cordially received. Skillful men, of the medical and <u>chirurgical</u> profession, were of rare occurrence in the colony. They seldom, it would appear, partook of the religious **zeal** that brought other **emigrants** across the Atlantic. In their researches into the human frame, it may be that the higher and more subtile **faculties** of such men were materialized, and that they lost the spiritual view of existence amid the intricacies of that wondrous mechanism, which seemed to involve art enough to comprise all of life within itself. At all events, the health of the good town of Boston, so far as medicine had aught to do with it, had hitherto lain in the guardianship of an aged deacon and apothecary, whose **piety** and godly deportment were stronger testimonials in his favor than any that he could have produced in the shape of a diploma. The only surgeon was one who combined the occasional exercise of that noble art with the daily and habitual flourish of a razor. To such a professional body Roger Chillingworth was a brilliant acquisition. He soon **manifested** his familiarity with the **ponderous** and **imposing** machinery of antique physic; in which every remedy contained a **multitude** of far-fetched and **heterogeneous** ingredients, as elaborately compounded as if the proposed result had been the **elixir** of Life. In his Indian captivity, moreover, he had gained much knowledge of the properties of native herbs and roots; nor did he conceal from his patients, that these simple medicines,

BOON *n.*
a blessing, something to be thankful for
Synonyms: windfall, favor, treasure, benefit

EXEMPLARY (ihg <u>zehm</u> pluhr ee) *adj.*
excellent, perfect
Synonyms: commendable, meritorious, ideal,
superlative, admirable

DIVINE (dih <u>vien</u>) *n.*
a clergyman
Synonyms: theologian, churchman, cleric

RENOWN (rih <u>nown</u>) *n.*
fame, widespread acclaim
Synonyms: eminence, distinction, prestige,
standing, celebrity

FERVENT (<u>fuhr</u> vehnt) *adj.*
passionate, intense, zealous
Synonyms: vehement, eager, enthusiastic, avid

SCRUPULOUS (<u>skroop</u> yuh luhs) *adj.*
careful and precise, honest
Synonyms: conscientious, painstaking, meticulous,
punctilious, principled

PAROCHIAL (puh <u>roh</u> kee uhl) *adj.*
relating to a parish; of limited scope or outlook
Synonyms: religious; narrow, restricted, insular

OBSCURE (uhb <u>skyoor</u>) *v.* **-ing,-ed.**
to make dim or unclear
Synonyms: hide, conceal, blur, veil

HUMILITY (hyoo <u>mihl</u> ih tee) *n.*
humbleness
Synonyms: modesty, reserve, lowliness

PROVIDENCE (<u>prah</u> vih dehnts) *n. (See page 230.)*

EMACIATED (ih <u>may</u> shee ay tihd) *adj.*
very thin due to hunger or disease, feeble
Synonyms: bony, gaunt, haggard, skeletal

MELANCHOLY (<u>mehl</u> uhn kahl ee) *adj.*
sad, depressed
Synonyms: dejected, despondent, woeful, sorrowful

Nature's **boon** to the untutored savage, had quite as large a share of his own confidence as the European pharmacopeia, which so many learned doctors had spent centuries in elaborating.

This learned stranger was **exemplary**, as regarded, at least, the outward forms of a religious life, and, early after his arrival, had chosen for his spiritual guide the Reverend Mr. Dimmesdale. The young **divine**, whose scholarlike **renown** still lived in Oxford, was considered by his more **fervent** admirers as little less than a heavenly-ordained apostle, destined, should he live and labor for the ordinary term of life, to do as great deeds for the now feeble New England Church, as the early Fathers had achieved for the infancy of the Christian faith. About this period, however, the health of Mr. Dimmesdale had evidently begun to fail. By those best acquainted with his habits, the paleness of the young minister's cheek was accounted for by his too earnest devotion to study, his **scrupulous** fulfilment of **parochial** duty, and, more than all, by the fasts and vigils of which he made a frequent practice, in order to keep the grossness of this earthly state from clogging and **obscuring** his spiritual lamp. Some declared, that, if Mr. Dimmesdale were really going to die, it was cause enough that the world was not worthy to be any longer trodden by his feet. He himself, on the other hand, with characteristic **humility**, avowed his belief, that, if **Providence** should see fit to remove him, it would be because of his own unworthiness to perform its humblest mission here on earth. With all this difference of opinion as to the cause of his decline, there could be no question of the fact. His form grew **emaciated**; his voice, though still rich and sweet, had a certain **melancholy** prophecy of decay in it; he was often observed, on any slight alarm or other sudden accident, to put his hand

QUERY (<u>kweh</u> ree) *n.*
question
Synonyms: inquiry, interrogation

EMINENT (<u>ehm</u> uh nuhnt) *adj.*
celebrated, distinguished, outstanding, towering
Synonyms: noted, famous, prominent, important,
illustrious

INCLINE (ihn <u>klien</u>) *v.* **-ing,-ed.**
to have a specific tendency, to be predisposed
Synonyms: lean toward, influence, impel, prefer

PROVIDENTIAL (prah vih <u>dehnt</u> shuhl) *adj.*
resulting from divine control or direction by God
Synonyms: heaven-sent, miraculous

OPPORTUNE (ah pohr <u>toon</u>) *adj.*
appropriate, favorable
Synonyms: seasonable, timely, advantageous

COUNTENANCE (<u>kown</u> tuh nuhns) *v.* **-ing,-ed.**
to approve or support, give permission
Synonyms: condone, permit, consent

MANIFEST (<u>maan</u> uh fehst) *v.* **-ing,-ed.**
to make evident or certain by display
Synonyms: exhibit, showcase, expose

over his heart, with first a flush and then a paleness, indicative of pain.

Such was the young clergyman's condition, and so imminent the prospect that his dawning light would be extinguished, all untimely, when Roger Chillingworth made his advent to the town. His first entry on the scene, few people could tell whence, dropping down, as it were, out of the sky, or starting from the nether earth, had an aspect of mystery, which was easily heightened to the miraculous. He was now known to be a man of skill; it was observed that he gathered herbs, and the blossoms of wild-flowers, and dug up roots, and plucked off twigs from the forest trees, like one acquainted with hidden virtues in what was valueless to common eyes. He was heard to speak of Sir Kenelm Digby, and other famous men—whose scientific attainments were esteemed hardly less than supernatural—as having been his correspondents or associates. Why, with such rank in the learned world, had he come hither? What could he, whose sphere was in great cities, be seeking in the wilderness? In answer to this **query**, a rumor gained ground—and, however absurd, was entertained by some very sensible people—that Heaven had wrought an absolute miracle by transporting an **eminent** Doctor of Physic from a German university bodily through the air and setting him down at the door of Mr. Dimmesdale's study! Individuals of wiser faith, indeed, who knew that Heaven promotes its purposes without aiming at the stage-effect of what is called miraculous interposition, were **inclined** to see a **providential** hand in Roger Chillingworth's so **opportune** arrival.

This idea was **countenanced** by the strong interest which the physician ever **manifested** in the young clergyman; he attached himself to him as a parishioner, and sought to win a friendly regard and confidence from his naturally reserved sensibility. He expressed great alarm

DESPONDENT (dih <u>spahn</u> duhnt) *adj.*
feeling discouraged and dejected
Synonyms: sad, depressed, desolate, forlorn

IMPORTUNATE (ihm <u>pohr</u> chuh niht) *adj.*
pleading; extremely urgent; persistant
Synonyms: craving, beseeching; earnest, imperative;
troublesome

REPEL (rih <u>pehl</u>) *v.* **-ling,-led.**
to rebuff, repulse; disgust, offend
Synonyms: reject, spurn, parry; nauseate, revolt

ENTREATY (ehn <u>tree</u> tee) *n.*
a plea or request
Synonyms: imploration, prayer, petition

TREMULOUS (<u>treh</u> myoo luhs) *adj.*
trembling, quivering; fearful, timid
Synonyms: shaking, palsied; timorous, anxious

SOLEMNLY (<u>sah</u> luhm lee) *adv.*
seriously or somberly
Synonyms: quietly, earnestly, ceremonially

PROVIDENCE (<u>prah</u> vih dehnts) *n.*
divine control and direction by God; preparation
and foresight
Synonyms: fate, destiny, good luck; prudence,
precaution

MANIFESTLY (<u>maan</u> uh fehst lee) *adv.*
evidently, certainly
Synonyms: clearly, apparently, obviously

IMPOSED (ihm <u>pohzd</u>) *adj.*
forced, fake, obligatory, compulsory
Synonyms: dictated, decreed, demanded, ordained

at his pastor's state of health, but was anxious to attempt the cure, and, if early undertaken, seemed not **despondent** of a favorable result. The elders, the deacons, the motherly dames, and the young and fair maidens of Mr. Dimmesdale's flock, were alike **importunate** that he should make trial of the physician's frankly offered skill. Mr. Dimmesdale gently **repelled** their **entreaties**.

"I need no medicine," said he.

But how could the young minister say so, when, with every successive Sabbath, his cheek was paler and thinner, and his voice more **tremulous** than before—when it had now become a constant habit, rather than a casual gesture, to press his hand over his heart? Was he weary of his labors? Did he wish to die? These questions were **solemnly** propounded to Mr. Dimmesdale by the elder ministers of Boston and the deacons of his church, who, to use their own phrase, "dealt with him" on the sin of rejecting the aid which **Providence** so **manifestly** held out. He listened in silence, and finally promised to confer with the physician.

"Were it God's will," said the Reverend Mr. Dimmesdale, when, in fulfilment of this pledge, he requested old Roger Chillingworth's professional advice, "I could be well content that my labors, and my sorrows, and my sins, and my pains, should shortly end with me, and what is earthly of them be buried in my grave, and the spiritual go with me to my eternal state, rather than that you should put your skill to the proof in my behalf."

"Ah," replied Roger Chillingworth, with that quietness which, whether **imposed** or natural, marked all his deportment, "it is thus that a young clergyman is apt to speak. Youthful men, not having taken a deep root, give up their hold of life so easily! And saintly men, who walk with God on earth, would fain be away, to walk with him on the golden pavements of the New Jerusalem."

BALM (bahm) *n.*
a soothing, healing influence or substance
Synonyms: succor, comfort, palliative, anodyne, salve

SOLEMN (<u>sah</u> luhm) *adj.*
somberly impressive, deeply serious
Synonyms: dignified, earnest, ceremonial

MODERATE (<u>mah</u> duhr iht) *adj.*
average, reasonable
Synonyms: mediocre, temperate

REVERENTIAL (rehv uhr <u>ehn</u> shuhl) *adj.*
expressing great awe and respect
Synonyms: faithful, deferential

SENTIMENT (<u>sehn</u> tuh muhnt) *n.*
an attitude, thought, or judgment prompted by feeling
Synonym: emotion

IMPEL (ihm <u>pehl</u>) *v.* **-ling,-led.**
to urge forward as if driven by a strong moral pressure
Synonyms: push, prompt, incite, instigate

CREED (kreed) *n.*
a statement of belief or principle
Synonyms: tenet, credo, doctrine, dogma, precept

LIBERAL (<u>lihb</u> uh ruhl) (<u>lihb</u> ruhl) *adj.*
tolerant, broad-minded; generous, lavish
Synonyms: progressive, permissive; bounteous, munificent

TREMULOUS (<u>treh</u> myoo luhs) *adj.*
trembling, quivering; fearful, timid
Synonyms: shaking, palsied; timorous, anxious

"Nay," rejoined the young minister, putting his hand to his heart, with a flush of pain flitting over his brow, "were I worthier to walk there, I could be better content to toil here."

"Good men ever interpret themselves too meanly," said the physician.

In this manner, the mysterious old Roger Chillingworth became the medical adviser of the Reverend Mr. Dimmesdale. As not only the disease interested the physician, but he was strongly moved to look into the character and qualities of the patient, these two men, so different in age, came gradually to spend much time together. For the sake of the minister's health, and to enable the leech to gather plants with healing **balm** in them, they took long walks on the sea-shore, or in the forest; mingling various talk with the plash and murmur of the waves, and the **solemn** wind-anthem among the tree-tops. Often, likewise, one was the guest of the other in his place of study and retire-ment. There was a fascination for the minister in the company of the man of science, in whom he recognized an intellectual cultivation of no **moderate** depth or scope; together with a range and freedom of ideas that he would have vainly looked for among the members of his own profession. In truth, he was startled, if not shocked, to find this attribute in the physician. Mr. Dimmesdale was a true priest, a true religionist, with the **reverential sentiment** largely developed, and an order of mind that **impelled** itself powerfully along the track of a **creed**, and wore its passage continually deeper with the lapse of time. In no state of society would he have been what is called a man of **liberal** views; it would always be essential to his peace to feel the pressure of a faith about him, supporting, while it confined him within its iron framework. Not the less, however, though with a **tremulous** enjoyment, did he feel the occasional

MEDIUM (<u>mee</u> dee uhm) *n.*

a substance or object that is used to transmit or
accomplish something

Synonyms: means, instrument, vehicle, mechanism

STIFLED (<u>stie</u> fuhld) *adj.*

smothering or suffocating; suppressed or held back

Synonyms: stuffy; muted, muffled, restrained

ORTHODOX (<u>ohr</u> thuh dahks) *adj.*

accepted, conservative, traditional

Synonyms: conventional, standard, customary

SCRUTINIZE (<u>skroot</u> ihn iez) *v.* **-ing,-ed.**

to observe carefully

Synonyms: examine, study, survey

NOVELTY (<u>nah</u> vuhl tee) *n.*

something new and original

Synonyms: surprise, change, innovation

TINGE (tihnj) *v.* **-ing,-ed.**

to affect or modify in character; to color with a
slight shade, stain, odor, or taste

Synonyms: tarnish, sully, mar; dye, imbue, hue, tint

INFIRMITY (ihn <u>fuhr</u> mih tee) *n.*

weakness; disease, ailment

Synonyms: frailty; illness, affliction

DELVE (dehlv) *v.* **-ing,-ed.**

to search or explore intensely; to dig

Synonyms: probe, examine, research; shovel,
excavate

PRY (prie) *v.* **-ing,-ied.**

to look closely at; to meddle; force open

Synonyms: probe; snoop, nose, spy; lever

SAGACITY (suh <u>gaa</u> sih tee) *n.*

shrewdness, intelligence

Synonyms: perspicacity, wisdom, knowledge

INTUITION (ihn too <u>ih</u> shihn) *n.*

instinct, innate knowledge that is not learned

Synonyms: insight, clairvoyance, premonition

relief of looking at the universe through the **medium** of another kind of intellect than those with which he habitually held converse. It was as if a window were thrown open, admitting a freer atmosphere into the close and **stifled** study, where his life was wasting itself away, amid lamplight, or obstructed day-beams, and the musty fragrance, be it sensual or moral, that exhales from books. But the air was too fresh and chill to be long breathed with comfort. So the minister, and the physician with him, withdrew again within the limits of what their church defined as **orthodox**.

Thus Roger Chillingworth **scrutinized** his patient carefully, both as he saw him in his ordinary life, keeping an accustomed pathway in the range of thoughts familiar to him, and as he appeared when thrown amidst other moral scenery, the **novelty** of which might call out something new to the surface of his character. He deemed it essential, it would seem, to know the man, before attempting to do him good. Wherever there is a heart and an intellect, the diseases of the physical frame are **tinged** with the peculiarities of these. In Arthur Dimmesdale, thought and imagination were so active, and sensibility so intense, that the bodily **infirmity** would be likely to have its groundwork there. So Roger Chillingworth—the man of skill, the kind and friendly physician—strove to go deep into his patient's bosom, **delving** among his principles, **prying** into his recollections, and probing everything with a cautious touch, like a treasure-seeker in a dark cavern. Few secrets can escape an investigator, who has opportunity and license to undertake such a quest, and skill to follow it up. A man burdened with a secret should especially avoid the intimacy of his physician. If the latter possess native **sagacity**, and a nameless something more—let us call it **intuition**; if he show no intrusive egotism, nor disagreeably prominent characteristics of his own; if he have the power, which must be

SAT Vocabulary

AFFINITY (uh <u>fih</u> nih tee) *n.*
similarity, resemblance; fondness, liking
Synonyms: agreement; partiality, penchant, inclination

TUMULT (<u>tuh</u> muhlt) *n.*
state of confusion, agitation
Synonyms: disturbance, turmoil, din, commotion

INARTICULATE (ihn ahr <u>tihk</u> yuh liht) *adj.*
tongue-tied, unable to speak clearly, without speech
Synonyms: incomprehensible, unintelligible

INEVITABLE (ihn <u>ehv</u> ih tuh buhl) *adj.*
certain, unavoidable
Synonyms: inescapable, sure, predictable

EBB (ehb) *n.*
a period of decline or recession; the reflux of the tide
Synonyms: retreat, abatement, waning, withdrawal; flow

born with him, to bring his mind into such **affinity** with his patient's, that this last shall unawares have spoken what he imagines himself only to have thought; if such revelations be received without **tumult**, and acknowledged not so often by an uttered sympathy as by silence, an **inarticulate** breath, and here and there a word, to indicate that all is understood; if to these qualifications of a confidant be joined the advantages afforded by his recognized character as a physician—then, at some **inevitable** moment, will the soul of the sufferer be dissolved, and flow forth in a dark, but transparent stream, bringing all its mysteries into the daylight.

Roger Chillingworth possessed all, or most, of the attributes above enumerated. Nevertheless, time went on; a kind of intimacy, as we have said, grew up between these two cultivated minds, which had as wide a field as the whole sphere of human thought and study to meet upon; they discussed every topic of ethics and religion, of public affairs and private character; they talked much, on both sides, of matters that seemed personal to themselves; and yet no secret, such as the physician fancied must exist there, ever stole out of the minister's consciousness into his companion's ear. The latter had his suspicions, indeed, that even the nature of Mr. Dimmesdale's bodily disease had never fairly been revealed to him. It was a strange reserve!

After a time, at a hint from Roger Chillingworth, the friends of Mr. Dimmesdale effected an arrangement by which the two were lodged in the same house; so that every **ebb** and flow of the minister's life-tide might pass under the eye of his anxious and attached physician. There was much joy throughout the town when this greatly desirable object was attained. It was held to be the best possible measure for the young clergyman's welfare; unless, indeed, as often urged by such as felt authorized to do so, he had selected some one of the many blooming

PREVAIL (prih <u>vayl</u>) *v.* **-ing,-ed.**
to persuade; to overcome; to succeed lastingly
Synonyms: induce, convince; dominate, triumph;
persist, endure

UNSAVORY (uhn <u>say</u> vuhr ee) *adj.*
not agreeable in taste or smell
Synonyms: unappetizing, flavorless, rancid, gross

SAGACIOUS (suh <u>gay</u> shuhs) *adj.*
shrewd, intelligent
Synonyms: astute, perspicacious, wise

BENEVOLENT (buh <u>neh</u> vuh luhnt) *adj.*
kind, compassionate
Synonyms: charitable, altruistic, beneficent,
generous, good

CONCORD (<u>kahn</u> kohrd) *n.*
agreement or harmony
Synonyms: accord, concurrence, consensus,
solidarity, concert

PATERNAL (puh <u>tuhr</u> nuhl) *adj.* *(See page 208.)*
REVERENTIAL (rehv uhr <u>ehn</u> shuhl) *adj.* *(See page 244.)*
PIOUS (<u>pie</u> uhs) *adj.* *(See page 220.)*
VENERABLE (<u>veh</u> nehr uh buhl) *adj.* *(See page 214.)*
ADAPTED (uh <u>daap</u> tihd) *adj.* *(See page 202.)*
PROPHET (<u>prah</u> feht) *n.*
a person who has the ability to foretell events
Synonyms: clairvoyant, predictor, seer, oracle

DENOUNCING (dih <u>nown</u> sihng) *adj.*
accusing, blaming
Synonyms: criticizing, condemning, vilifying, branding

ERUDITION (ehr yuh <u>dih</u> shuhn) (ehr uh <u>dih</u> shuhn) *n.*
serious, scholarly learning
Synonyms: knowledge, education

DIVINE (dih <u>vien</u>) *n.* *(See page 238.)*
VILIFY (<u>vih</u> luh fie) *v.* **-ing,-ied.**
to slander, defame
Synonyms: abuse, bad-mouth, disparage

CONSTRAIN (kuhn <u>strayn</u>) *v.* **-ing,-ed.**
to force, impel; restrain
Synonyms: prompt, urge; restrict, control, calculate

AVAIL (uh <u>vayl</u>) *v.* **-ing,-ed.** *(See page 160.)*

damsels, spiritually devoted to him, to become his devoted wife. This latter step, however, there was no present prospect that Arthur Dimmesdale would be **prevailed** upon to take; he rejected all suggestions of the kind, as if priestly celibacy were one of his articles of church-discipline. Doomed by his own choice, therefore, as Mr. Dimmesdale so evidently was, to eat his **unsavory** morsel always at another's board, and endure the lifelong chill which must be his lot who seeks to warm himself only at another's fireside, it truly seemed that this **sagacious**, experienced, **benevolent** old physician, with his **concord** of **paternal** and **reverential** love for the young pastor, was the very man of all mankind, to be constantly within reach of his voice.

The new abode of the two friends was with a **pious** widow, of good social rank, who dwelt in a house covering pretty nearly the site on which the **venerable** structure of King's Chapel has since been built. It had the graveyard, originally Isaac Johnson's home-field, on one side, and so was well **adapted** to call up serious reflections, suited to their respective employments, in both minister and man of physic. The motherly care of the good widow assigned to Mr. Dimmesdale a front apartment, with a sunny exposure, and heavy window-curtains to create a noontide shadow, when desirable. The walls were hung round with tapestry, said to be from the Gobelin looms, and at all events, representing the Scriptural story of David and Bathsheba, and Nathan the **prophet**, in colors still unfaded, but which made the fair woman of the scene almost as grimly picturesque as the woe-**denouncing** seer. Here, the pale clergyman piled up his library, rich with parchment-bound folios of the Fathers, and the lore of Rabbis, and monkish **erudition**, of which the Protestant **divines**, even while they **vilified** and decried that class of writers, were yet **constrained** often to **avail** themselves. On the other side of the house, old Roger

DISTILLING (dihs tih lihng) *adj.*
relating to the evaporation and collection of a liquid
by condensing as a means of purifying
Synonyms: clarifying, vaporizing, precipitating

ALCHEMIST (<u>aal</u> kuh mihst) *n.*
one who practices the medieval chemical philosophy
aimed at trying to change metal into gold, curing all
diseases, and lengthening human life
Synonyms: doctor, magician, scientist

COMMODIOUSNESS (kuh <u>moh</u> dee uhs nehs) *n.*
roominess, spaciousness
Synonym: largeness

BESTOW (bih <u>stoh</u>) *v.* **-ing,-ed.** *(See page 162.)*

DISCERNING (dihs <u>uhr</u> nihng) *adj.*
perceptive
Synonyms: observant, attentive, watchful

INTIMATE (<u>ihn</u> tuh mayt) *v.* **-ing,-ed.**
to hint or suggest obscurely
Synonyms: implicate, allude, insinuate

PROVIDENCE (<u>prah</u> vih dehnts) *n.* *(See page 242.)*

MULTITUDE (<u>muhl</u> tuh tood) *n.*
a crowd; the state of being many, a great number
Synonyms: throng; mass, myriad

INTUITION (ihn too <u>ih</u> shihn) *n.* *(See page 246.)*

PROFOUND (pruh <u>fownd</u>) (proh <u>fownd</u>) *adj.*
deep; having intellectual depth
Synonyms: bottomless; serious, thorough, weighty

REFUTATION (rih fyoo <u>tay</u> shuhn) *n.*
contradiction or defense of something or someone
Synonyms: denial, refusal, disproof, objection

CONJURER (<u>kahn</u> juhr uhr) *n.*
one who summons a devil or spirit by invocation,
one who practices magic or witchcraft
Synonyms: sorcerer, magician, illusionist

IMPLICATE (<u>ihm</u> pluh kayt) *v.* **-ing,-ed.**
to involve in a crime, incriminate
Synonyms: embroil, ensnare

Chillingworth arranged his study and laboratory; not such as a modern man of science would reckon even tolerably complete, but provided with a **distilling** apparatus, and the means of compounding drugs and chemicals, which the practiced **alchemist** knew well how to turn to purpose. With such **commodiousness** of situation, these two learned persons sat themselves down, each in his own domain, yet familiarly passing from one apartment to the other, and **bestowing** a mutual and not incurious inspection into one another's business.

And the Reverend Arthur Dimmesdale's best **discerning** friends, as we have **intimated**, very reasonably imagined that the hand of **Providence** had done all this, for the purpose—besought in so many public, and domestic, and secret prayers—of restoring the young minister to health. But—it must now be said—another portion of the community had latterly begun to take its own view of the relation betwixt Mr. Dimmesdale and the mysterious old physician. When an uninstructed **multitude** attempts to see with its eyes, it is exceedingly apt to be deceived. When, however, it forms its judgment, as it usually does, on the **intuitions** of its great and warm heart, the conclusions thus attained are often so **profound** and so unerring, as to possess the character of truths supernaturally revealed. The people, in the case of which we speak, could justify its prejudice against Roger Chillingworth by no fact or argument worthy of serious **refutation**. There was an aged handicraftsman, it is true, who had been a citizen of London at the period of Sir Thomas Overbury's murder, now some thirty years agone; he testified to having seen the physician, under some other name which the narrator of the story had now forgotten, in company with Doctor Forman, the famous old **conjurer**, who was **implicated** in the affair of Overbury. Two or three individuals hinted, that the man of skill, during his Indian captivity, had enlarged his

SOBER (<u>soh</u> buhr) *adj.*
 self-controlled; serious; not intoxicated
  Synonyms: subdued, sedate; grave; dry, not drunk

AFFIRM (uh <u>fihrm</u>) *v.* **-ing,-ed.**
 to state positively, to assert as valid or confirmed
  Synonyms: declare, avow, maintain

INFERNAL (ihn <u>fuhr</u> nuhl) *adj.*
 relating to the dead or hell; devilish
  Synonyms: damned, accursed; fiendish, awful,
  malicious

VISAGE (<u>vih</u> sihj) *n.*
 the appearance of a person or place, face
  Synonyms: expression, look, style, manner

DIFFUSED (dih <u>fyoozd</u>) *adj.*
 widely spread out
  Synonyms: scattered, dispersed

SANCTITY (<u>saank</u> tih tee) *n.*
 holiness, saintliness
  Synonyms: devoutness, divinity, piety

DIABOLICAL (die uh <u>bah</u> lih kuhl) *adj.*
 characteristic of the devil
  Synonyms: fiendish, wicked, evil

medical attainments by joining in the <u>incantations</u> of the savage priests, who were universally acknowledged to be powerful enchanters, often performing seemingly miraculous cures by their skill in the black art. A large number—and many of these were persons of such **sober** sense and practical observation that their opinions would have been valuable in other matters—**affirmed** that Roger Chillingworth's aspect had undergone a remarkable change while he had dwelt in town, and especially since his abode with Mr. Dimmesdale. At first, his expression had been calm, meditative, scholar-like. Now, there was something ugly and evil in his face, which they had not previously noticed, and which grew still the more obvious to sight the oftener they looked upon him. According to the vulgar idea, the fire in his laboratory had been brought from the lower regions, and was fed with **infernal** fuel; and so, as might be expected, his **visage** was getting sooty with the smoke.

To sum up the matter, it grew to be a widely **diffused** opinion, that the Reverend Arthur Dimmesdale, like many other personages of especial **sanctity**, in all ages of the Christian world, was haunted either by Satan himself, or Satan's <u>emissary</u>, in the guise of old Roger Chillingworth. This **diabolical** agent had the divine permission, for a season, to burrow into the clergyman's intimacy, and plot against his soul. No sensible man, it was confessed, could doubt on which side the victory would turn. The people looked, with an unshaken hope, to see the minister come forth out of the conflict <u>transfigured</u> with the glory which he would unquestionably win. Meanwhile, nevertheless, it was sad to think of the perchance mortal agony through which he must struggle towards his triumph.

Alas, to judge from the gloom and terror in the depths of the poor minister's eyes, the battle was a sore one, and the victory anything but secure!

TEMPERAMENT (<u>tehm</u> puhr uh mehnt) *n.*
a manner of behaving, an attitude
Synonyms: disposition, mood, mentality

INTEGRITY (ihn <u>tehg</u> rih tee) *n.*
decency, honesty, wholeness
Synonyms: honor, probity, rectitude, virtue

DELVE (dehlv) *v.* **-ing,-ed.**
to dig; to search or explore intensely
Synonyms: shovel, excavate; probe, examine, research

OMINOUS (<u>ah</u> mihn uhs) *adj.*
menacing, threatening, indicating misfortune
Synonyms: inauspicious, sinister, dire, baleful

The Leech and His Patient
Chapter 10

Old Roger Chillingworth, throughout life, had been calm in **temperament**, kindly, though not of warm affections, but ever, and in all his relations with the world, a pure and upright man. He had begun an investigation, as he imagined, with the severe and equal **integrity** of a judge, desirous only of truth, even as if the question involved no more than the air-drawn lines and figures of a geometrical problem, instead of human passions and wrongs inflicted on himself. But, as he proceeded, a terrible fascination, a kind of fierce, though still calm, necessity seized the old man within its gripe and never set him free again until he had done all its bidding. He now dug into the poor clergyman's heart, like a miner searching for gold; or, rather, like a sexton **delving** into a grave, possibly in quest of a jewel that had been buried on the dead man's bosom, but likely to find nothing save mortality and corruption. Alas for his own soul, if these were what he sought!

Sometimes, a light glimmered out of the physician's eyes, burning blue and **ominous**, like the reflection of a furnace, or, let us say, like one of those gleams of ghastly fire that darted from Bunyan's awful doorway in the hillside and quivered on the pilgrim's face. The soil where this dark miner was working had perchance shown indications that encouraged him.

"This man," said he, at one such moment, to himself, "pure as they deem him—all spiritual as he seems—hath inherited a strong animal nature from his father or his mother. Let us dig a little further in the direction of this vein!"

ASPIRATION (aa spuhr <u>ay</u> shuhn) *n.*
a great hope or goal
Synonyms: intention, purpose, expectation

SENTIMENT (<u>sehn</u> tuh muhnt) *n.*
an attitude, thought, or judgment prompted by feeling
Synonym: emotion

PIETY (<u>pie</u> eh tee) *n.*
devoutness
Synonyms: devotion, reverence

STEALTHILY (<u>stehl</u> thuh lee) *adv.*
quietly and cautiously
Synonyms: furtively, secretly, surreptitiously,
covertly

WARY (<u>way</u> ree) *adj.*
careful, cautious
Synonyms: watchful, vigilant, alert, guarded,
suspicious

INTUITION (ihn too <u>ih</u> shihn) *n.*
instinct, innate knowledge that is not learned
Synonyms: insight, clairvoyance, premonition

INIMICAL (ih <u>nihm</u> ih kuhl) *adj.*
hostile, unfriendly
Synonyms: injurious, harmful, adverse, antagonistic

INTUITIVE (ihn <u>too</u> ih tihv) *adj.*
instinctive, untaught
Synonyms: visceral, innate

MORBIDNESS (<u>mohr</u> bihd nehs) *n.*
the quality of having an unhealthy mentality
Synonyms: unwholesomeness, pessimism, dread

Then, after long search into the minister's dim interior, and turning over many precious materials, in the shape of high **aspirations** for the welfare of his race, warm love of souls, pure **sentiments**, natural **piety**, strengthened by thought and study, and illuminated by revelation—all of which invaluable gold was perhaps no better than rubbish to the seeker—he would turn back discouraged, and begin his quest towards another point. He groped along as **stealthily**, with as cautious a tread, and as **wary** an outlook, as a thief entering a chamber where a man lies only half asleep—or, it may be, broad awake—with purpose to steal the very treasure which this man guards as the apple of his eye. In spite of his premeditated carefulness, the floor would now and then creak; his garments would rustle; the shadow of his presence, in a forbidden proximity, would be thrown across his victim. In other words, Mr. Dimmesdale, whose sensibility of nerve often produced the effect of spiritual **intuition**, would become vaguely aware that something **inimical** to his peace had thrust itself into relation with him. But old Roger Chillingworth, too, had perceptions that were almost **intuitive**; and when the minister threw his startled eyes towards him, there the physician sat; his kind, watchful, sympathizing, but never intrusive friend.

Yet Mr. Dimmesdale would perhaps have seen this individual's character more perfectly, if a certain **morbidness**, to which sick hearts are liable, had not rendered him suspicious of all mankind. Trusting no man as his friend, he could not recognize his enemy when the latter actually appeared. He therefore still kept up a familiar <u>intercourse</u> with him, daily receiving the old physician in his study; or visiting the laboratory, and, for recreation's sake, watching the processes by which weeds were converted into drugs of potency.

One day, leaning his forehead on his hand, and his

INANIMATE (ihn <u>aan</u> ih miht) *adj.*
not active or alive, lacking energy
Synonyms: dead, lifeless, dull, soulless

MANIFEST (<u>maan</u> uh fehst) *adj.*
evidently obvious
Synonyms: apparent, distinct, prominent, glaring

FOREBODE (fohr <u>bohd</u>) *v.* **-ing,-ed.**
to have a presentiment of upcoming evil
Synonyms: predict, portend, foretell, anticipate

DISCLOSE (dihs <u>klohs</u>) *v.* **-ing,-ed.**
to open up, divulge
Synonyms: confide, reveal, impart

DISCLOSURE (dihs <u>kloh</u> shuhr) *n.*
exposure, divulgence
Synonyms: confession, revelation

RETRIBUTION (reh trih <u>byoo</u> shuhn) *n.*
something which is justly deserved, such as
repayment or punishment
Synonyms: vengeance, payback, compensation

elbow on the sill of the open window that looked towards the graveyard, he talked with Roger Chillingworth while the old man was examining a bundle of unsightly plants.

"Where," asked he, with a look <u>askance</u> at them—for it was the clergyman's peculiarity that he seldom, nowadays, looked straightforward at any object, whether human or **inanimate**—"where, my kind doctor, did you gather those herbs, with such a dark, flabby leaf?"

"Even in the graveyard here at hand," answered the physician, continuing his employment. "They are new to me. I found them growing on a grave which bore no tombstone, nor other memorial of the dead man, save these ugly weeds, that have taken upon themselves to keep him in remembrance. They grew out of his heart, and typify, it may be, some hideous secret that was buried with him, and which he had done better to confess during his lifetime."

"Perchance," said Mr. Dimmesdale, "he earnestly desired it, but could not."

"And wherefore?" rejoined the physician. "Wherefore not; since all the powers of nature call so earnestly for the confession of sin, that these black weeds have sprung up out of a buried heart, to make **manifest** an unspoken crime?"

"That, good Sir, is but a fantasy of yours," replied the minister. "There can be, if I **forebode** aright, no power, short of the divine mercy, to **disclose**, whether by uttered words, or by type or emblem, the secrets that may be buried with a human heart. The heart, making itself guilty of such secrets, must perforce hold them, until the day when all hidden things shall be revealed. Nor have I so read or interpreted Holy Writ, as to understand that the **disclosure** of human thoughts and deeds, then to be made, is intended as a part of the **retribution**. That, surely, were a shallow view of it. No; these revelations,

AVAIL (uh <u>vayl</u>) *v.* **-ing,-ed.**
to make use of; to result in; to be of use or advantage to
Synonyms: employ; transpire, eventuate; help,
serve, benefit

SOLACE (<u>sah</u> lihs) *n.*
comfort in distress, consolation
Synonyms: succor, balm, cheer, condolence

AFFLICT (uh <u>flihkt</u>) *v.* **-ing,-ed.**
to distress severely so as to cause persistent anguish
Synonyms: harass, trouble, torment, wound

IMPORTUNATE (ihm <u>pohr</u> chuh niht) *adj.*
persistant; pleading; extremely urgent
Synonyms: troublesome; craving, beseeching;
earnest, imperative

STIFLE (<u>stie</u> fuhl) *v.* **-ing,-ed.**
to smother or suffocate; to suppress or hold back
Synonyms: mute, muffle; restrain

CONSTITUTION (kahn stih <u>too</u> shuhn) *n.*
the physical structure or health of something or
someone; the sum of components, composition
Synonyms: disposition, nature, stature; formation,
design, architecture, make-up

RETAIN (rih <u>tayn</u>) *v.* **-ing,-ed.**
to hold, keep possession of
Synonyms: withhold, reserve

ZEAL (zeel) *n.*
passion or devotion to a cause
Synonyms: fanaticism, enthusiasm

unless I greatly err, are meant merely to promote the intellectual satisfaction of all intelligent beings, who will stand waiting, on that day, to see the dark problem of this life made plain. A knowledge of men's hearts will be needful to the completest solution of that problem. And I conceive, moreover, that the hearts holding such miserable secrets as you speak of will yield them up, at that last day, not with reluctance, but with a joy unutterable."

"Then why not reveal them here?" asked Roger Chillingworth, glancing quietly aside at the minister. "Why should not the guilty ones sooner **avail** themselves of this unutterable **solace**?"

"They mostly do," said the clergyman, griping hard at his breast, as if **afflicted** with an **importunate** throb of pain. "Many, many a poor soul hath given its confidence to me, not only on the death-bed, but while strong in life, and fair in reputation. And ever, after such an outpouring, oh, what a relief have I witnessed in those sinful brethren, even as in one who at last draws free air, after long **stifling** with his own polluted breath. How can it be otherwise? Why should a wretched man, guilty, we will say, of murder, prefer to keep the dead corpse buried in his own heart, rather than fling it forth at once, and let the universe take care of it!"

"Yet some men bury their secrets thus," observed the calm physician.

"True; there are such men," answered Mr. Dimmesdale. "But, not to suggest more obvious reasons, it may be that they are kept silent by the very **constitution** of their nature. Or—can we not suppose—guilty as they may be, **retaining**, nevertheless, a **zeal** for God's glory and man's welfare, they shrink from displaying themselves black and filthy in the view of men; because, thenceforward, no good can be achieved by them; no evil of the past be redeemed by better service. So, to their own unutterable torment, they go about among their

INIQUITY (ih <u>nihk</u> wih tee) *n.*
  sin, evil act
    Synonyms: immorality, injustice, wickedness, vice
ZEAL (zeel) *n. (See page 262.)*
IMPULSE (<u>ihm</u> puhls) *n. (See page 224.)*
PROPAGATE (<u>prah</u> puh gayt) *v.* **-ing,-ed.**
  to breed; to spread or proliferate
    Synonyms: reproduce, procreate; distribute,
    circulate, disseminate
MANIFEST (<u>maan</u> uh fehst) *adj.*
  evidently obvious
    Synonyms: apparent, distinct, prominent, glaring
CONSTRAIN (kuhn <u>strayn</u>) *v.* **-ing,-ed. *(See page 250.)***
PENITENTIAL (peh nih <u>tehn</u> shuhl) *adj.*
  relating to sorrow expressed for sins or offenses
    Synonyms: remorseful, apologetic, repentant
ABASEMENT (uh <u>bays</u> mehnt) *n.*
  shame, disgrace
    Synonyms: corruption, humiliation, downfall
PIOUS (<u>pie</u> uhs) *adj. (See page 220.)*
INDIFFERENTLY (ihn <u>dihf</u> ruhnt lee) *adv.*
  in an uncaring manner; without bias
    Synonyms: disinterestedly, apathetically; impartially
WAIVE (wayv) *v.* **-ing,-ed.**
  to refrain from enforcing; to give up
    Synonyms: relinquish, yield; resign, surrender, cede
FACULTY (<u>faa</u> kuhl tee) *n. (See page 236.)*
AGITATE (<u>aa</u> gih tayt) *v.* **-ing,-ed.**
  to upset or excite; to make uneasy
    Synonyms: disturb, fluster, bother
TEMPERAMENT (<u>tehm</u> puhr uh mehnt) *n. (See pg. 256.)*
ADJACENT (uh <u>jay</u> suhnt) *adj.*
  next to, close, bordering
    Synonyms: neighboring, adjoining, abutting
TRAVERSE (truh <u>vuhrs</u>) *v.* **-ing,-ed. *(See page 66.)***
PERVERSE (puhr <u>vuhrs</u>) *adj.*
  1. having the tendency to oppose or contradict
    Synonyms: contrary, improper, obstinate
  2. immoral, disobedient
    Synonyms: corrupted, mean, depraved

fellow-creatures, looking pure as new-fallen snow while their hearts are all speckled and spotted with **iniquity** of which they cannot rid themselves."

"These men deceive themselves," said Roger Chillingworth, with somewhat more emphasis than usual, and making a slight gesture with his forefinger. "They fear to take up the shame that rightfully belongs to them. Their love for man, their **zeal** for God's service—these holy **impulses** may or may not coexist in their hearts with the evil inmates to which their guilt has unbarred the door, and which must needs **propagate** a hellish breed within them. But, if they seek to glorify God, let them not lift heavenward their unclean hands! If they would serve their fellow-men, let them do it by making **manifest** the power and reality of conscience, in **constraining** them to **penitential** self-**abasement**! Wouldst thou have me to believe, O wise and **pious** friend, that a false show can be better—can be more for God's glory, or man's welfare—than God's own truth? Trust me, such men deceive themselves!"

"It may be so," said the young clergyman, **indifferently**, as **waiving** a discussion that he considered irrelevant or unreasonable. He had a ready **faculty**, indeed, of escaping from any topic that **agitated** his too sensitive and nervous **temperament**. "But, now, I would ask of my well-skilled physician, whether, in good sooth, he deems me to have profited by his kindly care of this weak frame of mine?"

Before Roger Chillingworth could answer, they heard the clear, wild laughter of a young child's voice, proceeding from the **adjacent** burial-ground. Looking instinctively from the open window—for it was summertime—the minister beheld Hester Prynne and little Pearl passing along the footpath that **traversed** the enclosure. Pearl looked as beautiful as the day, but was in one of those moods of **perverse** merriment which,

SAT Vocabulary

IRREVERENTLY (ih <u>rehv</u> uhr uhnt lee) *adv.*
disrespectfully, in a manner of humorous mocking
Synonyms: impiously, iconoclastically, satirically

ENTREATY (ehn <u>tree</u> tee) *n.*
a plea or request
Synonyms: imploration, prayer, petition

DECOROUSLY (deh <u>kohr</u> uhs lee) *adv.*
properly, tastefully, in a socially correct manner
Synonyms: politely, courteously, appropriately

TENACIOUSLY (tuh <u>nay</u> shuhs lee) *adv.*
stubbornly, with strength
Synonyms: persistently, doggedly, obstinately

ADHERE (aad <u>heer</u>) *v.* **-ing,-ed.**
to cling; to follow through without deviation
Synonyms: cleave, stick; carry out

REVERENCE (<u>reh</u> vuhr ehnts) *n.*
deep respect, awe
Synonyms: veneration, adoration, admiration

MIRTH (muhrth) *n.*
frivolity, gaiety, laughter
Synonyms: merriment, jollity, hilarity, glee

whenever they occurred, seemed to remove her entirely out of the sphere of sympathy or human contact. She now skipped **irreverently** from one grave to another; until, coming to the broad, flat, armorial tombstone of a departed worthy—perhaps of Isaac Johnson himself—she began to dance upon it. In reply to her mother's command and **entreaty** that she would behave more **decorously**, little Pearl paused to gather the prickly burrs from a tall burdock which grew beside the tomb. Taking a handful of these, she arranged them along the lines of the scarlet letter that decorated the maternal bosom, to which the burrs, as their nature was, **tenaciously adhered**. Hester did not pluck them off.

Roger Chillingworth had by this time approached the window, and smiled grimly down.

"There is no law, nor **reverence** for authority, no regard for human ordinances or opinions, right or wrong, mixed up with that child's composition," remarked he, as much to himself as to his companion. "I saw her, the other day, bespatter the Governor himself with water, at the cattle-trough in Spring Lane. What, in Heaven's name, is she? Is the imp altogether evil? Hath she affections? Hath she any discoverable principle of being?"

"None—save the freedom of a broken law," answered Mr. Dimmesdale, in a quiet way, as if he had been discussing the point within himself. "Whether capable of good, I know not."

The child probably overheard their voices; for, looking up to the window, with a bright, but naughty smile of **mirth** and intelligence, she threw one of the prickly burrs at the Reverend Mr. Dimmesdale. The sensitive clergyman shrunk, with nervous dread, from the light missile. Detecting his emotion, Pearl clapped her little hands in the most extravagant ecstasy. Hester Prynne, likewise, had involuntarily looked up; and all these four

DRAW *v.* **-ing, drew, drawn.**
　1. to pull, drag; to attract
　　Synonyms: haul, tow, lug; lure, entice
　2. to move steadily
　　Synonyms: proceed, continue, progress

DEMERIT (dih <u>mayr</u> iht) *n.*
　a characterictic worthy of blame or disrespect
　　Synonyms: fault, failure, sin, deficiency

GRIEVOUS (<u>gree</u> vuhs) *adj.*
　causing grief and sorrow, serious and distressing
　　Synonyms: grave, dire, mournful, dolorous

VERILY (<u>veh</u> rih lee) *adv.*
　truly, with accuracy and confidence
　　Synonyms: truthfully, reliably, assuredly

WARY (<u>way</u> ree) *adj.*
　careful, cautious
　　Synonyms: watchful, vigilant, alert, guarded,
　　suspicious

persons, old and young, regarded one another in silence, till the child laughed aloud, and shouted, "Come away, Mother! Come away, or yonder old <u>Black Man</u> will catch you! He hath got hold of the minister already. Come away, Mother, or he will catch you! But he cannot catch little Pearl!"

So she **drew** her mother away, skipping, dancing, and frisking fantastically, among the hillocks of the dead people, like a creature that had nothing in common with a bygone and buried generation, nor owned herself akin to it. It was as if she had been made afresh, out of new elements, and must perforce be permitted to live her own life, and be a law unto herself, without her eccentricities being reckoned to her for a crime.

"There goes a woman," resumed Roger Chillingworth, after a pause, "who, be her **demerits** what they may, hath none of that mystery of hidden sinfulness which you deem so **grievous** to be borne. Is Hester Prynne the less miserable, think you, for that scarlet letter on her breast?"

"I do **verily** believe it," answered the clergyman. "Nevertheless, I cannot answer for her. There was a look of pain in her face, which I would gladly have been spared the sight of. But still, methinks, it must needs be better for the sufferer to be free to show his pain, as this poor woman Hester is, than to cover it all up in his heart."

There was another pause; and the physician began anew to examine and arrange the plants which he had gathered.

"You inquired of me, a little time agone," said he, at length, "my judgment as touching your health."

"I did," answered the clergyman, "and would gladly learn it. Speak frankly, I pray you, be it for life or death."

"Freely, then, and plainly," said the physician, still busy with his plants, but keeping a **wary** eye on Mr.

MANIFEST (<u>maan</u> uh fehst) *v.* **-ing,-ed.**
to make evident or certain by display
Synonyms: exhibit, showcase, expose

PROVIDENCE (<u>prah</u> vih dehnts) *n.*
divine control and direction by God; preparation
and foresight
Synonyms: fate, destiny, good luck; prudence,
precaution

IMBUE (ihm <u>byoo</u>) *v.* **-ing,-ed.**
to infuse; to dye, wet
Synonyms: permeate; moisten

Dimmesdale, "the disorder is a strange one; not so much in itself, nor as outwardly **manifested**—in so far, at least, as the symptoms have been laid open to my observation. Looking daily at you, my good Sir, and watching the tokens of your aspect, now for months gone by, I should deem you a man sore sick, it may be, yet not so sick but that an instructed and watchful physician might well hope to cure you. But—I know not what to say— the disease is what I seem to know, yet know it not."

"You speak in riddles, learned Sir," said the pale minister, glancing aside out of the window.

"Then to speak more plainly," continued the physician, "and I crave pardon, Sir—should it seem to require pardon—for this needful plainness of my speech. Let me ask—as your friend—as one having charge, under **Providence**, of your life and physical well-being—hath all the operation of this disorder been fairly laid open and recounted to me?"

"How can you question it?" asked the minister. "Surely, it were child's play to call in a physician, and then hide the sore!"

"You would tell me, then, that I know all?" said Roger Chillingworth, deliberately, and fixing an eye, bright with intense and concentrated intelligence, on the minister's face. "Be it so! But again! He to whom only the outward and physical evil is laid open, knoweth, oftentimes, but half the evil which he is called upon to cure. A bodily disease, which we look upon as whole and entire within itself, may, after all, be but a symptom of some ailment in the spiritual part. Your pardon, once again, good Sir, if my speech give the shadow of offence. You, Sir, of all men whom I have known, are he whose body is the closest conjoined, and **imbued**, and identified, so to speak, with the spirit whereof it is the instrument."

"Then I need ask no further," said the clergyman,

EMACIATED (ih <u>may</u> shee ay tihd) *adj.*
very thin due to hunger or disease, feeble
Synonyms: bony, gaunt, haggard, skeletal

MANIFESTATION (maan uh fehs <u>tay</u> shuhn) *n.*
a clear appearance or display
Synonyms: expression, exhibition, indication

MEDDLE (<u>meh</u> duhl) *v.* **-ing,-ed.**
to interfere in others' affairs, to impose
Synonyms: tamper, encroach

PIOUS (<u>pie</u> uhs) *adj.*
dedicated, devout; extremely religious
Synonyms: observant, reverent; sanctimonious

somewhat hastily rising from his chair. "You deal not, I take it, in medicine for the soul!"

"Thus, a sickness," continued Roger Chillingworth, going on, in an unaltered tone, without heeding the interruption—but standing up and confronting the **emaciated** and white-cheeked minister with his low, dark, and misshapen figure—"a sickness, a sore place, if we may so call it, in your spirit, hath immediately its appropriate **manifestation** in your bodily frame. Would you, therefore, that your physician heal the bodily evil? How may this be, unless you first lay open to him the wound or trouble in your soul?"

"No—not to thee—not to an earthly physician!" cried Mr. Dimmesdale passionately, and turning his eyes, full and bright, and with a kind of fierceness, on old Roger Chillingworth. "Not to thee! But, if it be the soul's disease, then do I commit myself to the one Physician of the soul! He, if it stand with His good pleasure, can cure; or He can kill! Let Him do with me as, in His justice and wisdom, He shall see good. But who art thou, that **meddlest** in this matter—that darest thrust himself between the sufferer and his God?"

With a frantic gesture, he rushed out of the room.

"It is as well to have made this step," said Roger Chillingworth to himself, looking after the minister with a grave smile. "There is nothing lost. We shall be friends again anon. But see, now, how passion takes hold upon this man, and hurrieth him out of himself! As with one passion, so with another! He hath done a wild thing ere now, this **pious** Master Dimmesdale, in the hot passion of his heart!"

It proved not difficult to reestablish the intimacy of the two companions, on the same footing and in the same degree as heretofore. The young clergyman, after a few hours of privacy, was sensible that the disorder of his nerves had hurried him into an unseemly outbreak

PALLIATE (<u>paa</u> lee ayt) *v.* **-ing,-ed.**
to make less serious, ease
Synonyms: extenuate, mitigate, alleviate, assuage

BESTOW (bih <u>stoh</u>) *v.* **-ing,-ed.**
to apply or devote time or effort; to give as a gift
Synonyms: allocate, dedicate; endow, confer, present

REMORSEFUL (rih <u>mohrs</u> fuhl) *adj.*
distressed, having strong feelings of guilt
Synonyms: anguished, rueful, shameful, penitent

AMPLE (<u>aam</u> puhl) *adj.*
abundant, plentiful
Synonyms: substantial, generous

ASSENT (uh <u>sehnt</u>) *v.* **-ing,-ed.**
to agree
Synonyms: accede, concur, acquiesce

PROFOUND (pruh <u>fownd</u>) (proh <u>fownd</u>) *adj.*
deep; having intellectual depth
Synonyms: bottomless; serious, thorough, weighty

REPOSE (rih <u>pohz</u>) *n.*
sleep, rest, ease; a state of peace or tranquility
Synonyms: relaxation, leisure, idleness; calmness,
serenity

of temper which there had been nothing in the physician's words to excuse or **palliate**. He marvelled, indeed, at the violence with which he had thrust back the kind old man, when merely proffering the advice which it was his duty to **bestow**, and which the minister himself had expressly sought. With these **remorseful** feelings, he lost no time in making the **amplest** apologies, and besought his friend still to continue the care, which, if not successful in restoring him to health, had, in all probability, been the means of prolonging his feeble existence to that hour. Roger Chillingworth readily **assented**, and went on with his medical supervision of the minister; doing his best for him, in all good faith, but always quitting the patient's apartment at the close of a professional interview, with a mysterious and puzzled smile upon his lips. This expression was invisible in Mr. Dimmesdale's presence, but grew strongly evident as the physician crossed the threshold.

"A rare case!" he muttered. "I must look deeper into it. A strange sympathy betwixt soul and body! Were it only for the art's sake, I must search this matter to the bottom!"

It came to pass, not long after the scene above recorded, that the Reverend Mr. Dimmesdale, at noonday, and entirely unawares, fell into a deep, deep slumber, sitting in his chair, with a large black-letter volume open before him on the table. It must have been a work of vast ability in the somniferous school of literature. The **profound** depth of the minister's **repose** was the more remarkable, inasmuch as he was one of those persons whose sleep, ordinarily, is as light, as fitful, and as easily scared away, as a small bird hopping on a twig. To such an unwonted remoteness, however, had his spirit now withdrawn into itself, that he stirred not in his chair when old Roger Chillingworth, without any extraordinary precaution, came into the room. The

RAPTURE (<u>raap</u> chuhr) *n.*
ecstasy or extreme joy; deep absorption
Synonyms: exaltation; immersion

MANIFEST (<u>maan</u> uh fehst) *adj.*
evidently obvious
Synonyms: apparent, distinct, prominent, glaring

physician advanced directly in front of his patient, laid his hand upon his bosom, and thrust aside the vestment that, hitherto, had always covered it even from the professional eye.

Then, indeed, Mr. Dimmesdale shuddered, and slightly stirred.

After a brief pause, the physician turned away.

But with what a wild look of wonder, joy, and horror! With what a ghastly **rapture**, as, it were, too mighty to be expressed only by the eye and features, and therefore bursting forth through the whole ugliness of his figure, and making itself even riotously **manifest** by the extravagant gestures with which he threw up his arms towards the ceiling, and stamped his foot upon the floor! Had a man seen old Roger Chillingworth, at that moment of his ecstasy, he would have had no need to ask how Satan comports himself when a precious human soul is lost to Heaven and won into his kingdom.

But what distinguished the physician's ecstasy from Satan's was the trait of wonder in it!

MALICE (<u>maal</u> ihs) *n.*
  animosity, spite, hatred
    Synonyms: malevolence, cruelty, hostility

LATENT (<u>lay</u> tnt) *adj.*
  present but hidden; potential
    Synonyms: dormant, quiescent; capable

REMORSE (rih <u>mohrs</u>) *n.*
  a gnawing distress arising from a sense of guilt
    Synonyms: anguish, ruefulness, shame, penitence

REPENTANCE (rih <u>pehn</u> tehnts) *n.*
  sorrow expressed for sins or offenses, penitence
    Synonyms: remorse, contrition, apology

LAVISH (<u>laa</u> vihsh) *v.* **-ing,-ed.**
  to shower with abundance or extravagance; to waste
  or spend excessively
    Synonyms: cram, overflow, saturate, teem; squander

VENGEANCE (<u>vehn</u> juhns) *n.*
  punishment inflicted in retaliation; vehemence
    Synonyms: revenge, repayment; wrath

BALK (bawk) *v.* **-ing,-ed.**
  to resist or refuse, shirk
    Synonyms: evade, thwart, stop, check

INCLINE (ihn <u>klien</u>) *v.* **-ing,-ed.**
  to have a specific tendency, to be predisposed
    Synonyms: lean toward, influence, impel, prefer

PROVIDENCE (<u>prah</u> vih dehnts) *n.*
  divine control and direction by God; preparation and
  foresight
    Synonyms: fate, destiny, good luck; prudence,
    precaution

AVENGER (uh <u>vehn</u> juhr) *n.*
  one who retaliates or takes revenge for an injury or
  crime
    Synonyms: punisher, vindicator

SUBSEQUENT (<u>suhb</u> suh kwehnt) *adj.*
  following in time or order
    Synonyms: succeeding, next, after

The Interior of a Heart

Chapter 11

After the incident last described, the <u>intercourse</u> between the clergyman and the physician, though externally the same, was really of another character than it had previously been. The intellect of Roger Chillingworth had now a sufficiently plain path before it. It was not, indeed, precisely that which he had laid out for himself to tread. Calm, gentle, passionless as he appeared, there was yet, we fear, a quiet depth of **malice**, hitherto **latent**, but active now, in this unfortunate old man, which led him to imagine a more intimate revenge than any mortal had ever wreaked upon an enemy. To make himself the one trusted friend, to whom should be confided all the fear, the **remorse**, the agony, the ineffectual **repentance**, the backward rush of sinful thoughts, expelled in vain! All that guilty sorrow, hidden from the world, whose great heart would have pitied and forgiven, to be revealed to him, the Pitiless, to him, the Unforgiving! All that dark treasure to be **lavished** on the very man, to whom nothing else could so adequately pay the debt of **vengeance**!

The clergyman's shy and sensitive reserve had **balked** this scheme. Roger Chillingworth, however, was **inclined** to be hardly, if at all, less satisfied with the aspect of affairs which **Providence**—using the **avenger** and his victim for its own purposes, and, perchance, pardoning where it seemed most to punish—had substituted for his black devices. A revelation, he could almost say, had been granted to him. It mattered little, for his object, whether celestial, or from what other region. By its aid, in all the **subsequent** relations <u>betwixt</u> him and Mr. Dimmesdale, not merely the external presence, but the

SUBTLETY (<u>suh</u> tuhl tee) *n.*

the quality of being hard to detect or describe
Synonyms: nuance, tact

DEFORMED (dih <u>fohrmd</u>) *adj.*

disfigured, spoiled
Synonyms: contorted, twisted, marred, misshapen

GAIT (gayt) *n.*

the way one moves on foot, a manner of walking
Synonyms: tread, walk, march, pace

INDIFFERENT (ihn <u>dihf</u> ruhnt) (ihn <u>dihf</u> uhr uhnt) *adj.*

uncaring, unbiased
Synonyms: unconcerned, detached, uninterested, apathetic

ODIOUS (<u>oh</u> dee uhs) *adj.*

hateful, contemptible
Synonyms: detestable, obnoxious, offensive, repellent, loathsome

IMPLICITLY (ihm <u>plih</u> siht lee) *adv.*

undoubtedly; in a way that is not directly expressed
Synonyms: unquestionably; tacitly

ANTIPATHY (aan <u>tih</u> puh thee) *n.*

dislike, hostility, extreme opposition or aversion
Synonyms: antagonism, enmity, malice

ABHORRENCE (uhb <u>hohr</u> ehnts) *n.*

loathing, detestation
Synonyms: hatred, condemnation, abomination

MORBID (<u>mohr</u> bihd) *adj.*

1. having an unhealthy mentality; relating to disease
   Synonyms: unwholesome; pathological
2. abnormally terrible and gloomy; gruesome
   Synonyms: dismal, dreary; grisly, macabre

PRESENTIMENT (prih <u>sehn</u> tih mehnt) *n.*

the anticipation or sense that something may happen
Synonyms: expectation, premonition

very inmost soul of the latter seemed to be brought out before his eyes, so that he could see and comprehend its every movement. He became, thenceforth, not a spectator only, but a chief actor, in the poor minister's interior world. He could play upon him as he chose. Would he arouse him with a throb of agony? The victim was forever on the rack; it needed only to know the spring that controlled the engine; and the physician knew it well! Would he startle him with sudden fear? As at the waving of a magician's wand, uprose a grisly phantom—uprose a thousand phantoms—in many shapes, of death, or more awful shame, all flocking round about the clergyman, and pointing with their fingers at his breast!

All this was accomplished with a **subtlety** so perfect, that the minister, though he had constantly a dim perception of some evil influence watching over him, could never gain a knowledge of its actual nature. True, he looked doubtfully, fearfully—even, at times, with horror and the bitterness of hatred—at the **deformed** figure of the old physician. His gestures, his **gait**, his grizzled beard, his slightest and most **indifferent** acts, the very fashion of his garments, were **odious** in the clergyman's sight; a token **implicitly** to be relied on, of a deeper **antipathy** in the breast of the latter than he was willing to acknowledge to himself. For, as it was impossible to assign a reason for such distrust and **abhorrence**, so Mr. Dimmesdale, conscious that the poison of one **morbid** spot was infecting his heart's entire substance, attributed all his **presentiments** to no other cause. He took himself to task for his bad sympathies in reference to Roger Chillingworth, disregarded the lesson that he should have drawn from them, and did his best to root them out. Unable to accomplish this, he nevertheless, as a matter of principle, continued his habits of social familiarity with the old man, and thus gave him constant opportunities for perfecting the purpose to

FORLORN (fohr <u>lohrn</u>) *adj.*
hopeless, despairing; dreary, deserted; unhappy
Synonyms: dejected, despondent; desolate;
downcast, depressed

AVENGER (uh <u>vehn</u> juhr) *n.* *(See page 278.)*

MACHINATION (mahk uh <u>nay</u> shuhn) *n.*
a plot or scheme
Synonyms: conspiracy, intrigue, design

PRETERNATURAL (pree tuhr <u>naach</u> uh ruhl) *adj.*
extraordinary or unnatural
Synonyms: abnormal, mysterious, odd, unearthly

SOBER (<u>soh</u> buhr) *adj.* *(See page 254.)*

EMINENT (<u>ehm</u> uh nuhnt) *adj.* *(See page 240.)*

PROFOUNDLY (proh <u>fownd</u> lee) *adv.*
deeply, extremely, infinitely
Synonyms: intensely, thoroughly, severely

ENDOW (ehn <u>dow</u>) *v.* **-ing,-ed.** *(See page 224.)*

DOCTRINAL (<u>dahk</u> truh nuhl) *adj.*
rigidly devoted to theories
Synonyms: inflexible, dogmatic, opinionated,
authoritative

CONSTITUTE (kahn stih <u>toot</u>) *v.* **-ing,-ed.** *(See pg. 112.)*

EFFICACIOUS (eff uh <u>kay</u> shuhs) *adj.*
effective, efficient
Synonyms: effectual, potent

UNAMIABLE (uhn <u>ay</u> mee uh buhl) *adj.*
unfriendly, unpleasant, unlikable
Synonyms: disagreeable, rude, discourteous

FACULTY (<u>faa</u> kuhl tee) *n.* *(See page 236.)*

ETHEREALIZE (ih <u>theer</u> ee uh liez) *v.* **-ing,-ed.**
to become or make heavenly
Synonym: spiritualize

DESCEND (dih <u>sehnd</u>) (dee <u>sehnd</u>) *v.* **-ing,-ed.**
to pass from a higher place to a lower place
Synonyms: fall, dismount, gravitate

which—poor, **forlorn** creature that he was, and more wretched than his victim—the **avenger** had devoted himself.

While thus suffering under bodily disease, and gnawed and tortured by some black trouble of the soul, and given over to the **machinations** of his deadliest enemy, the Reverend Mr. Dimmesdale had achieved a brilliant popularity in his sacred office. He won it, indeed, in great part, by his sorrows. His intellectual gifts, his moral perceptions, his power of experiencing and communicating emotion, were kept in a state of **preternatural** activity by the prick and anguish of his daily life. His fame, though still on its upward slope, already overshadowed the **soberer** reputations of his fellow-clergymen, **eminent** as several of them were. There were scholars among them, who had spent more years in acquiring <u>abstruse</u> lore connected with the divine profession, than Mr. Dimmesdale had lived; and who might well, therefore, be more **profoundly** versed in such solid and valuable attainments than their youthful brother. There were men, too, of a sturdier texture of mind than his, and **endowed** with a far greater share of shrewd, hard, iron, or granite understanding; which, duly mingled with a fair proportion of **doctrinal** ingredient, **constitutes** a highly respectable, **efficacious**, and **unamiable** variety of the clerical species. There were others, again, true saintly fathers, whose **faculties** had been elaborated by weary toil among their books, and by patient thought, and **etherealized**, moreover, by spiritual communications with the better world, into which their purity of life had almost introduced these holy personages, with their garments of mortality still clinging to them. All that they lacked was the gift that **descended** upon the chosen disciples at Pentecost, in tongues of flame; symbolizing, it would seem, not the power of speech in foreign and unknown languages, but that of

ATTESTATION (uh tehs <u>tay</u> shuhn) *n.*
testimony, confession
Synonyms: admission, confirmation, substantiation

MEDIUM (<u>mee</u> dee uhm) *n.*
a substance or object that is used to transmit or
accomplish something
Synonyms: means, instrument, vehicle, mechanism

SANCTITY (<u>saank</u> tih tee) *n.*
holiness, saintliness
Synonyms: devoutness, divinity, piety

THWART (thwahrt) *v.* **-ing,-ed.**
to block or prevent from happening; to frustrate
Synonyms: oppose, defeat, foil, balk; hinder, baffle

TOTTER (<u>tah</u> tuhr) *v.* **-ing,-ed.**
to stand with much unsteadiness
Synonyms: wobble, sway, reel, stagger

ETHEREAL (ih <u>theer</u> ee uhl) *adj.*
not earthly, spiritual; intangible
Synonyms: heavenly; diaphanous, airy, gossamer,
sheer

ELOQUENCE (<u>eh</u> luh kwuhns) *n.*
persuasive and effective speech
Synonyms: expressiveness, fluency

REBUKE (ree <u>byook</u>) *n.*
a reprimand, scolding, punishment
Synonyms: admonition, reproof, reproach

SANCTIFIED (<u>saank</u> tih fied) *adj.*
pious; holy, sacred
Synonyms: self-righteous; consecrated, divine

IMBUE (ihm <u>byoo</u>) *v.* **-ing,-ed.**
to infuse; to dye, wet
Synonyms: permeate; moisten

SENTIMENT (<u>sehn</u> tuh muhnt) *n.*
an attitude, thought, or judgment prompted by feeling
Synonym: emotion

addressing the whole human brotherhood in the heart's native language. These fathers, otherwise so <u>apostolic</u>, lacked Heaven's last and rarest **attestation** of their office, the Tongue of Flame. They would have vainly sought—had they ever dreamed of seeking—to express the highest truths through the humblest **medium** of familiar words and images. Their voices came down, afar and indistinctly, from the upper heights where they habitually dwelt.

Not improbably, it was to this latter class of men that Mr. Dimmesdale, by many of his traits of character, naturally belonged. To the high mountain-peaks of faith and **sanctity** he would have climbed, had not the tendency been **thwarted** by the burden, whatever it might be, of crime or anguish, beneath which it was his doom to **totter**. It kept him down, on a level with the lowest; him, the man of **ethereal** attributes, whose voice the angels might else have listened to and answered! But this very burden it was that gave him sympathies so intimate with the sinful brotherhood of mankind, so that his heart vibrated in unison with theirs, and received their pain into itself, and sent its own throb of pain through a thousand other hearts, in gushes of sad, persuasive **eloquence**. Oftenest persuasive, but sometimes terrible! The people knew not the power that moved them thus. They deemed the young clergyman a miracle of holiness. They fancied him the mouthpiece of Heaven's messages of wisdom, and **rebuke**, and love. In their eyes, the very ground on which he trod was **sanctified**. The virgins of his church grew pale around him, victims of a passion so **imbued** with religious **sentiment** that they imagined it to be all religion, and brought it openly, in their white bosoms, as their most acceptable sacrifice before the altar. The aged members of his flock, beholding Mr. Dimmesdale's frame so feeble, while they were themselves so rugged in their

INFIRMITY (ihn <u>fuhr</u> mih tee) *n.*
weakness; disease, ailment
Synonyms: frailty; illness, affliction

ENJOIN (ehn <u>joyn</u>) *v.* **-ing,-ed.**
to order, urge, command; forbid or prohibit, as by judicial order
Synonyms: direct, instruct; proscribe

VENERATION (veh nehr <u>ay</u> shuhn) *n.*
adoration, honor, respect
Synonyms: homage, reverence, deference, esteem

IMPULSE (<u>ihm</u> puhls) *n.*
sudden tendency, inclination
Synonyms: urge, whim

DEVOID (dih <u>voyd</u>) *adj.*
being without, lacking
Synonyms: destitute, empty, vacant, null, bare

ASCEND (uh <u>sehnd</u>) *v.* **-ing,-ed.**
to rise to another level or climb; to move upward
Synonyms: elevate, escalate, mount; hoist, lift

OMNISCIENCE (ahm <u>nih</u> shehnts) *n.*
the ability to be all-knowing, infinite knowledge
Synonyms: wisdom, magnificence

DISCERN (dihs <u>uhrn</u>) *v.* **-ing,-ed.**
to perceive or recognize something
Synonyms: descry, observe, glimpse, distinguish

SANCTITY (<u>saank</u> tih tee) *n.*
holiness, saintliness
Synonyms: devoutness, divinity, piety

REVERENCE (<u>reh</u> vuhr ehnts) *v.* **-ing,-ed.**
to worship, regard with awe
Synonyms: venerate, adore, idolize, admire

TREMULOUS (<u>treh</u> myoo luhs) *adj.*
trembling, quivering; fearful, timid
Synonyms: shaking, palsied; timorous, anxious

infirmity, believed that he would go heavenward before them, and **enjoined** it upon their children, that their old bones should be buried close to their young pastor's holy grave. And, all this time, perchance, when poor Mr. Dimmesdale was thinking of his grave, he questioned with himself whether the grass would ever grow on it, because an accursed thing must there be buried!

It is inconceivable, the agony with which this public **veneration** tortured him! It was his genuine **impulse** to adore the truth, and to reckon all things shadow-like, and utterly **devoid** of weight or value, that had not its divine essence as the life within their life. Then, what was he—a substance—or the dimmest of all shadows? He longed to speak out from his own pulpit, at the full height of his voice, and tell the people what he was. "I, whom you behold in these black garments of the priesthood—I, who **ascend** the sacred desk, and turn my pale face heavenward, taking upon myself to hold communion, in your behalf, with the Most High **Omniscience**— I, in whose daily life you **discern** the **sanctity** of Enoch—I, whose footsteps, as you suppose, leave a gleam along my earthly track, whereby the pilgrims that shall come after me may be guided to the regions of the blest—I, who have laid the hand of baptism upon your children—I, who have breathed the parting prayer over your dying friends, to whom the amen sounded faintly from a world which they had quitted—I, your pastor, whom you so **reverence** and trust, am utterly a pollution and a lie!"

More than once, Mr. Dimmesdale had gone into the pulpit, with a purpose never to come down its steps until he should have spoken words like the above. More than once, he had cleared his throat and drawn in the long, deep, and **tremulous** breath, which, when sent forth again, would come burdened with the black secret of his soul. More than once—nay, more than a hundred

VILE (viel) *adj.*
  wretched, offensive, disgusting
    Synonyms: despicable, nasty, depraved

ABOMINATION (uh bahm ih <u>nay</u> shuhn) *n.*
  something which causes disgust and hatred
    Synonyms: abhorrence, horror, evil

INIQUITY (ih <u>nihk</u> wih tee) *n. (See page 264.)*

WRATH (raath) *n.*
  anger, rage
    Synonyms: fury, ire, resentment, indignation

IMPULSE (<u>ihm</u> puhls) *n.*
  sudden tendency, inclination
    Synonyms: urge, whim

DEFILE (dih <u>fiel</u>) *v.* **-ing,-ed.**
  to disgrace, dishonor; to dirty, spoil
    Synonyms: debase, degrade, desecrate; corrupt,
    besmear

REVERENCE (<u>reh</u> vuhr ehnts) *v* **-ing,-ed.** *(See pg. 286.)*

PURPORT (puhr <u>pohrt</u>) *n. (See page 168.)*

LURK (luhrk) *v.* **-ing,-ed.**
  to hide, to lie hidden or unsuspected; to prowl, sneak
    Synonyms: conceal; stalk, creep, skulk, slink

DISCERN (dihs <u>uhrn</u>) *v.* **-ing,-ed.** *(See page 286.)*

REMORSEFUL (rih <u>mohrs</u> fuhl) *adj.*
  distressed, having strong feelings of guilt
    Synonyms: anguished, rueful, shameful, penitent

HYPOCRITE (<u>hih</u> puh kriht) *n.*
  person claiming beliefs or virtues he or she doesn't
  really possess
    Synonyms: fraud, liar, sham, fake, phony

CONSTITUTION (kahn stih <u>too</u> shuhn) *n. (See pg. 262.)*

LOATHE (lohth) *v.* **-ing,-ed.**
  to abhor, despise, hate
    Synonyms: abominate, execrate, detest, condemn

DIVINE (dih <u>vien</u>) *n. (See page 238.)*

times—he had actually spoken! Spoken! But how? He had told his hearers that he was altogether **vile**, a **viler** companion of the **vilest**, the worst of sinners, an **abomination**, a thing of unimaginable **iniquity**; and that the only wonder was that they did not see his wretched body shrivelled up before their eyes by the burning **wrath** of the Almighty! Could there be plainer speech than this? Would not the people start up in their seats, by a simultaneous **impulse**, and tear him down out of the pulpit which he **defiled**? Not so, indeed! They heard it all, and did but **reverence** him the more. They little guessed what deadly **purport lurked** in those self-condemning words. "The godly youth!" said they among themselves. "The saint on earth! Alas, if he **discern** such sinfulness in his own white soul, what horrid spectacle would he behold in thine or mine!" The minister well knew—subtile, but **remorseful hypocrite** that he was—the light in which his vague confession would be viewed. He had striven to put a cheat upon himself by making the avowal of a guilty conscience, but had gained only one other sin, and a self-acknowledged shame, without the momentary relief of being self-deceived. He had spoken the very truth, and transformed it into the veriest falsehood. And yet, by the **constitution** of his nature, he loved the truth and **loathed** the lie, as few men ever did. Therefore, above all things else, he **loathed** his miserable self!

His inward trouble drove him to practices more in accordance with the old, corrupted faith of Rome than with the better light of the church in which he had been born and bred. In Mr. Dimmesdale's secret closet, under lock and key, there was a bloody scourge. Oftentimes, this Protestant and Puritan **divine** had plied it on his own shoulders; laughing bitterly at himself the while, and smiting so much the more pitilessly because of that bitter laugh. It was his custom, too, as it has

PIOUS (pie uhs) *adj.*
extremely religious; dedicated, devout
Synonyms: sanctimonious; reverent, observant

MEDIUM (mee dee uhm) *n.*
a substance or object that is used to transmit or accomplish something
Synonyms: means, instrument, vehicle, mechanism

RIGOROUSLY (rih guhr uhs lee) *adv.*
intensely, strictly, exactly
Synonyms: rigidly, severely, dogmatically, sternly

PENANCE (peh nihns) *n.*
voluntary suffering to repent for a wrong
Synonyms: atonement, reparation, chastening, reconciliation

INTROSPECTION (ihn truh spehk shuhn) *n.*
the contemplation of one's own thoughts and feelings
Synonyms: reflection, meditation

DIABOLIC (die uh bah lih) *adj.*
characteristic of the devil
Synonyms: fiendish, wicked, evil

ETHEREAL (ih theer ee uhl) *adj.*
not earthly, spiritual; intangible
Synonyms: heavenly; diaphanous, airy, gossamer, sheer

DISCERN (dihs uhrn) *v.* **-ing,-ed.**
to perceive or recognize something
Synonyms: descry, observe, glimpse, distinguish

BRAZEN (bray zihn) *adj.*
1. made of brass
Synonyms: brassy, shiny
2. shameless, defiant
Synonyms: brash, audacious, forward

DIVINITY (dih vihn ih tee) *n.*
the study of religion
Synonym: theology

been that of many other **pious** Puritans, to fast—not, however, like them, in order to purify the body and render it the fitter **medium** of celestial illumination, but **rigorously**, and until his knees trembled beneath him, as an act of **penance**. He kept vigils, likewise, night after night, sometimes in utter darkness; sometimes with a glimmering lamp; and sometimes, viewing his own face in a looking-glass, by the most powerful light which he could throw upon it. He thus typified the constant **introspection** wherewith he tortured, but could not purify, himself. In these lengthened vigils, his brain often reeled, and visions seemed to flit before him; perhaps seen doubtfully, and by a faint light of their own, in the remote dimness of the chamber, or more vividly, and close beside him, within the looking-glass. Now it was a herd of **diabolic** shapes that grinned and mocked at the pale minister, and beckoned him away with them; now a group of shining angels, who flew upward heavily, as sorrow-laden, but grew more **ethereal** as they rose. Now came the dead friends of his youth, and his white-bearded father, with a saint-like frown, and his mother, turning her face away as she passed by. Ghost of a mother—thinnest fantasy of a mother—methinks she might yet have thrown a pitying glance towards her son! And now, through the chamber which these spectral thoughts had made so ghastly, glided Hester Prynne, leading along little Pearl in her scarlet garb, and pointing her forefinger, first at the scarlet letter on her bosom, and then at the clergyman's own breast.

None of these visions ever quite deluded him. At any moment, by an effort of his will, he could **discern** substances through their misty lack of substance, and convince himself that they were not solid in their nature, like yonder table of carved oak, or that big, square, leathern-bound and **brazen**-clasped volume of **divinity**. But, for all that, they were, in one sense, the truest and

SUBSTANTIAL (suhb <u>staan</u> shuhl) *adj.*
　having substance; large in size or amount
　　Synonyms: important, significant; ample, hearty,
　　strong

IMPALPABLE (ihm <u>paalp</u> uh buhl) *adj.*
　unreal, intangible
　　Synonyms: imperceptible, tenuous, unsubstantial

UNDISSEMBLED (uhn dihs <u>sehm</u> buhld) *adj.*
　displayed or shown clearly without disguise
　　Synonyms: revealed, exposed, demonstrated

FORBEAR (fohr <u>bayr</u>) *v.* **-ing,-bore,-borne.**
　to hold back or refrain
　　Synonyms: resist, evade, abstain, shun

most **substantial** things which the poor minister now dealt with. It is the unspeakable misery of a life so false as his, that it steals the pith and substance out of whatever realities there are around us, and which were meant by Heaven to be the spirit's joy and nutriment. To the untrue man, the whole universe is false—it is **impalpable**—it shrinks to nothing within his grasp. And he himself, in so far as he shows himself in a false light, becomes a shadow, or, indeed, ceases to exist. The only truth that continued to give Mr. Dimmesdale a real existence on this earth was the anguish in his inmost soul, and the **undissembled** expression of it in his aspect. Had he once found power to smile, and wear a face of gayety, there would have been no such man!

On one of those ugly nights, which we have faintly hinted at, but **forborne** to picture forth, the minister started from his chair. A new thought had struck him. There might be a moment's peace in it. Attiring himself with as much care as if it had been for public worship, and precisely in the same manner, he stole softly down the staircase, undid the door, and issued forth.

IGNOMINY (<u>ihg</u> nuh mih nee) *n.*
  disgrace and dishonor
    Synonyms: degradation, debasement

ASCEND (uh <u>sehnd</u>) *v.* **-ing,-ed.**
  to rise to another level or climb; to move upward
    Synonyms: elevate, escalate, mount; hoist, lift

OBSCURE (uhb <u>skyoor</u>) *adj.*
  dim, unclear; not well known
    Synonyms: dark, faint; remote, minor

ZENITH (<u>zee</u> nihth) *n.*
  highest point, summit
    Synonyms: acme, apex, climax, crown, pinnacle

MULTITUDE (<u>muhl</u> tuh tood) *n.*
  a crowd; the state of being many, a great number
    Synonyms: throng; mass, myriad

SUSTAIN (suh <u>stayn</u>) *v.* **-ing,-ed.**
  to endure, undergo; to support, uphold
    Synonyms: withstand; maintain, prop, encourage

DISCERN (dihs <u>uhrn</u>) *v.* **-ing,-ed.**
  to perceive or recognize something
    Synonyms: descry, observe, glimpse, distinguish

PERIL (<u>pehr</u> ihl) *n.*
  danger
    Synonyms: trouble, hazard, harm

PENITENCE (<u>peh</u> nih tehnts) *n.*
  sorrow expressed for sins or offenses, repentance
    Synonyms: remorse, contrition, apology

TRIFLE (<u>trie</u> fuhl) *v.* **-ing,-ed.**
  to toy around with; to waste time or money
    Synonyms: putter, fidget; squander

The Minister's Vigil
Chapter 12

Walking in the shadow of a dream, as it were, and perhaps actually under the influence of a species of <u>somnambulism</u>, Mr. Dimmesdale reached the spot where, now so long since, Hester Prynne had lived through her first hours of public **ignominy**. The same platform or scaffold, black and weather-stained with the storm or sunshine of seven long years, and footworn, too, with the tread of many culprits who had since **ascended** it, remained standing beneath the balcony of the meeting-house. The minister went up the steps.

It was an **obscure** night of early May. An unvaried pall of cloud muffled the whole expanse of sky from **zenith** to horizon. If the same **multitude** which had stood as eye-witnesses while Hester Prynne **sustained** her punishment could now have been summoned forth, they would have **discerned** no face above the platform, nor hardly the outline of a human shape, in the dark gray of the midnight. But the town was all asleep. There was no **peril** of discovery. The minister might stand there, if it so pleased him, until morning should redden in the east, without other risk than that the dank and chill night-air would creep into his frame, and stiffen his joints with rheumatism, and clog his throat with catarrh and cough, thereby defrauding the expectant audience of tomorrow's prayer and sermon. No eye could see him, save that ever-wakeful one which had seen him in his closet, wielding the bloody scourge. Why, then, had he come hither? Was it but the mockery of **penitence**? A mockery, indeed, but in which his soul **trifled** with itself! A mockery at which angels blushed and wept, while

IMPULSE (<u>ihm</u> puhls) *n.*
sudden tendency, inclination
Synonyms: urge, whim

REMORSE (rih <u>mohrs</u>) *n.*
a gnawing distress arising from a sense of guilt
Synonyms: anguish, ruefulness, shame, penitence

DOG (dawg) *v.* **-ging,-ged.**
to follow persistently
Synonyms: track, trail, chase, hound

INVARIABLY (ihn <u>vaa</u> ree uh blee) *adv.*
without change, constantly
Synonyms: always, repeatedly, perpetually

TREMULOUS (<u>treh</u> myoo luhs) *adj.*
trembling, quivering; fearful, timid
Synonyms: shaking, palsied; timorous, anxious

DISCLOSURE (dihs <u>kloh</u> shuhr) *n.*
exposure, divulgence
Synonyms: confession, revelation

INFIRMITY (ihn <u>fuhr</u> mih tee) *n.*
weakness; disease, ailment
Synonyms: frailty; illness, affliction

INEXTRICABLE (ihn <u>ehk</u> strih kuh buhl) *adj.*
difficult to disentangle; difficult to solve
Synonyms: permanent, inflexible, stuck;
unsolvable, mysterious

REPENTANCE (rih <u>pehn</u> tehnts) *n.*
sorrow expressed for sins or offenses, penitence
Synonyms: remorse, contrition, apology

EXPIATION (ehk spee <u>ay</u> shuhn) *n.*
atonement, compensation for wrongdoing
Synonyms: amends, payment, redemption

RESTRAIN (rih <u>strayn</u>) *v.* **-ing,-ed.**
to control, repress, restrict, hold back
Synonyms: hamper, bridle, curb, check

fiends rejoiced with jeering laughter! He had been driven hither by the **impulse** of that **remorse** which **dogged** him everywhere, and whose own sister and closely linked companion was that Cowardice which **invariably** drew him back, with her **tremulous** gripe, just when the other **impulse** had hurried him to the verge of a **disclosure**. Poor, miserable man! What right had **infirmity** like his to burden itself with crime? Crime is for the iron-nerved, who have their choice either to endure it, or, if it press too hard, to exert their fierce and savage strength for a good purpose, and fling it off at once! This feeble and most sensitive of spirits could do neither, yet continually did one thing or another, which intertwined, in the same **inextricable** knot, the agony of heaven-defying guilt and vain **repentance**.

And thus, while standing on the scaffold, in this vain show of **expiation**, Mr. Dimmesdale was overcome with a great horror of mind, as if the universe were gazing at a scarlet token on his naked breast, right over his heart. On that spot, in very truth, there was, and there had long been, the gnawing and poisonous tooth of bodily pain. Without any effort of his will, or power to **restrain** himself, he shrieked aloud; an outcry that went pealing through the night, and was beaten back from one house to another, and reverberated from the hills in the background; as if a company of devils, detecting so much misery and terror in it, had made a plaything of the sound, and were bandying it to and fro.

"It is done!" muttered the minister, covering his face with his hands. "The whole town will awake, and hurry forth, and find me here!"

But it was not so. The shriek had perhaps sounded with a far greater power, to his own startled ears, than it actually possessed. The town did not awake; or, if it did, the drowsy slumberers mistook the cry either for something frightful in a dream, or for the noise of witches;

MAGISTRATE (<u>maa</u> juh strayt) *n.*
an official who can administrate laws
Synonyms: judge, arbiter, authority, marshal

EVOKE (ih <u>vohk</u>) *v.* **-ing,-ed.**
to summon or call forth, to inspire memories, to
produce a reaction
Synonyms: conjure, educe, elicit, arouse

VENERABLE (<u>veh</u> nehr uh buhl) *adj.*
respected because of age
Synonyms: distinguished, elderly

MULTITUDINOUS (muhl tih <u>too</u> dih nihs) *adj.*
many, numerous
Synonyms: myriad, countless

CLAMOR (<u>klaa</u> muhr) *n.*
noisy outcry or loudness
Synonyms: din, cacophony, racket, uproar

WARY (<u>way</u> ree) *adj.*
careful, cautious
Synonyms: watchful, vigilant, alert, guarded,
suspicious

whose voices, at that period, were often heard to pass over the settlements or lonely cottages, as they rode with Satan through the air. The clergyman, therefore, hearing no symptoms of disturbance, uncovered his eyes and looked about him. At one of the chamber-windows of Governor Bellingham's mansion, which stood at some distance, on the line of another street, he beheld the appearance of the old **magistrate** himself, with a lamp in his hand, a white nightcap on his head, and a long white gown enveloping his figure. He looked like a ghost, **evoked** unseasonably from the grave. The cry had evidently startled him. At another window of the same house, moreover, appeared old Mistress Hibbins, the Governor's sister, also with a lamp, which, even thus far off, revealed the expression of her sour and discontented face. She thrust forth her head from the lattice, and looked anxiously upward. Beyond the shadow of a doubt, this **venerable** witch-lady had heard Mr. Dimmesdale's outcry, and interpreted it, with its **multitudinous** echoes and reverberation, as the **clamor** of the fiends and night-hags, with whom she was well known to make excursions into the forest.

Detecting the gleam of Governor Bellingham's lamp, the old lady quickly extinguished her own, and vanished. Possibly, she went up among the clouds. The minister saw nothing further of her motions. The **magistrate**, after a **wary** observation of the darkness— into which, nevertheless, he could see but little farther than he might into a mill-stone—retired from the window.

The minister grew comparatively calm. His eyes, however, were soon greeted by a little, glimmering light, which, at first a long way off, was approaching up the street. It threw a gleam of recognition on here a post, and there a garden fence, and here a latticed window-pane, and there a pump, with its full trough of water, and here, again, an arched door of oak, with an iron

MINUTE (mie <u>noot</u>) (mih <u>noot</u>) *adj.*
   precise, detailed; very small
      Synonyms: critical; tiny, diminutive, infinitesimal

CONJECTURE (kuhn <u>jehk</u> shuhr) *v.* **-ing,-ed.**
   to infer, predict, guess
      Synonyms: postulate, hypothesize, suppose, surmise

LUMINARY (<u>loo</u> muh nehr ee) *n.*
   a bright object; celebrity or source of inspiration
      Synonyms: light; hero, dignitary

RESTRAIN (rih <u>strayn</u>) *v.* **-ing,-ed.**
   to control, repress, restrict, hold back
      Synonyms: hamper, bridle, curb, check

VENERABLE (<u>veh</u> nehr uh buhl) *adj.*
   respected because of age
      Synonyms: distinguished, elderly

knocker, and a rough log for the doorstep. The Reverend Mr. Dimmesdale noted all these **minute** particulars, even while firmly convinced that the doom of his existence was stealing onward, in the footsteps which he now heard; and that the gleam of the lantern would fall upon him, in a few moments more, and reveal his long-hidden secret. As the light drew nearer, he beheld, within its illuminated circle, his brother clergyman—or, to speak more accurately, his professional father, as well as highly valued friend—the Reverend Mr. Wilson; who, as Mr. Dimmesdale now **conjectured**, had been praying at the bedside of some dying man. And so he had. The good old minister came freshly from the death-chamber of Governor Winthrop, who had passed from Earth to Heaven within that very hour. And now, surrounded, like the saint-like personages of olden times, with a radiant halo, that glorified him amid this gloomy night of sin—as if the departed Governor had left him an inheritance of his glory, or as if he had caught upon himself the distant shine of the celestial city, while looking thitherward to see the triumphant pilgrim pass within its gates—now, in short, good Father Wilson was moving homeward, aiding his footsteps with a lighted lantern! The glimmer of this **luminary** suggested the above conceits to Mr. Dimmesdale, who smiled—nay, almost laughed at them—and then wondered if he were going mad.

As the Reverend Mr. Wilson passed beside the scaffold, closely muffling his Geneva cloak about him with one arm and holding the lantern before his breast with the other, the minister could hardly **restrain** himself from speaking.

"A good evening to you, **venerable** Father Wilson! Come up hither, I pray you, and pass a pleasant hour with me!"

Good heavens! Had Mr. Dimmesdale actually

VENERABLE (<u>veh</u> nehr uh buhl) *adj.*
respected because of age
Synonyms: distinguished, elderly

LURID (<u>loor</u> ihd) *adj.*
harshly shocking, revolting; glowing
Synonyms: ghastly, garish, gruesome, grisly,
macabre; fiery

SOLEMN (<u>sah</u> luhm) *adj.*
somberly impressive, deeply serious
Synonyms: dignified, earnest, ceremonial

DESCEND (dih <u>sehnd</u>) (dee <u>sehnd</u>) *v.* **-ing,-ed.**
to pass from a higher place to a lower place
Synonyms: fall, dismount, gravitate

DEFUNCT (dih <u>fuhnkt</u>) *adj.*
no longer existing, dead, extinct
Synonyms: gone, vanished, deceased, departed,
extinguished

TRANSGRESSOR (traans <u>greh</u> suhr) *n.*
violator; a trespasser
Synonyms: sinner, offender; overstepper

TUMULT (<u>tuh</u> muhlt) *n.*
state of confusion, agitation
Synonyms: disturbance, turmoil, din, commotion

WAX (waaks) *v.* **-ing,-ed.**
to increase gradually; to begin to be
Synonyms: enlarge, expand, swell; become, grow

PATRIARCH (<u>pay</u> tree ahrk) *n.*
an old well-respected man, often the head of a
family; a high member or head of a church
Synonyms: elder, leader; bishop, dignitary

DECOROUS (<u>deh</u> kuhr uhs) (deh <u>kohr</u> uhs) *adj.*
proper, tasteful, socially correct
Synonyms: polite, courteous, appropriate

AWRY (uh <u>rie</u>) *adv.*
crooked, askew, amiss
Synonyms: aslant, wrong

spoken? For one instant, he believed that these words had passed his lips. But they were uttered only within his imagination. The **venerable** Father Wilson continued to step slowly onward, looking carefully at the muddy pathway before his feet, and never once turning his head towards the guilty platform. When the light of the glimmering lantern had faded quite away, the minister discovered, by the faintness which came over him, that the last few moments had been a crisis of terrible anxiety; although his mind had made an involuntary effort to relieve itself by a kind of **lurid** playfulness.

Shortly afterwards, the like grisly sense of the humorous again stole in among the **solemn** phantoms of his thought. He felt his limbs growing stiff with the unaccustomed chilliness of the night, and doubted whether he should be able to **descend** the steps of the scaffold. Morning would break, and find him there. The neighborhood would begin to rouse itself. The earliest riser, coming forth in the dim twilight, would perceive a vaguely defined figure aloft on the place of shame; and, half crazed <u>betwixt</u> alarm and curiosity, would go, knocking from door to door, summoning all the people to behold the ghost—as he needs must think it—of some **defunct transgressor**. A dusky **tumult** would flap its wings from one house to another. Then—the morning light still **waxing** stronger—old **patriarchs** would rise up in great haste, each in his flannel gown, and matronly dames, without pausing to put off their night-gear. The whole tribe of **decorous** personages, who had never heretofore been seen with a single hair of their heads **awry**, would start into public view, with the disorder of a nightmare in their aspects. Old Governor Bellingham would come grimly forth, with his King James's <u>ruff</u> fastened askew; and Mistress Hibbins, with some twigs of the forest clinging to her skirts, and looking sourer than ever, as having hardly got a wink of sleep after her night

VISAGE (<u>vih</u> sihj) *n.*
   the appearance of a person or place, face
      Synonyms: expression, look, style, manner

DISCERN (dihs <u>uhrn</u>) *v.* **-ing,-ed.**
   to perceive or recognize something
      Synonyms: descry, observe, glimpse, distinguish

ACUTE (uh <u>kyoot</u>) *adj.*
   sharp, pointed, severe; clever, shrewd
      Synonyms: intense, fierce; ingenious, keen

SUPPRESS (suh <u>prehs</u>) *v.* **-ing,-ed.**
   to restrain (like a whisper), to hold back
      Synonyms: subdue, stifle, muffle, quell, curb

ride; and good Father Wilson, too, after spending half the night at a death-bed and liking ill to be disturbed, thus early, out of his dreams about the glorified saints. Hither, likewise, would come the elders and deacons of Mr. Dimmesdale's church, and the young virgins who so idolized their minister, and had made a shrine for him in their white bosoms; which now, by the by, in their hurry and confusion, they would scantly have given themselves time to cover with their kerchiefs. All people, in a word, would come stumbling over their thresholds, and turning up their amazed and horror-stricken **visages** around the scaffold. Whom would they **discern** there, with the red eastern light upon his brow? Whom, but the Reverend Arthur Dimmesdale, half frozen to death, overwhelmed with shame, and standing where Hester Prynne had stood!

Carried away by the grotesque horror of this picture, the minister, unawares, and to his own infinite alarm, burst into a great peal of laughter. It was immediately responded to by a light, airy, childish laugh, in which, with a thrill of the heart—but he knew not whether of exquisite pain, or pleasure as **acute**—he recognized the tones of little Pearl.

"Pearl! Little Pearl!" cried he, after a moment's pause; then, **suppressing** his voice, "Hester! Hester Prynne! Are you there?"

"Yes, it is Hester Prynne!" she replied, in a tone of surprise; and the minister heard her footsteps approaching from the sidewalk, along which she had been passing. "It is I, and my little Pearl."

"Whence come you, Hester?" asked the minister. "What sent you hither?"

"I have been watching at a death-bed," answered Hester Prynne, "at Governor Winthrop's death-bed, and have taken his measure for a robe, and am now going homeward to my dwelling."

ASCEND (uh sehnd) *v.* **-ing,-ed.**
to rise to another level or climb; to move upward
Synonyms: elevate, escalate, mount; hoist, lift

TUMULTUOUS (tuh muhl choo uhs) *adj.*
agitated, confusing or disorderly
Synonyms: turbulent, chaotic, hectic, disturbed

TORPID (tohr pihd) *adj.*
dormant; lethargic, unable to move
Synonyms: hibernating, inactive, inert; apathetic,
sluggish

"Come up hither, Hester, thou and little Pearl," said the Reverend Mr. Dimmesdale. "Ye have both been here before, but I was not with you. Come up hither once again, and we will stand all three together!"

She silently **ascended** the steps, and stood on the platform, holding little Pearl by the hand. The minister felt for the child's other hand, and took it. The moment that he did so, there came what seemed a **tumultuous** rush of new life, other life than his own, pouring like a torrent into his heart, and hurrying through all his veins, as if the mother and the child were communicating their vital warmth to his half-**torpid** system. The three formed an electric chain.

"Minister!" whispered little Pearl.

"What wouldst thou say, child?" asked Mr. Dimmesdale.

"Wilt thou stand here with Mother and me, tomorrow noontide?" inquired Pearl.

"Nay, not so, my little Pearl," answered the minister; for, with the new energy of the moment, all the dread of public exposure, that had so long been the anguish of his life, had returned upon him; and he was already trembling at the conjunction in which—with a strange joy, nevertheless—he now found himself. "Not so, my child. I shall, indeed, stand with thy mother and thee one other day, but not tomorrow."

Pearl laughed, and attempted to pull away her hand. But the minister held it fast.

"A moment longer, my child!" said he.

"But wilt thou promise," asked Pearl, "to take my hand, and Mother's hand, tomorrow noontide?"

"Not then, Pearl," said the minister, "but another time."

"And what other time?" persisted the child.

"At the great judgment day," whispered the minister—and, strangely enough, the sense that he was a

IMPEL (ihm <u>pehl</u>) *v.* **-ling,-led.**
  to urge forward as if driven by a strong moral pressure
    Synonyms: push, prompt, incite, instigate

MEDIUM (<u>mee</u> dee uhm) *n.*
  a substance or object that is used to transmit or
  accomplish something
    Synonyms: means, instrument, vehicle, mechanism

IMPART (ihm <u>pahrt</u>) *v.* **-ing,-ed.**
  to give or share, to pass on
    Synonyms: bestow, contribute, reveal, convey

SINGULARITY (sihn gyuh <u>layr</u> ih tee) *n.*
  uncommonness, peculiarity
    Synonyms: difference, oddity, rarity, uniqueness,
    individuality

SOLEMN (<u>sah</u> luhm) *adj.*
  somberly impressive, deeply serious
    Synonyms: dignified, earnest, ceremonial

professional teacher of the truth **impelled** him to answer the child so. "Then, and there, before the judgment seat, thy mother, and thou, and I, must stand together. But the daylight of this world shall not see our meeting!"

Pearl laughed again.

But, before Mr. Dimmesdale had done speaking, a light gleamed far and wide over all the muffled sky. It was doubtless caused by one of those meteors, which the night-watcher may so often observe, burning out to waste, in the vacant regions of the atmosphere. So powerful was its radiance, that it thoroughly illuminated the dense **medium** of cloud betwixt the sky and earth. The great vault brightened, like the dome of an immense lamp. It showed the familiar scene of the street, with the distinctness of mid-day, but also with the awfulness that is always **imparted** to familiar objects by an unaccustomed light. The wooden houses, with their jutting stories and quaint gable-peaks; the doorsteps and thresholds, with the early grass springing up about them; the garden-plots, black with freshly-turned earth; the wheel-track, little worn, and, even in the market-place, margined with green on either side—all were visible, but with a **singularity** of aspect that seemed to give another moral interpretation to the things of this world than they had ever borne before. And there stood the minister, with his hand over his heart; and Hester Prynne, with the embroidered letter glimmering on her bosom; and little Pearl, herself a symbol, and the connecting link between those two. They stood in the noon of that strange and **solemn** splendor, as if it were the light that is to reveal all secrets and the daybreak that shall unite all who belong to one another.

There was witchcraft in little Pearl's eyes and her face, as she glanced upward at the minister, wore that naughty smile which made its expression frequently so elfish. She withdrew her hand from Mr. Dimmesdale's,

ZENITH (<u>zee</u> nihth) *n.*
highest point, summit
Synonyms: acme, apex, climax, crown, pinnacle

PESTILENCE (<u>peh</u> stihl ehnts) *n.*
epidemic, plague, illness
Synonyms: contagion, scourge, sickness, disease

FOREBODE (fohr <u>bohd</u>) *v.* **-ing,-ed.**
to have a presentiment of upcoming evil
Synonyms: predict, portend, foretell, anticipate

MULTITUDE (<u>muhl</u> tuh tood) *n.*
a crowd; the state of being many, a great number
Synonyms: throng; mass, myriad

MEDIUM (<u>mee</u> dee uhm) *n.*
a substance or object that is used to transmit or
accomplish something
Synonyms: means, instrument, vehicle, mechanism

PROVIDENCE (<u>prah</u> vih dehnts) *n.*
divine control and direction by God; preparation
and foresight
Synonyms: fate, destiny, good luck; prudence,
precaution

MORBIDLY (<u>mohr</u> bihd lee) *adv.*
gloomily, gruesomely
Synonyms: darkly, psychotically, horridly

IMPUTE (ihm <u>pyoot</u>) *v.* **-ing,-ed.**
to attribute
Synonyms: ascribe, credit

and pointed across the street. But he clasped both his hands over his breast, and cast his eyes towards the **zenith**.

Nothing was more common, in those days, than to interpret all meteoric appearances, and other natural phenomena, that occurred with less regularity than the rise and set of sun and moon, as so many revelations from a supernatural source. Thus, a blazing spear, a sword of flame, a bow, or a sheaf of arrows, seen in the midnight sky, prefigured Indian warfare. **Pestilence** was known to have been **foreboded** by a shower of crimson light. We doubt whether any marked event, for good or evil, ever befell New England, from its settlement down to Revolutionary times, of which the inhabitants had not been previously warned by some spectacle of this nature. Not seldom, it had been seen by **multitudes**. Oftener, however, its credibility rested on the faith of some lonely eye-witness, who beheld the wonder through the colored, magnifying, and distorting **medium** of his imagination, and shaped it more distinctly in his afterthought. It was, indeed, a majestic idea, that the destiny of nations should be revealed, in these awful hieroglyphics, on the cope of Heaven. A scroll so wide might not be deemed too expansive for **Providence** to write a people's doom upon. The belief was a favorite one with our forefathers, as betokening that their infant commonwealth was under a celestial guardianship of peculiar intimacy and strictness. But what shall we say when an individual discovers a revelation addressed to himself alone, on the same vast sheet of record! In such a case, it could only be the symptom of a highly disordered mental state, when a man, rendered **morbidly** self-contemplative by long, intense, and secret pain, had extended his egotism over the whole expanse of nature, until the firmament itself should appear no more than a fitting page for his soul's history and fate!

We **impute** it, therefore, solely to the disease in his

ZENITH (<u>zee</u> nihth) *n.*
highest point, summit
Synonyms: acme, apex, climax, crown, pinnacle

SINGULAR (<u>sihn</u> gyuh luhr) *adj.*
uncommon, peculiar
Synonyms: unusual, odd, rare, unique, individual

DISCERN (dihs <u>uhrn</u>) *v.* **-ing,-ed.**
to perceive or recognize something
Synonyms: descry, observe, glimpse, distinguish

IMPART (ihm <u>pahrt</u>) *v.* **-ing,-ed.**
to give or share, to pass on
Synonyms: bestow, contribute, reveal, convey

MALEVOLENCE (muh <u>lehv</u> uh luhnts) *n.*
ill-will, desire to cause evil or harm to others; hatred
Synonyms: spite, unkindness; animosity, malice

KINDLE (<u>kihn</u> duhl) *v.* **-ing,-ed.**
to set fire to or ignite; to excite or inspire
Synonyms: light, spark; arouse, awaken

DISCLOSE (dihs <u>klohs</u>) *v.* **-ing,-ed.**
to expose, divulge
Synonyms: confess, reveal, impart

ADMONISH (aad <u>mahn</u> ihsh) *v.* **-ing,-ed.**
to caution or reprimand
Synonyms: reprove, chide, upbraid, berate, rebuke

ARCH (ahrch) *adj.*
having the highest rank, most important;
mischievous, roguish
Synonyms: chief, top; impish, saucy, ironic
Note: an "arch-fiend" refers to the devil

own eye and heart, that the minister, looking upward to the **zenith**, beheld there the appearance of an immense letter—the letter A—marked out in lines of dull red light. Not but the meteor may have shown itself at that point, burning duskily through a veil of cloud; but with no such shape as his guilty imagination gave it; or, at least, with so little definiteness, that another's guilt might have seen another symbol in it.

There was a **singular** circumstance that characterized Mr. Dimmesdale's psychological state at this moment. All the time that he gazed upward to the **zenith**, he was, nevertheless, perfectly aware that little Pearl was pointing her finger towards old Roger Chillingworth, who stood at no great distance from the scaffold. The minister appeared to see him, with the same glance that **discerned** the miraculous letter. To his features, as to all other objects, the meteoric light **imparted** a new expression; or it might well be that the physician was not careful then, as at all other times, to hide the **malevolence** with which he looked upon his victim. Certainly, if the meteor **kindled** up the sky, and **disclosed** the earth, with an awfulness that **admonished** Hester Prynne and the clergyman of the day of judgment, then might Roger Chillingworth have passed with them for the **arch**-fiend, standing there with a smile and scowl, to claim his own. So vivid was the expression, or so intense the minister's perception of it, that it seemed still to remain painted on the darkness, after the meteor had vanished, with an effect as if the street and all things else were at once annihilated.

"Who is that man, Hester?" gasped Mr. Dimmesdale, overcome with terror. "I shiver at him! Dost thou know the man? I hate him, Hester!"

She remembered her oath, and was silent.

"I tell thee, my soul shivers at him!" muttered the

ERUDITE (<u>ehr</u> yuh diet) (<u>ehr</u> uh diet) *adj.*
   learned, scholarly
      Synonyms: knowledgeable, cultured, well-read,
      educated, literate

PIOUS (<u>pie</u> uhs) *adj.*
   dedicated, devout; extremely religious
      Synonyms: observant, reverent; sanctimonious

BESEECH (bih <u>seech</u>) *v.* **-ing,-ed.**
   to beg, plead, implore
      Synonyms: petition, supplicate, entreat

minister again. "Who is he? Who is he? Canst thou do nothing for me? I have a nameless horror of the man!"

"Minister," said little Pearl, "I can tell thee who he is!"

"Quickly, then, child!" said the minister, bending his ear close to her lips. "Quickly!—and as low as thou canst whisper."

Pearl mumbled something into his ear that sounded, indeed, like human language, but was only such gibberish as children may be heard amusing themselves with by the hour together. At all events, if it involved any secret information in regard to old Roger Chillingworth, it was in a tongue unknown to the **erudite** clergyman, and did but increase the bewilderment of his mind. The elfish child then laughed aloud.

"Dost thou mock me now?" said the minister.

"Thou wast not bold! Thou wast not true!" answered the child. "Thou wouldst not promise to take my hand, and Mother's hand, tomorrow noontide!"

"Worthy Sir," answered the physician, who had now advanced to the foot of the platform. "**Pious** Master Dimmesdale! Can this be you? Well, well, indeed! We men of study, whose heads are in our books, have need to be straitly looked after! We dream in our waking moments, and walk in our sleep. Come, good Sir, and my dear friend, I pray you, let me lead you home!"

"How knewest thou that I was here?" asked the minister, fearfully.

"Verily, and in good faith," answered Roger Chillingworth, "I knew nothing of the matter. I had spent the better part of the night at the bedside of the worshipful Governor Winthrop, doing what my poor skill might to give him ease. He going home to a better world, I, likewise, was on my way homeward, when this strange light shone out. Come with me, I **beseech** you, Reverend Sir; else you will be poorly able to do Sabbath duty tomorrow. Aha! See now, how they trouble the brain, these books, these books!

WHIMSEY or WHIMSY (<u>wihm</u> zee) *n.*
a fanciful idea; an act of spontaneity
Synonyms: notion, fantasy; impulse, outburst, bout

DESPONDENCY (dih <u>spahn</u> duhn see) *n.*
discouragement, dejection
Synonyms: sadness, depression, desolation

DISCOURSE (<u>dihs</u> kohrs) *n.*
a formal, orderly, and extended expression of
thought; the verbal exchange of ideas
Synonyms: dialogue, conversation; speech

REPLETE (rih <u>pleet</u>) *adj.*
abundantly supplied
Synonyms: abounding, satiated, gorged, stuffed, full

EFFICACY (<u>eff</u> uh kuh see) *n.*
effectiveness, efficiency
Synonym: potency

SCURRILOUS (<u>skuhr</u> uh luhs) *adj.*
vulgar, low, indecent
Synonyms: coarse, abusive, foul-mouthed

REVERENCE (<u>reh</u> vuhr ehnts) *n.*
the state of being well respected; deep respect, awe
Synonyms: veneration, adoration, admiration

PORTENT (<u>pohr</u> tehnt) *n.*
an omen, a sign of what is to come
Synonyms: token, prodigy

You should study less, good Sir, and take a little pastime; or these night-**whimseys** will grow upon you."

"I will go home with you," said Mr. Dimmesdale.

With a chill **despondency**, like one awaking, all nerveless from an ugly dream, he yielded himself to the physician, and was led away.

The next day, however, being the Sabbath, he preached a **discourse** which was held to be the richest and most powerful, and the most **replete** with heavenly influences, that had ever proceeded from his lips. Souls, it is said more souls than one, were brought to the truth by the **efficacy** of that sermon, and vowed within themselves to cherish a holy gratitude towards Mr. Dimmesdale throughout the long hereafter. But, as he came down the pulpit steps, the gray-bearded sexton met him, holding up a black glove, which the minister recognized as his own.

"It was found," said the sexton, "this morning, on the scaffold where evil-doers are set up to public shame. Satan dropped it there, I take it, intending a **scurrilous** jest against your **reverence**. But, indeed, he was blind and foolish, as he ever and always is. A pure hand needs no glove to cover it!"

"Thank you, my good friend," said the minister, gravely, but startled at heart; for, so confused was his remembrance, that he had almost brought himself to look at the events of the past night as visionary. "Yes, it seems to be my glove, indeed!"

"And, since Satan saw fit to steal it, your **reverence** must needs handle him without gloves, henceforward," remarked the old sexton, grimly smiling. "But did your **reverence** hear of the **portent** that was seen last night? A great red letter in the sky—the letter A, which we interpret to stand for Angel. For, as our good Governor Winthrop was made an angel this past night, it was doubtless held fit that there should be some notice thereof!"

"No," answered the minister, "I had not heard of it."

SINGULAR (<u>sihn</u> gyuh luhr) *adj.*
uncommon, peculiar
Synonyms: rare, unusual, odd, unique, individual

ABASE (uh <u>bays</u>) *v.* **-ing-ed.**
to shame, disgrace
Synonyms: humble, humiliate, demean

GROVEL (<u>grah</u> vuhl) *v.* **-ling,-led.**
to humble oneself in a demeaning way
Synonyms: cringe, fawn, kowtow, bootlick

FACULTY (<u>faa</u> kuhl tee) *n.*
the ability to act or do
Synonyms: aptitude, capability, sense, skill

RETAIN (rih <u>tayn</u>) *v.* **-ing,-ed.**
to hold, keep possession of
Synonyms: withhold, reserve

PRISTINE (prih <u>steen</u>) *adj.*
untouched, uncorrupted
Synonyms: pure, clean

MORBID (<u>mohr</u> bihd) *adj.*
1. having an unhealthy mentality; relating to disease
   Synonyms: unwholesome; pathological
2. abnormally terrible and gloomy; gruesome
   Synonyms: dismal, dreary; grisly, macabre

REPOSE (rih <u>pohz</u>) *n.*
a state of peace or tranquility; sleep, rest, ease
Synonyms: calmness, serenity; relaxation, leisure, idleness

SECLUSION (sih <u>cloo</u> zhuhn) *n.*
isolation, detachment
Synonyms: separation, privacy, solitude

Another View of Hester
Chapter 13

In her late **singular** interview with Mr. Dimmesdale, Hester Prynne was shocked at the condition to which she found the clergyman reduced. His nerve seemed absolutely destroyed. His moral force was **abased** into more than childish weakness. It **grovelled** helpless on the ground, even while his intellectual **faculties retained** their **pristine** strength, or had perhaps acquired a **morbid** energy, which disease only could have given them. With her knowledge of a train of circumstances hidden from all others, she could readily infer that, besides the legitimate action of his own conscience, a terrible machinery had been brought to bear, and was still operating, on Mr. Dimmesdale's well-being and **repose**. Knowing what this poor, fallen man had once been, her whole soul was moved by the shuddering terror with which he had appealed to her—the outcast woman—for support against his instinctively discovered enemy. She decided, moreover, that he had a right to her utmost aid. Little accustomed, in her long **seclusion** from society, to measure her ideas of right and wrong by any standard external to herself, Hester saw—or seemed to see—that there lay a responsibility upon her in reference to the clergyman, which she owed to no other, nor to the whole world besides. The links that united her to the rest of human kind—links of flowers, or silk, or gold, or whatever the material—had all been broken. Here was the iron link of mutual crime, which neither he nor she could break. Like all other ties, it brought along with it its obligations.

Hester Prynne did not now occupy precisely the same

IGNOMINY (<u>ihg</u> nuh mih nee) *n.*
disgrace and dishonor
Synonyms: degradation, debasement

IMPEDE (ihm <u>peed</u>) *v.* **-ing,-ed.**
to obstruct, to act as a barrier
Synonyms: delay, thwart, interfere, hinder, block

REQUITAL (rih <u>kwie</u> tuhl) *n.*
repayment, compensation
Synonyms: reciprocation, reimbursement

INFAMY (<u>ihn</u> fuh mee) *n.*
reputation for bad deeds
Synonyms: disgrace, dishonor, shame

PAUPER (<u>paw</u> puhr) *n.*
a very poor person
Synonym: beggar

GIBE (jieb) *n.*
a heckling or taunting remark
Synonyms: ridicule, mockery, derision, jeer, jab

position in which we beheld her during the earlier periods of her **ignominy**. Years had come and gone. Pearl was now seven years old. Her mother, with the scarlet letter on her breast, glittering in its fantastic embroidery, had long been a familiar object to the townspeople. As is apt to be the case when a person stands out in any prominence before the community, and, at the same time, interferes neither with public nor individual interests and conveniences, a species of general regard had ultimately grown up in reference to Hester Prynne. It is to the credit of human nature, that, except where its self-ishness is brought into play, it loves more readily than it hates. Hatred, by a gradual and quiet process, will even be transformed to love, unless the change be **impeded** by a continually new irritation of the original feeling of hostility. In this matter of Hester Prynne, there was neither irritation nor irksomeness. She never battled with the public, but submitted, uncomplainingly, to its worst usage; she made no claim upon it in **requital** for what she suffered; she did not weigh upon its sympathies. Then, also, the blameless purity of her life during all these years in which she had been set apart to **infamy**, was reckoned largely in her favor. With nothing now to lose, in the sight of mankind, and with no hope, and seemingly no wish, of gaining anything, it could only be a genuine regard for virtue that had brought back the poor wanderer to its paths.

It was perceived, too, that while Hester never put forward even the humblest title to share in the world's privileges—further than to breathe the common air, and earn daily bread for little Pearl and herself by the faithful labor of her hands—she was quick to acknowledge her sisterhood with the race of man, whenever benefits were to be conferred. None so ready as she to give of her little substance to every demand of poverty; even though the bitter-hearted **pauper** threw back a **gibe** in

REQUITAL (rih <u>kwie</u> tuhl) *n.*
repayment, compensation
  Synonyms: reciprocation, reimbursement

PESTILENCE (<u>peh</u> stihl ehnts) *n.*
 illness, epidemic, plague
  Synonyms: contagion, scourge, sickness, disease

STALK (stahk) *v.* **-ing,-ed.**
to hunt, pursue
  Synonyms: track, shadow, trail

CALAMITY (kuh <u>laam</u> ih tee) *n.*
misfortune; state of despair
  Synonyms: disaster, cataclysm; misery

MEDIUM (<u>mee</u> dee uhm) *n.*
a substance or object that is used to transmit or
accomplish something
  Synonyms: means, instrument, vehicle, mechanism

ZEALOUSLY (<u>zeh</u> luhs lee) *adv.*
passionately, devotedly
  Synonyms: fanatically, enthusiastically, militantly,
  radically

requital of the food brought regularly to his door, or the garments wrought for him by the fingers that could have embroidered a monarch's robe. None so self-devoted as Hester, when **pestilence stalked** through the town. In all seasons of **calamity**, indeed, whether general or of individuals, the outcast of society at once found her place. She came, not as a guest, but as a rightful inmate, into the household that was darkened by trouble; as if its gloomy twilight were a **medium** in which she was entitled to hold <u>intercourse</u> with her fellow-creatures. There glimmered the embroidered letter, with comfort in its unearthly ray. Elsewhere the token of sin, it was the taper of the sick-chamber. It had even thrown its gleam, in the sufferer's hard extremity, across the verge of time. It had shown him where to set his foot, while the light of earth was fast becoming dim, and ere the light of futurity could reach him. In such emergencies, Hester's nature showed itself warm and rich; a well-spring of human tenderness, unfailing to every real demand, and inexhaustible by the largest. Her breast, with its badge of shame, was but the softer pillow for the head that needed one. She was self-ordained a Sister of Mercy; or, we may rather say, the world's heavy hand had so ordained her, when neither the world nor she looked forward to this result. The letter was the symbol of her calling. Such helpfulness was found in her—so much power to do and power to sympathize—that many people refused to interpret the scarlet A by its original signification. They said that it meant Able; so strong was Hester Prynne, with a woman's strength.

It was only the darkened house that could contain her. When sunshine came again, she was not there. Her shadow had faded across the threshold. The helpful inmate had departed, without one backward glance to gather up the <u>meed</u> of gratitude, if any were in the hearts of those whom she had served so **zealously**.

SAT Vocabulary

RESOLUTE (reh suh <u>loot</u>) *adj.*
determined; with a clear purpose
Synonyms: firm, unwavering; intent, resolved

ACCOST (uh <u>cahst</u>) (uh <u>kawst</u>) *v.* **-ing,-ed.**
to approach and speak to someone, often in an
aggressive way
Synonyms: address, confront

HUMILITY (hyoo <u>mihl</u> ih tee) *n.*
humbleness
Synonyms: modesty, reserve, lowliness

DESPOTIC (dehs <u>pah</u> tihk) *adj.*
tyrannical, oppressive
Synonyms: dictatorial, authoritarian

DESPOT (<u>dehs</u> puht) (<u>dehs</u> paht) *n.*
a tyrannical ruler, totalitarian
Synonyms: autocrat, dictator

INCLINE (ihn <u>klien</u>) *v.* **-ing,-ed.** *(See page 278.)*

BENIGN (bih <u>nien</u>) *adj.*
kindly, gentle, or harmless
Synonyms: innocuous, mild, safe

COUNTENANCE (<u>kown</u> tuh nuhns) *n.*
appearance, facial expression
Synonyms: face, features, visage

FORTIFY (<u>fohr</u> tih fie) *v.* **-ing,-ed.**
to make strong, to reinforce or secure
Synonyms: invigorate, strengthen, energize, support

BENEVOLENCE (buh <u>neh</u> vuh luhnts) *n. (See page 216.)*

EMINENT (<u>ehm</u> uh nuhnt) *adj. (See page 240.)*

IMPOSE (ihm <u>pohz</u>) *v.* **-ing,-ed.** *(See page 180.)*

PENANCE (<u>peh</u> nihns) *n. (See page 194.)*

AFFLICTED (uh <u>flihk</u> tihd) *adj.*
severely distressed, anguished
Synonyms: troubled, tormented, wounded

PROPENSITY (pruh <u>pehn</u> suh tee) *n.*
inclination, tendency
Synonyms: predilection, bias, penchant

Meeting them in the street, she never raised her head to receive their greeting. If they were **resolute** to **accost** her, she laid her finger on the scarlet letter, and passed on. This might be pride, but was so like **humility**, that it produced all the softening influence of the latter quality on the public mind. The public is **despotic** in its temper; it is capable of denying common justice, when too strenuously demanded as a right; but quite as frequently it awards more than justice when the appeal is made, as **despots** love to have it made, entirely to its generosity. Interpreting Hester Prynne's deportment as an appeal of this nature, society was **inclined** to show its former victim a more **benign countenance** than she cared to be favored with, or, perchance, than she deserved.

The rulers, and the wise and learned men of the community, were longer in acknowledging the influence of Hester's good qualities than the people. The prejudices which they shared in common with the latter were **fortified** in themselves by an iron framework of reasoning, that made it a far tougher labor to expel them. Day by day, nevertheless, their sour and rigid wrinkles were relaxing into something which, in the due course of years, might grow to be an expression of almost **benevolence**. Thus it was with the men of rank, on whom their **eminent** position **imposed** the guardianship of the public morals. Individuals in private life, meanwhile, had quite forgiven Hester Prynne for her frailty; nay, more, they had begun to look upon the scarlet letter as the token, not of that one sin, for which she had borne so long and dreary a **penance**, but of her many good deeds since. "Do you see that woman with the embroidered badge?" they would say to strangers. "It is our Hester—the town's own Hester, who is so kind to the poor, so helpful to the sick, so comforting to the **afflicted**!" Then, it is true, the **propensity** of human nature to tell the very worst of itself, when embodied in

CONSTRAIN (kuhn strayn) *v.* **-ing,-ed.**
  to force, impel; restrain
    Synonyms: prompt, urge; restrict, control, calculate

IMPART (ihm pahrt) *v.* **-ing,-ed.**
  to give or share, to pass on
    Synonyms: bestow, contribute, reveal, convey

PERIL (pehr ihl) *n.*
  danger
    Synonyms: trouble, hazard, harm

REPULSIVE (rih puhl sihv) *adj.*
  sickening, disgusting, repellant
    Synonyms: nauseating, offensive

REPEL (rih pehl) *v.* **-ling,-led.**
  to disgust, offend; to rebuff, repulse
    Synonyms: nauseate, revolt; reject, spurn, parry

AUSTERITY (aw stayr ih tee) *n.*
  lack of adornment; strictness or severity of manner
    Synonyms: bareness, simplicity; discipline

LUXURIANT (luhg zhoor ee ehnt) *adj.*
  lavish, elegant
    Synonyms: rich, abundant, profuse

the person of another, would **constrain** them to whisper the black scandal of bygone years. It was nonetheless a fact, however, that, in the eyes of the very men who spoke thus, the scarlet letter had the effect of the cross on a nun's bosom. It **imparted** to the wearer a kind of sacredness which enabled her to walk securely amid all **peril**. Had she fallen among thieves, it would have kept her safe. It was reported, and believed by many, that an Indian had drawn his arrow against the badge, and that the missile struck it, but fell harmless to the ground.

The effect of the symbol—or, rather, of the position in respect to society that was indicated by it—on the mind of Hester Prynne herself, was powerful and peculiar. All the light and graceful foliage of her character had been withered up by this red-hot brand, and had long ago fallen away, leaving a bare and harsh outline which might have been **repulsive**, had she possessed friends or companions to be **repelled** by it. Even the attractiveness of her person had undergone a similar change. It might be partly owing to the studied **austerity** of her dress, and partly to the lack of demonstration in her manners. It was a sad transformation, too, that her rich and **luxuriant** hair had either been cut off, or was so completely hidden by a cap, that not a shining lock of it ever once gushed into the sunshine. It was due in part to all these causes, but still more to something else, that there seemed to be no longer anything in Hester's face for Love to dwell upon; nothing in Hester's form, though majestic and statue-like, that Passion would ever dream of clasping in its embrace; nothing in Hester's bosom, to make it ever again the pillow of affection. Some attribute had departed from her, the permanence of which had been essential to keep her a woman. Such is frequently the fate, and such the stern development, of the feminine character and person, when the woman has encountered, and lived through, an experience of

RETRIEVE (rih <u>treev</u>) *v.* **-ing,-ed.**
to reclaim; to bring, fetch
Synonyms: recover, regain, recoup; get, return

EMANCIPATED (ih <u>maan</u> suh pay tihd) *adj.*
freed, liberated
Synonyms: independent, released

STIGMATIZE (<u>stihg</u> muh tiez) *v.* **-ing,-ed.**
to mark with disgrace or inferiority
Synonyms: scandalize, denounce, brand

PERILOUS (<u>pehr</u> uh luhs) *adj.*
full of danger
Synonyms: risky, hazardous, unsafe

peculiar severity. If she be all tenderness, she will die. If she survives, the tenderness will either be crushed out of her, or—and the outward semblance is the same—crushed so deeply into her heart that it can never show itself more. The latter is perhaps the truest theory. She who has once been woman, and ceased to be so, might at any moment become a woman again if there were only the magic touch to effect the <u>transfiguration</u>. We shall see whether Hester Prynne were ever afterwards so touched, and <u>transfigured</u>.

Much of the marble coldness of Hester's impression was to be attributed to the circumstance, that her life had turned, in a great measure, from passion and feeling to thought. Standing alone in the world—alone, as to any dependence on society, and with little Pearl to be guided and protected—alone, and hopeless of **retrieving** her position, even had she not scorned to consider it desirable—she cast away the fragments of a broken chain. The world's law was no law for her mind. It was an age in which the human intellect, newly **emancipated**, had taken a more active and a wider range than for many centuries before. Men of the sword had overthrown nobles and kings. Men bolder than these had overthrown and rearranged—not actually, but within the sphere of theory, which was their most real abode—the whole system of ancient prejudice, wherewith was linked much of ancient principle. Hester Prynne <u>imbibed</u> this spirit. She assumed a freedom of speculation, then common enough on the other side of the Atlantic, but which our forefathers, had they known it, would have held to be a deadlier crime than that **stigmatized** by the scarlet letter. In her lonesome cottage, by the seashore, thoughts visited her, such as dared to enter no other dwelling in New England; shadowy guests that would have been as **perilous** as demons to

SAT Vocabulary

CONFORM (kuhn <u>fohrm</u>) *v.* **-ing,-ed.**
to comply with accepted rules and customs
Synonyms: adapt, obey, agree

QUIETUDE (<u>kwie</u> eh tood) *n.*
peace or tranquility
Synonyms: calm, ease, contentment, serenity

PROPHETESS (<u>prah</u> feh tihs) *n.*
a woman who has the ability to foretell events
Synonyms: clairvoyant, predictor, seer, oracle

UNDERMINE (uhn duhr <u>mien</u>) *v.* **-ing,-ed.**
to sabotage, thwart
Synonyms: weaken, sap, undercut, subvert, impair

PROVIDENCE (<u>prah</u> vih dehnts) *n.*
divine control and direction by God; preparation
and foresight
Synonyms: fate, destiny, good luck; prudence,
precaution

AMISS (uh <u>mihs</u>) *adv.*
accidentally, mistakenly; in a defective way
Synonyms: astray, awry; faultily

IMPEL (ihm <u>pehl</u>) *v.* **-ling,-led.**
to urge forward as if driven by a strong moral pressure
Synonyms: push, prompt, incite, instigate

DISCERN (dihs <u>uhrn</u>) *v.* **-ing,-ed.**
to perceive or recognize something
Synonyms: descry, observe, glimpse, distinguish

their entertainer, could they have been seen so much as knocking at her door.

It is remarkable that persons who speculate the most boldly often **conform** with the most perfect **quietude** to the external regulations of society. The thought suffices them, without investing itself in the flesh and blood of action. So it seemed to be with Hester. Yet, had little Pearl never come to her from the spiritual world, it might have been far otherwise. Then, she might have come down to us in history, hand in hand with Ann Hutchinson, as the foundress of a religious sect. She might, in one of her phases, have been a **prophetess**. She might, and not improbably would, have suffered death from the stern tribunals of the period, for attempting to **undermine** the foundations of the Puritan establishment. But, in the education of her child, the mother's enthusiasm of thought had something to wreak itself upon. **Providence**, in the person of this little girl, had assigned to Hester's charge the germ and blossom of womanhood, to be cherished and developed amid a host of difficulties. Everything was against her. The world was hostile. The child's own nature had something wrong in it, which continually betokened that she had been born **amiss**—the effluence of her mother's lawless passion—and often **impelled** Hester to ask, in bitterness of heart, whether it were for ill or good that the poor little creature had been born at all.

Indeed, the same dark question often rose into her mind, with reference to the whole race of womanhood. Was existence worth accepting, even to the happiest among them? As concerned her own individual existence, she had long ago decided in the negative, and dismissed the point as settled. A tendency to speculation, though it may keep woman quiet, as it does man, yet makes her sad. She **discerns**, it may be, such a hopeless task before her. As a first step, the whole system of

OBVIATE (<u>ahb</u> vee ayt) *v.* **-ing,-ed.**
to anticipate and prevent, to make unnecessary
Synonyms: eliminate, preclude, avert, forestall, deter

ETHEREAL (ih <u>theer</u> ee uhl) *adj.*
not earthly, spiritual; intangible
Synonyms: heavenly; diaphanous, airy, gossamer, sheer

LABYRINTH (<u>laab</u> uh rihnth) *n.*
maze
Synonyms: entanglement, mesh, web

INSURMOUNTABLE (ihn suhr <u>mownt</u> uh buhl) *adj.*
impossible, unable to be overcome
Synonyms: unachievable, insuperable, unattainable

PRECIPICE (<u>prehs</u> ih pihs) *n.*
edge, steep overhang
Synonyms: crag, cliff, brink

EFFICACY (<u>eff</u> uh kuh see) *n.*
effectiveness, efficiency
Synonym: potency

REMORSE (rih <u>mohrs</u>) *n.*
a gnawing distress arising from a sense of guilt
Synonyms: anguish, ruefulness, shame, penitence

VENOM (<u>vehn</u> uhm) *n.*
poison; malice or spite
Synonyms: toxin; harm, hatred

INFUSE (ihn <u>fyooz</u>) *v.* **-ing,-ed.**
to permeate with something that alters; to inspire or animate
Synonyms: introduce, pervade; instill, impart

society is to be torn down and built up anew. Then, the very nature of the opposite sex, or its long hereditary habit, which has become like nature, is to be essentially modified, before woman can be allowed to assume what seems a fair and suitable position. Finally, all other difficulties being **obviated**, woman cannot take advantage of these preliminary reforms, until she herself has undergone a still mightier change; in which, perhaps, the **ethereal** essence, wherein she has her truest life, will be found to have evaporated. A woman never overcomes these problems by any exercise of thought. They are not to be solved, or only in one way. If her heart chance to come uppermost, they vanish. Thus, Hester Prynne, whose heart had lost its regular and healthy throb, wandered without a clue in the dark **labyrinth** of mind; now turned aside by an **insurmountable precipice**; now starting back from a deep chasm. There was wild and ghastly scenery all around her, and a home and comfort nowhere. At times, a fearful doubt strove to possess her soul, whether it were not better to send Pearl at once to Heaven, and go herself to such futurity as Eternal Justice should provide.

The scarlet letter had not done its office.

Now, however, her interview with the Reverend Mr. Dimmesdale, on the night of his vigil, had given her a new theme of reflection, and held up to her an object that appeared worthy of any exertion and sacrifice for its attainment. She had witnessed the intense misery beneath which the minister struggled, or, to speak more accurately, had ceased to struggle. She saw that he stood on the verge of lunacy, if he had not already stepped across it. It was impossible to doubt, that, whatever painful **efficacy** there might be in the secret sting of **remorse**, a deadlier **venom** had been **infused** into it by the hand that proffered relief. A secret enemy had been continually by his side, under the semblance of a friend and helper, and

SAT Vocabulary

AVAIL (uh <u>vayl</u>) *v.* **-ing,-ed.**
  to make use of; to result in; to be of use or advantage to
    Synonyms: employ; transpire, eventuate; help, serve, benefit

FOREBODE (fohr <u>bohd</u>) *v.* **-ing,-ed.**
  to have a presentiment of upcoming evil
    Synonyms: predict, portend, foretell, anticipate

AUSPICIOUS (aw <u>spih</u> shuhs) *adj.*
  having favorable prospects, promising
    Synonyms: encouraging, hopeful, positive

DISCERN (dihs <u>uhrn</u>) *v.* **-ing,-ed.**
  to perceive or recognize something
    Synonyms: descry, observe, glimpse, distinguish

ACQUIESCE (aak wee <u>ehs</u>) *v.* **-ing,-ed.**
  to comply quietly; to agree
    Synonyms: submit; accede, consent

IMPULSE (<u>ihm</u> puhls) *n.*
  sudden tendency, inclination
    Synonyms: urge, whim

SOLEMN (<u>sah</u> luhm) *adj.*
  somberly impressive, deeply serious
    Synonyms: dignified, earnest, ceremonial

ABASED (uh <u>baysd</u>) *adj.*
  shamed, disgraced
    Synonyms: humbled, humiliated, demeaned

IGNOMINY (<u>ihg</u> nuh mih nee) *n.*
  disgrace and dishonor
    Synonyms: degradation, debasement

RESOLVE (rih <u>sahlv</u>) *v.* **-ing,-ed.**
  to determine or to make a firm decision about
    Synonyms: solve, decide, clear up

had **availed** himself of the opportunities thus afforded for tampering with the delicate springs of Mr. Dimmesdale's nature. Hester could not but ask herself, whether there had not originally been a defect of truth, courage, and loyalty, on her own part in allowing the minister to be thrown into a position where so much evil was to be **foreboded**, and nothing **auspicious** to be hoped. Her only justification lay in the fact that she had been able to **discern** no method of rescuing him from the blacker ruin that had overwhelmed herself, except by **acquiescing** in Roger Chillingworth's scheme of disguise. Under that **impulse**, she had made her choice, and had chosen, as it now appeared, the more wretched alternative of the two. She determined to redeem her error, so far as it might yet be possible. Strengthened by years of hard and **solemn** trial, she felt herself no longer so inadequate to cope with Roger Chillingworth as on that night, **abased** by sin, and half maddened by the **ignominy**, that was still new, when they had talked together in the prison-chamber. She had climbed her way, since then, to a higher point. The old man, on the other hand, had brought himself nearer to her level, or perhaps below it, by the revenge which he had stooped for.

In fine, Hester Prynne **resolved** to meet her former husband, and do what might be in her power for the rescue of the victim on whom he had so evidently set his gripe. The occasion was not long to seek. One afternoon, walking with Pearl in a retired part of the peninsula, she beheld the old physician, with a basket on one arm and a staff in the other hand, stooping along the ground, in quest of roots and herbs to concoct his medicines withal.

AGITATED (<u>aa</u> gih tay tihd) *adj.*
moving in a sudden or physically violent way; upset or uneasy
Synonyms: churning, convulsing, rocking; disturbed, flustered, bothered

ACCOST (uh <u>cahst</u>) (uh <u>kawst</u>) *v.* **-ing,-ed.**
to approach and speak to someone, often in an aggressive way
Synonyms: address, confront

MAGISTRATE (<u>maa</u> juh strayt) *n.*
an official who can administrate laws
Synonyms: judge, arbiter, authority, marshal

DISCOURSE (<u>dihs</u> kohrs) *v.* **-ing,-ed.**
to talk or converse
Synonyms: speak, discuss, lecture

Hester and the Physician
Chapter 14

Hester bade little Pearl run down to the margin of the water, and play with the shells and tangled seaweed, until she should have talked awhile with yonder gatherer of herbs. So the child flew away like a bird, and, making bare her small white feet, went pattering along the moist margin of the sea. Here and there she came to a full stop, and peeped curiously into a pool, left by the retiring tide as a mirror for Pearl to see her face in. Forth peeped at her, out of the pool, with dark, glistening curls around her head, and an elf-smile in her eyes, the image of a little maid, whom Pearl, having no other playmate, invited to take her hand and run a race with her. But the visionary little maid, on her part, beckoned likewise, as if to say—"This is a better place! Come thou into the pool!" And Pearl, stepping in, mid-leg deep, beheld her own white feet at the bottom; while, out of a still lower depth, came the gleam of a kind of fragmentary smile, floating to and fro in the **agitated** water.

Meanwhile, her mother had **accosted** the physician.

"I would speak a word with you," said she, "a word that concerns us much."

"Aha! And is it Mistress Hester that has a word for old Roger Chillingworth?" answered he, raising himself from his stooping posture. "With all my heart! Why, Mistress, I hear good tidings of you on all hands! No longer ago than yester-eve, a **magistrate**, a wise and godly man, was **discoursing** of your affairs, Mistress Hester, and whispered me that there had been question concerning you in the council. It was debated whether or no, with safety to the common weal, yonder scarlet

ENTREATY (ehn <u>tree</u> tee) *n.*
a plea or request
Synonyms: imploration, prayer, petition

MAGISTRATE (<u>maa</u> juh strayt) *n.*
an official who can administrate laws
Synonyms: judge, arbiter, authority, marshal

PURPORT (puhr <u>pohrt</u>) *n.*
intention, purpose
Synonyms: importance, meaning

DISCERN (dihs <u>uhrn</u>) *v.* **-ing,-ed.**
to perceive or recognize something
Synonyms: descry, observe, glimpse, distinguish

RETAIN (rih <u>tayn</u>) *v.* **-ing,-ed.**
to hold, keep possession of
Synonyms: withhold, reserve

VIGOR (<u>vih</u> guhr) *n.*
physical or mental energy
Synonyms: strength, vitality, power, capability

VISAGE (<u>vih</u> sihj) *n.*
face, the appearance of a person or place
Synonyms: expression, look, style, manner

DERISIVELY (dih <u>rie</u> sihv lee) *adv.*
in a mocking or ridiculing manner
Synonyms: tauntingly, insultingly, scoffingly

FACULTY (<u>faa</u> kuhl tee) *n.*
the ability to act or do
Synonyms: aptitude, capability, sense, skill

letter might be taken off your bosom. On my life, Hester, I made my **entreaty** to the worshipful **magistrate** that it might be done forthwith!"

"It lies not in the pleasure of the **magistrates** to take off this badge," calmly replied Hester. "Were I worthy to be quit of it, it would fall away of its own nature, or be transformed into something that should speak a different **purport**."

"Nay, then, wear it, if it suit you better," rejoined he. "A woman must needs follow her own fancy, touching the adornment of her person. The letter is gayly embroidered, and shows right bravely on your bosom!"

All this while, Hester had been looking steadily at the old man, and was shocked, as well as wonder-smitten, to **discern** what a change had been wrought upon him within the past seven years. It was not so much that he had grown older; for though the traces of advancing life were visible, he bore his age well, and seemed to **retain** a wiry **vigor** and alertness. But the former aspect of an intellectual and studious man, calm and quiet, which was what she best remembered in him, had altogether vanished, and been succeeded by an eager, searching, almost fierce, yet carefully guarded look. It seemed to be his wish and purpose to mask this expression with a smile; but the latter played him false, and flickered over his **visage** so **derisively**, that the spectator could see his blackness all the better for it. Ever and anon, too, there came a glare of red light out of his eyes; as if the old man's soul were on fire, and kept on smouldering duskily within his breast, until, by some casual puff of passion, it was blown into a momentary flame. This he repressed, as speedily as possible, and strove to look as if nothing of the kind had happened.

In a word, old Roger Chillingworth was a striking evidence of man's **faculty** of transforming himself into a devil, if he will only, for a reasonable space of time,

DERIVE (dih <u>riev</u>) *v.* **-ing,-ed.**
   to receive from a source, to originate
      Synonyms: infer, descend, deduce, come (from)

EXTORT (ihk <u>stohrt</u>) *v.* **-ing,-ed.**
   to obtain something by threat or force
      Synonyms: wring, coerce, blackmail, bully

MISGIVING (mihs <u>gihv</u> ihng) *n.*
   a feeling of apprehension, doubt, sense of foreboding
      Synonyms: distrust, presentiment, qualm, disquiet

undertake a devil's office. This unhappy person had effected such a transformation, by devoting himself, for seven years, to the constant analysis of a heart full of torture, and **deriving** his enjoyment thence, and adding fuel to those fiery tortures which he analyzed and gloated over.

The scarlet letter burned on Hester Prynne's bosom. Here was another ruin, the responsibility of which came partly home to her.

"What see you in my face," asked the physician, "that you look at it so earnestly?"

"Something that would make me weep, if there were any tears bitter enough for it," answered she. "But let it pass! It is of yonder miserable man that I would speak."

"And what of him?" cried Roger Chillingworth, eagerly, as if he loved the topic, and were glad of an opportunity to discuss it with the only person of whom he could make a confidant. "Not to hide the truth, Mistress Hester, my thoughts happen just now to be busy with the gentleman. So speak freely; and I will make answer."

"When we last spake together," said Hester, "now seven years ago, it was your pleasure to **extort** a promise of secrecy, as touching the former relation <u>betwixt</u> yourself and me. As the life and good fame of yonder man were in your hands, there seemed no choice to me, save to be silent, in accordance with your <u>behest</u>. Yet it was not without heavy **misgivings** that I thus bound myself; for, having cast off all duty towards other human beings, there remained a duty towards him; and something whispered me that I was betraying it, in pledging myself to keep your counsel. Since that day, no man is so near to him as you. You tread behind his every footstep. You are beside him, sleeping and waking. You search his thoughts. You burrow and <u>rankle</u> in his heart! Your clutch is on his life, and you cause him to die daily

PERPETRATION (puhr peh <u>tray</u> shuhn) *n.*
the act of committing a crime, an evil action
Synonyms: wrongdoing, action, performance

LURID (<u>loor</u> ihd) *adj.*
harshly shocking, revolting; glowing
Synonyms: ghastly, garish, gruesome, grisly,
macabre; fiery

REMORSE (rih <u>mohrs</u>) *n.*
a gnawing distress arising from a sense of guilt
Synonyms: anguish, ruefulness, shame, penitence

a living death; and still he knows you not. In permitting this, I have surely acted a false part by the only man to whom the power was left me to be true!"

"What choice had you?" asked Roger Chillingworth. "My finger, pointed at this man, would have hurled him from his pulpit into a dungeon—thence, peradventure, to the gallows!"

"It had been better so!" said Hester Prynne.

"What evil have I done the man?" asked Roger Chillingworth again. "I tell thee, Hester Prynne, the richest fee that ever physician earned from monarch could not have bought such care as I have wasted on this miserable priest! But for my aid, his life would have burned away in torments within the first two years after the **perpetration** of his crime and thine. For, Hester, his spirit lacked the strength that could have borne up, as thine has, beneath a burden like thy scarlet letter. Oh, I could reveal a goodly secret! But enough! What art can do, I have exhausted on him. That he now breathes, and creeps about on earth, is owing all to me!"

"Better he had died at once!" said Hester Prynne.

"Yea, woman, thou sayest truly!" cried old Roger Chillingworth, letting the **lurid** fire of his heart blaze out before her eyes. "Better had he died at once! Never did mortal suffer what this man has suffered. And all, all, in the sight of his worst enemy! He has been conscious of me. He has felt an influence dwelling always upon him like a curse. He knew, by some spiritual sense—for the Creator never made another being so sensitive as this—he knew that no friendly hand was pulling at his heart-strings, and that an eye was looking curiously into him, which sought only evil, and found it. But he knew not that the eye and hand were mine! With the superstition common to his brotherhood, he fancied himself given over to a fiend, to be tortured with frightful dreams, and desperate thoughts, the sting of **remorse**,

VILELY (viel lee) *adv.*
   wretchedly, offensively, disgustingly
      Synonyms: despicably, wickedly, sickeningly

PERPETUAL (puhr <u>peht</u> chyoo uhl) *adj.*
   endless, lasting
      Synonyms: continuous, constant, ceaseless, eternal, perennial

USURP (yoo <u>suhrp</u>) *v.* **-ing,-ed.**
   to occupy instead, to assume a position; to seize by force
      Synonyms: preempt, displace; arrogate, appropriate

BESTOW (bih <u>stoh</u>) *v.* **-ing,-ed.**
   to apply or devote time or effort; to give as a gift
      Synonyms: allocate, dedicate; endow, confer, present

and despair of pardon; as a foretaste of what awaits him beyond the grave. But it was the constant shadow of my presence—the closest <u>propinquity</u> of the man whom he had most **vilely** wronged—and who had grown to exist only by this **perpetual** poison of the direst revenge! Yea, indeed—he did not err—there was a fiend at his elbow! A mortal man, with once a human heart, has become a fiend for his special torment!"

The unfortunate physician, while uttering these words, lifted his hands with a look of horror, as if he had beheld some frightful shape, which he could not recognize, **usurping** the place of his own image in a glass. It was one of those moments—which sometimes occur only at the interval of years when a man's moral aspect is faithfully revealed to his mind's eye. Not improbably, he had never before viewed himself as he did now.

"Hast thou not tortured him enough?" said Hester, noticing the old man's look. "Has he not paid thee all?"

"No—no! He has but increased the debt!" answered the physician; and as he proceeded, his manner lost its fiercer characteristics, and subsided into gloom. "Dost thou remember me, Hester, as I was nine years agone? Even then, I was in the autumn of my days, nor was it the early autumn. But all my life had been made up of earnest, studious, thoughtful, quiet years, **bestowed** faithfully for the increase of mine own knowledge, and faithfully, too, though this latter object was but casual to the other—faithfully for the advancement of human welfare. No life had been more peaceful and innocent than mine; few lives so rich with benefits conferred. Dost thou remember me? Was I not, though you might deem me cold, nevertheless a man thoughtful for others, craving little for himself—kind, true, just, and of constant, if not warm affections? Was I not all this?"

"All this, and more," said Hester.

"And what am I now?" demanded he, looking into

AVENGE (uh <u>vehn</u>j) *v.* **-ing,-ed.**
   to retaliate or take revenge for an injury or crime
     Synonyms: punish, vindicate

DISCERN (dihs <u>uhrn</u>) *v.* **-ing,-ed.**
   to perceive or recognize something
     Synonyms: descry, observe, glimpse, distinguish

BANE (bayn) *n.*
   something causing death, destruction, or ruin
     Synonyms: undoer, curse, scourge, poison

IMPLORE (ihm <u>plohr</u>) *v.* **-ing,-ed.**
   to call upon in supplication, beg
     Synonyms: plead, entreat, solicit

RESTRAIN (rih <u>strayn</u>) *v.* **-ing,-ed.**
   to control, repress, restrict, hold back
     Synonyms: hamper, bridle, curb, check

her face, and permitting the whole evil within him to be written on his features. "I have already told thee what I am! A fiend! Who made me so?"

"It was myself!" cried Hester, shuddering. "It was I, not less than he. Why hast thou not **avenged** thyself on me?"

"I have left thee to the scarlet letter," replied Roger Chillingworth. "If that have not **avenged** me, I can do no more!"

He laid his finger on it, with a smile.

"It has **avenged** thee!" answered Hester Prynne.

"I judged no less," said the physician. "And now, what wouldst thou with me touching this man?"

"I must reveal the secret," answered Hester, firmly. "He must **discern** thee in thy true character. What may be the result, I know not. But this long debt of confidence, due from me to him, whose **bane** and ruin I have been, shall at length be paid. So far as concerns the overthrow or preservation of his fair fame and his earthly state, and perchance his life, he is in thy hands. Nor do I—whom the scarlet letter has disciplined to truth, though it be the truth of red-hot iron, entering into the soul—nor do I perceive such advantages in his living any longer a life of ghastly emptiness, that I shall stoop to **implore** thy mercy. Do with him as thou wilt! There is no good for him—no good for me—no good for thee! There is no good for little Pearl! There is no path to guide us out of this dismal maze!"

"Woman, I could well <u>nigh</u> pity thee!" said Roger Chillingworth, unable to **restrain** a thrill of admiration too; for there was a quality almost majestic in the despair which she expressed. "Thou hadst great elements. <u>Peradventure</u>, hadst thou met earlier with a better love than mine, this evil had not been. I pity thee, for the good that has been wasted in thy nature!"

"And I thee," answered Hester Prynne, "for the

PURGE (puhrj) *v.* **-ing,-ed.**
to cleanse or free from impurities
Synonyms: purify, eliminate, rid

RETRIBUTION (reh trih <u>byoo</u> shuhn) *n.*
something which is justly deserved, such as
repayment or punishment
Synonyms: vengeance, payback, compensation

AWRY (uh <u>rie</u>) *adv.*
amiss, crooked, askew
Synonyms: wrong, aslant

hatred that has transformed a wise and just man to a fiend! Wilt thou yet **purge** it out of thee, and be once more human? If not for his sake, then doubly for thine own! Forgive, and leave his further **retribution** to the Power that claims it! I said, but now, that there could be no good event for him, or thee, or me, who are here wandering together in this gloomy maze of evil, and stumbling at every step, over the guilt wherewith we have strewn our path. It is not so! There might be good for thee, and thee alone, since thou hast been deeply wronged, and hast it at thy will to pardon. Wilt thou give up that only privilege? Wilt thou reject that priceless benefit?"

"Peace, Hester, peace!" replied the old man, with gloomy sternness. "It is not granted me to pardon. I have no such power as thou tellest me of. My old faith, long forgotten, comes back to me, and explains all that we do, and all we suffer. By thy first step **awry**, thou didst plant the germ of evil; but since that moment, it has all been a dark necessity. Ye that have wronged me are not sinful, save in a kind of typical illusion; neither am I fiend-like, who have snatched a fiend's office from his hands. It is our fate. Let the black flower blossom as it may! Now go thy ways, and deal as thou wilt with yonder man."

He waved his hand, and betook himself again to his employment of gathering herbs.

DEFORMED (dih fohrmd) *adj.*
disfigured, spoiled
Synonyms: contorted, twisted, marred, misshapen

BLIGHT (bliet) *v.* **-ing,-ed.**
to afflict, destroy
Synonyms: damage, plague

VERDURE (vuhr juhr) *n.*
lushness of flourishing vegetation; inexperience
Synonyms: greenery, foliage, woodedness;
immaturity

SEDULOUS (seh juh luhs) *adj.*
constant and persevering
Synonyms: persistent, careful, attentive, diligent

DELETERIOUS (dehl ih teer ee uhs) *adj.*
subtly or unexpectedly harmful
Synonyms: injurious, adverse, hurtful

MALIGNANT (muh lihg nehnt) *adj.*
evil in influence or effect; aggressively malicious;
tending to produce death
Synonyms: vindictive, threatening; destructive,
harmful; lethal, fatal

OMINOUS (ah mihn uhs) *adj.*
menacing, threatening, indicating misfortune
Synonyms: inauspicious, sinister, dire, baleful

DEFORMITY (dih fohr mih tee) *n.*
disfigurement
Synonyms: malformation, disproportion

LUXURIANCE (luhg zhoor ee ehnts) *n.*
abundance; elegance, lavishness
Synonyms: excess, overload, profusion; richness

Hester and Pearl
Chapter 15

So Roger Chillingworth—a **deformed** old figure, with a face that haunted men's memories longer than they liked—took leave of Hester Prynne, and went stooping away along the earth. He gathered here and there an herb, or grubbed up a root, and put it into the basket on his arm. His gray beard almost touched the ground, as he crept onward. Hester gazed after him a little while, looking with a half-fantastic curiosity to see whether the tender grass of early spring would not be **blighted** beneath him, and show the wavering track of his footsteps, <u>sere</u> and brown, across its cheerful **verdure**. She wondered what sort of herbs they were, which the old man was so **sedulous** to gather. Would not the earth, quickened to an evil purpose by the sympathy of his eye, greet him with poisonous shrubs, of species hitherto unknown, that would start up under his fingers? Or might it suffice him that every wholesome growth should be converted into something **deleterious** and **malignant** at his touch? Did the sun, which shone so brightly everywhere else, really fall upon him? Or was there, as it rather seemed, a circle of **ominous** shadow moving along with his **deformity**, whichever way he turned himself? And whither was he now going? Would he not suddenly sink into the earth, leaving a barren and blasted spot, where, in due course of time, would be seen deadly nightshade, dogwood, henbane, and whatever else of vegetable wickedness the climate could produce, all flourishing with hideous **luxuriance**? Or would he spread bat's wings and flee away, looking so much the uglier, the higher he rose towards Heaven?

351

UPBRAID (uhp <u>brayd</u>) *v.* **-ing,-ed.**
to scold sharply
Synonyms: berate, reproach, rebuke, chide

SENTIMENT (<u>sehn</u> tuh muhnt) *n.*
an attitude, thought, or judgment prompted by feeling
Synonym: emotion

SECLUSION (sih <u>cloo</u> zhuhn) *n.*
isolation, detachment
Synonyms: separation, privacy, solitude

MEDIUM (<u>mee</u> dee uhm) *n.*
a substance or object that is used to transmit or
accomplish something
Synonyms: means, instrument, vehicle, mechanism

SUBSEQUENT (<u>suhb</u> suh kwehnt) *adj.*
following in time or order
Synonyms: succeeding, next, after

REPENT (rih <u>pehnt</u>) *v.* **-ing,-ed.**
to regret a past action
Synonyms: rue, atone, apologize

RECIPROCATE (rih <u>sihp</u> ruh kayt) *v.* **-ing,-ed.**
to give or feel in return, to interact mutually
Synonym: exchange

REPROACH (rih <u>prohch</u>) *v.* **-ing,-ed.**
to express disappointment or displeasure; to disgrace
Synonyms: blame, rebuke, admonish; discredit

IMPOSE (ihm <u>pohz</u>) *v.* **-ing,-ed.**
to inflict, force upon
Synonyms: dictate, decree, demand, ordain

"Be it sin or no," said Hester Prynne, bitterly, as she still gazed after him, "I hate the man!"

She **upbraided** herself for the **sentiment**, but could not overcome or lessen it. Attempting to do so, she thought of those long-past days, in a distant land, when he used to emerge at eventide from the **seclusion** of his study, and sit down in the firelight of their home, and in the light of her nuptial smile. He needed to bask himself in that smile, he said, in order that the chill of so many lonely hours among his books might be taken off the scholar's heart. Such scenes had once appeared not otherwise than happy; but now, as viewed through the dismal **medium** of her **subsequent** life, they classed themselves among her ugliest remembrances. She marvelled how such scenes could have been! She marvelled how she could ever have been wrought upon to marry him! She deemed it her crime most to be **repented** of that she had ever endured, and **reciprocated**, the lukewarm grasp of his hand, and had suffered the smile of her lips and eyes to mingle and melt into his own. And it seemed a fouler offence committed by Roger Chillingworth, than any which had since been done him, that, in the time when her heart knew no better, he had persuaded her to fancy herself happy by his side.

"Yes, I hate him!" repeated Hester, more bitterly than before. "He betrayed me! He has done me worse wrong than I did him!"

Let men tremble to win the hand of woman, unless they win along with it the utmost passion of her heart! Else it may be their miserable fortune, as it was Roger Chillingworth's, when some mightier touch than their own may have awakened all her sensibilities, to be **reproached** even for the calm content, the marble image of happiness, which they will have **imposed** upon her as the warm reality. But Hester ought long ago to have done with this injustice. What did it <u>betoken</u>? Had seven long

REPENTANCE (rih <u>pehn</u> tehnts) *n.*
  sorrow expressed for sins or offenses, penitence
    Synonyms: remorse, contrition, apology

FLAG (flaag) *v.* **-ging,-ged.**
  to decline in vigor, strength, or interest
    Synonyms: wane, subside, ebb, dwindle, slacken

IMPALPABLE (ihm <u>paalp</u> uh buhl) *adj.*
  unreal, intangible
    Synonyms: imperceptible, tenuous, unsubstantial

FOUNDER (<u>fown</u> duhr) *v.* **-ing,-ed.**
  to sink, to fall helplessly
    Synonyms: immerse, plunge

DEXTERITY (dehk <u>stayr</u> ih tee) *n.*
  physical or mental skill, ability
    Synonyms: aptitude, adroitness, proficiency

years, under the torture of the scarlet letter, inflicted so much of misery, and wrought out no **repentance**?

The emotions of that brief space, while she stood gazing after the crooked figure of old Roger Chillingworth, threw a dark light on Hester's state of mind, revealing much that she might not otherwise have acknowledged to herself.

He being gone, she summoned back her child.

"Pearl! Little Pearl! Where are you?"

Pearl, whose activity of spirit never **flagged**, had been at no loss for amusement while her mother talked with the old gatherer of herbs. At first, as already told, she had flirted fancifully with her own image in a pool of water, beckoning the phantom forth, and—as it declined to venture—seeking a passage for herself into its sphere of **impalpable** earth and unattainable sky. Soon finding, however, that either she or the image was unreal, she turned elsewhere for better pastime. She made little boats out of birch-bark, and freighted them with snail-shells, and sent out more ventures on the mighty deep than any merchant in New England; but the larger part of them **foundered** near the shore. She seized a live horseshoe by the tail, and made prize of several five-fingers, and laid out a jelly-fish to melt in the warm sun. Then she took up the white foam, that streaked the line of the advancing tide, and threw it upon the breeze, scampering after it with winged footsteps, to catch the great snow-flakes ere they fell. Perceiving a flock of beach-birds, that fed and fluttered along the shore, the naughty child picked up her apron full of pebbles, and, creeping from rock to rock after these small sea-fowl, displayed remarkable **dexterity** in pelting them. One little gray bird with a white breast, Pearl was almost sure, had been hit by a pebble, and fluttered away with a broken wing. But then the elf-child sighed, and gave up her sport; because it grieved her to have done harm to a little being that was as wild as the sea-breeze, or as wild as Pearl herself.

PURPORT (puhr <u>pohrt</u>) *n.*
intention, purpose
  Synonyms: importance, meaning

SINGULAR (<u>sihn</u> gyuh luhr) *adj.*
peculiar, uncommon
  Synonyms: unique, individual, unusual, odd, rare

MORBID (<u>mohr</u> bihd) *adj.*
  1. having an unhealthy mentality; relating to disease
    Synonyms: unwholesome; pathological
  2. abnormally terrible and gloomy; gruesome
    Synonyms: dismal, dreary; grisly, macabre

ASCERTAIN (aa suhr <u>tayn</u>) *v.* **-ing,-ed.**
to determine, discover, make certain of
  Synonyms: verify, calculate, detect

Her final employment was to gather sea-weed of various kinds, and make herself a scarf, or mantle, and a head-dress, and thus assume the aspect of a little mermaid. She inherited her mother's gift for devising drapery and costume. As the last touch to her mermaid's garb, Pearl took some eel-grass, and imitated, as best she could, on her own bosom, the decoration with which she was so familiar on her mother's. A letter—the letter A—but freshly green, instead of scarlet! The child bent her chin upon her breast, and contemplated this device with strange interest; even as if the one only thing for which she had been sent into the world was to make out its hidden import.

"I wonder if Mother will ask me what it means?" thought Pearl.

Just then she heard her mother's voice, and flitting along as lightly as one of the little sea-birds, appeared before Hester Prynne, dancing, laughing, and pointing her finger to the ornament upon her bosom.

"My little Pearl!" said Hester, after a moment's silence, "the green letter, and on thy childish bosom, has no **purport**. But dost thou know, my child, what this letter means which thy mother is doomed to wear?"

"Yes, Mother," said the child. "It is the great letter A. Thou hast taught me in the hornbook."

Hester looked steadily into her little face; but, though there was that **singular** expression which she had so often remarked in her black eyes, she could not satisfy herself whether Pearl really attached any meaning to the symbol. She felt a **morbid** desire to **ascertain** the point.

"Dost thou know, child, wherefore thy mother wears this letter?"

"Truly do I!" answered Pearl, looking brightly into her mother's face. "It is for the same reason that the minister keeps his hand over his heart!"

"And what reason is that?" asked Hester, half smiling

INCONGRUITY (ihn kuhn <u>groo</u> it tee) *n.*
incompatibility, lack of agreement
    Synonyms: inconsistency, unsuitability,
    disharmony

CAPRICIOUS (kuh <u>pree</u> shuhs) (kuh <u>prih</u> shuhs) *adj.*
impulsive, whimsical, without much thought
    Synonyms: erratic, fickle, flighty, inconstant,
    wayward

PETULANT (<u>peh</u> chuh luhnt) *adj.*
rude, peevish
    Synonyms: irritable, querulous, testy, fretful

REQUITAL (rih <u>kwie</u> tuhl) *n.*
repayment, compensation
    Synonyms: reciprocation, reimbursement

DISPOSITION (dihs puh <u>zih</u> shuhn) *n.*
  1. mood or temperament
    Synonyms: behavior, nature
  2. a habitual tendency, an inclination
    Synonyms: willingness, propensity

UNAMIABLE (uhn <u>ay</u> mee uh buhl) *adj.*
unfriendly, unpleasant, unlikable
    Synonyms: disagreeable, rude, discourteous

PRECOCITY (prih <u>cah</u> sih tee) *n.*
unusually advanced intelligence at an early age
    Synonyms: brightness, talent, aptitude

ACUTENESS (uh <u>kyoot</u> nehs) *n.*
intelligence, keen wit; sharpness, severity
    Synonyms: genius, cleverness; intensity

at the absurd **incongruity** of the child's observation; but, on second thoughts, turning pale. "What has the letter to do with any heart, save mine?"

"Nay, Mother, I have told all I know," said Pearl more seriously than she was wont to speak. "Ask yonder old man whom thou hast been talking with! It may be he can tell. But in good earnest now, Mother dear, what does this scarlet letter mean? And why dost thou wear it on thy bosom? And why does the minister keep his hand over his heart?"

She took her mother's hand in both her own, and gazed into her eyes with an earnestness that was seldom seen in her wild and **capricious** character. The thought occurred to Hester that the child might really be seeking to approach her with childlike confidence, and doing what she could, and as intelligently as she knew how, to establish a meeting-point of sympathy. It showed Pearl in an unwonted aspect. Heretofore, the mother, while loving her child with the intensity of a sole affection, had schooled herself to hope for little other return than the waywardness of an April breeze, which spends its time in airy sport, and has its gusts of inexplicable passion, and is **petulant** in its best of moods, and chills oftener than caresses you, when you take it to your bosom; in **requital** of which misdemeanors, it will sometimes, of its own vague purpose, kiss your cheek with a kind of doubtful tenderness, and play gently with your hair, and then be gone about its other idle business, leaving a dreamy pleasure at your heart. And this, moreover, was a mother's estimate of the child's **disposition**. Any other observer might have seen few but **unamiable** traits, and have given them a far darker coloring. But now the idea came strongly into Hester's mind, that Pearl, with her remarkable **precocity** and **acuteness**, might already have approached the age when she could be made a friend, and intrusted with as much of a mother's sorrow as could be

IMPART (ihm <u>pahrt</u>) *v.* **-ing,-ed.** *(See page 326.)*

IRREVERENCE (ih <u>rehv</u> uhr uhnts) *n.*
disrespect, gentle or humorous mockery
Synonyms: rudeness, discourtesy, impudence

CHAOS (<u>kay</u> ahs) *n.*
extreme disorder
Synonyms: incoherence, randomness, disorganization

STEADFAST (<u>stehd</u> faast) *adj.*
unwavering, loyal
Synonyms: faithful, true, constant, fast, staunch

TAINT (taynt) *n.*
a moral flaw; a smear or stain
Synonyms: fault, shame, corruption;
contamination, blemish, pollution

ACRID (<u>aak</u> rihd) *adj.*
harsh, bitter
Synonyms: sharp, pungent, caustic

INEVITABLE (ihn <u>ehv</u> ih tuh buhl) *adj. (See page 248.)*

ENIGMA (eh <u>nihg</u> mah) *n.*
a puzzle, something that cannot be explained
Synonyms: mystery, riddle

INNATE (ih <u>nayt</u>) (<u>ihn</u> ayt) *adj.*
natural, inborn
Synonyms: congenital, inherent, intrinsic

EPOCH (<u>eh</u> pihk) *n. (See page 192.)*

PROVIDENCE (<u>prah</u> vih dehnts) *n. (See page 330.)*

RETRIBUTION (reh trih <u>byoo</u> shuhn) *n. (See page 348.)*

ENDOW (ehn <u>dow</u>) *v.* **-ing,-ed.** *(See page 224.)*

PROPENSITY (pruh <u>pehn</u> suh tee) *n.*
inclination, tendency
Synonyms: predilection, bias, penchant

BENEFICENCE (buh <u>neh</u> fih sihnts) *n.*
kindness and goodness
Synonyms: benevolence, graciousness, philanthropy

VIVACITY (vih <u>vahs</u> ih tee) *n.*
liveliness, spiritedness
Synonyms: vibrance, zest

imparted, without **irreverence** either to the parent or the child. In the little **chaos** of Pearl's character, there might be seen emerging—and could have been, from the very first—the **steadfast** principles of an unflinching courage—an uncontrollable will—a sturdy pride, which might be disciplined into self-respect—and a bitter scorn of many things, which, when examined, might be found to have the **taint** of falsehood in them. She possessed affections, too, though hitherto **acrid** and disagreeable, as are the richest flavors of unripe fruit. With all these sterling attributes, thought Hester, the evil which she inherited from her mother must be great indeed, if a noble woman do not grow out of this elfish child.

Pearl's **inevitable** tendency to hover about the **enigma** of the scarlet letter seemed an **innate** quality of her being. From the earliest **epoch** of her conscious life, she had entered upon this as her appointed mission. Hester had often fancied that **Providence** had a design of justice and **retribution**, in **endowing** the child with this marked **propensity**; but never, until now, had she bethought herself to ask, whether, linked with that design, there might not likewise be a purpose of mercy and **beneficence**. If little Pearl were entertained with faith and trust, as a spirit messenger no less than an earthly child, might it not be her errand to soothe away the sorrow that lay cold in her mother's heart, and converted it into a tomb—and to help her to overcome the passion, once so wild, and even yet neither dead nor asleep, but only imprisoned within the same tomblike heart?

Such were some of the thoughts that now stirred in Hester's mind, with as much **vivacity** of impression as if they had actually been whispered into her ear. And there was little Pearl, all this while holding her mother's hand in both her own, and turning her face upward, while she put these searching questions, once, and again, and still a third time.

TALISMAN (<u>taa</u> lihs mehn) *n.*
   a magical object that is believed to bring protection
   or supernatural powers to its keeper
      Synonyms: lucky charm, amulet, idol

ASPERITY (uh <u>spayr</u> ih tee) *n.*
   harshness, meanness
      Synonyms: sharpness, irritability, crossness

"What does the letter mean, Mother? And why dost thou wear it? And why does the minister keep his hand over his heart?"

What shall I say? thought Hester to herself. No! If this be the price of the child's sympathy, I cannot pay it.

Then she spoke aloud.

"Silly Pearl," said she, "what questions are these? There are many things in this world that a child must not ask about. What know I of the minister's heart? And as for the scarlet letter, I wear it for the sake of its gold-thread."

In all the seven bygone years, Hester Prynne had never before been false to the symbol on her bosom. It may be that it was the **talisman** of a stern and severe, but yet a guardian spirit, who now forsook her; as recognizing that, in spite of his strict watch over her heart, some new evil had crept into it, or some old one had never been expelled. As for little Pearl, the earnestness soon passed out of her face.

But the child did not see fit to let the matter drop. Two or three times, as her mother and she went homeward, and as often at supper-time, and while Hester was putting her to bed, and once after she seemed to be fairly asleep, Pearl looked up, with mischief gleaming in her black eyes.

"Mother," said she, "what does the scarlet letter mean?"

And the next morning, the first indication the child gave of being awake was by popping up her head from the pillow and making that other inquiry, which she had so unaccountably connected with her investigations about the scarlet letter:

"Mother! Mother! Why does the minister keep his hand over his heart?"

"Hold thy tongue, naughty child!" answered her mother, with an **asperity** that she had never permitted to herself before. "Do not tease me; else I shall shut thee into the dark closet!"

RESOLVE (rih <u>sahlv</u>) *n.*
determination, a firm decision
Synonyms: dedication, perseverance, willpower

PERIL (<u>pehr</u> ihl) *n.*
danger
Synonyms: trouble, hazard, harm

PENITENT (peh nih <u>tehnt</u>) *adj.*
sorrowful for one's sins or offenses
Synonyms: remorseful, apologetic, repentant

IMPUTE (ihm <u>pyoot</u>) *v.* **-ing,-ed.**
to attribute
Synonyms: ascribe, credit

A Forest Walk

Chapter 16

Hester Prynne remained constant in her **resolve** to make known to Mr. Dimmesdale, at whatever risk of present pain or ulterior consequences, the true character of the man who had crept into his intimacy. For several days, however, she vainly sought an opportunity of addressing him in some of the meditative walks which she knew him to be in the habit of taking, along the shores of the peninsula, or on the wooded hills of the neighboring country. There would have been no scandal, indeed, nor **peril** to the holy whiteness of the clergyman's good fame, had she visited him in his own study, where many a **penitent** person, ere now, had confessed sins of perhaps as deep a dye as the one betokened by the scarlet letter. But, partly that she dreaded the secret or undisguised interference of old Roger Chillingworth, and partly that her conscious heart **imputed** suspicion where none could have been felt, and partly that both the minister and she would need the whole wide world to breathe in while they talked together—for all these reasons, Hester never thought of meeting him in any narrower privacy than beneath the open sky.

At last, while attending in a sick-chamber, whither the Reverend Mr. Dimmesdale had been summoned to make a prayer, she learnt that he had gone the day before to visit the Apostle Eliot, among his Indian converts. He would probably return, by a certain hour, in the afternoon of the morrow. Betimes, therefore, the next day, Hester took little Pearl—who was necessarily the companion of all her mother's expeditions, however inconvenient her presence—and set forth.

The road, after the two wayfarers had crossed from

SAT Vocabulary

PRIMEVAL (prie <u>mee</u> vuhl) *adj.*
ancient, primitive
> Synonyms: primordial, original, archaic, antediluvian

DISCLOSE (dihs <u>klohs</u>) *v.* **-ing,-ed.**
to open up, divulge
> Synonyms: confide, reveal, impart

AMISS (uh <u>mihs</u>) *adv.*
mistakenly, accidentally; in a defective way
> Synonyms: astray, awry; faultily

SOMBRE or SOMBER (<u>sahm</u> buhr) *adj.*
melancholy, dismal, dark and gloomy
> Synonyms: serious, grave, mournful, lugubrious, funereal

SPORTIVE (<u>spohr</u> tihv) *adj.*
frolicsome, playful
> Synonyms: frisky, merry, lively

PENSIVENESS (<u>pehn</u> sihv nehs) *n.*
serious or deep thoughtfulness
> Synonyms: contemplativeness, meditativeness

SCINTILLATE (<u>sihn</u> tuhl ayt) *v.* **-ing,-ed.**
to sparkle, flash
> Synonyms: gleam, glisten, glitter, shimmer, twinkle

VIVACITY (vih <u>vahs</u> ih tee) *n.*
liveliness, spiritedness
> Synonyms: vibrance, zest

DRAW *v.* **-ing, drew, drawn.**
1. to move steadily
> Synonyms: proceed, continue, progress
2. to pull, drag; to attract
> Synonyms: haul, tow, lug; lure, entice

the peninsula to the mainland, was no other than a foot-path. It straggled onward into the mystery of the **primeval** forest. This hemmed it in so narrowly, and stood so black and dense on either side, and **disclosed** such imperfect glimpses of the sky above, that, to Hester's mind, it imaged not **amiss** the moral wilderness in which she had so long been wandering. The day was chill and **sombre**. Overhead was a gray expanse of cloud, slightly stirred, however, by a breeze, so that a gleam of flickering sunshine might now and then be seen at its solitary play along the path. This flitting cheerfulness was always at the farther extremity of some long vista through the forest. The **sportive** sunlight—feebly **sportive**, at best, in the predominant **pensiveness** of the day and scene—withdrew itself as they came <u>nigh</u>, and left the spots where it had danced the drearier, because they had hoped to find them bright.

"Mother," said little Pearl, "the sunshine does not love you. It runs away and hides itself, because it is afraid of something on your bosom. Now see! There it is, playing, a good way off. Stand you here, and let me run and catch it. I am but a child. It will not flee from me, for I wear nothing on my bosom yet!"

"Nor ever will, my child, I hope," said Hester.

"And why not, Mother?" asked Pearl, stopping short, just at the beginning of her race. "Will not it come of its own accord, when I am a woman grown?"

"Run away, child," answered her mother, "and catch the sunshine! It will soon be gone."

Pearl set forth, at a great pace, and, as Hester smiled to perceive, did actually catch the sunshine, and stood laughing in the midst of it, all brightened by its splendor, and **scintillating** with the **vivacity** excited by rapid motion. The light lingered about the lonely child, as if glad of such a playmate, until her mother had **drawn** almost <u>nigh</u> enough to step into the magic circle too.

VIGOR (<u>vih</u> guhr) *n.*
 physical or mental energy
  Synonyms: strength, vitality, power, capability

VIVACITY (vih <u>vahs</u> ih tee) *n.*
 liveliness, spiritedness
  Synonyms: vibrance, zest

IMPART (ihm <u>pahrt</u>) *v.* **-ing,-ed.**
 to give or share, to pass on
  Synonyms: bestow, contribute, reveal, convey

"It will go now," said Pearl, shaking her head.

"See!" answered Hester, smiling. "Now I can stretch out my hand, and grasp some of it."

As she attempted to do so, the sunshine vanished; or, to judge from the bright expression that was dancing in Pearl's features, her mother could have fancied that the child had absorbed it into herself, and would give it forth again, with a gleam about her path, as they should plunge into some gloomier shade. There was no other attribute that so much impressed her with a sense of new and untransmitted **vigor** in Pearl's nature, as this never-failing **vivacity** of spirits; she had not the disease of sadness, which almost all children, in these latter days, inherit, with the scrofula, from the troubles of their ancestors. Perhaps this too was a disease, and but the reflex of the wild energy with which Hester had fought against her sorrows before Pearl's birth. It was certainly a doubtful charm, **imparting** a hard, metallic lustre to the child's character. She wanted—what some people want throughout life—a grief that should deeply touch her, and thus humanize and make her capable of sympathy. But there was time enough yet for little Pearl.

"Come, my child!" said Hester, looking about her from the spot where Pearl had stood still in the sunshine. "We will sit down a little way within the wood, and rest ourselves."

"I am not aweary, Mother," replied the little girl. "But you may sit down, if you will tell me a story meanwhile."

"A story, child!" said Hester. "And about what?"

"Oh, a story about the Black Man," answered Pearl, taking hold of her mother's gown, and looking up, half earnestly, half mischievously, into her face. "How he haunts this forest, and carries a book with him—a big, heavy book, with iron clasps; and how this ugly Black Man offers his book and an iron pen to everybody that

LUXURIANT (luhg <u>zhoor</u> ee ehnt) *adj.*
   elegant, lavish
     Synonyms: rich, abundant, profuse
EPOCH (<u>eh</u> pihk) *n.*
   a specific time in history; a particular day or time
     Synonyms: period, era, generation; date

meets him here among the trees; and they are to write their names with their own blood. And then he sets his mark on their bosoms! Didst thou ever meet the <u>Black Man</u>, Mother?"

"And who told you this story, Pearl?" asked her mother, recognizing a common superstition of the period.

"It was the old dame in the chimney-corner, at the house where you watched last night," said the child. "But she fancied me asleep while she was talking of it. She said that a thousand and a thousand people had met him here, and had written in his book, and have his mark on them. And that ugly-tempered lady, old Mistress Hibbins, was one. And, Mother, the old dame said that this scarlet letter was the <u>Black Man's</u> mark on thee, and that it glows like a red flame when thou meetest him at midnight, here in the dark wood. Is it true, Mother? And dost thou go to meet him in the night-time?"

"Didst thou ever awake, and find thy mother gone?" asked Hester.

"Not that I remember," said the child. "If thou fearest to leave me in our cottage, thou mightest take me along with thee. I would very gladly go! But, Mother, tell me now! Is there such a <u>Black Man</u>? And didst thou ever meet him? And is this his mark?"

"Wilt thou let me be at peace, if I once tell thee?" asked her mother.

"Yes, if thou tellest me all," answered Pearl.

"Once in my life I met the <u>Black Man</u>!" said her mother. "This scarlet letter is his mark!"

Thus conversing, they entered sufficiently deep into the wood to secure themselves from the observation of any casual passenger along the forest track. Here they sat down on a **luxuriant** heap of moss, which, at some **epoch** of the preceding century, had been a gigantic pine, with

COMPEL (kuhm <u>pehl</u>) *v.* **-ling,-led.**
to urge or force
Synonyms: coerce, oblige, constrain

LOQUACITY (loh <u>kwah</u> sih tee) *n.*
talkativeness
Synonyms: garrulousness, verbosity, wordiness

MELANCHOLY (<u>mehl</u> uhn kahl ee) *adj.*
sad, depressed
Synonyms: dejected, despondent, woeful, sorrowful

SOMBRE or SOMBER (<u>sahm</u> buhr) *adj.*
melancholy, dismal, dark and gloomy
Synonyms: serious, grave, mournful, lugubrious,
funereal

SOLEMN (<u>sah</u> luhm) *adj.*
somberly impressive, deeply serious
Synonyms: dignified, earnest, ceremonial

its root and trunk in the darksome shade, and its head aloft in the upper atmosphere. It was a little dell where they had seated themselves, with a leaf-strewn bank rising gently on either side, and a brook flowing through the midst over a bed of fallen and drowned leaves. The trees impending over it had flung down great branches, from time to time, which choked up the current and **compelled** it to form eddies and black depths at some points, while, in its swifter and livelier passages, there appeared a channelway of pebbles, and brown, sparkling sand. Letting the eyes follow along the course of the stream, they could catch the reflected light from its water, at some short distance within the forest, but soon lost all traces of it amid the bewilderment of tree-trunks and underbrush, and here and there a huge rock covered over with gray lichens. All these giant trees and boulders of granite seemed intent on making a mystery of the course of this small brook; fearing, perhaps, that, with its never-ceasing **loquacity**, it should whisper tales out of the heart of the old forest whence it flowed, or mirror its revelations on the smooth surface of a pool. Continually, indeed, as it stole onward, the streamlet kept up a babble, kind, quiet, soothing, but **melancholy**, like the voice of a young child that was spending its infancy without playfulness, and knew not how to be merry among sad acquaintance and events of **sombre** hue.

"O brook! O foolish and tiresome little brook!" cried Pearl, after listening awhile to its talk. "Why art thou so sad? Pluck up a spirit, and do not be all the time sighing and murmuring!"

But the brook, in the course of its little lifetime among the forest-trees, had gone through so **solemn** an experience that it could not help talking about it, and seemed to have nothing else to say. Pearl resembled the brook, inasmuch as the current of her life gushed from a wellspring as mysterious, and had flowed through

PRATTLE (<u>praa</u> tuhl) *v.* **-ing,-ed.**
to talk foolishly and meaninglessly
Synonyms: chatter, babble, drivel, blather

CADENCE (<u>kay</u> dihnts) *n.*
a series of musical chords, a balanced rhythm
Synonyms: measure, beat, tempo, meter

MELANCHOLY (<u>mehl</u> uhn kahl ee) *adj.*
sad, depressed
Synonyms: dejected, despondent, woeful, sorrowful

PROPHETIC (pruh <u>feh</u> tihk) *adj.*
relating to the ability to foretell events
Synonyms: intuitive, clairvoyant, predictive

LAMENTATION (laa mehn <u>tay</u> shuhn) *n.*
an expression of grief or sorrow, a loud cry
Synonyms: complaint, moaning, sobbing, tears

scenes shadowed as heavily with gloom. But, unlike the little stream, she danced and sparkled, and **prattled** airily along her course.

"What does this sad little brook say, Mother?" inquired she.

"If thou hadst a sorrow of thine own, the brook might tell thee of it," answered her mother, "even as it is telling me of mine! But now, Pearl, I hear a footstep along the path, and the noise of one putting aside the branches. I would have thee betake thyself to play, and leave me to speak with him that comes yonder."

"Is it the <u>Black Man</u>?" asked Pearl.

"Wilt thou go and play, child?" repeated her mother. "But do not stray far into the wood. And take heed that thou come at my first call."

"Yes, Mother," answered Pearl. "But if it be the <u>Black Man</u>, wilt thou not let me stay a moment, and look at him, with his big book under his arm?"

"Go, silly child!" said her mother, impatiently. "It is no <u>Black Man</u>! Thou canst see him now, through the trees. It is the minister!"

"And so it is!" said the child. "And, Mother, he has his hand over his heart! Is it because, when the minister wrote his name in the book, the <u>Black Man</u> set his mark in that place? But why does he not wear it outside his bosom, as thou dost, Mother?"

"Go now, child, and thou shalt tease me as thou wilt another time," cried Hester Prynne. "But do not stray far. Keep where thou canst hear the babble of the brook."

The child went singing away, following up the current of the brook, and striving to mingle a more lightsome **cadence** with its **melancholy** voice. But the little stream would not be comforted, and still kept telling its unintelligible secret of some very mournful mystery that had happened—or making a **prophetic lamentation** about

DESPONDENCY (dih <u>spahn</u> duhn see) *n.*
discouragement, dejection
Synonyms: sadness, depression, desolation

SECLUSION (sih <u>cloo</u> zhuhn) *n.*
isolation, detachment
Synonyms: separation, privacy, solitude

LISTLESSNESS (<u>lihst</u> lihs nehs) *n.*
lack of energy and enthusiasm
Synonyms: lethargy, sluggishness, languor,
indolence

GAIT (gayt) *n.*
the way one moves on foot, a manner of walking
Synonyms: tread, walk, march, pace

VIVACIOUS (vie <u>vay</u> shuhs) *adj.*
lively, spirited
Synonyms: animated, dynamic, vibrant, zesty

something that was yet to happen—within the verge of the dismal forest. So Pearl, who had enough of shadow in her own little life, chose to break off all acquaintance with this repining brook. She set herself, therefore, to gathering violets and wood-anemones, and some scarlet columbines that she found growing in the crevices of a high rock.

When her elf-child had departed, Hester Prynne made a step or two towards the track that led through the forest, but still remained under the deep shadow of the trees. She beheld the minister advancing along the path, entirely alone, and leaning on a staff which he had cut by the wayside. He looked haggard and feeble, and betrayed a nerveless **despondency** in his air, which had never so remarkably characterized him in his walks about the settlement, nor in any other situation where he deemed himself liable to notice. Here it was woefully visible, in this intense **seclusion** of the forest, which, of itself, would have been a heavy trial to the spirits. There was a **listlessness** in his **gait**; as if he saw no reason for taking one step farther, nor felt any desire to do so, but would have been glad, could he be glad of anything, to fling himself down at the root of the nearest tree, and lie there passive, forevermore. The leaves might bestrew him and the soil gradually accumulate and form a little hillock over his frame, no matter whether there were life in it or no. Death was too definite an object to be wished for, or avoided.

To Hester's eye, the Reverend Mr. Dimmesdale exhibited no symptom of positive and **vivacious** suffering, except that, as little Pearl had remarked, he kept his hand over his heart.

SOMBRE or SOMBER (<u>sahm</u> buhr) *adj.*
melancholy, dismal, dark and gloomy
Synonyms: serious, grave, mournful, lugubrious,
funereal

The Pastor and His Parishioner

Chapter 17

Slowly as the minister walked, he had almost gone by before Hester Prynne could gather voice enough to attract his observation. At length, she succeeded.

"Arthur Dimmesdale!" she said, faintly at first; then louder, but hoarsely. "Arthur Dimmesdale!"

"Who speaks?" answered the minister.

Gathering himself quickly up, he stood more erect, like a man taken by surprise in a mood to which he was reluctant to have witnesses. Throwing his eyes anxiously in the direction of the voice, he indistinctly beheld a form under the trees, clad in garments so **sombre**, and so little relieved from the gray twilight into which the clouded sky and the heavy foliage had darkened the noontide, that he knew not whether it were a woman or a shadow. It may be, that his pathway through life was haunted thus, by a spectre that had stolen out from among his thoughts.

He made a step nigher, and discovered the scarlet letter.

"Hester! Hester Prynne!" said he. "Is it thou? Art thou in life?"

"Even so!" she answered. "In such life as has been mine these seven years past! And thou, Arthur Dimmesdale, dost thou yet live?"

It was no wonder that they thus questioned one another's actual and bodily existence, and even doubted of their own. So strangely did they meet, in the dim wood, that it was like the first encounter, in the world beyond the grave, of two spirits who had been intimately connected in their former life, but now stood coldly shuddering, in mutual dread; as not yet familiar with their state, nor wonted to the companionship of disembodied beings. Each a ghost, and awe-stricken at the other ghost!

EPOCH (<u>eh</u> pihk) *n.*
    a specific time in history; a particular day or time
        Synonyms: period, era, generation; date

TREMULOUSLY (<u>treh</u> myoo luhs lee) *adv.*
    in a trembling, quivering manner; fearfully, timidly
        Synonyms: unsteadily, weakly; timorously,
        anxiously

BROOD *v.* **-ing,-ed.**
    1. to think about in a gloomy or serious way
        Synonyms: ponder, worry, obsess
    2. to hang over in a threatening manner
        Synonyms: loom, hover

ESTRANGE (ih <u>straynj</u>) *v.* **-ing,-ed.**
    to alienate, keep at a distance
        Synonyms: disaffect, separate, divorce

DEVOID (dih <u>voyd</u>) *adj.*
    being without, lacking
        Synonyms: destitute, empty, vacant, null, bare

They were awe-stricken likewise at themselves; because the crisis flung back to them their consciousness, and revealed to each heart its history and experience, as life never does, except at such breathless **epochs**. The soul beheld its features in the mirror of the passing moment. It was with fear, and **tremulously**, and, as it were, by a slow, reluctant necessity, that Arthur Dimmesdale put forth his hand, chill as death, and touched the chill hand of Hester Prynne. The grasp, cold as it was, took away what was dreariest in the interview. They now felt themselves, at least, inhabitants of the same sphere.

Without a word more spoken—neither he nor she assuming the guidance, but with an unexpressed consent—they glided back into the shadow of the woods whence Hester had emerged, and sat down on the heap of moss where she and Pearl had before been sitting. When they found voice to speak, it was at first only to utter remarks and inquiries such as any two acquaintances might have made, about the gloomy sky, the threatening storm, and, next, the health of each. Thus they went onward, not boldly, but step by step, into the themes that were **brooding** deepest in their hearts. So long **estranged** by fate and circumstances, they needed something slight and casual to run before, and throw open the doors of intercourse, so that their real thoughts might be led across the threshold.

After a while, the minister fixed his eyes on Hester Prynne's.

"Hester," said he, "hast thou found peace?"

She smiled drearily, looking down upon her bosom.

"Hast thou?" she asked.

"None! Nothing but despair!" he answered. "What else could I look for being what I am, and leading such a life as mine? Were I an atheist—a man **devoid** of conscience—a wretch with coarse and brutal instincts—I might have found peace, long ere now. Nay, I never should

REVERENCE (<u>reh</u> vuhr ehnts) *v.* **-ing,-ed.**
to regard with awe, to worship
Synonyms: idolize, admire, venerate, adore

REVERENCE (<u>reh</u> vuhr ehnts) *n.*
deep respect, awe
Synonyms: veneration, adoration, admiration

CONSOLATION (kahn suh <u>lay</u> shuhn) *n.*
something providing comfort or solace for a loss or hardship
Synonym: condolence

DISCERN (dihs <u>uhrn</u>) *v.* **-ing,-ed.**
to perceive or recognize something
Synonyms: descry, observe, glimpse, distinguish

REPENT (rih <u>pehnt</u>) *v.* **-ing,-ed.**
to regret a past action
Synonyms: rue, atone, apologize

PENITENCE (<u>peh</u> nih tehnts) *n.*
sorrow expressed for sins or offenses, repentance
Synonyms: remorse, contrition, apology

PENANCE (<u>peh</u> nihns) *n.*
voluntary suffering to repent for a wrong
Synonyms: atonement, reparation, chastening, reconciliation

have lost it! But, as matters stand with my soul, whatever of good capacity there originally was in me, all of God's gifts that were the choicest have become the ministers of spiritual torment. Hester, I am most miserable!"

"The people **reverence** thee," said Hester. "And surely thou workest good among them! Doth this bring thee no comfort?"

"More misery, Hester—only the more misery!" answered the clergyman, with a bitter smile. "As concerns the good which I may appear to do, I have no faith in it. It must needs be a delusion. What can a ruined soul like mine, effect towards the redemption of other souls? Or a polluted soul towards their purification? And as for the people's **reverence**, would that it were turned to scorn and hatred! Canst thou deem it, Hester, a **consolation**, that I must stand up in my pulpit and meet so many eyes turned upward to my face, as if the light of Heaven were beaming from it—must see my flock hungry for the truth, and listening to my words as if a tongue of Pentecost were speaking—and then look inward, and **discern** the black reality of what they idolize? I have laughed, in bitterness and agony of heart, at the contrast between what I seem and what I am! And Satan laughs at it!"

"You wrong yourself in this," said Hester, gently. "You have deeply and sorely **repented**. Your sin is left behind you, in the days long past. Your present life is no less holy, in very truth, than it seems in people's eyes. Is there no reality in the **penitence** thus sealed and witnessed by good works? And wherefore should it not bring you peace?"

"No, Hester, no!" replied the clergyman. "There is no substance in it! It is cold and dead, and can do nothing for me! Of **penance**, I have had enough! Of **penitence**, there has been none! Else, I should long ago have thrown off these garments of mock holiness and have shown myself to mankind as they will see me at the judgment-seat. Happy are you, Hester, that wear the scarlet letter

383

VILE (viel) *adj.*
wretched, offensive, disgusting
Synonyms: despicable, nasty, depraved

RESTRAINED (rih <u>straynd</u>) *adj.*
controlled, repressed, restricted
Synonyms: hampered, bridled, curbed, checked

VEHEMENTLY (<u>vee</u> huh muhnt lee) *adv.*
strongly, urgently
Synonyms: intensely, passionately, ardently

INTERPOSE (ihn tuhr <u>pohz</u>) *v.* **-ing,-ed.**
to interject or interrupt; to come between
Synonyms: encroach, butt in, intrude; interfere,
divide, meddle

MALEVOLENT (muh <u>lehv</u> uh luhnt) *adj.*
ill-willed, causing evil or harm to others
Synonyms: malicious, malignant, spiteful, baneful

MISANTHROPY (mihz <u>aan</u> thruh pee) *n.*
a dislike or mistrust for human nature or mankind
Synonyms: cynicism, pessimism

openly upon your bosom! Mine burns in secret! Thou little knowest what a relief it is, after the torment of a seven years' cheat, to look into an eye that recognizes me for what I am! Had I one friend—or were it my worst enemy—to whom, when sickened with the praises of all other men, I could daily betake myself and be known as the **vilest** of all sinners, methinks my soul might keep itself alive thereby. Even thus much of truth would save me! But, now, it is all falsehood—all emptiness—all death!"

Hester Prynne looked into his face, but hesitated to speak. Yet, uttering his long-**restrained** emotions so **vehemently** as he did, his words here offered her the very point of circumstances in which to **interpose** what she came to say. She conquered her fears, and spoke.

"Such a friend as thou hast even now wished for," said she, "with whom to weep over thy sin, thou hast in me, the partner of it!" Again she hesitated, but brought out the words with an effort. "Thou hast long had such an enemy, and dwellest with him, under the same roof!"

The minister started to his feet, gasping for breath, and clutching at his heart, as if he would have torn it out of his bosom.

"Ha! What sayest thou!" cried he. "An enemy! And under mine own roof! What mean you?"

Hester Prynne was now fully sensible of the deep injury for which she was responsible to this unhappy man, in permitting him to lie for so many years, or, indeed, for a single moment, at the mercy of one whose purposes could not be other than **malevolent**. The very contiguity of his enemy, beneath whatever mask the latter might conceal himself, was enough to disturb the magnetic sphere of a being so sensitive as Arthur Dimmesdale. There had been a period when Hester was less alive to this consideration; or, perhaps, in the **misanthropy** of her own trouble, she left the minister to bear what she might picture to herself as a more tolerable

INVIGORATED (ihn <u>vih</u> guh ray tihd) *adj.*
   made lively or energetic
      Synonyms: stimulated, strengthened, revitalized

MALIGNITY (muh <u>lihg</u> nih tee) *n.*
   evil or aggressive malice; something that produces
   death
      Synonyms: bitterness, resentment; malevolence

INFIRMITY (ihn <u>fuhr</u> mih tee) *n.*
   weakness; disease, ailment
      Synonyms: frailty; illness, affliction

ALIENATION (ay lee uhn <u>ay</u> shuhn) *n.*
   separation or isolation; derangement of the mind
      Synonyms: estrangement, disaffection; madness,
      insanity

GRIEVOUS (<u>gree</u> vuhs) *adj.*
   causing grief and sorrow, serious and distressing
      Synonyms: grave, dire, mournful, dolorous

doom. But of late, since the night of his vigil, all her sympathies towards him had been both softened and **invigorated**. She now read his heart more accurately. She doubted not that the continual presence of Roger Chillingworth—the secret poison of his **malignity**, infecting all the air about him—and his authorized interference, as a physician, with the minister's physical and spiritual **infirmities**—that these bad opportunities had been turned to a cruel purpose. By means of them, the sufferer's conscience had been kept in an irritated state, the tendency of which was, not to cure by wholesome pain, but to disorganize and corrupt his spiritual being. Its result, on earth, could hardly fail to be insanity, and, hereafter, that eternal **alienation** from the Good and True, of which madness is perhaps the earthly type.

Such was the ruin to which she had brought the man, once—nay, why should we not speak it?—still so passionately loved! Hester felt that the sacrifice of the clergyman's good name, and death itself, as she had already told Roger Chillingworth, would have been infinitely preferable to the alternative which she had taken upon herself to choose. And now, rather than have had this **grievous** wrong to confess, she would gladly have lain down on the forest leaves and died there, at Arthur Dimmesdale's feet.

"O Arthur," cried she, "forgive me! In all things else, I have striven to be true! Truth was the one virtue which I might have held fast, and did hold fast, through all extremity; save when thy good—thy life—thy fame—were put in question! Then I consented to a deception. But a lie is never good, even though death threaten on the other side! Dost thou not see what I would say? That old man—the physician, he whom they call Roger Chillingworth—he was my husband!"

The minister looked at her, for an instant, with all that violence of passion, which—intermixed, in more shapes

than one, with his higher, purer, softer qualities—was, in fact, the portion of him which the Devil claimed, and through which he sought to win the rest. Never was there a blacker or a fiercer frown than Hester now encountered. For the brief space that it lasted, it was a dark <u>transfiguration</u>. But his character had been so much enfeebled by suffering, that even its lower energies were incapable of more than a temporary struggle. He sank down on the ground, and buried his face in his hands.

"I might have known it," murmured he. "I did know it! Was not the secret told me, in the natural recoil of my heart, at the first sight of him, and as often as I have seen him since? Why did I not understand? O Hester Prynne, thou little, little knowest all the horror of this thing! And the shame—the indelicacy—the horrible ugliness of this exposure of a sick and guilty heart to the very eye that would gloat over it! Woman, woman, thou art accountable for this! I cannot forgive thee!"

"Thou shalt forgive me!" cried Hester, flinging herself on the fallen leaves beside him. "Let God punish! Thou shalt forgive!"

With sudden and desperate tenderness, she threw her arms around him, and pressed his head against her bosom; little caring though his cheek rested on the scarlet letter. He would have released himself, but strove in vain to do so. Hester would not set him free, lest he should look her sternly in the face. All the world had frowned on her—for seven long years had it frowned upon this lonely woman—and still she bore it all, nor ever once turned away her firm, sad eyes. Heaven, likewise, had frowned upon her, and she had not died. But the frown of this pale, weak, sinful, and sorrow-stricken man was what Hester could not bear and live!

"Wilt thou yet forgive me?" she repeated over and over again. "Wilt thou not frown? Wilt thou forgive?"

"I do forgive you, Hester," replied the minister, at

SANCTITY (<u>saank</u> tih tee) *n.*
holiness, saintliness, pureness
Synonyms: devoutness, divinity, piety

CONSECRATION (kahn suh <u>kray</u> shuhn) *n.*
a declaration of sacredness, a dedication to a
purpose or to worship something specific
Synonyms: sanctification, devotion, commitment

OBSCURE (uhb <u>skyoor</u>) *adj.*
dim, unclear; not well known
Synonyms: dark, faint; remote, minor

SOLEMN (<u>sah</u> luhm) *adj.*
somberly impressive, deeply serious
Synonyms: dignified, earnest, ceremonial

DOLEFULLY (<u>dohl</u> fuhl lee) *adv.*
sadly, mournfully
Synonyms: funereally, somberly, lugubriously,
dismally, woefully

CONSTRAIN (kuhn <u>strayn</u>) *v.* **-ing,-ed.**
to force, impel; restrain
Synonyms: prompt, urge; restrict, control,
calculate

FOREBODE (fohr <u>bohd</u>) *v.* **-ing,-ed.**
to have a presentiment of upcoming evil
Synonyms: predict, portend, foretell, anticipate

IGNOMINY (<u>ihg</u> nuh mih nee) *n.*
disgrace and dishonor
Synonyms: degradation, debasement

length, with a deep utterance, out of an abyss of sadness, but no anger. "I freely forgive you now. May God forgive us both! We are not, Hester, the worst sinners in the world. There is one worse than even the polluted priest! That old man's revenge has been blacker than my sin. He has violated, in cold blood, the **sanctity** of a human heart. Thou and I, Hester, never did so!"

"Never, never!" whispered she. "What we did had a **consecration** of its own. We felt it so! We said so to each other! Hast thou forgotten it?"

"Hush, Hester!" said Arthur Dimmesdale, rising from the ground. "No! I have not forgotten!"

They sat down again, side by side, and hand clasped in hand, on the mossy trunk of the fallen tree. Life had never brought them a gloomier hour; it was the point whither their pathway had so long been tending, and darkening ever, as it stole along; and yet it enclosed a charm that made them linger upon it, and claim another, and another, and, after all, another moment. The forest was **obscure** around them, and creaked with a blast that was passing through it. The boughs were tossing heavily above their heads; while one **solemn** old tree groaned **dolefully** to another, as if telling the sad story of the pair that sat beneath, or **constrained** to **forebode** evil to come.

And yet they lingered. How dreary looked the forest track that led backward to the settlement, where Hester Prynne must take up again the burden of her **ignominy**, and the minister the hollow mockery of his good name! So they lingered an instant longer. No golden light had ever been so precious as the gloom of this dark forest. Here, seen only by his eyes, the scarlet letter need not burn into the bosom of the fallen woman! Here, seen only by her eyes, Arthur Dimmesdale, false to God and man, might be, for one moment, true!

He started at a thought that suddenly occurred to him.

"Hester," cried he, "here is a new horror! Roger

SATIATE (<u>say</u> shee ayt) *v.* **-ing,-ed.**
   to satisfy
      Synonyms: sate, cloy, glut, gorge

RESOLVE (rih <u>sahlv</u>) *v.* **-ing,-ed.**
   to determine or to make a firm decision about
      Synonyms: solve, decide, clear up

Chillingworth knows your purpose to reveal his true character. Will he continue, then, to keep our secret? What will now be the course of his revenge?"

"There is a strange secrecy in his nature," replied Hester thoughtfully, "and it has grown upon him by the hidden practices of his revenge. I deem it not likely that he will betray the secret. He will doubtless seek other means of **satiating** his dark passion."

"And I—how am I to live longer, breathing the same air with this deadly enemy?" exclaimed Arthur Dimmesdale, shrinking within himself, and pressing his hand nervously against his heart—a gesture that had grown involuntary with him. "Think for me, Hester! Thou art strong. **Resolve** for me!"

"Thou must dwell no longer with this man," said Hester, slowly and firmly. "Thy heart must be no longer under his evil eye!"

"It were far worse than death!" replied the minister. "But how to avoid it? What choice remains to me? Shall I lie down again on these withered leaves, where I cast myself when thou didst tell me what he was? Must I sink down here, and die at once?"

"Alas, what a ruin has befallen thee!" said Hester, with the tears gushing into her eyes. "Wilt thou die for very weakness? There is no other cause!"

"The judgment of God is on me," answered the conscience-stricken priest. "It is too mighty for me to struggle with!"

"Heaven would show mercy," rejoined Hester, "hadst thou but the strength to take advantage of it."

"Be thou strong for me!" answered he. "Advise me what to do."

"Is the world, then, so narrow?" exclaimed Hester Prynne, fixing her deep eyes on the minister's, and instinctively exercising a magnetic power over a spirit so shattered and subdued that it could hardly hold itself

VESTIGE (<u>veh</u> stihj) *n.*
    trace, remnant
        Synonyms: relic, remains, token

PROVIDENCE (<u>prah</u> vih dehnts) *n.*
    divine control and direction by God; preparation
    and foresight
        Synonyms: fate, destiny, good luck; prudence,
        precaution

SENTINEL (<u>sehn</u> tih nuhl) *n.*
    a watch guard
        Synonyms: scout, lookout, protector, watchman

FERVENTLY (<u>fuhr</u> vehnt lee) *adv.*
    passionately, intensely, zealously
        Synonyms: vehemently, eagerly, enthusiastically,
        avidly

RESOLVE (rih <u>sahlv</u>) *v.* **-ing,-ed.**
    to determine or to make a firm decision about
        Synonyms: solve, decide, clear up

erect. "Doth the universe lie within the compass of yonder town, which only a little time ago was but a leaf-strewn desert, as lonely as this around us? Whither leads yonder forest-track? Backward to the settlement, thou sayest! Yes, but onward, too! Deeper it goes, and deeper, into the wilderness, less plainly to be seen at every step, until, some few miles hence, the yellow leaves will show no **vestige** of the white man's tread. There thou art free! So brief a journey would bring thee from a world where thou hast been most wretched, to one where thou mayest still be happy! Is there not shade enough in all this boundless forest to hide thy heart from the gaze of Roger Chillingworth?"

"Yes, Hester, but only under the fallen leaves!" replied the minister, with a sad smile.

"Then there is the broad pathway of the sea!" continued Hester. "It brought thee hither. If thou so choose, it will bear thee back again. In our native land, whether in some remote rural village or in vast London— or surely, in Germany, in France, in pleasant Italy—thou wouldst be beyond his power and knowledge! And what hast thou to do with all these iron men, and their opinions? They have kept thy better part in bondage too long already!"

"It cannot be!" answered the minister, listening as if he were called upon to realize a dream. "I am powerless to go! Wretched and sinful as I am, I have had no other thought than to drag on my earthly existence in the sphere where **Providence** hath placed me. Lost as my own soul is, I would still do what I may for other human souls! I dare not quit my post, though an unfaithful **sentinel**, whose sure reward is death and dishonor, when his dreary watch shall come to an end!"

"Thou art crushed under this seven years' weight of misery," replied Hester, **fervently resolved** to buoy him up with her own energy. "But thou shalt leave it all behind thee! It shall not cumber thy steps as thou treadest along

MEDDLE (<u>meh</u> duhl) *v.* **-ing,-ed.**
  to interfere in others' affairs, to impose
    Synonyms: tamper, encroach

RENOWNED (rih <u>nownd</u>) *adj.*
  famed, having widespread acclaim
    Synonyms: eminent, distinguished, prestigious

REPENT (rih <u>pehnt</u>) *v.* **-ing,-ed.**
  to regret a past action
    Synonyms: rue, atone, apologize

KINDLE (<u>kihn</u> duhl) *v.* **-ing,-ed.**
  to excite or inspire; to set fire to or ignite
    Synonyms: arouse, awaken; light, spark

TOTTER (<u>tah</u> tuhr) *v.* **-ing,-ed.**
  to stand with much unsteadiness
    Synonyms: wobble, sway, reel, stagger

DESPONDENCY (dih <u>spahn</u> duhn see) *n.*
  discouragement, dejection
    Synonyms: sadness, depression, desolation

the forest-path; neither shalt thou freight the ship with it, if thou prefer to cross the sea. Leave this wreck and ruin here where it hath happened. **Meddle** no more with it! Begin all anew! Hast thou exhausted possibility in the failure of this one trial? Not so! The future is yet full of trial and success. There is happiness to be enjoyed! There is good to be done! Exchange this false life of thine for a true one. Be, if thy spirit summon thee to such a mission, the teacher and apostle of the red men. Or—as is more thy nature—be a scholar and a sage among the wisest and the most **renowned** of the cultivated world. Preach! Write! Act! Do anything, save to lie down and die! Give up this name of Arthur Dimmesdale, and make thyself another, and a high one, such as thou canst wear without fear or shame. Why shouldst thou <u>tarry</u> so much as one other day in the torments that have gnawed into thy life—that have made thee feeble to will and to do—that will leave thee powerless even to **repent**! Up, and away!"

"O Hester!" cried Arthur Dimmesdale, in whose eyes a fitful light, **kindled** by her enthusiasm, flashed up and died away, "thou tellest of running a race to a man whose knees are **tottering** beneath him! I must die here! There is not the strength or courage left me to venture into the wide, strange, difficult world, alone!"

It was the last expression of the **despondency** of a broken spirit. He lacked energy to grasp the better fortune that seemed within his reach.

He repeated the word.

"Alone, Hester!"

"Thou shalt not go alone!" answered she, in a deep whisper.

Then, all was spoken!

ESTRANGED (ih <u>straynjd</u>) *adj.*
alienated, kept at a distance
Synonyms: disaffected, separated, divorced

REVERENCE (<u>reh</u> vuhr ehnts) *n.*
deep respect, awe
Synonyms: veneration, adoration, admiration

AMISS (uh <u>mihs</u>) *adv.*
in a defective way; mistakenly, accidentally
Synonyms: faultily; astray, awry

TRANSGRESS (traans <u>grehs</u>) *v.* **-ing,-ed.**
to violate a law or command; to trespass
Synonyms: sin, disobey, offend; overstep

A Flood of Sunshine

Chapter 18

Arthur Dimmesdale gazed into Hester's face with a look in which hope and joy shone out, indeed, but with fear <u>betwixt</u> them, and a kind of horror at her boldness, who had spoken what he vaguely hinted at, but dared not speak.

But Hester Prynne, with a mind of native courage and activity, and for so long a period not merely **estranged**, but outlawed, from society, had habituated herself to such latitude of speculation as was altogether foreign to the clergyman. She had wandered, without rule or guidance, in a moral wilderness; as vast, as intricate and shadowy, as the untamed forest, amid the gloom of which they were now holding a <u>colloquy</u> that was to decide their fate. Her intellect and heart had their home, as it were, in desert places, where she roamed as freely as the wild Indian in his woods. For years past she had looked from this **estranged** point of view at human institutions, and whatever priests or legislators had established; criticizing all with hardly more **reverence** than the Indian would feel for the clerical band, the judicial robe, the <u>pillory</u>, the gallows, the fireside, or the church. The tendency of her fate and fortunes had been to set her free. The scarlet letter was her passport into regions where other women dared not tread. Shame, Despair, Solitude! These had been her teachers—stern and wild ones—and they had made her strong, but taught her much **amiss**.

The minister, on the other hand, had never gone through an experience calculated to lead him beyond the scope of generally received laws; although, in a single instance, he had so fearfully **transgressed** one of the

EPOCH (<u>eh</u> pihk) *n.* *(See page 370.)*

MORBID (<u>mohr</u> bihd) *adj.* *(See page 356.)*

ZEAL (zeel) *n.* *(See page 262.)*

MINUTENESS (mie <u>noot</u> nehs) (mih <u>noot</u> nehs) *n.*
precision, attention to detail; the state of being tiny
Synonyms: accuracy, exactness, carefulness; smallness

INEVITABLY (ihn <u>ehv</u> ih tuh blee) *adv.* *(See page 202.)*

IGNOMINY (<u>ihg</u> nuh mih nee) *n.* *(See page 390.)*

EXTENUATION (ihk stehn yoo <u>ay</u> shuhn) *n.*
the act of lessening the seriousness, strength, or effect of
Synonyms: mitigation, lightening

AVAIL (uh <u>vayl</u>) *v.* **-ing,-ed.** *(See page 160.)*

REMORSE (rih <u>mohrs</u>) *n.* *(See page 342.)*

HARROW (<u>haa</u> roh) *v.* **-ing,-ed.**
to torment, terrify
Synonyms: agonize, dismay, upset, disturb, frighten

HYPOCRITE (<u>hih</u> puh kriht) *n.*
person claiming beliefs or virtues he or she doesn't
really possess
Synonyms: fraud, liar, sham, fake, phony

PERIL (<u>pehr</u> ihl) *n.* *(See page 364.)*

INFAMY (<u>ihn</u> fuh mee) *n.* *(See page 320.)*

INSCRUTABLE (ihn <u>skroo</u> tuh buhl) *adj.* *(See pg. 176.)*

MACHINATION (mahk uh <u>nay</u> shuhn) *n.*
a plot or scheme
Synonyms: conspiracy, intrigue, design

EXPIATE (<u>ehk</u> spee ayt) *v.* **-ing,-ed.**
to atone for, make amends for
Synonyms: answer, compensate, pay

BREACH (breech) *n.*
a break, tear or rupture; a violation
Synonyms: gap, lapse, rift; contravention, dereliction

CITADEL (<u>sih</u> tih dehl) *n.*
a fortress which provides safety and where
commands are delegated, the center of control
Synonyms: stronghold, castle, station, support

SUBSEQUENT (<u>suhb</u> suh kwehnt) *adj.* *(See page 352.)*

most sacred of them. But this had been a sin of passion, not of principle, nor even purpose. Since that wretched **epoch**, he had watched, with **morbid zeal** and **minuteness**, not his acts—for those it was easy to arrange—but each breath of emotion, and his every thought. At the head of the social system, as the clergy-men of that day stood, he was only the more trammelled by its regulations, its principles, and even its prejudices. As a priest, the framework of his order **inevitably** hemmed him in. As a man who had once sinned, but who kept his conscience all alive and painfully sensitive by the fretting of an unhealed wound, he might have been supposed safer within the line of virtue than if he had never sinned at all.

Thus, we seem to see that, as regarded Hester Prynne, the whole seven years of outlaw and **ignominy** had been little other than a preparation for this very hour. But Arthur Dimmesdale! Were such a man once more to fall, what plea could be urged in **extenuation** of his crime? None; unless it **avail** him somewhat, that he was broken down by long and exquisite suffering; that his mind was darkened and confused by the very **remorse** which **harrowed** it; that, between fleeing as an avowed criminal, and remaining as a **hypocrite**, conscience might find it hard to strike the balance; that it was human to avoid the **peril** of death and **infamy**, and the **inscrutable machinations** of an enemy; that, finally, to this poor pil-grim, on his dreary and desert path, faint, sick, miserable, there appeared a glimpse of human affection and sympa-thy, a new life, and a true one, in exchange for the heavy doom which he was now **expiating**. And be the stern and sad truth spoken, that the **breach** which guilt has once made into the human soul is never, in this mortal state, repaired. It may be watched and guarded, so that the enemy shall not force his way again into the **citadel** and might even, in his **subsequent** assaults, select some other

STEALTHY (<u>stehl</u> thee) *adj.*
    sly and cautious, sneaky
        Synonyms: furtive, secretive, unperceived

RESOLVE (rih <u>sahlv</u>) *v.* **-ing,-ed.**
    to determine or to make a firm decision about
        Synonyms: solve, decide, clear up

IRREVOCABLY (ih rehv <u>oh</u> kuh blee) *adv.*
    conclusively, irreversibly
        Synonyms: permanently, indelibly, irreparably

SOLACE (<u>sah</u> lihs) *n.*
    comfort in distress, consolation
        Synonyms: succor, balm, cheer, condolence

EXECUTION (ehk sih <u>kyoo</u> shuhn) *n.*
    1. the act of putting to death
        Synonyms: killing, suicide, murder
    2. the act of performing or carrying out a task
        Synonyms: accomplishment, achievement

SUSTAIN (suh <u>stayn</u>) *v.* **-ing,-ed.**
    to endure, undergo; to support, uphold
        Synonyms: withstand; maintain, prop, encourage

EXHILARATING (ihg <u>zihl</u> uh ray tihng) *adj.*
    energizing or filling with happiness
        Synonyms: elating, euphoric, exuberant

GROVEL (<u>grah</u> vuhl) *v.* **-ling,-led.**
    to humble oneself in a demeaning way
        Synonyms: cringe, fawn, kowtow, bootlick

TEMPERAMENT (<u>tehm</u> puhr uh mehnt) *n.*
    an attitude, a manner of behaving
        Synonyms: disposition, mood, mentality

INEVITABLY (ihn <u>ehv</u> ih tuh blee) *adv.*
    certainly, unavoidably
        Synonyms: inescapably, surely, predictably

TINGE (tihnj) *n.*
    a slight shade of color, stain, odor, or taste
        Synonyms: hint, hue, tincture, tone, wash

avenue, in preference to that where he had formerly succeeded. But there is still the ruined wall, and, near it, the **stealthy** tread of the foe that would win over again his unforgotten triumph.

The struggle, if there were one, need not be described. Let it suffice, that the clergyman **resolved** to flee, and not alone.

"If, in all these past seven years," thought he, "I could recall one instant of peace or hope, I would yet endure for the sake of that earnest of Heaven's mercy. But now—since I am **irrevocably** doomed—wherefore should I not snatch the **solace** allowed to the condemned culprit before his **execution**? Or, if this be the path to a better life, as Hester would persuade me, I surely give up no fairer prospect by pursuing it! Neither can I any longer live without her companionship; so powerful is she to **sustain**—so tender to soothe! O Thou to whom I dare not lift mine eyes, wilt Thou yet pardon me!"

"Thou wilt go," said Hester, calmly, as he met her glance.

The decision once made, a glow of strange enjoyment threw its flickering brightness over the trouble of his breast. It was the **exhilarating** effect—upon a prisoner just escaped from the dungeon of his own heart—of breathing the wild, free atmosphere of an unredeemed, unchristianized, lawless region. His spirit rose, as it were, with a bound, and attained a nearer prospect of the sky, than throughout all the misery which had kept him **grovelling** on the earth. Of a deeply religious **temperament**, there was **inevitably** a **tinge** of the devotional in his mood.

"Do I feel joy again!" cried he, wondering at himself. "Methought the germ of it was dead in me! O Hester, thou art my better angel! I seem to have flung myself— sick, sin-stained, and sorrow-blackened—down upon

STIGMA (<u>stihg</u> mah) *n.*
  a mark of disgrace or inferiority
    Synonyms: stain, blot, brand, taint

IMPULSE (<u>ihm</u> puhls) *n.*
  sudden tendency, inclination
    Synonyms: urge, whim

IMPART (ihm <u>pahrt</u>) *v.* **-ing,-ed.**
  to give or share, to pass on
    Synonyms: bestow, contribute, reveal, convey

IRREVOCABLE (ih rehv <u>oh</u> kuh buhl) *adj.*
  conclusive, irreversible
    Synonyms: permanent, indelible, irreparable

these forest leaves, and to have risen up all made anew, and with new powers to glorify Him that hath been merciful! This is already the better life! Why did we not find it sooner?"

"Let us not look back," answered Hester Prynne. "The past is gone! Wherefore should we linger upon it now? See! With this symbol, I undo it all, and make it as it had never been!"

So speaking, she undid the clasp that fastened the scarlet letter, and, taking it from her bosom, threw it to a distance among the withered leaves. The mystic token alighted on the hither verge of the stream. With a hand's-breadth farther flight it would have fallen into the water, and have given the little brook another woe to carry onward, besides the unintelligible tale which it still kept murmuring about. But there lay the embroidered letter, glittering like a lost jewel, which some ill-fated wanderer might pick up, and thenceforth be haunted by strange phantoms of guilt, sinkings of the heart, and unaccountable misfortune.

The **stigma** gone, Hester heaved a long, deep sigh, in which the burden of shame and anguish departed from her spirit. Oh, exquisite relief! She had not known the weight until she felt the freedom! By another **impulse**, she took off the formal cap that confined her hair; and down it fell upon her shoulders, dark and rich, with at once a shadow and a light in its abundance, and **imparting** the charm of softness to her features. There played around her mouth, and beamed out of her eyes, a radiant and tender smile, that seemed gushing from the very heart of womanhood. A crimson flush was glowing on her cheek, that had been long so pale. Her sex, her youth, and the whole richness of her beauty, came back from what men call the **irrevocable** past, and clustered themselves, with her maiden hope and a happiness before unknown, within the magic circle of this

OBSCURE (uhb <u>skyoor</u>) *adj.*
  dim, unclear; not well known
    Synonyms: dark, faint; remote, minor

TRANSMUTE (traans <u>myoot</u>) *v.* **-ing,-ed.**
  to change in appearance or shape
    Synonyms: transform, convert, metamorphose

SOLEMN (<u>sah</u> luhm) *adj.*
  somberly impressive, deeply serious
    Synonyms: dignified, earnest, ceremonial

HEATHEN (<u>hee</u> thuhn) *adj.*
  pagan, uncivilized and irreligious
    Synonyms: idolatrous, polytheistic, unbelieving

SUBJUGATE (<u>suhb</u> juh gayt) *v.* **-ing,-ed.**
  to conquer, subdue, enslave
    Synonyms: defeat, vanquish

The Scarlet Letter

hour. And, as if the gloom of the earth and sky had been but the effluence of these two mortal hearts, it vanished with their sorrow. All at once, as with a sudden smile of Heaven, forth burst the sunshine, pouring a very flood into the **obscure** forest, gladdening each green leaf, **transmuting** the yellow fallen ones to gold, and gleaming adown the gray trunks of the **solemn** trees. The objects that had made a shadow hitherto embodied the brightness now. The course of the little brook might be traced by its merry gleam afar into the wood's heart of mystery, which had become a mystery of joy.

Such was the sympathy of Nature—that wild, **heathen** Nature of the forest, never **subjugated** by human law, nor illumined by higher truth—with the bliss of these two spirits! Love, whether newly born, or aroused from a deathlike slumber, must always create a sunshine, filling the heart so full of radiance that it overflows upon the outward world. Had the forest still kept its gloom, it would have been bright in Hester's eyes, and bright in Arthur Dimmesdale's!

Hester looked at him with the thrill of another joy.

"Thou must know Pearl!" said she. "Our little Pearl! Thou hast seen her—yes, I know it—but thou wilt see her now with other eyes. She is a strange child! I hardly comprehend her! But thou wilt love her dearly, as I do, and wilt advise me how to deal with her."

"Dost thou think the child will be glad to know me?" asked the minister, somewhat uneasily. "I have long shrunk from children, because they often show a distrust—a backwardness to be familiar with me. I have even been afraid of little Pearl!"

"Ah, that was sad!" answered the mother. "But she will love thee dearly, and thou her. She is not far off. I will call her! Pearl! Pearl!"

"I see the child," observed the minister. "Yonder she is, standing in a streak of sunshine, a good way off, on

407

SOMBRE or SOMBER (<u>sahm</u> buhr) *adj.*
melancholy, dismal, dark and gloomy
Synonyms: serious, grave, mournful, lugubrious, funereal

DENIZEN (<u>dehn</u> ih zehn) *n.*
a native, one who is very familiar with a certain place
Synonyms: resident, citizen, inhabitant

REPENT (rih <u>pehnt</u>) *v.* **-ing,-ed.**
to regret a past action
Synonyms: rue, atone, apologize

CHOLERIC (<u>kah</u> luhr ihk) *adj.*
easily angered, short-tempered
Synonyms: irritable, surly, wrathful, irate

the other side of the brook. So thou thinkest the child will love me?"

Hester smiled, and again called to Pearl, who was visible at some distance, as the minister had described her, like a bright-apparelled vision in a sunbeam, which fell down upon her through an arch of boughs. The ray quivered to and fro, making her figure dim or distinct—now like a real child, now like a child's spirit—as the splendor went and came again. She heard her mother's voice, and approached slowly through the forest.

Pearl had not found the hour pass wearisomely while her mother sat talking with the clergyman. The great black forest—stern as it showed itself to those who brought the guilt and troubles of the world into its bosom—became the playmate of the lonely infant, as well as it knew how. **Sombre** as it was, it put on the kindest of its moods to welcome her. It offered her the partridge-berries, the growth of the preceding autumn, but ripening only in the spring, and now red as drops of blood upon the withered leaves. These Pearl gathered, and was pleased with their wild flavor. The small **denizens** of the wilderness hardly took pains to move out of her path. A partridge, indeed, with a brood of ten behind her, ran forward threateningly, but soon **repented** of her fierceness, and clucked to her young ones not to be afraid. A pigeon, alone on a low branch, allowed Pearl to come beneath, and uttered a sound as much of greeting as alarm. A squirrel from the lofty depths of his domestic tree, chattered either in anger or merriment—for a squirrel is such a **choleric** and humorous little personage, that it is hard to distinguish between his moods—so he chattered at the child, and flung down a nut upon her head. It was a last year's nut, and already gnawed by his sharp tooth. A fox, startled from his sleep by her light footstep on the leaves, looked inquisitively at Pearl, as doubting whether it were better

to steal off, or renew his nap on the same spot. A wolf, it is said—but here the tale has surely lapsed into the improbable—came up, and smelt of Pearl's robe, and offered his savage head to be patted by her hand. The truth seems to be, however, that the mother-forest, and these wild things which it nourished, all recognized a kindred wildness in the human child.

And she was gentler here than in the grassy-margined streets of the settlement, or in her mother's cottage. The flowers appeared to know it; and one and another whispered as she passed, "Adorn thyself with me, thou beautiful child, adorn thyself with me!" And, to please them, Pearl gathered the violets, and anemones, and columbines, and some twigs of the freshest green, which the old trees held down before her eyes. With these she decorated her hair, and her young waist, and became a nymph-child, or an infant <u>dryad</u>, or whatever else was in closest sympathy with the antique wood. In such guise had Pearl adorned herself, when she heard her mother's voice, and came slowly back.

Slowly, for she saw the clergyman!

MANIFEST (<u>maan</u> uh fehst) *adj.*
  evidently obvious
    Synonyms: apparent, distinct, prominent, glaring

PROPHET (<u>prah</u> feht) *n.*
  a person who has the ability to foretell events
    Synonyms: clairvoyant, predictor, seer, oracle

The Child at the Brookside

Chapter 19

"Thou wilt love her dearly," repeated Hester Prynne, as she and the minister sat watching little Pearl. "Dost thou not think her beautiful? And see with what natural skill she has made those simple flowers adorn her! Had she gathered pearls, and diamonds, and rubies, in the wood, they could not have become her better. She is a splendid child! But I know whose brow she has!"

"Dost thou know, Hester," said Arthur Dimmesdale, with an unquiet smile, "that this dear child, tripping about always at thy side, hath caused me many an alarm? Methought—O Hester, what a thought is that, and how terrible to dread it—that my own features were partly repeated in her face, and so strikingly that the world might see them! But she is mostly thine!"

"No, no! Not mostly!" answered the mother, with a tender smile. "A little longer, and thou needest not to be afraid to trace whose child she is. But how strangely beautiful she looks, with those wild flowers in her hair! It is as if one of the fairies, whom we left in our dear old England, had decked her out to meet us."

It was with a feeling which neither of them had ever before experienced, that they sat and watched Pearl's slow advance. In her was visible the tie that united them. She had been offered to the world, these seven years past, as the living <u>hieroglyphic</u>, in which was revealed the secret they so darkly sought to hide—all written in this symbol—all plainly **manifest**—had there been a **prophet** or magician skilled to read the character of flame! And Pearl was the oneness of their being. Be the foregone evil what it might, how could they doubt that their earthly

ACCOST (uh <u>cahst</u>) (uh <u>kawst</u>) *v.* **-ing,-ed.**
to approach and speak to someone, often in an
aggressive way
    Synonyms: address, confront

PRATTLE (<u>praa</u> tuhl) *v.* **-ing,-ed.**
to talk foolishly and meaninglessly
    Synonyms: chatter, babble, drivel, blather

lives and future destinies were conjoined, when they beheld at once the material union, and the spiritual idea, in whom they met, and were to dwell immortally together? Thoughts like these—and perhaps other thoughts, which they did not acknowledge or define—threw an awe about the child, as she came onward.

"Let her see nothing strange—no passion nor eagerness—in thy way of **accosting** her," whispered Hester. "Our Pearl is a fitful and fantastic little elf, sometimes. Especially, she is seldom tolerant of emotion, when she does not fully comprehend the why and wherefore. But the child hath strong affections! She loves me, and will love thee!"

"Thou canst not think," said the minister, glancing aside at Hester Prynne, "how my heart dreads this interview, and yearns for it! But, in truth, as I already told thee, children are not readily won to be familiar with me. They will not climb my knee, nor **prattle** in my ear, nor answer to my smile; but stand apart, and eye me strangely. Even little babes, when I take them in my arms, weep bitterly. Yet Pearl, twice in her little lifetime, hath been kind to me! The first time—thou knowest it well! The last was when thou ledst her with thee to the house of yonder stern old Governor."

"And thou didst plead so bravely in her behalf and mine!" answered the mother. "I remember it; and so shall little Pearl. Fear nothing! She may be strange and shy at first, but will soon learn to love thee!"

By this time Pearl had reached the margin of the brook and stood on the farther side, gazing silently at Hester and the clergyman, who still sat together on the mossy tree-trunk, waiting to receive her. Just where she had paused, the brook chanced to form a pool, so smooth and quiet that it reflected a perfect image of her little figure, with all the brilliant picturesqueness of her beauty, in its adornment of flowers and wreathed

SAT Vocabulary

INTANGIBLE (ihn <u>taan</u> juh buhl) *adj.*
    not perceptible to the touch, not material
        Synonyms: impalpable, imponderable, illusory,
        abstract

STEADFASTLY (<u>stehd</u> faast lee) *adv.*
    with persistence, without wavering, loyally
        Synonyms: relentlessly, faithfully, constantly,
        staunchly

MEDIUM (<u>mee</u> dee uhm) *n.*
    a substance or object that is used to transmit or
    accomplish something
        Synonyms: means, instrument, vehicle, mechanism

ESTRANGE (ih <u>straynj</u>) *v.* **-ing,-ed.**
    to alienate, keep at a distance
        Synonyms: disaffect, separate, divorce

IMPART (ihm <u>pahrt</u>) *v.* **-ing,-ed.**
    to give or share, to pass on
        Synonyms: bestow, contribute, reveal, convey

foliage, but more refined and spiritualized than the reality. This image, so nearly identical with the living Pearl, seemed to communicate somewhat of its own shadowy and **intangible** quality to the child herself. It was strange, the way in which Pearl stood, looking so **steadfastly** at them through the dim **medium** of the forest-gloom; herself, meanwhile, all glorified with a ray of sunshine that was attracted thitherward as by a certain sympathy. In the brook beneath stood another child—another and the same—with likewise its ray of golden light. Hester felt herself, in some indistinct and tantalizing manner, **estranged** from Pearl; as if the child, in her lonely ramble through the forest, had strayed out of the sphere in which she and her mother dwelt together, and was now vainly seeking to return to it.

There was both truth and error in the impression; the child and mother were **estranged**, but through Hester's fault, not Pearl's. Since the latter rambled from her side, another inmate had been admitted within the circle of the mother's feelings, and so modified the aspect of them all, that Pearl, the returning wanderer, could not find her wonted place, and hardly knew where she was.

"I have a strange fancy," observed the sensitive minister, "that this brook is the boundary between two worlds, and that thou canst never meet thy Pearl again. Or is she an elfish spirit, who, as the legends of our childhood taught us, is forbidden to cross a running stream? Pray hasten her; for this delay has already **imparted** a tremor to my nerves."

"Come, dearest child!" said Hester encouragingly, and stretching out both her arms. "How slow thou art! When hast thou been so sluggish before now? Here is a friend of mine, who must be thy friend also. Thou wilt have twice as much love, henceforward, as thy mother alone could give thee! Leap across the brook and come to us. Thou canst leap like a young deer!"

SINGULAR (<u>sihn</u> gyuh luhr) *adj.*
uncommon, peculiar
Synonyms: unusual, odd, rare, unique, individual

IMPERIOUS (ihm <u>pihr</u> ee uhs) *adj.*
arrogantly self-assured, domineering, overbearing
Synonyms: authoritarian, despotic

INURE (ihn <u>yoor</u>) *v.* **-ing,-ed.**
to accustom, harden, become used to
Synonyms: habituate, familiarize, condition

MOLLIFY (<u>mahl</u> uh fie) *v.* **-ing,-ied.**
to calm or make less severe
Synonyms: pacify, conciliate, appease, placate,
moderate

ENTREATY (ehn <u>tree</u> tee) *n.*
a plea or request
Synonyms: imploration, prayer, petition

GESTICULATE (jeh <u>stih</u> kyuh layt) *v.* **-ing,-ed.**
to make expressive gestures
Synonyms: motion, indicate, signal

Pearl, without responding in any manner to these honey-sweet expressions, remained on the other side of the brook. Now she fixed her bright, wild eyes on her mother, now on the minister, and now included them both in the same glance, as if to detect and explain to herself the relation which they bore to one another. For some unaccountable reason, as Arthur Dimmesdale felt the child's eyes upon himself, his hand—with that gesture so habitual as to have become involuntary—stole over his heart. At length, assuming a **singular** air of authority, Pearl stretched out her hand, with the small forefinger extended, and pointing evidently towards her mother's breast. And beneath, in the mirror of the brook, there was the flower-girdled and sunny image of little Pearl, pointing her small forefinger too.

"Thou strange child, why dost thou not come to me?" exclaimed Hester.

Pearl still pointed with her forefinger; and a frown gathered on her brow, the more impressive from the childish, the almost baby-like aspect of the features that conveyed it. As her mother still kept beckoning to her and arraying her face in a holiday suit of unaccustomed smiles, the child stamped her foot with a yet more **imperious** look and gesture. In the brook, again, was the fantastic beauty of the image, with its reflected frown, its pointed finger, and **imperious** gesture, giving emphasis to the aspect of little Pearl.

"Hasten, Pearl, or I shall be angry with thee!" cried Hester Prynne, who, however **inured** to such behavior on the elf-child's part at other seasons, was naturally anxious for a more seemly deportment now. "Leap across the brook, naughty child, and run hither! Else I must come to thee!"

But Pearl, not a <u>whit</u> startled at her mother's threats any more than **mollified** by her **entreaties**, now suddenly burst into a fit of passion, **gesticulating** violently, and

WRATH (raath) *n.*
anger, rage
Synonyms: fury, ire, resentment, indignation

MULTITUDE (<u>muhl</u> tuh tood) *n.*
a crowd; the state of being many, a great number
Synonyms: throng; mass, myriad

GESTICULATE (jeh <u>stih</u> kyuh layt) *v.* **-ing,-ed.**
to make expressive gestures
Synonyms: motion, indicate, signal

PACIFY (<u>paa</u> suh fie) *v.* **-ing,-ied.**
to restore calm, bring peace
Synonyms: mollify, conciliate, appease, placate

PRETERNATURAL (pree tuhr <u>naach</u> uh ruhl) *adj.*
extraordinary or unnatural
Synonyms: abnormal, mysterious, odd, unearthly

PALLOR (<u>paal</u> uhr) *n.*
extreme paleness of the skin
Synonyms: lividity, wanness

throwing her small figure into the most extravagant contortions. She accompanied this wild outbreak with piercing shrieks, which the woods reverberated on all sides; so that, alone as she was in her childish and unreasonable **wrath**, it seemed as if a hidden **multitude** were lending her their sympathy and encouragement. Seen in the brook, once more, was the shadowy **wrath** of Pearl's image, crowned and girdled with flowers, but stamping its foot, wildly **gesticulating**, and, in the midst of all, still pointing its small forefinger at Hester's bosom!

"I see what ails the child," whispered Hester to the clergyman, and turning pale in spite of a strong effort to conceal her trouble and annoyance. "Children will not abide any, the slightest, change in the accustomed aspect of things that are daily before their eyes. Pearl misses something which she has always seen me wear."

"I pray you," answered the minister, "if thou hast any means of **pacifying** the child, do it forthwith! Save it were the cankered **wrath** of an old witch, like Mistress Hibbins," added he, attempting to smile, "I know nothing that I would not sooner encounter than this passion in a child. In Pearl's young beauty, as in the wrinkled witch, it has a **preternatural** effect. **Pacify** her, if thou lovest me!"

Hester turned again towards Pearl with a crimson blush upon her cheek, a conscious glance aside at the clergyman, and then a heavy sigh; while, even before she had time to speak, the blush yielded to a deadly **pallor**.

"Pearl," said she, sadly, "look down at thy feet! There!—before thee!—on the hither side of the brook!"

The child turned her eyes to the point indicated; and there lay the scarlet letter, so close upon the margin of the stream that the gold embroidery was reflected in it.

"Bring it hither!" said Hester.

"Come thou and take it up!" answered Pearl.

INEVITABLE (ihn <u>ehv</u> ih tuh buhl) *adj.*
  certain, unavoidable
    Synonyms: inescapable, sure, predictable

REPROACHFULLY (rih <u>prohch</u> fuh lee) *adv.*
  in a disappointed or critical manner, disparagingly
    Synonyms: disapprovingly, shamefully, meanly,
    abusively

"Was ever such a child!" observed Hester, aside to the minister. "Oh, I have much to tell thee about her! But, in very truth, she is right as regards this hateful token. I must bear its torture yet a little longer—only a few days longer—until we shall have left this region and look back hither as to a land which we have dreamed of. The forest cannot hide it! The mid-ocean shall take it from my hand, and swallow it up forever!"

With these words, she advanced to the margin of the brook, took up the scarlet letter, and fastened it again into her bosom. Hopefully, but a moment ago, as Hester had spoken of drowning it in the deep sea, there was a sense of **inevitable** doom upon her, as she thus received back this deadly symbol from the hand of fate. She had flung it into infinite space—she had drawn an hour's free breath—and here again was the scarlet misery, glittering on the old spot! So it ever is, whether thus typified or no, that an evil deed invests itself with the character of doom. Hester next gathered up the heavy tresses of her hair, and confined them beneath her cap. As if there were a withering spell in the sad letter, her beauty, the warmth and richness of her womanhood, departed, like fading sunshine; and a gray shadow seemed to fall across her.

When the dreary change was wrought, she extended her hand to Pearl.

"Dost thou know thy mother now, child?" asked she, **reproachfully**, but with a subdued tone. "Wilt thou come across the brook and own thy mother, now that she has her shame upon her—now that she is sad?"

"Yes, now I will!" answered the child, bounding across the brook, and clasping Hester in her arms. "Now thou art my mother indeed! And I am thy little Pearl!"

In a mood of tenderness that was not usual with her, she drew down her mother's head, and kissed her brow

IMPEL (ihm <u>pehl</u>) *v.* **-ling,-led.**
to urge forward as if driven by a strong moral pressure
Synonyms: push, prompt, incite, instigate

ENTREAT (ehn <u>treet</u>) *v.* **-ing,-ed.**
to plead, beg
Synonyms: beseech, implore, importune, request

ACUTE (uh <u>kyoot</u>) *adj.*
clever, shrewd; sharp, pointed, severe
Synonyms: ingenious, keen; intense, fierce

CAPRICE (kuh <u>prees</u>) *n.*
an impulsive change of mind, fickleness
Synonym: whim

MANIFEST (<u>maan</u> uh fehst) *v.* **-ing,-ed.**
to make evident or certain by display
Synonyms: exhibit, showcase, expose

GRIMACE (<u>grih</u> muhs) (grih <u>mays</u>) *n.*
a facial expression showing pain or disgust
Synonyms: scowl, leer, glare

SINGULAR (<u>sihn</u> gyuh luhr) *adj.*
peculiar, uncommon
Synonyms: unique, individual, unusual, odd, rare

PHYSIOGNOMY (fih zee <u>ahg</u> nuh mee) *n.*
characteristic facial features; the art of judging one's
character from facial features
Synonyms: visage, expression; divination

TALISMAN (<u>taa</u> lihs mehn) *n.*
a magical object that is believed to bring protection
or supernatural powers to its keeper
Synonyms: lucky charm, amulet, idol

and both her cheeks. But then—by a kind of necessity that always **impelled** this child to <u>alloy</u> whatever comfort she might chance to give with a throb of anguish—Pearl put up her mouth, and kissed the scarlet letter too!

"That was not kind!" said Hester. "When thou hast shown me a little love, thou mockest me!"

"Why doth the minister sit yonder?" asked Pearl.

"He waits to welcome thee," replied her mother. "Come thou, and **entreat** his blessing! He loves thee, my little Pearl, and loves thy mother too. Wilt thou not love him? Come! He longs to greet thee!"

"Doth he love us?" said Pearl, looking up with **acute** intelligence into her mother's face. "Will he go back with us, hand in hand, we three together, into the town?"

"Not now, dear child," answered Hester. "But in days to come he will walk hand in hand with us. We will have a home and fireside of our own; and thou shalt sit upon his knee; and he will teach thee many things, and love thee dearly. Thou wilt love him; wilt thou not?"

"And will he always keep his hand over his heart?" inquired Pearl.

"Foolish child, what a question is that!" exclaimed her mother. "Come and ask his blessing!"

But, whether influenced by the jealousy that seems instinctive with every petted child towards a dangerous rival, or from whatever **caprice** of her freakish nature, Pearl would show no favor to the clergyman. It was only by an exertion of force that her mother brought her up to him, hanging back and **manifesting** her reluctance by odd **grimaces**; of which, ever since her babyhood, she had possessed a **singular** variety, and could transform her mobile **physiognomy** into a series of different aspects, with a new mischief in them, each and all. The minister—painfully embarrassed, but hoping that a kiss might prove a **talisman** to admit him into the child's

DIFFUSE (dih <u>fyooz</u>) *v.* **-ing,-ed.**
    to spread out widely
        Synonyms: scatter, disperse

SOLITUDE (<u>sahl</u> ih tood) *n.*
    aloneness, social isolation
        Synonyms: loneliness; seclusion, withdrawal,
        retirement

MULTITUDINOUS (muhl tih <u>too</u> dih nihs) *adj.*
    many, numerous
        Synonyms: myriad, countless

MELANCHOLY (<u>mehl</u> uhn kahl ee) *adj.*
    sad, depressed
        Synonyms: dejected, despondent, woeful, sorrowful

kindlier regards—bent forward, and impressed one on her brow. Hereupon, Pearl broke away from her mother, and, running to the brook, stooped over it, and bathed her forehead, until the unwelcome kiss was quite washed off, and **diffused** through a long lapse of the gliding water. She then remained apart, silently watching Hester and the clergyman, while they talked together, and made such arrangements as were suggested by their new position, and the purposes soon to be fulfilled.

And now this fateful interview had come to a close. The dell was to be left a **solitud**e among its dark, old trees, which, with their **multitudinous** tongues, would whisper long of what had passed there, and no mortal be the wiser. And the **melancholy** brook would add this other tale to the mystery with which its little heart was already overburdened, and whereof it still kept up a murmuring babble, with not a whit more cheerfulness of tone than for ages heretofore.

VICISSITUDE (vih <u>sih</u> sih tood) *n.*
 change or variation, ups and downs
  Synonyms: mutability, inconstancy, wavering

ANTIQUITY (aan <u>tih</u> kwih tee) *n.*
 ancient times; the quality of being very old
  Synonyms: history; hoariness, antiqueness

SOLACE (<u>sah</u> lihs) *n.*
 comfort in distress, consolation
  Synonyms: succor, balm, cheer, condolence

DUPLICITY (doo <u>plih</u> sih tee) *n.*
 the quality of being double; deception, dishonesty
  Synonyms: duality, two-facedness; infidelity,
  disloyalty

VEX (vehks) *v.* **-ing,-ed.**
 to confuse, puzzle; to irritate, annoy
  Synonyms: perplex, perturb; bother, plague, afflict,
  irk

DISQUIETUDE (dihs <u>kwie</u> eh tood) *n.*
 anxiety, lack of peace or tranquility
  Synonyms: edginess, uneasiness

SUSTAIN (suh <u>stayn</u>) *v.* **-ing,-ed.**
 to endure, undergo; to support, uphold
  Synonyms: withstand; maintain, prop, encourage

The Minister in a Maze

Chapter 20

As the minister departed, in advance of Hester Prynne and little Pearl, he threw a backward glance, half expecting that he should discover only some faintly traced features or outline of the mother and the child slowly fading into the twilight of the woods. So great a **vicissitude** in his life could not at once be received as real. But there was Hester, clad in her gray robe, still standing beside the tree-trunk, which some blast had overthrown a long **antiquity** ago, and which time had ever since been covering with moss, so that these two fated ones, with earth's heaviest burden on them, might there sit down together, and find a single hour's rest and **solace**. And there was Pearl, too, lightly dancing from the margin of the brook—now that the intrusive third person was gone—and taking her old place by her mother's side. So the minister had not fallen asleep, and dreamed!

In order to free his mind from this indistinctness and **duplicity** of impression, which **vexed** it with a strange **disquietude**, he recalled and more thoroughly defined the plans which Hester and himself had sketched for their departure. It had been determined between them that the Old World, with its crowds and cities, offered them a more eligible shelter and concealment than the wilds of New England, or all America, with its alternatives of an Indian wigwam, or the few settlements of Europeans, scattered thinly along the seaboard. Not to speak of the clergyman's health, so inadequate to **sustain** the hardships of a forest life, his native gifts, his culture, and his entire development would secure him a home only in the midst of civilization and refinement; the higher the state,

ADAPTED (uh <u>daap</u> tihd) *adj.*
adjusted, changed, fit
Synonyms: accustomed, altered, conformed

HONORABLE (<u>ah</u> nuhr uh buhl) *adj.*
illustrious, praiseworthy, deserving
Synonyms: respectable, dignified, noble

EPOCH (<u>eh</u> pihk) *n.*
a particular day or time; a specific time in history
Synonyms: date; period, era, generation

EXEMPLARY (ihg <u>zehm</u> pluhr ee) *adj.*
excellent, perfect
Synonyms: commendable, meritorious, ideal, superlative, admirable

INTROSPECTION (ihn truh <u>spehk</u> shuhn) *n.*
the contemplation of one's own thoughts and feelings
Synonyms: reflection, meditation

PROFOUND (pruh <u>fownd</u>) (proh <u>fownd</u>) *adj.*
deep; having intellectual depth
Synonyms: bottomless; serious, thorough, weighty

ACUTE (uh <u>kyoot</u>) *adj.*
clever, shrewd; sharp, pointed, severe
Synonyms: ingenious, keen; intense, fierce

APPREHEND (aa pree <u>hehnd</u>) *v.* **-ing,-ed.**
1. to anticipate fearfully; to become aware of something through one's senses; to understand
Synonyms: dread; perceive; comprehend, grasp
2. to arrest
Synonyms: capture, seize, take, nab

SUBTLE (<u>suh</u> tuhl) *adj.*
hard to detect or describe
Synonyms: elusive, abstruse, clever, devious, insinuating

the more delicately **adapted** to it the man. In furtherance of his choice, it so happened that a ship lay in the harbor; one of those questionable cruisers, frequent at that day, which, without being absolutely outlaws of the deep, yet roamed over its surface with a remarkable irresponsibility of character. This vessel had recently arrived from the Spanish Main, and, within three days' time would sail for Bristol. Hester Prynne—whose vocation, as a self-enlisted Sister of Charity, had brought her acquainted with the captain and crew—could take upon herself to secure the passage of two individuals and a child, with all the secrecy which circumstances rendered more than desirable.

The minister had inquired of Hester, with no little interest, the precise time at which the vessel might be expected to depart. It would probably be on the fourth day from the present. "That is most fortunate!" he had then said to himself. Now, why the Reverend Mr. Dimmesdale considered it so very fortunate, we hesitate to reveal. Nevertheless—to hold nothing back from the reader—it was because on the third day from the present he was to preach the Election Sermon; and, as such an occasion formed an **honorable epoch** in the life of a New England clergyman, he could not have chanced upon a more suitable mode and time of terminating his professional career. "At least they shall say of me," thought this **exemplary** man, "that I leave no public duty unperformed, nor ill performed!" Sad, indeed, that an **introspection** so **profound** and **acute** as this poor minister's should be so miserably deceived! We have had, and may still have, worse things to tell of him; but none, we **apprehend**, so pitiably weak; no evidence, at once so slight and <u>irrefragable</u>, of a **subtle** disease, that had long since begun to eat into the real substance of his character. No man, for any considerable period can wear one

MULTITUDE (<u>muhl</u> tuh tood) *n.*
a crowd; the state of being many, a great number
Synonyms: throng; mass, myriad

UNCOUTH (uhn <u>kooth</u>) *adj.*
lacking in refinement, awkward and uncultivated in
appearance or manner
Synonyms: crude, clumsy, ungraceful

ASCENT (uh <u>sehnt</u>) *n.*
an upward slope; a climb or rising to another level;
movement upward
Synonyms: incline, upgrade; mounting; scaling,
escalation

IMPORTUNATELY (ihm <u>pohr</u> chuh niht lee) *adv.*
in a pleading or extremely urgent manner
Synonyms: beseechingly, earnestly, imperatively

BESTOW (bih <u>stoh</u>) *v.* **-ing,-ed.**
to give as a gift; to apply or devote time or effort
Synonyms: endow, confer, present; allocate, dedicate

MUTABILITY (myoo tuh <u>bihl</u> uh tee) *n.*
changeability, inconsistency
Synonym: impermanence

face to himself and another to the **multitude**, without finally getting bewildered as to which may be the true.

The excitement of Mr. Dimmesdale's feelings as he returned from his interview with Hester, lent him unaccustomed physical energy, and hurried him townward at a rapid pace. The pathway among the woods seemed wilder, more **uncouth** with its rude natural obstacles, and less trodden by the foot of man, than he remembered it on his outward journey. But he leaped across the plashy places, thrust himself through the clinging underbrush, climbed the **ascent**, plunged into the hollow, and overcame, in short, all the difficulties of the track with an unweariable activity that astonished him. He could not but recall how feebly, and with what frequent pauses for breath, he had toiled over the same ground only two days before. As he drew near the town, he took an impression of change from the series of familiar objects that presented themselves. It seemed not yesterday, not one, nor two, but many days, or even years ago, since he had quitted them. There, indeed, was each former trace of the street, as he remembered it, and all the peculiarities of the houses, with the due **multitude** of gable-peaks, and a weathercock at every point where his memory suggested one. Not the less, however, came this **importunately** obtrusive sense of change. The same was true as regarded the acquaintances whom he met, and all the well-known shapes of human life, about the little town. They looked neither older nor younger now; the beards of the aged were no whiter, nor could the creeping babe of yesterday walk on his feet today; it was impossible to describe in what respect they differed from the individuals on whom he had so recently **bestowed** a parting glance; and yet the minister's deepest sense seemed to inform him of their **mutability**. A similar impression struck him most remarkably as he passed under the walls of his own

EDIFICE (<u>eh</u> duh fuhs) *n.*
a large structure
Synonyms: building, construction, skyscraper

MELANCHOLY (<u>mehl</u> uhn kahl ee) *adj.*
sad, depressed
Synonyms: dejected, despondent, woeful, sorrowful

EMACIATED (ih <u>may</u> shee ay tihd) *adj.*
very thin due to hunger or disease, feeble
Synonyms: bony, gaunt, haggard, skeletal

IMPULSE (<u>ihm</u> puhls) *n.*
sudden tendency, inclination
Synonyms: urge, whim

INCITE (ihn <u>siet</u>) *v.* **-ing,-ed.**
to move to action, to activate, to urge on
Synonyms: encourage, actuate, motivate, stimulate

PROFOUND (pruh <u>fownd</u>) (proh <u>fownd</u>) *adj.*
deep; having intellectual depth
Synonyms: bottomless; serious, thorough, weighty

PATERNAL (puh <u>tuhr</u> nuhl) *adj.*
fatherly, related to the characteristics of fatherhood;
inherited from the father
Synonyms: parental; hereditary

PATRIARCHAL (pay tree <u>ahr</u> kuhl) *adj.*
relating to the qualities of an old, well-respected
man, often the head of a family or a high member of
a church
Synonyms: dignified, experienced, reverenced

The Scarlet Letter

church. The **edifice** had so very strange, and yet so familiar, an aspect, that Mr. Dimmesdale's mind vibrated between two ideas; either that he had seen it only in a dream hitherto, or that he was merely dreaming about it now.

This phenomenon, in the various shapes which it assumed, indicated no external change, but so sudden and important a change in the spectator of the familiar scene, that the intervening space of a single day had operated on his consciousness like the lapse of years. The minister's own will, and Hester's will, and the fate that grew between them, had wrought this transformation. It was the same town as heretofore; but the same minister returned not from the forest. He might have said to the friends who greeted him, "I am not the man for whom you take me! I left him yonder in the forest, withdrawn into a secret dell, by a mossy tree-trunk, and near a **melancholy** brook! Go seek your minister, and see if his **emaciated** figure, his thin cheek, his white, heavy, pain-wrinkled brow, be not flung down there, like a cast-off garment!" His friends, no doubt, would still have insisted with him—"Thou art thyself the man!"—but the error would have been their own, not his.

Before Mr. Dimmesdale reached home, his inner man gave him other evidences of a revolution in the sphere of thought and feeling. In truth, nothing short of a total change of dynasty and moral code, in that interior kingdom, was adequate to account for the **impulses** now communicated to the unfortunate and startled minister. At every step he was **incited** to do some strange, wild, wicked thing or other, with a sense that it would be at once involuntary and intentional; in spite of himself, yet growing out of a **profounder** self than that which opposed the **impulse**. For instance, he met one of his own deacons. The good old man addressed him with the **paternal** affection and **patriarchal** privilege, which his

VENERABLE (<u>veh</u> nehr uh buhl) *adj.*
respected because of age
Synonyms: distinguished, elderly

ENJOIN (ehn <u>joyn</u>) *v.* **-ing,-ed.**
to order, urge, command; forbid or prohibit, as by
judicial order
Synonyms: direct, instruct; proscribe

ENDOWMENT (ehn <u>dow</u> mehnt) (ihn <u>dow</u> mehnt) *n.*
a talent; a gift
Synonyms: ability, aptitude; grant, benefit

HOARY (<u>hohr</u> ee) (<u>haw</u> ree) *adj.*
very old; whitish or gray from age
Synonyms: antediluvian, antique, vintage, ancient

BLASPHEMOUS (<u>blaas</u> fuh muhs) *adj.*
cursing, profane, irreverent
Synonyms: sacrilegious, impious

SANCTIFIED (<u>saank</u> tih fied) *adj.*
pious; holy, sacred
Synonyms: self-righteous; consecrated, divine

PATRIARCHAL (pay tree <u>ahr</u> kuhl) *adj.* *(See pg. 434.)*

IMPIETY (ihm <u>pie</u> uh tee) *n.*
lack of religious devoutness
Synonyms: irreverence, profanity, immorality

PIOUS (<u>pie</u> uhs) *adj.*
extremely religious; dedicated, devout
Synonyms: sanctimonious; observant, reverent

EXEMPLARY (ihg <u>zehm</u> pluhr ee) *adj.* *(See page 430.)*

REMINISCENCE (reh muh <u>nihs</u> ehnts) *n.* *(See pg. 114.)*

SOLEMN (<u>sah</u> luhm) *adj.* *(See page 406.)*

DEVOUT (dih <u>vowt</u>) *adj.*
devoted, as to religion
Synonyms: pious, observant, sincere, earnest

CONSOLATION (kahn suh <u>lay</u> shuhn) *n.*
something providing comfort or solace for a loss or
hardship
Synonym: condolence

venerable age, his upright and holy character, and his station in the Church entitled him to use; and, conjoined with this, the deep, almost worshipping respect which the minister's professional and private claims alike demanded. Never was there a more beautiful example of how the majesty of age and wisdom may comport with the <u>obeisance</u> and respect **enjoined** upon it, as from a lower social rank, and inferior order of **endowment**, towards a higher. Now, during a conversation of some two or three moments between the Reverend Mr. Dimmesdale and this excellent and **hoary** bearded deacon, it was only by the most careful self-control that the former could refrain from uttering certain **blasphemous** suggestions that rose into his mind, respecting the communion supper. He absolutely trembled and turned pale as ashes, lest his tongue should wag itself, in utterance of these horrible matters, and plead his own consent for so doing, without his having fairly given it. And, even with this terror in his heart, he could hardly avoid laughing, to imagine how the **sanctified** old **patriarchal** deacon would have been petrified by his minister's **impiety**!

Again, another incident of the same nature. Hurrying along the street, the Reverend Mr. Dimmesdale encountered the eldest female member of his church; a most **pious** and **exemplary** old dame; poor, widowed, lonely, and with a heart as full of **reminiscences** about her dead husband and children, and her dead friends of long ago, as a burial-ground is full of storied gravestones. Yet all this, which would else have been such heavy sorrow, was made almost a **solemn** joy to her **devout** old soul, by religious **consolations** and the truths of Scripture, wherewith she had fed herself continually for more than thirty years. And, since Mr. Dimmesdale had taken her in charge, the good grandam's chief earthly comfort—which, unless it had

RAPTUROUSLY (<u>raap</u> chuhr uhs lee) *adv.*
with extreme joy or ecstasy
Synonyms: blissfully, delightfully

PITHY (<u>pih</u> thee) *adj.*
concise, succinct, to the point with a precise purpose
Synonyms: brief, compact

INFUSION (ihn <u>fyoo</u> zhuhn) *n.*
a solution that is introduced into the body
Synonyms: pervasion, preparation, concoction

IMPART (ihm <u>pahrt</u>) *v.* **-ing,-ed.**
to give or share, to pass on
Synonyms: bestow, contribute, reveal, convey

PROVIDENCE (<u>prah</u> vih dehnts) *n.*
divine control and direction by God; preparation
and foresight
Synonyms: fate, destiny, good luck; prudence,
precaution

TRANSITORY (<u>traan</u> sih tohr ee) *adj.*
short-lived, existing only briefly
Synonyms: transient, ephemeral, fleeting, fugitive,
momentary

SANCTITY (<u>saank</u> tih tee) *n.*
holiness, saintliness
Synonyms: devoutness, divinity, piety

been likewise a heavenly comfort, could have been none at all—was to meet her pastor, whether casually, or of set purpose, and be refreshed with a word of warm, fragrant, heaven-breathing Gospel truth, from his beloved lips into her dulled but **rapturously** attentive ear. But, on this occasion, up to the moment of putting his lips to the old woman's ear, Mr. Dimmesdale, as the great enemy of souls would have it, could recall no text of Scripture, nor aught else, except a brief, **pithy**, and, as it then appeared to him, unanswerable argument against the immortality of the human soul. The instilment thereof into her mind would probably have caused this aged sister to drop down dead at once, as by the effect of an intensely poisonous **infusion**. What he really did whisper, the minister could never afterwards recollect. There was, perhaps, a fortunate disorder in his utterance, which failed to **impart** any distinct idea to the good widow's comprehension, or which **Providence** interpreted after a method of its own. Assuredly, as the minister looked back, he beheld an expression of divine gratitude and ecstasy that seemed like the shine of the celestial city on her face, so wrinkled and ashy pale.

Again, a third instance. After parting from the old church member, he met the youngest sister of them all. It was a maiden newly won—and won by the Reverend Mr. Dimmesdale's own sermon, on the Sabbath after his vigil—to barter the **transitory** pleasures of the world for the heavenly hope that was to assume brighter substance as life grew dark around her, and which would gild the utter gloom with final glory. She was fair and pure as a lily that had bloomed in Paradise. The minister knew well that he was himself enshrined within the stainless **sanctity** of her heart, which hung its snowy curtains about his image, **imparting** to religion the warmth of love, and to love a religious purity. Satan, that afternoon, had surely led the poor young girl away

ARCH (ahrch) *adj.*
having the highest rank, most important;
mischievous, roguish
Synonyms: chief, top; impish, saucy, ironic
Note: an "arch-fiend" refers to the devil

BLIGHT (bliet) *v.* **-ing,-ed.**
to afflict, destroy
Synonyms: damage, plague

SUSTAIN (suh <u>stayn</u>) *v.* **-ing,-ed.**
to endure, undergo; to support, uphold
Synonyms: withstand; maintain, prop, encourage

IMPULSE (<u>ihm</u> puhls) *n.*
sudden tendency, inclination
Synonyms: urge, whim

LUDICROUS (<u>loo</u> dih kruhs) *adj.*
laughable, ridiculous
Synonyms: hilarious, absurd, foolish, silly,
preposterous

FORBEAR (fohr <u>bayr</u>) *v.* **-ing,-bore,-borne.**
to hold back or refrain
Synonyms: resist, evade, abstain, shun

VOLLEY (<u>vah</u> lee) *n.*
a series of things bursting forward; a flight of
missiles, a round of gunshots
Synonyms: rupture, outburst, explosion;
discharge, barrage, salvo, fusillade, hail

from her mother's side, and thrown her into the pathway of this sorely tempted, or—shall we not rather say?— this lost and desperate man. As she drew <u>nigh</u>, the **arch**-fiend whispered him to condense into small compass and drop into her tender bosom a germ of evil that would be sure to blossom darkly soon, and bear black fruit <u>betimes</u>. Such was his sense of power over this virgin soul, trusting him as she did, that the minister felt potent to **blight** all the field of innocence with but one wicked look, and develop all its opposite with but a word. So—with a mightier struggle than he had yet **sustained**—he held his Geneva cloak before his face, and hurried onward, making no sign of recognition, and leaving the young sister to digest his rudeness as she might. She ransacked her conscience—which was full of harmless little matters, like her pocket or her workbag— and took herself to task, poor thing, for a thousand imaginary faults; and went about her household duties with swollen eyelids the next morning.

Before the minister had time to celebrate his victory over this last temptation, he was conscious of another **impulse**, more **ludicrous**, and almost as horrible. It was—we blush to tell it—it was to stop short in the road, and teach some very wicked words to a knot of little <u>Puritan</u> children who were playing there, and had but just begun to talk. Denying himself this freak, as unworthy of his cloth, he met a drunken seaman, one of the ship's crew from the Spanish Main. And, here, since he had so valiantly **forborne** all other wickedness, poor Mr. Dimmesdale longed, at least, to shake hands with the <u>tarry</u> <u>blackguard</u>, and recreate himself with a few improper jests, such as dissolute sailors so abound with, and a **volley** of good, round, solid, satisfactory, and heaven-defying oaths! It was not so much a better principle, as partly his natural good taste, and still more his

SAT Vocabulary

DECORUM (deh <u>kuhr</u> uhm) (deh <u>kohr</u> uhm) *n.*
propriety, taste, social correctness
  Synonyms: politeness, courtesy, appropriateness

POTENTATE (poh <u>tehn</u> tayt) *n.*
a monarch or ruler with great power
  Synonyms: leader, emperor, king, prince, czar

IMPERATIVE (ihm <u>pehr</u> uh tihv) *adj.*
essential, immediate, urgent
  Synonyms: necessary, crucial, critical

PURPORT (puhr <u>pohrt</u>) *n.*
intention, purpose
  Synonyms: importance, meaning

buckramed habit of clerical **decorum**, that carried him safely through the latter crisis.

"What is it that haunts and tempts me thus?" cried the minister to himself, at length, pausing in the street, and striking his hand against his forehead. "Am I mad or am I given over utterly to the fiend? Did I make a contract with him in the forest, and sign it with my blood? And does he now summon me to its fulfilment, by suggesting the performance of every wickedness which his most foul imagination can conceive?"

At the moment when the Reverend Mr. Dimmesdale thus communed with himself, and struck his forehead with his hand, old Mistress Hibbins, the reputed witch-lady, is said to have been passing by. She made a very grand appearance; having on a high headdress, a rich gown of velvet, and a ruff done up with the famous yellow starch, of which Ann Turner, her special friend, had taught her the secret, before this last good lady had been hanged for Sir Thomas Overbury's murder. Whether the witch had read the minister's thoughts or no, she came to a full stop, looked shrewdly into his face, smiled craftily, and—though little given to converse with clergymen—began a conversation.

"So, Reverend Sir, you have made a visit into the forest," observed the witch-lady, nodding her high headdress at him. "The next time, I pray you to allow me only a fair warning, and I shall be proud to bear you company. Without taking overmuch upon myself, my good word will go far towards gaining any strange gentleman a fair reception from yonder **potentate** you wot of!"

"I profess, madam," answered the clergyman, with a grave obeisance, such as the lady's rank demanded, and his own good-breeding made **imperative**—"I profess, on my conscience and character, that I am utterly bewildered as touching the **purport** of your words! I went not into the forest to seek a **potentate**; neither do I, at any

PIOUS (<u>pie</u> uhs) *adj.*
dedicated, devout; extremely religious
Synonyms: observant, reverent; sanctimonious

HEATHENDOM (<u>hee</u> thuhn duhm) *n.*
an uncivilized or irreligious lifestyle
Synonyms: idolatry, polytheism, paganism

DIFFUSE (dih <u>fyooz</u>) *v.* **-ing,-ed.**
to spread out widely
Synonyms: scatter, disperse

IMPULSE (<u>ihm</u> puhls) *n.*
sudden tendency, inclination
Synonyms: urge, whim

UNPROVOKED (uhn proh <u>vohkd</u>) *adj.*
not prompted or stimulated by something
Synonyms: unjustified, unwarranted

MALIGNITY (muh <u>lihg</u> nih tee) *n.*
evil or aggressive malice; something that produces
death
Synonyms: bitterness, resentment; malevolence

GRATUITOUS (gruh <u>too</u> uh tuhs) *adj.*
unnecessary and unjustified; free, voluntary
Synonyms: unwarranted; complimentary, gratis

PERVERTED (puhr <u>vuhr</u> tihd) *adj.*
immoral, abnormal
Synonyms: corrupted, debased, debauched,
depraved, warped

IMPEL (ihm <u>pehl</u>) *v.* **-ling,-led.**
to urge forward as if driven by a strong moral pressure
Synonyms: push, prompt, incite, instigate

future time, design a visit thither, with a view to gaining the favor of such a personage. My one sufficient object was to greet that **pious** friend of mine, the Apostle Eliot, and rejoice with him over the many precious souls he hath won from **heathendom**!"

"Ha, ha, ha!" cackled the old witch-lady, still nodding her high head-dress at the minister. "Well, well, we must needs talk thus in the daytime! You carry it off like an old hand! But at midnight, and in the forest, we shall have other talk together!"

She passed on with her aged stateliness, but often turning back her head and smiling at him, like one willing to recognize a secret intimacy of connection.

"Have I then sold myself," thought the minister, "to the fiend whom, if men say true, this yellow-starched and velveted old hag has chosen for her prince and master!"

The wretched minister! He had made a bargain very like it! Tempted by a dream of happiness, he had yielded himself, with deliberate choice, as he had never done before, to what he knew was deadly sin. And the infectious poison of that sin had been thus rapidly **diffused** throughout his moral system. It had stupefied all blessed **impulses**, and awakened into vivid life the whole brotherhood of bad ones. Scorn, bitterness, **unprovoked malignity**, **gratuitous** desire of ill, ridicule of whatever was good and holy, all awoke, to tempt, even while they frightened him. And his encounter with old Mistress Hibbins, if it were a real incident, did but show his sympathy and fellowship with wicked mortals, and the world of **perverted** spirits.

He had, by this time, reached his dwelling, on the edge of the burial ground, and, hastening up the stairs, took refuge in his study. The minister was glad to have reached this shelter, without first betraying himself to the world by any of those strange and wicked eccentricities to which he had been continually **impelled** while

PROPHET (<u>prah</u> feht) *n.*
  a person who has the ability to foretell events
    Synonyms: clairvoyant, predictor, seer, oracle

DEVOID (dih <u>voyd</u>) *adj.*
  being without, lacking
    Synonyms: destitute, empty, vacant, null, bare

REQUISITE (<u>reh</u> kwih ziht) *adj.*
  essential, necessary
    Synonyms: required, indispensable

passing through the streets. He entered the accustomed room, and looked around him on its books, its windows, its fireplace, and the tapestried comfort of the walls, with the same perception of strangeness that had haunted him throughout his walk from the forest-dell into the town, and thitherward. Here he had studied and written; here, gone through fast and vigil, and come forth half alive; here, striven to pray; here, borne a hundred thousand agonies! There was the Bible, in its rich old Hebrew, with Moses and the **prophets** speaking to him, and God's voice through all! There, on the table, with the inky pen beside it, was an unfinished sermon, with a sentence broken in the midst, where his thoughts had ceased to gush out upon the page, two days before. He knew that it was himself, the thin and white-cheeked minister, who had done and suffered these things, and written thus far into the Election Sermon! But he seemed to stand apart, and eye this former self with scornful, pitying, but half-envious curiosity. That self was gone. Another man had returned out of the forest; a wiser one, with a knowledge of hidden mysteries which the simplicity of the former never could have reached. A bitter kind of knowledge that!

While occupied with these reflections, a knock came at the door of the study, and the minister said, "Come in!"—not wholly **devoid** of an idea that he might behold an evil spirit. And so he did! It was old Roger Chillingworth that entered. The minister stood, white and speechless, with one hand on the Hebrew Scriptures, and the other spread upon his breast.

"Welcome home, Reverend Sir," said the physician. "And how found you that godly man, the Apostle Eliot? But methinks, dear Sir, you look pale; as if the travel through the wilderness had been too sore for you. Will not my aid be **requisite** to put you in heart and strength to preach your Election Sermon?"

SINGULAR (<u>sihn</u> gyuh luhr) *adj.*
peculiar, uncommon
Synonyms: unique, individual, unusual, odd, rare

APPREHENSION (aa prih <u>hehn</u> shuhn) *n.*
suspicion or fear of future or unknown evil; the act
of perceiving or comprehending; a legal seizure
Synonyms: concern, worry; understanding; capture

SUSTAIN (suh <u>stayn</u>) *v.* **-ing,-ed.**
to support, uphold; to endure, undergo
Synonyms: maintain, prop, encourage; withstand

VIGOROUS (<u>vih</u> guhr uhs) *adj.*
having great physical or mental energy
Synonyms: strong, powerful, intense

DISCOURSE (<u>dihs</u> kohrs) *n.*
a formal, orderly, and extended expression of
thought; the verbal exchange of ideas
Synonyms: dialogue, conversation; speech

APPREHEND (aa pree <u>hehnd</u>) *v.* **-ing,-ed.**
1. to anticipate fearfully; to become aware of something through one's senses; to understand
Synonyms: dread; perceive; comprehend, grasp
2. to arrest
Synonyms: capture, seize, take, nab

PIOUS (<u>pie</u> uhs) *adj.*
dedicated, devout; extremely religious
Synonyms: observant, reverent; sanctimonious

"Nay, I think not so," rejoined the Reverend Mr. Dimmesdale. "My journey, and the sight of the holy Apostle yonder, and the free air which I have breathed, have done me good, after so long confinement in my study. I think to need no more of your drugs, my kind physician, good though they be, and administered by a friendly hand."

All this time, Roger Chillingworth was looking at the minister with the grave and intent regard of a physician towards his patient. But, in spite of this outward show, the latter was almost convinced of the old man's knowledge, or, at least, his confident suspicion, with respect to his own interview with Hester Prynne. The physician knew then, that, in the minister's regard, he was no longer a trusted friend, but his bitterest enemy. So much being known, it would appear natural that a part of it should be expressed. It is **singular**, however, how long a time often passes before words embody things; and with what security two persons, who choose to avoid a certain subject, may approach its very verge, and retire without disturbing it. Thus, the minister felt no **apprehension** that Roger Chillingworth would touch, in express words, upon the real position which they **sustained** towards one another. Yet did the physician, in his dark way, creep frightfully near the secret.

"Were it not better," said he, "that you use my poor skill tonight? Verily, dear Sir, we must take pains to make you strong and **vigorous** for this occasion of the Election **discourse**. The people look for great things from you, **apprehending** that another year may come about, and find their pastor gone."

"Yea, to another world," replied the minister, with **pious** resignation. "Heaven grant it be a better one; for, in good sooth, I hardly think to <u>tarry</u> with my flock through the flitting seasons of another year! But,

SOLEMN (<u>sah</u> luhm) *adj.*
somberly impressive, deeply serious
Synonyms: dignified, earnest, ceremonial

REQUITE (rih <u>kwiet</u>) *v.* **-ing,-ed.**
to return or repay
Synonyms: reciprocate, avenge, compensate, reimburse

RECOMPENSE (<u>reh</u> kuhm pehns) *n.*
something given as a means of compensation
Synonyms: payment, reward, remuneration

RAVENOUS (<u>raa</u> vehn uhs) *adj.*
extremely hungry
Synonyms: voracious, gluttonous, rapacious, predatory, famished

IMPULSIVE (ihm <u>puhl</u> sihv) *adj.*
sudden, spontaneous
Synonyms: whimsical, unprompted, involuntary

ORACLE (<u>or</u> ah kuhl) *n.*
a person who foresees the future and gives advice
Synonyms: seer, prophet, soothsayer, sibyl, fortuneteller

touching your medicine, kind Sir, in my present frame of body, I need it not."

"I joy to hear it," answered the physician. "It may be that my remedies, so long administered in vain, begin now to take due effect. Happy man were I, and well deserving of New England's gratitude, could I achieve this cure!"

"I thank you from my heart, most watchful friend," said the Reverend Mr. Dimmesdale, with a **solemn** smile. "I thank you, and can but **requite** your good deeds with my prayers."

"A good man's prayers are golden **recompense**!" rejoined old Roger Chillingworth, as he took his leave. "Yea, they are the current gold coin of the New Jerusalem, with the King's own mint-mark on them!"

Left alone, the minister summoned a servant of the house and requested food, which, being set before him, he ate with **ravenous** appetite. Then, flinging the already written pages of the Election Sermon into the fire, he forthwith began another, which he wrote with such an **impulsive** flow of thought and emotion, that he fancied himself inspired; and only wondered that Heaven should see fit to transmit the grand and **solemn** music of its **oracles** through so foul an organ-pipe as he. However, leaving that mystery to solve itself or go unsolved forever, he drove his task onward, with earnest haste and ecstasy. Thus the night fled away, as if it were a winged steed, and he careering on it; morning came, and peeped, blushing, through the curtains; and at last sunrise threw a golden beam into the study, and laid it right across the minister's bedazzled eyes. There he was, with the pen still between his fingers, and a vast, immeasurable tract of written space behind him!

PLEBEIAN (<u>plee</u> bee uhn) *adj.*
low-class, crude, vulgar
Synonyms: unrefined, coarse, common

QUIETUDE (<u>kwie</u> eh tood) *n.*
peace or tranquility
Synonyms: calm, ease, contentment, serenity

PRETERNATURALLY (pree tuhr <u>naach</u> uh ruh lee) *adj.*
extraordinarily or unnaturally
Synonyms: abnormally, mysteriously, oddly,
unearthly

COUNTENANCE (<u>kown</u> tuh nuhns) *n.*
appearance, facial expression
Synonyms: face, features, visage

MIEN (meen) *n.*
characteristics expressive of attitude or personality
Synonyms: manner, demeanor, expression, style

SUSTAIN (suh <u>stayn</u>) *v.* **-ing,-ed.**
to endure, undergo; to support, uphold
Synonyms: withstand; maintain, prop, encourage

MULTITUDE (<u>muhl</u> tuh tood) *n.*
a crowd; the state of being many, a great number
Synonyms: throng; mass, myriad

The New England Holiday

Chapter 21

Betimes in the morning of the day on which the new Governor was to receive office at the hands of the people Hester Prynne and little Pearl came into the market-place. It was already thronged with the craftsmen and other **plebeian** inhabitants of the town, in considerable numbers; among whom, likewise, were many rough figures, whose attire of deer-skins marked them as belonging to some of the forest settlements, which surrounded the little metropolis of the colony.

On this public holiday, as on all other occasions, for seven years past, Hester was clad in a garment of coarse gray cloth. Not more by its hue than by some indescribable peculiarity in its fashion, it had the effect of making her fade personally out of sight and outline; while, again, the scarlet letter brought her back from this twilight indistinctness and revealed her under the moral aspect of its own illumination. Her face, so long familiar to the townspeople, showed the marble **quietude** which they were accustomed to behold there. It was like a mask; or, rather, like the frozen calmness of a dead woman's features; owing this dreary resemblance to the fact that Hester was actually dead, in respect to any claim of sympathy, and had departed out of the world, with which she still seemed to mingle.

It might be, on this one day, that there was an expression unseen before, nor, indeed, vivid enough to be detected, now; unless some **preternaturally** gifted observer should have first read the heart, and have afterwards sought a corresponding development in the **countenance** and **mien**. Such a spiritual seer might have conceived that, after **sustaining** the gaze of the **multitude**

PENANCE (<u>peh</u> nihns) *n.*
voluntary suffering to repent for a wrong
Synonyms: atonement, reparation, chastening,
reconciliation

PERPETUALLY (puhr <u>peht</u> chyoo uh lee) *adv.*
endlessly, lastingly
Synonyms: continuously, constantly, ceaselessly,
eternally, perennially

EXHILARATING (ihg <u>zihl</u> uh ray tihng) *adj.*
energizing or filling with happiness
Synonyms: elating, euphoric, exuberant

INEVITABLE (ihn <u>ehv</u> ih tuh buhl) *adj.*
certain, unavoidable
Synonyms: inescapable, sure, predictable

LANGUOR (<u>laang</u> uhr) *n.*
lack of energy, indifference, a lazy mood
Synonyms: weakness, listlessness, sluggishness

APPARITION (aa puh <u>rih</u> shuhn) *n.*
an unexpected or unusual sight or appearance; a
ghostly figure
Synonyms: illusion; spirit, specter

REQUISITE (<u>reh</u> kwih ziht) *adj.*
essential, necessary
Synonyms: required, indispensable

CONTRIVE (kuhn <u>triev</u>) *v.* **-ing,-ed.**
to form in an artistic manner; to devise, plan, or
manage
Synonyms: create, design; concoct, scheme

IMPART (ihm <u>pahrt</u>) *v.* **-ing,-ed.**
to give or share, to pass on
Synonyms: bestow, contribute, reveal, convey

MANIFESTATION (maan uh fehs <u>tay</u> shuhn) *n.*
a clear appearance or display
Synonyms: expression, exhibition, indication

through seven miserable years as a necessity, a **penance**, and something which it was a stern religion to endure, she now, for one last time more, encountered it freely and voluntarily, in order to convert what had so long been agony into a kind of triumph. "Look your last on the scarlet letter and its wearer!" the people's victim and life-long bond-slave, as they fancied her, might say to them. "Yet a little while, and she will be beyond your reach! A few hours longer, and the deep, mysterious ocean will quench and hide forever the symbol which ye have caused to burn upon her bosom!" Nor were it an inconsistency too improbable to be assigned to human nature, should we suppose a feeling of regret in Hester's mind, at the moment when she was about to win her freedom from the pain which had been thus deeply incorporated with her being. Might there not be an irresistible desire to <u>quaff</u> a last, long, breathless draught of the cup of wormwood and aloes, with which nearly all her years of womanhood had been **perpetually** flavored? The wine of life, henceforth to be presented to her lips, must be indeed rich, delicious, and **exhilarating**, in its chased and golden beaker; or else leave an **inevitable** and weary **languor**, after the lees of bitterness wherewith she had been drugged, as with a cordial of intensest potency.

Pearl was decked out with airy gayety. It would have been impossible to guess that this bright and sunny **apparition** owed its existence to the shape of gloomy gray; or that a fancy, at once so gorgeous and so delicate as must have been **requisite** to **contrive** the child's apparel, was the same that had achieved a task perhaps more difficult, in **imparting** so distinct a peculiarity to Hester's simple robe. The dress, so proper was it to little Pearl, seemed an effluence, or **inevitable** development and outward **manifestation** of her character, no more to be separated from her than the many-hued brilliancy

SINGULAR (<u>sihn</u> gyuh luhr) *adj.*
  peculiar, uncommon
    Synonyms: unique, individual, unusual, odd, rare

INQUIETUDE (ihn <u>kwie</u> eh tood) *n.*
  restlessness, uneasiness
    Synonyms: discontentment, edginess, anxiety

AGITATION (aa gih <u>tay</u> shuhn) *n.*
  uneasiness; commotion, excitement
    Synonyms: restlessness, anxiety; disturbance

EFFERVESCENCE (eh fuhr <u>vehs</u> ihnts) *n.*
  liveliness, a show of high spirits; bubbliness
    Synonyms: excitement; foaming, fizzing

INARTICULATE (ihn ahr <u>tihk</u> yuh liht) *adj.*
  unable to be understood, tongue-tied, without speech
    Synonyms: incomprehensible, unintelligible

BUSTLE (<u>buh</u> suhl) *n.*
  busy and energetic activity
    Synonyms: chaos, commotion, hubbub

from a butterfly's wing or the painted glory from the leaf of a bright flower. As with these, so with the child; her garb was all of one idea with her nature. On this eventful day, moreover, there was a certain **singular inquietude** and excitement in her mood, resembling nothing so much as the shimmer of a diamond, that sparkles and flashes with the varied throbbings of the breast on which it is displayed. Children have always a sympathy in the **agitations** of those connected with them; always, especially, a sense of any trouble or impending revolution, of whatever kind, in domestic circumstances; and therefore Pearl, who was the gem on her mother's unquiet bosom, betrayed, by the very dance of her spirits, the emotions which none could detect in the marble passiveness of Hester's brow.

This **effervescence** made her flit with a bird-like movement, rather than walk by her mother's side. She broke continually into shouts of a wild, **inarticulate**, and sometimes piercing music. When they reached the market-place, she became still more restless, on perceiving the stir and **bustle** that enlivened the spot; for it was usually more like the broad and lonesome green before a village meeting-house than the centre of a town's business.

"Why, what is this, Mother?" cried she. "Wherefore have all the people left their work today? Is it a play-day for the whole world? See, there is the blacksmith! He has washed his sooty face, and put on his Sabbath-day clothes and looks as if he would gladly be merry, if any kind body would only teach him how! And there is Master Brackett, the old jailer, nodding and smiling at me. Why does he do so, Mother?"

"He remembers thee as a little babe, my child," answered Hester.

"He should not nod and smile at me, for all that—the black, grim, ugly-eyed old man!" said Pearl. "He may nod at thee, if he will; for thou art clad in gray, and

MAGISTRATE (<u>maa</u> juh strayt) *n.*
an official who can administrate laws
Synonyms: judge, arbiter, authority, marshal

wearest the scarlet letter. But see, Mother, how many faces of strange people, and Indians among them, and sailors! What have they all come to do, here in the market-place?"

"They wait to see the procession pass," said Hester. "For the Governor and the **magistrates** are to go by, and the ministers, and all the great people and good people, with the music and the soldiers marching before them."

"And will the minister be there?" asked Pearl. "And will he hold out both his hands to me, as when thou ledst me to him from the brook-side?"

"He will be there, child," answered her mother. "But he will not greet thee today; nor must thou greet him."

"What a strange, sad man is he!" said the child, as if speaking partly to herself. "In the dark night-time he calls us to him, and holds thy hand and mine, as when we stood with him on the scaffold yonder! And in the deep forest, where only the old trees can hear, and the strip of sky see it, he talks with thee, sitting on a heap of moss! And he kisses my forehead, too, so that the little brook would hardly wash it off! But here, in the sunny day, and among all the people, he knows us not; nor must we know him! A strange, sad man is he, with his hand always over his heart!"

"Be quiet, Pearl! Thou understandest not these things," said her mother. "Think not now of the minister, but look about thee, and see how cheery is everybody's face today. The children have come from their schools, and the grown people from their workshops and their fields, on purpose to be happy. For today a new man is beginning to rule over them; and so—as has been the custom of mankind ever since a nation was first gathered—they make merry and rejoice; as if a good and golden year were at length to pass over the poor old world!"

MIRTH (muhrth) *n.*
frivolity, gaiety, laughter
Synonyms: merriment, jollity, hilarity, glee

INFIRMITY (ihn <u>fuhr</u> mih tee) *n.*
weakness; disease, ailment
Synonyms: frailty; illness, affliction

DISPEL (dihs <u>pehl</u>) *v.* **-ling,-led.**
to drive out or scatter
Synonyms: disband, disperse

AFFLICTION (uh <u>flihk</u> shuhn) *n.*
severe distress, persistent anguish
Synonyms: hurt, adversity, hardship, plight,
suffering

TINGE (tihnj) *n.*
a slight shade of color, stain, odor, or taste
Synonyms: hint, hue, tincture, tone, wash

EPOCH (<u>eh</u> pihk) *n.*
a specific time in history; a particular day or time
Synonyms: period, era, generation; date

IMPRACTICABLE (ihm <u>praak</u> tih kuh buhl) *adj.*
incapable of being performed by the means
employed; impassable
Synonyms: imprudent, impossible; blocked

MIRTHFUL (<u>muhrth</u> fuhl) *adj.*
happy, cheerful, carefree
Synonyms: merry, jolly, hilarious, gleeful

SOLEMNITY (suh <u>lehm</u> nih tee) *n.*
dignified seriousness
Synonyms: ceremoniousness, formality

MAGISTRATE (<u>maa</u> juh strayt) *n.*
an official who can administrate laws
Synonyms: judge, arbiter, authority, marshal

It was as Hester said, in regard to the unwonted jollity that brightened the faces of the people. Into this festal season of the year—as it already was, and continued to be during the greater part of two centuries—the <u>Puritans</u> compressed whatever **mirth** and public joy they deemed allowable to human **infirmity**; thereby so far **dispelling** the customary cloud, that, for the space of a single holiday, they appeared scarcely more grave than most other communities at a period of general **affliction**.

But we perhaps exaggerate the gray or sable **tinge**, which undoubtedly characterized the mood and manners of the age. The persons now in the market-place of Boston had not been born to an inheritance of <u>Puritanic</u> gloom. They were native Englishmen, whose fathers had lived in the sunny richness of the Elizabethan **epoch**; a time when the life of England, viewed as one great mass, would appear to have been as stately, magnificent, and joyous, as the world has ever witnessed. Had they followed their hereditary taste, the New England settlers would have illustrated all events of public importance by bonfires, banquets, pageantries, and processions. Nor would it have been **impracticable**, in the observance of majestic ceremonies, to combine **mirthful** recreation with **solemnity**, and give, as it were, a grotesque and brilliant embroidery to the great robe of state, which a nation, at such festivals, puts on. There was some shadow of an attempt of this kind in the mode of celebrating the day on which the political year of the colony commenced. The dim reflection of a remembered splendor, a colorless and manifold diluted repetition of what they had beheld in proud old London—we will not say at a royal coronation, but at a Lord Mayor's show—might be traced in the customs which our forefathers instituted, with reference to the annual installation of **magistrates**. The fathers and founders of the commonwealth—the statesman, the

SAT Vocabulary

EMINENCE (<u>ehm</u> uh nuhnts) *n.*
1. a position of distinction or superiority
   Synonyms: prominence, importance
2. a prominent place, something which projects outward
   Synonyms: elevation, summit, peak

IMPART (ihm <u>pahrt</u>) *v.* **-ing,-ed.**
to give or share, to pass on
   Synonyms: bestow, contribute, reveal, convey

COUNTENANCE (<u>kown</u> tuh nuhns) *v.* **-ing,-ed.**
to approve or support, give permission
   Synonyms: condone, permit, consent

MIMIC (<u>mih</u> mihk) *adj.*
imitation
   Synonym: mock

MULTITUDE (<u>muhl</u> tuh tood) *n.*
a crowd; the state of being many, a great number
   Synonyms: throng; mass, myriad

MIRTHFUL (<u>muhrth</u> fuhl) *adj.*
happy, cheerful, carefree
   Synonyms: merry, jolly, hilarious, gleeful

JOCULARITY (jahk yuh <u>laar</u> ih tee) *n.*
jovial and playful activity, humorous fun
   Synonyms: joking, merriment

SENTIMENT (<u>sehn</u> tuh muhnt) *n.*
an attitude, thought, or judgment prompted by feeling
   Synonym: emotion

priest, and the soldier—deemed it a duty then to assume the outward state and majesty, which, in accordance with antique style, was looked upon as the proper garb of public or social **eminence**. All came forth, to move in procession before the people's eye, and thus **impart** a needed dignity to the simple frame-work of a government so newly constructed.

Then, too, the people were **countenanced**, if not encouraged, in relaxing the severe and close application to their various modes of rugged industry, which, at all other times, seemed of the same piece and material with their religion. Here, it is true, were none of the appliances which popular merriment would so readily have found in the England of Elizabeth's time, or that of James; no rude shows of a theatrical kind; no minstrel, with his harp and legendary ballad, nor gleeman, with an ape dancing to his music; no juggler, with his tricks of **mimic** witchcraft; no Merry Andrew, to stir up the **multitude** with jests, perhaps hundreds of years old, but still effective, by their appeals to the very broadest sources of **mirthful** sympathy. All such professors of the several branches of **jocularity** would have been sternly repressed, not only by the rigid discipline of law, but by the general **sentiment** which gives law its vitality. Not the less, however, the great, honest face of the people smiled, grimly, perhaps, but widely too. Nor were sports wanting, such as the colonists had witnessed, and shared in, long ago, at the country fairs and on the village-greens of England; and which it was thought well to keep alive on this new soil, for the sake of the courage and manliness that were essential in them. Wrestling-matches, in the different fashions of Cornwall and Devonshire, were seen here and there about the market-place; in one corner there was a friendly bout at quarterstaff; and—what attracted most interest of all—on the platform of the pillory, already so noted in our

INTERPOSITION (ihn tuhr puh <u>zih</u> shuhn) *n.*
an interjection or interruption
Synonyms: encroachment, intrusion, interference

CONSECRATED (<u>kahn</u> suh kray tihd) *adj.*
sacred, holy
Synonyms: sanctified, blessed, spirtual, adored

AFFIRM (uh <u>fihrm</u>) *v.* **-ing,-ed.**
to assert as valid or confirmed, to state positively
Synonyms: declare, avow, maintain

DESCENDANT (dih <u>sehn</u> dehnt) *n.*
an offspring or heir
Synonyms: child, kin, progeny

POSTERITY (pah <u>steh</u> ruh tee) *n.*
future generations; all of a person's descendants
Synonyms: progeny, offspring, line, lineage,
heritage

EMIGRANT (<u>eh</u> mih graant) *n.*
a person from another country or land
Synonym: foreigner

VISAGE (<u>vih</u> sihj) *n.*
the appearance of a person or place, face
Synonyms: expression, look, style, manner

SUBSEQUENT (<u>suhb</u> suh kwehnt) *adj.*
following in time or order
Synonyms: succeeding, next, after

COUNTENANCE (<u>kown</u> tuh nuhns) *n.*
appearance, facial expression
Synonyms: face, features, visage

BARBARIAN (baar <u>bayr</u> ee ihn) *n.*
a rude person who lacks culture and refinement
Synonyms: savage, brute, vandal, monster, rascal

SUSTAIN (suh <u>stayn</u>) *v.* **-ing,-ed.**
to support, uphold; to endure, undergo
Synonyms: maintain, prop, encourage; withstand

pages, two masters of defence were commencing an exhibition with the buckler and broadsword. But, much to the disappointment of the crowd, this latter business was broken off by the **interposition** of the town beadle, who had no idea of permitting the majesty of the law to be violated by such an abuse of one of its **consecrated** places.

It may not be too much to **affirm**, on the whole (the people being then in the first stages of joyless deportment, and the offspring of sires who had known how to be merry, in their day), that they would compare favorably, in point of holiday keeping, with their **descendants**, even at so long an interval as ourselves. Their immediate **posterity**, the generation next to the early **emigrants**, wore the blackest shade of Puritanism, and so darkened the national **visage** with it, that all the **subsequent** years have not sufficed to clear it up. We have yet to learn again the forgotten art of gayety.

The picture of human life in the market-place, though its general tint was the sad gray, brown, or black of the English **emigrants**, was yet enlivened by some diversity of hue. A party of Indians—in their savage finery of curiously embroidered deer-skin robes, wampum-belts, red and yellow ochre, and feathers, and armed with the bow and arrow and stone-headed spear—stood apart, with **countenances** of inflexible gravity, beyond what even the Puritan aspect could attain. Nor, wild as were these painted **barbarians**, were they the wildest feature of the scene. This distinction could more justly be claimed by some mariners—a part of the crew of the vessel from the Spanish Main—who had come ashore to see the humors of Election Day. They were rough-looking desperadoes, with sun-blackened faces, and an immensity of beard; their wide, short trousers were confined about the waist by belts, often clasped with a rough plate of gold, and **sustaining**

FEROCITY (fuhr <u>ah</u> sih tee) *n.*
fierceness, violence
Synonyms: fury, wildness, vehemence, turbulence

TRANSGRESS (traans <u>grehs</u>) *v.* **-ing,-ed.**
to violate a law or command; to trespass
Synonyms: sin, disobey, offend; overstep

SCRUPLE (<u>skroo</u> puhl) *n.*
a hesitation caused by moral conscience; an ethical
and moral belief that prevents action
Synonyms: restraint, qualm, misgiving; principle

ARRAIGN (uh <u>rayn</u>) *v.* **-ing,-ed.**
to call to court to answer an indictment, to blame
Synonyms: accuse, challenge, denounce, inculpate

PERIL (<u>pehr</u> ihl) *v.* **-ling,-led.**
to endanger, to make vulnerable
Synonyms: risk, jeopardize, threaten, expose

TEMPESTUOUS (tehm <u>pehs</u> tyoo uhs) *adj.*
stormy, raging, furious
Synonyms: tumultuous, blustery, inclement,
turbulent, torrential

RELINQUISH (rih <u>lihn</u> kwihsh) *v.* **-ing,-ed.**
to renounce or surrender something
Synonyms: yield, resign, abandon, cede, waive

PROBITY (<u>proh</u> buh tee) *n.*
honesty, high-mindedness
Synonyms: integrity, honor, rectitude, virtue

PIETY (<u>pie</u> eh tee) *n.* *(See page 258.)*

DISREPUTABLE (dihs <u>reh</u> pyuh tuh buhl) *adj.*
disgraceful, dishonorable, lacking respectability
Synonyms: infamous, shameful

UNBENIGNANTLY (uhn bih <u>nien</u> uhnt lee) *adv.*
unkindly, not in a gentle manner
Synonyms: unfavorably, hurtfully, meanly

CLAMOR (<u>klaa</u> muhr) *n.*
noisy outcry or loudness
Synonyms: din, cacophony, racket, uproar

REPUTABLE (<u>rehp</u> yuh tuh buhl) *adj.*
honorable, praiseworthy
Synonyms: trustworthy, favorable, dependable

always a long knife, and, in some instances, a sword. From beneath their broad-brimmed hats of palm-leaf gleamed eyes which, even in good-nature and merriment, had a kind of animal **ferocity**. They **transgressed**, without fear or **scruple**, the rules of behavior that were binding on all others; smoking tobacco under the beadle's very nose, although each whiff would have cost a townsman a shilling; and quaffing, at their pleasure, draughts of wine or aqua-vitæ from pocket-flasks, which they freely tendered to the gaping crowd around them. It remarkably characterized the incomplete morality of the age, rigid as we call it, that a license was allowed the seafaring class, not merely for their freaks on shore, but for far more desperate deeds on their proper element. The sailor of that day would go near to be **arraigned** as a pirate in our own. There could be little doubt, for instance, that this very ship's crew, though no unfavorable specimens of the nautical brotherhood, had been guilty, as we should phrase it, of depredations of the Spanish commerce, such as would have **perilled** all their necks in a modern court of justice.

But the sea in those old times heaved, swelled, and foamed, very much at its own will, or subject only to the **tempestuous** wind, with hardly any attempts at regulation by human law. The buccaneer on the wave might **relinquish** his calling, and become at once, if he chose, a man of **probity** and **piety** on land; nor, even in the full career of his reckless life, was he regarded as a personage with whom it was **disreputable** to traffic, or casually associate. Thus, the Puritan elders, in their black cloaks, starched bands, and steeple-crowned hats, smiled not **unbenignantly** at the **clamor** and rude deportment of these jolly seafaring men; and it excited neither surprise nor animadversion when so **reputable** a citizen as old Roger Chillingworth, the physician, was seen to enter

MULTITUDE (<u>muhl</u> tuh tood) *n.*
   a crowd; the state of being many, a great number
     Synonyms: throng; mass, myriad

PROFUSION (pruh <u>fyoo</u> zhuhn) *n.*
   abundance, outpouring
     Synonyms: plenty, extravagance

SURMOUNT (suhr <u>mownt</u>) *v.* **-ing,-ed.**
   1. to have something on top; to be on top of
   something
     Synonyms: cap, crown, cover
   2. to conquer, overcome
     Synonyms: clear, hurdle, leap, surpass, exceed

MAGISTRATE (<u>maa</u> juh strayt) *n.*
   an official who can administrate laws
     Synonyms: judge, arbiter, authority, marshal

INCUR (ihn <u>kuhr</u>) *v.* **-ring,-red.**
   to acquire or meet with, usually something negative
   or harmful; to become liable
     Synonyms: get, obtain, endure, sustain; oblige, owe

SOLITUDE (<u>sahl</u> ih tood) *n.*
   social isolation; time spent alone
     Synonyms: seclusion, withdrawal, retirement;
     loneliness

EMINENT (<u>ehm</u> uh nuhnt) *adj.*
   celebrated, distinguished, outstanding, towering
     Synonyms: noted, famous, prominent, important,
     illustrious

The Scarlet Letter

the market-place in close and familiar talk with the commander of the questionable vessel.

The latter was by far the most showy and gallant figure, so far as apparel went, anywhere to be seen among the **multitude**. He wore a **profusion** of ribbons on his garment, and gold-lace on his hat, which was also encircled by a gold chain and **surmounted** with a feather. There was a sword at his side, and a sword-cut on his forehead, which, by the arrangement of his hair, he seemed anxious rather to display than hide. A landsman could hardly have worn this garb and shown this face, and worn and shown them both with such a galliard air, without undergoing stern question before a **magistrate**, and probably **incurring** fine or imprisonment, or perhaps an exhibition in the stocks. As regarded the shipmaster, however, all was looked upon as pertaining to the character, as to a fish his glistening scales.

After parting from the physician, the commander of the Bristol ship strolled idly through the market-place; until, happening to approach the spot where Hester Prynne was standing, he appeared to recognize, and did not hesitate to address her. As was usually the case wherever Hester stood, a small vacant area—a sort of magic circle—had formed itself about her, into which, though the people were elbowing one another at a little distance, none ventured, or felt posed to intrude. It was a forcible type of the moral **solitude** in which the scarlet letter enveloped its fated wearer; partly by her own reserve, and partly by the instinctive, though no longer so unkindly, withdrawal of her fellow-creatures. Now, if never before, it answered a good purpose by enabling Hester and the seaman to speak together without risk of being overheard; and so changed was Hester Prynne's repute before the public, that the matron in town most **eminent** for rigid morality could not have held such intercourse with less result of scandal than herself.

PERIL (<u>pehr</u> ihl) *n.*
danger
Synonyms: trouble, hazard, harm

MIEN (meen) *n.*
characteristics expressive of attitude or personality
Synonyms: manner, demeanor, expression, style

CONSTERNATION (kahn stuhr <u>nay</u> shuhn) *n.*
amazement or distress that leads to confusion
Synonyms: alarm, bewilderment, perplexity

BUSTLING (<u>buh</u> slihng) *adj.*
busy and moving with much activity, energetic
Synonyms: scurrying, scrambling, dashing

"So, mistress," said the mariner, "I must bid the steward make ready one more berth than you bargained for! No fear of scurvy or ship-fever, this voyage! What with the ship's surgeon and this other doctor, our only danger will be from drug or pill; more by token, as there is a lot of apothecary's stuff aboard, which I traded for with a Spanish vessel."

"What mean you?" inquired Hester, startled more than she permitted to appear. "Have you another passenger?"

"Why, know you not," cried the shipmaster, "that this physician here—Chillingworth, he calls himself—is minded to try my cabin-fare with you? Ay, ay, you must have known it; for he tells me he is of your party, and a close friend to the gentleman you spoke of—he that is in **peril** from these sour old <u>Puritan</u> rulers!"

"They know each other well, indeed," replied Hester, with a **mien** of calmness, though in the utmost **consternation**. "They have long dwelt together."

Nothing further passed between the mariner and Hester Prynne. But, at that instant, she beheld old Roger Chillingworth himself, standing in the remotest corner of the market-place and smiling on her; a smile which—across the wide and **bustling** square, and through all the talk and laughter, and various thoughts, moods, and interests of the crowd—conveyed secret and fearful meaning.

DENOTE (dih <u>noht</u>) (dee <u>noht</u>) *v.* **-ing,-ed.**
to indicate, to stand for
Synonyms: show, signify, imply, symbolize, typify
MAGISTRATE (<u>maa</u> juh strayt) *n.*
an official who can administrate laws
Synonyms: judge, arbiter, authority, marshal
COMPLIANCE (kuhm <u>plie</u> uhnts) *n.*
conforming to submission, yielding
Synonyms: malleability, complacency, acquiescence
ADAPTED (uh <u>daap</u> tihd) *adj.*
adjusted, changed, fit
Synonyms: accustomed, altered, conformed
MULTITUDE (<u>muhl</u> tuh tood) *n.*
a crowd; the state of being many, a great number
Synonyms: throng; mass, myriad
IMPART (ihm <u>pahrt</u>) *v.* **-ing,-ed.**
to give or share, to pass on
Synonyms: bestow, contribute, reveal, convey
AGITATION (aa gih <u>tay</u> shuhn) *n.*
uneasiness; commotion, excitement
Synonyms: restlessness, anxiety; disturbance
EFFERVESCENCE (eh fuhr <u>vehs</u> ihnts) *n.*
liveliness, a show of high spirits; bubbliness
Synonyms: excitement; foaming, fizzing
HONORARY (<u>ah</u> nuhr ayr ee) *adj.*
holding a voluntary position; given an honor without
meeting normal standards
Synonyms: willing, unpaid; chosen, elected
SUSTAIN (suh <u>stayn</u>) *v.* **-ing,-ed.**
to support, uphold; to endure, undergo
Synonyms: maintain, prop, encourage; withstand
HONORABLE (<u>ah</u> nuhr uh buhl) *adj.*
illustrious, praiseworthy, deserving
Synonyms: respectable, dignified, noble
MERCENARY (<u>muhr</u> suhn ehr ee) *adj.*
motivated only by greed
Synonyms: venal, materialistic, avaricious

The Procession

Chapter 22

Before Hester Prynne could call together her thoughts and consider what was practicable to be done in this new and startling aspect of affairs, the sound of military music was heard approaching along a contiguous street. It **denoted** the advance of the procession of **magistrates** and citizens, on its way towards the meeting-house; where, in **compliance** with a custom thus early established, and ever since observed, the Reverend Mr. Dimmesdale was to deliver an Election Sermon.

Soon the head of the procession showed itself, with a slow and stately march, turning a corner and making its way across the market-place. First came the music. It comprised a variety of instruments, perhaps imperfectly **adapted** to one another and played with no great skill; but yet attaining the great object for which the harmony of drum and <u>clarion</u> addresses itself to the **multitude**— that of **imparting** a higher and more heroic air to the scene of life that passes before the eye. Little Pearl at first clapped her hands, but then lost, for an instant, the restless **agitation** that had kept her in a continual **effervescence** throughout the morning; she gazed silently and seemed to be borne upward, like a floating sea-bird, on the long heaves and swells of sound. But she was brought back to her former mood by the shimmer of the sunshine on the weapons and bright armor of the military company, which followed after the music, and formed the **honorary** escort of the procession. This body of soldiery—which still **sustains** a corporate existence and marches down from past ages with an ancient and **honorable** fame—was composed of no **mercenary** materials. Its ranks were filled with gentle-

MARTIAL (<u>mahr</u> shuhl) *adj.*
  warlike, pertaining to the military
    Synonyms: soldierly, combative
IMPULSE (<u>ihm</u> puhls) *n.*
  sudden tendency, inclination
    Synonyms: urge, whim
BURNISHED (<u>buhr</u> nihshd) *adj.*
  polished, smooth and bright
    Synonyms: shiny, buffed
ASPIRE (uh <u>spier</u>) *v.* **-ing,-ed.**
  to have great hopes, to aim at a goal
    Synonyms: intend, strive
CIVIL (<u>sih</u> vuhl) *adj.* *(See page 96.)*
EMINENCE (<u>ehm</u> uh nuhnts) *n.* *(See page 462.)*
DEMEANOR (dih <u>meen</u> uhr) *n.* *(See page 140.)*
HAUGHTY (<u>haw</u> tee) (<u>hah</u> tee) *adj.*
  arrogant and condescending
    Synonyms: proud, disdainful, supercilious,
    scornful
REVERENCE (<u>reh</u> vuhr ehnts) *n.*
  deep respect, awe
    Synonyms: veneration, adoration, admiration
DESCENDANT (dih <u>sehn</u> dehnt) *n.* *(See page 464.)*
FACULTY (<u>faa</u> kuhl tee) *n.*
  the ability to act or do
    Synonyms: aptitude, capability, sense, skill
BESTOW (bih <u>stoh</u>) *v.* **-ing,-ed.**
  to give as a gift; to apply or devote time or effort
    Synonyms: endow, confer, present; allocate, dedicate
VENERABLE (<u>veh</u> nehr uh buhl) *adj.*
  respected because of age
    Synonyms: distinguished, elderly
INTEGRITY (ihn <u>tehg</u> rih tee) *n.*
  decency, honesty, wholeness
    Synonyms: honor, probity, rectitude, virtue
ENDOWMENT (ehn <u>dow</u> mehnt) *n.* *(See page 436.)*

men, who felt the stirrings of **martial impulse** and sought to establish a kind of College of Arms, where, as in an association of Knights Templars, they might learn the science, and, so far as peaceful exercise would teach them, the practices of war. The high estimation then placed upon the military character might be seen in the lofty port of each individual member of the company. Some of them, indeed, by their services in the Low Countries and on other fields of warfare, had fairly won their title to assume the name and <u>pomp</u> of soldiership. The entire array, moreover, clad in **burnished** steel, and with plumage nodding over their bright <u>morions</u>, had a brilliancy of effect which no modern display can **aspire** to equal.

And yet the men of **civil eminence**, who came immediately behind the military escort, were better worth a thoughtful observer's eye. Even in outward **demeanor**, they showed a stamp of majesty that made the warrior's **haughty** stride look vulgar, if not absurd. It was an age when what we call talent had far less consideration than now, but the massive materials which produce stability and dignity of character a great deal more. The people possessed, by hereditary right, the quality of **reverence**; which, in their **descendants**, if it survive at all, exists in smaller proportion, and with a vastly diminished force, in the selection and estimate of public men. The change may be for good or ill, and is partly, perhaps, for both. In that old day, the English settler on these rude shores, having left king, nobles, and all degrees of awful rank behind, while still the **faculty** and necessity of **reverence** were strong in him, **bestowed** it on the white hair and **venerable** brow of age; on long-tried **integrity**; on solid wisdom and sad-colored experience; on **endowments** of that grave and weighty order which gives the idea of permanence, and comes under the general definition of respectability. These primitive statesmen, therefore—

PONDEROUS (<u>pahn</u> duhr uhs) *adj. (See page 236.)*

SOBRIETY (suh <u>brie</u> eh tee) *n.*
state of being serious or sober
Synonyms: gravity, moderation, temperance

FORTITUDE (<u>fohr</u> tih tood) (<u>fohr</u> tih tyood) *n.*
strength, stamina
Synonyms: endurance, hardiness, toughness, courage

PERIL (<u>pehr</u> ihl) *n. (See page 470.)*

TEMPESTUOUS (tehm <u>pehs</u> tyoo uhs) *adj. (See pg. 466.)*

COUNTENANCE (<u>kown</u> tuh nuhns) *n. (See page 464.)*

MAGISTRATE (<u>maa</u> juh strayt) *n. (See page 472.)*

DEMEANOR (dih <u>meen</u> uhr) *n. (See page 140.)*

PEER *n.*
a contemporary of equal standing
Synonyms: fellow, colleague

SOVEREIGN (<u>sah</u> vuhrn) *n.*
a ruler of a nation; a nation having supreme power
Synonyms: controller, monarch; territory, homeland

EMINENTLY (<u>ehm</u> uh nuhnt lee) *adv.*
in an outstanding and noticeable manner
Synonyms: notedly, famously, prominently,
importantly, illustriously

DIVINE (dih <u>vien</u>) *n. (See page 238.)*

DISCOURSE (<u>dihs</u> kohrs) *n. (See page 448.)*

INDUCEMENT (ih <u>doos</u> mehnt) *n.*
something that persuades, an incentive
Synonyms: motive, urging, encouragement

ASPIRING (uh <u>spier</u> ihng) *adj.*
having great hopes or goals
Synonyms: lofty, eager, striving, purposeful

GAIT (gayt) *n. (See page 376.)*

OMINOUSLY (<u>ah</u> mihn uhs lee) *adv.*
menacingly, threateningly
Synonym: sinisterly

IMPART (ihm <u>pahrt</u>) *v.* **-ing,-ed.** *(See page 472.)*

EXHILARATION (ihg zihl uh <u>ray</u> shuhn) *n.*
a state of being energetic or filled with happiness
Synonyms: elation, euphoria, exuberance, delight,
ebullience

Bradstreet, Endicott, Dudley, Bellingham, and their
<u>compeers</u>—who were elevated to power by the early
choice of the people, seem to have been not often brilliant, but distinguished by a **ponderous sobriety** rather
than activity of intellect. They had **fortitude** and self-
reliance, and, in time of difficulty or **peril**, stood up for
the welfare of the state like a line of cliffs against a
tempestuous tide. The traits of character here indicated
were well represented in the square cast of **countenance**
and large physical development of the new colonial
magistrates. So far as a **demeanor** of natural authority
was concerned, the mother country need not have
been ashamed to see these foremost men of an actual
democracy adopted into the House of **Peers**, or made
the Privy Council of the **sovereign**.

Next in order to the **magistrates** came the young and
eminently distinguished **divine**, from whose lips the religious **discourse** of the anniversary was expected. His
was the profession, at that era, in which intellectual
ability displayed itself far more than in political life;
for—leaving a higher motive out of the question—it
offered **inducements** powerful enough, in the almost
worshipping respect of the community, to win the most
aspiring ambition into its service. Even political
power—as in the case of Increase Mather—was within
the grasp of a successful priest.

It was the observation of those who beheld him now,
that never, since Mr. Dimmesdale first set his foot on
the New England shore, had he exhibited such energy as
was seen in the **gait** and air with which he kept his pace
in the procession. There was no feebleness of step, as at
other times; his frame was not bent; nor did his hand
rest **ominously** upon his heart. Yet, if the clergyman
were rightly viewed, his strength seemed not of the
body. It might be spiritual, and **imparted** to him by
angelic ministrations. It might be the **exhilaration** of

DISTILL (dihs <u>tihl</u>) *v.* **-ing,-ed.**
  to extract the essential parts; to evaporate and collect
  a liquid by condensing it as a means of purification
    Synonyms: clarify, separate; vaporize, precipitate
TEMPERAMENT (<u>tehm</u> puhr uh mehnt) *n.*
  a manner of behaving, an attitude
    Synonyms: disposition, mood, mentality
INVIGORATE (ihn <u>vih</u> guh rayt) *v.* **-ing,-ed.**
  to give life or energy to
    Synonyms: stimulate, strengthen, revitalize
ASCENDING (uh <u>sehn</u> dihng) *adj.*
  rising to another level or climbing; moving upward
    Synonyms: elevating, escalating, mounting;
    hoisting, lifting
PRETERNATURAL (pree tuhr <u>naach</u> uh ruhl) *adj.*
  extraordinary or unnatural
    Synonyms: abnormal, mysterious, odd, unearthly
MORBID (<u>mohr</u> bihd) *adj.*
  1. having an unhealthy mentality; relating to disease
    Synonyms: unwholesome; pathological
  2. abnormally terrible and gloomy; gruesome
    Synonyms: dismal, dreary; grisly, macabre
STEADFASTLY (<u>stehd</u> faast lee) *adv.*
  with persistence, without wavering, loyally
    Synonyms: relentlessly, faithfully, constantly,
    staunchly
SOLITUDE (<u>sahl</u> ih tood) *n.*
  social isolation; time spent alone
    Synonyms: seclusion, withdrawal, retirement;
    loneliness
MELANCHOLY (<u>mehl</u> uhn kahl ee) *adj.*
  sad, depressed
    Synonyms: dejected, despondent, woeful, sorrowful
VENERABLE (<u>veh</u> nehr uh buhl) *adj.*
  respected because of age
    Synonyms: distinguished, elderly

that potent cordial which is **distilled** only in the furnace glow of earnest and long-continued thought. Or, perchance, his sensitive **temperament** was **invigorated** by the loud and piercing music that swelled heavenward, and uplifted him on its **ascending** wave. Nevertheless, so abstracted was his look, it might be questioned whether Mr. Dimmesdale even heard the music. There was his body, moving onward, and with an unaccustomed force. But where was his mind? Far and deep in its own region, busying itself, with **preternatural** activity, to marshal a procession of stately thoughts that were soon to issue thence; and so he saw nothing, heard nothing, knew nothing, of what was around him; but the spiritual element took up the feeble frame, and carried it along, unconscious of the burden, and converting it to spirit like itself. Men of uncommon intellect, who have grown **morbid**, possess this occasional power of mighty effort, into which they throw the life of many days, and then are lifeless for as many more.

Hester Prynne, gazing **steadfastly** at the clergyman, felt a dreary influence come over her, but wherefore or whence she knew not; unless that he seemed so remote from her own sphere, and utterly beyond her reach. One glance of recognition, she had imagined, must needs pass between them. She thought of the dim forest, with its little dell of **solitude**, and love, and anguish, and the mossy tree-trunk, where, sitting hand in hand, they had mingled their sad and passionate talk with the **melancholy** murmur of the brook. How deeply had they known each other then! And was this the man? She hardly knew him now! He, moving proudly past, enveloped, as it were, in the rich music, with the procession of majestic and **venerable** fathers; he, so unattainable in his worldly position, and still more so in that far vista of his unsympathizing thoughts, through which she now beheld him! Her spirit sank with the idea

INTANGIBILITY (ihn taan juh <u>bihl</u> ih tee) *n.*
the quality of being imperceptible, illusory
Synonyms: impalpability, elusiveness, invisibility,
abstraction

SENTIMENT (<u>sehn</u> tuh muhnt) *n.*
an attitude, thought, or judgment prompted by feeling
Synonym: emotion

that all must have been a delusion, and that, vividly as she had dreamed it, there could be no real bond betwixt the clergyman and herself. And thus much of woman was there in Hester, that she could scarcely forgive him—least of all now, when the heavy footstep of their approaching Fate might be heard, nearer, nearer, nearer—for being able so completely to withdraw himself from their mutual world; while she groped darkly, and stretched forth her cold hands, and found him not.

Pearl either saw and responded to her mother's feelings, or herself felt the remoteness and **intangibility** that had fallen around the minister. While the procession passed, the child was uneasy, fluttering up and down like a bird on the point of taking flight. When the whole had gone by, she looked up into Hester's face.

"Mother," said she, "was that the same minister that kissed me by the brook?"

"Hold thy peace, dear little Pearl!" whispered her mother. "We must not always talk in the market-place of what happens to us in the forest."

"I could not be sure that it was he; so strange he looked," continued the child. "Else I would have run to him, and bid him kiss me now, before all the people; even as he did yonder among the dark old trees. What would the minister have said, Mother? Would he have clapped his hand over his heart, and scowled on me, and bid me be gone?"

"What should he say, Pearl," answered Hester, "save that it was no time to kiss, and that kisses are not to be given in the market-place? Well for thee, foolish child, that thou didst not speak to him!"

Another shade of the same **sentiment** in reference to Mr. Dimmesdale was expressed by a person whose eccentricities—or insanity, as we should term it—led her to do what few of the townspeople would have ventured on; to begin a conversation with the wearer of the

RENOWN (rih <u>nown</u>) *n.*
fame, widespread acclaim
Synonyms: eminence, distinction, prestige, standing, celebrity

SUBSEQUENTLY (<u>suhb</u> suh kwehnt lee) *adv.*
in time or order, in succession, behind
Synonyms: next, afterward

WARRANT (<u>wahr</u> ihnt) *v.* **-ing,-ed.**
to guarantee; to give a good reason for
Synonyms: endorse, promise, attest; justify

TRIFLE (<u>trie</u> fuhl) *n.*
something of slight worth or little importance; a slight degree or small amount
Synonyms: triviality, novelty, trinket, bit; speck, fraction, trace, dash

INFIRM (ihn <u>fuhrm</u>) *adj.*
ailing, diseased; weak
Synonyms: ill, afflicted; frail

scarlet letter, in public. It was Mistress Hibbins, who, arrayed in great magnificence, with a triple <u>ruff</u>, a broidered stomacher, a gown of rich velvet, and a gold-headed cane, had come forth to see the procession. As this ancient lady had the **renown** (which **subsequently** cost her no less a price than her life) of being a principal actor in all the works of <u>necromancy</u> that were continually going forward, the crowd gave way before her, and seemed to fear the touch of her garment, as if it carried the plague among its gorgeous folds. Seen in conjunction with Hester Prynne—kindly as so many now felt towards the latter—the dread inspired by Mistress Hibbins was doubled, and caused a general movement from that part of the market-place in which the two women stood.

"Now, what mortal imagination could conceive it!" whispered the old lady confidentially to Hester. "Yonder divine man! That saint on earth, as the people uphold him to be, and as—I must needs say—he really looks! Who, now, that saw him pass in the procession, would think how little while it is since he went forth out of his study—chewing a Hebrew text of Scripture in his mouth, I **warrant**—to take an airing in the forest! Aha! We know what that means, Hester Prynne! But, truly, forsooth, I find it hard to believe him the same man. Many a church-member saw I, walking behind the music, that has danced in the same measure with me, when Somebody was fiddler, and, it might be, an Indian powwow or a lapland wizard changing hands with us! That is but a **trifle**, when a woman knows the world. But this minister! Couldst thou surely tell, Hester, whether he was the same man that encountered thee on the forest-path?"

"Madam, I know not of what you speak," answered Hester Prynne, feeling Mistress Hibbins to be of **infirm** mind; yet strangely startled and awe-stricken by the

AFFIRM (uh <u>fihrm</u>) *v.* **-ing,-ed.**
to assert as valid or confirmed, to state positively
Synonyms: declare, avow, maintain

PIOUS (<u>pie</u> uhs) *adj.*
extremely religious; dedicated, devout
Synonyms: sanctimonious; observant, reverent

DISCLOSE (dihs <u>klohs</u>) *v.* **-ing,-ed.**
to open up, divulge
Synonyms: confide, reveal, impart

PROFOUND (pruh <u>fownd</u>) (proh <u>fownd</u>) *adj.*
deep; having intellectual depth
Synonyms: bottomless; serious, thorough, weighty

REVERENCE (<u>reh</u> vuhr ehnts) *n.*
an act of respect, such as a bow; deep respect, awe
Synonyms: curtsy; veneration, adoration,
admiration

DISCOURSE (<u>dihs</u> kohrs) *n.*
a formal, orderly, and extended expression of
thought; the verbal exchange of ideas
Synonyms: dialogue, conversation; speech

confidence with which she **affirmed** a personal connection between so many persons (herself among them) and the Evil One. "It is not for me to talk lightly of a learned and **pious** minister of the Word, like the Reverend Mr. Dimmesdale!"

"Fie, woman, fie!" cried the old lady, shaking her finger at Hester. "Dost thou think I have been to the forest so many times, and have yet no skill to judge who else has been there? Yea; though no leaf of the wild garlands, which they wore while they danced, be left in their hair! I know thee, Hester; for I behold the token. We may all see it in the sunshine; and it glows like a red flame in the dark. Thou wearest it openly; so there need be no question about that. But this minister! Let me tell thee, in thine ear! When the <u>Black Man</u> sees one of his own servants, signed and sealed, so shy of owning to the bond as is the Reverend Mr. Dimmesdale, he hath a way of ordering matters so that the mark shall be **disclosed** in open daylight to the eyes of all the world! What is it that the minister seeks to hide, with his hand always over his heart? Ha, Hester Prynne!"

"What is it, good Mistress Hibbins?" eagerly asked little Pearl. "Hast thou seen it?"

"No matter, darling!" responded Mistress Hibbins, making Pearl a **profound reverence**. "Thou thyself wilt see it, one time or another. They say, child, thou art of the lineage of the Prince of the Air! Wilt thou ride with me, some fine night, to see thy father? Then thou shalt know wherefore the minister keeps his hand over his heart!"

Laughing so shrilly that all the market-place could hear her, the weird old gentlewoman took her departure.

By this time the preliminary prayer had been offered in the meeting-house, and the accents of the Reverend Mr. Dimmesdale were heard commencing his **discourse**. An irresistible feeling kept Hester near the spot. As the

SAT Vocabulary

EDIFICE (<u>eh</u> duh fuhs) *n.*
a large structure
Synonyms: building, construction, skyscraper
AUDITOR (<u>aw</u> dih tuhr) *n.*
a listener; one who formally examines financial records
Synonyms: hearer, attendee; reviewer, corrector
ENDOWMENT (ehn <u>dow</u> mehnt) (ihn <u>dow</u> mehnt) *n.*
a talent; a gift
Synonyms: ability, aptitude; grant, benefit
CADENCE (<u>kay</u> dihnts) *n. (See page 374.)*
PATHOS (<u>pay</u> thahs) *n.*
a quality that causes deeply emotional feelings; a
feeling of deep emotion
Synonyms: poignancy; suffering, sadness, passion
MEDIUM (<u>mee</u> dee uhm) *n. (See page 416.)*
REPOSE (rih <u>pohz</u>) *v.* **-ing,-ed.**
to relax or rest, to lie
Synonyms: sleep, slumber
ASCEND (uh <u>sehnd</u>) *v.* **-ing,-ed.**
to rise to another level or climb; to move upward
Synonyms: elevate, escalate, mount; hoist, lift
GRADATION (gray <u>day</u> shuhn) *n.*
one stage in a process that occurs by regular degrees;
variation in tone or color
Synonyms: subtlety, nuance; shade, step
SOLEMN (<u>sah</u> luhm) *adj.*
somberly impressive, deeply serious
Synonyms: dignified, earnest, ceremonial
PLAINTIVENESS (<u>playn</u> tihv nehs) *n.*
sadness, lamentation
Synonyms: mourning, melancholy
DESOLATE (<u>deh</u> soh liht) *adj.*
devoid of warmth or comfort; showing the effects of
abandonment or neglect
Synonyms: cheerless, somber, wretched; barren,
bleak, forsaken, vacant
DIFFUSE (dih <u>fyooz</u>) *v.* **-ing,-ed.**
to spread out widely
Synonyms: scatter, disperse

sacred **edifice** was too much thronged to admit another **auditor**, she took up her position close beside the scaffold of the <u>pillory</u>. It was in sufficient proximity to bring the whole sermon to her ears, in the shape of an indistinct, but varied, murmur and flow of the minister's very peculiar voice.

This vocal organ was in itself a rich **endowment**; insomuch that a listener, comprehending nothing of the language in which the preacher spoke, might still have been swayed to and fro by the mere tone and **cadence**. Like all other music, it breathed passion and **pathos**, and emotions high or tender, in a tongue native to the human heart, wherever educated. Muffled as the sound was by its passage through the church-walls, Hester Prynne listened with such intentness, and sympathized so intimately, that the sermon had throughout a meaning for her, entirely apart from its indistinguishable words. These, perhaps, if more distinctly heard, might have been only a grosser **medium**, and have clogged the spiritual sense. Now she caught the low undertone, as of the wind sinking down to **repose** itself; then **ascended** with it, as it rose through progressive **gradations** of sweetness and power, until its volume seemed to envelop her with an atmosphere of awe and **solemn** grandeur. And yet, majestic as the voice sometimes became, there was forever in it an essential character of **plaintiveness**. A loud or low expression of anguish—the whisper, or the shriek, as it might be conceived, of suffering humanity, that touched a sensibility in every bosom! At times this deep strain of **pathos** was all that could be heard, and scarcely heard, sighing amid a **desolate** silence. But even when the minister's voice grew high and commanding—when it gushed irrepressibly upward—when it assumed its utmost breadth and power, so overfilling the church as to burst its way through the solid walls and **diffuse** itself in the open air—still, if the **auditor**

BESEECH (bih <u>seech</u>) *v.* **-ing,-ed.**
to beg, plead, implore
Synonyms: petition, supplicate, entreat

PROFOUND (pruh <u>fownd</u>) (proh <u>fownd</u>) *adj.*
having intellectual depth; deep
Synonyms: serious, thorough, weighty; bottomless

INEVITABLE (ihn <u>ehv</u> ih tuh buhl) *adj. (See page 454.)*

IGNOMINY (<u>ihg</u> nuh mih nee) *n.*
disgrace and dishonor
Synonyms: degradation, debasement

SOMBRE or SOMBER (<u>sahm</u> buhr) *adj. (See page 408.)*

ERRATIC (ih <u>raat</u> ihk) *adj.*
unpredictable, irregular, inconsistent
Synonyms: eccentric, capricious, unstable

UNDULATING (<u>uhn</u> dyoo lay tihng) *adj.*
rolling along in a rippled motion, moving in waves
Synonyms: oscillating, fluctuating, billowing,
surging, pulsating

VIVACITY (vih <u>vahs</u> ih tee) *n.*
liveliness, spiritedness
Synonyms: vibrance, zest

INDEFATIGABLE (ihn dih <u>faat</u> ih guh buhl) *adj.*
incapable of being tired
Synonyms: unflagging, weariless, inexhaustible

DISQUIETUDE (dihs <u>kwie</u> eh tood) *n.*
anxiety, lack of peace or tranquility
Synonyms: edginess, uneasiness

MINUTE (mie <u>noot</u>) (mih <u>noot</u>) *adj.*
very small; precise, detailed
Synonyms: tiny, diminutive, infinitesimal; critical

REQUITAL (rih <u>kwie</u> tuhl) *n.*
repayment, compensation
Synonyms: reciprocation, reimbursement

INCLINE (ihn <u>klien</u>) *v.* **-ing,-ed.**
to have a specific tendency, to be predisposed
Synonyms: lean toward, influence, impel, prefer

listened intently, and for the purpose, he could detect the same cry of pain. What was it? The complaint of a human heart, sorrow-laden, perchance guilty, telling its secret, whether of guilt or sorrow, to the great heart of mankind; **beseeching** its sympathy or forgiveness—at every moment—in each accent—and never in vain! It was this **profound** and continual undertone that gave the clergyman his most appropriate power.

During all this time, Hester stood, statue-like, at the foot of the scaffold. If the minister's voice had not kept her there, there would nevertheless have been an **inevitable** magnetism in that spot, whence she dated the first hour of her life of **ignominy**. There was a sense within her—too ill-defined to be made a thought, but weighing heavily on her mind—that her whole orb of life, both before and after, was connected with this spot, as with the one point that gave it unity.

Little Pearl, meanwhile, had quitted her mother's side, and was playing at her own will about the market-place. She made the **sombre** crowd cheerful by her **erratic** and glistening ray; even as a bird of bright plumage illuminates a whole tree of dusky foliage by darting to and fro, half seen and half concealed amid the twilight of the clustering leaves. She had an **undulating**, but, oftentimes, a sharp and irregular movement. It indicated the restless **vivacity** of her spirit, which today was doubly **indefatigable** in its tiptoe dance, because it was played upon and vibrated with her mother's **disquietude**. Whenever Pearl saw anything to excite her ever-active and wandering curiosity, she flew thitherward, and, as we might say, seized upon that man or thing as her own property, so far as she desired it; but without yielding the **minutest** degree of control over her motions in **requital**. The Puritans looked on, and, if they smiled, were none the less **inclined** to pronounce the child a demon offspring, from the indescribable

AUDACITY (aw <u>daa</u> sih tee) *n.*
boldness, daring
Synonyms: courage, bravery, recklessness

TEMPEST (<u>tehm</u> pehst) *n.*
a storm; rage or fury
Synonyms: inclemency; tumult, turbulence, torrent

charm of beauty and eccentricity that shone through her little figure, and sparkled with its activity. She ran and looked the wild Indian in the face; and he grew conscious of a nature wilder than his own. Thence, with native **audacity**, but still with a reserve as characteristic, she flew into the midst of a group of mariners, the swarthy-cheeked wild men of the ocean, as the Indians were of the land; and they gazed wonderingly and admiringly at Pearl, as if a flake on the sea-foam had taken the shape of a little maid, and were gifted with a soul of the sea-fire that flashes beneath the prow in the night-time.

One of these seafaring men—the shipmaster, indeed, who had spoken to Hester Prynne—was so smitten with Pearl's aspect, that he attempted to lay hands upon her, with purpose to snatch a kiss. Finding it as impossible to touch her as to catch a humming-bird in the air, he took from his hat the gold chain that was twisted about it, and threw it to the child. Pearl immediately twined it around her neck and waist, with such happy skill that, once seen there, it became a part of her, and it was difficult to imagine her without it.

"Thy mother is yonder woman with the scarlet letter," said the seaman. "Wilt thou carry her a message from me?"

"If the message pleases me, I will," answered Pearl.

"Then tell her," rejoined he, "that I spake again with the <u>black-a-visaged</u> hump-shouldered old doctor, and he engages to bring his friend, the gentleman she <u>wots</u> of, aboard with him. So let thy mother take no thought, save for herself and thee. Wilt thou tell her this, thou witch-baby?"

"Mistress Hibbins says my father is the Prince of the Air!" cried Pearl, with a naughty smile. "If thou callest me that ill name, I shall tell him of thee, and he will chase thy ship with a **tempest**!"

STEADFASTLY (<u>stehd</u> faast lee) *adv.*
with persistence, without wavering, loyally
Synonyms: relentlessly, faithfully, constantly, staunchly

COUNTENANCE (<u>kown</u> tuh nuhns) *n.*
appearance, facial expression
Synonyms: face, features, visage

INEVITABLE (ihn <u>ehv</u> ih tuh buhl) *adj.*
certain, unavoidable
Synonyms: inescapable, sure, predictable

LABYRINTH (<u>laab</u> uh rihnth) *n.*
maze
Synonyms: entanglement, mesh, web

PERPLEXITY (puhr <u>plek</u> sih tee) *n.*
the state of being puzzled or confused
Synonyms: bewilderment, distraction, disorientation

BOORISH (<u>bohr</u> ihsh) *adj.*
crude, lacking manners or taste
Synonyms: vulgar, impolite, gruff, uncivilized

UNSCRUPULOUS (uhn <u>skroop</u> yuh luhs) *adj.*
unaware of what is right and wrong, dishonest; hasty and imprecise
Synonyms: shameless, unprincipled, deceitful; unconscientious

REPUGNANCE (rih <u>puhg</u> nehnts) *n.*
strong dislike, distaste, or antagonism; an instance of contradiction or inconsistency
Synonyms: repulsion, aversion; incompatibility

PURPORT (puhr <u>pohrt</u>) *n.*
intention, purpose
Synonyms: importance, meaning

LANGUIDLY (<u>laang</u> gwihd lee) *adv.*
slowly, without energy, indifferently
Synonyms: weakly, listlessly, sluggishly

Pursuing a zigzag course across the market-place, the child returned to her mother and communicated what the mariner had said. Hester's strong, calm, **steadfastly** enduring spirit almost sank, at last, on beholding this dark and grim **countenance** of an **inevitable** doom, which—at the moment when a passage seemed to open for the minister and herself out of their **labyrinth** of misery—showed itself, with an unrelenting smile, right in the midst of their path.

With her mind harassed by the terrible **perplexity** in which the shipmaster's intelligence involved her, she was also subjected to another trial. There were many people present from the country round about who had often heard of the scarlet letter, and to whom it had been made terrific by a hundred false or exaggerated rumors, but who had never beheld it with their own bodily eyes. These, after exhausting other modes of amusement, now thronged about Hester Prynne with rude and **boorish** intrusiveness. **Unscrupulous** as it was, however, it could not bring them nearer than a circuit of several yards. At that distance they accordingly stood, fixed there by the centrifugal force of the **repugnance** which the mystic symbol inspired. The whole gang of sailors, likewise, observing the press of spectators, and learning the **purport** of the scarlet letter, came and thrust their sunburnt and desperado-looking faces into the ring. Even the Indians were affected by a sort of cold shadow of the white man's curiosity, and, gliding through the crowd, fastened their snake-like black eyes on Hester's bosom, conceiving, perhaps, that the wearer of this brilliantly embroidered badge must needs be a personage of high dignity among her people. Lastly, the inhabitants of the town (their own interest in this worn-out subject **languidly** reviving itself, by sympathy with what they saw others feel) lounged idly to the same quarter, and tormented Hester Prynne, perhaps more than all the

IGNOMINY (<u>ihg</u> nuh mih nee) *n.*
disgrace and dishonor
Synonyms: degradation, debasement

IRREVERENT (ih <u>rehv</u> uhr uhnt) *adj.*
disrespectful, gently or humorously mocking
Synonyms: impious, iconoclastic, satirical

SURMISE (suhr <u>miez</u>) *v.* **-ing,-ed.**
to make an educated guess.
Synonyms: conjecture, speculate, infer

STIGMA (<u>stihg</u> mah) *n.*
a mark of disgrace or inferiority
Synonyms: stain, blot, brand, taint

rest, with their cool, well-acquainted gaze at her familiar shame. Hester saw and recognized the self-same faces of that group of matrons, who had awaited her forthcoming from the prison-door, seven years ago; all save one, the youngest and only compassionate among them, whose burial-robe she had since made. At the final hour, when she was so soon to fling aside the burning letter, it had strangely become the centre of more remark and excitement, and was thus made to sear her breast more painfully than at any time since the first day she put it on.

While Hester stood in that magic circle of **ignominy** where the cunning cruelty of her sentence seemed to have fixed her forever, the admirable preacher was looking down from the sacred pulpit upon an audience whose very inmost spirits had yielded to his control. The sainted minister in the church! The woman of the scarlet letter in the market-place! What imagination would have been **irreverent** enough to **surmise** that the same scorching **stigma** was on them both!

ELOQUENT (<u>eh</u> luh kwuhnt) *adj.*
persuasive and effective, with regards to speech
Synonyms: expressive, fluent

PROFOUND (pruh <u>fownd</u>) (proh <u>fownd</u>) *adj.*
having intellectual depth; deep
Synonyms: serious, thorough, weighty; bottomless

ORACLE (<u>or</u> ah kuhl) *n.*
a person who foresees the future and gives advice
Synonyms: seer, prophet, soothsayer, sibyl,
fortuneteller

TUMULT (<u>tuh</u> muhlt) *n.*
state of confusion, agitation
Synonyms: disturbance, turmoil, din, commotion

AUDITOR (<u>aw</u> dih tuhr) *n.*
a listener; one who formally examines financial
records
Synonyms: hearer, attendee; reviewer, corrector

RAPTURE (<u>raap</u> chuhr) *n.*
deep absorption; ecstasy or extreme joy
Synonyms: immersion; exaltation

DESCEND (dih <u>sehnd</u>) (dee <u>sehnd</u>) *v.* **-ing,-ed.**
1. to arrive in an overwhelming way
Synonyms: overtake, cascade, surge
2. to pass from a higher place to a lower place
Synonyms: fall, dismount, gravitate

DISCOURSE (<u>dihs</u> kohrs) *n.*
a formal, orderly, and extended expression of
thought; the verbal exchange of ideas
Synonyms: speech; dialogue, conversation

The Revelation of the Scarlet Letter

Chapter 23

The **eloquent** voice, on which the souls of the listening audience had been borne aloft as on the swelling waves of the sea, at length came to a pause. There was a momentary silence, **profound** as what should follow the utterance of **oracles**. Then ensued a murmur and half-hushed **tumult**; as if the **auditors**, released from the high spell that had transported them into the region of another's mind, were returning into themselves, with all their awe and wonder still heavy on them. In a moment more, the crowd began to gush forth from the doors of the church. Now that there was an end, they needed other breath, more fit to support the gross and earthly life into which they relapsed, than that atmosphere which the preacher had converted into words of flame and had burdened with the rich fragrance of his thought.

In the open air their **rapture** broke into speech. The street and the market-place absolutely babbled, from side to side, with applauses of the minister. His hearers could not rest until they had told one another of what each knew better than he could tell or hear. According to their united testimony, never had man spoken in so wise, so high, and so holy a spirit, as he that spake this day; nor had inspiration ever breathed through mortal lips more evidently than it did through his. Its influence could be seen, as it were, **descending** upon him, and possessing him, and continually lifting him out of the written **discourse** that lay before him, and filling him with ideas that must have been as marvellous to himself as to his audience. His subject, it appeared, had been the

CONSTRAIN (kuhn <u>strayn</u>) *v.* **-ing,-ed.**
   to force, impel; restrain
     Synonyms: prompt, urge; restrict, control, calculate
PROPHET (<u>prah</u> feht) *n.*
   a person who has the ability to foretell events
     Synonyms: clairvoyant, predictor, seer, oracle
DENOUNCE (dih <u>nowns</u>) *v.* **-ing,-ed.**
   1. to pronounce
     Synonyms: proclaim, proscribe
   2. to condemn; to accuse, blame
     Synonyms: censure; criticize, vilify, brand
DISCOURSE (<u>dihs</u> kohrs) *n. (See page 496.)*
PATHOS (<u>pay</u> thahs) *n.*
   a quality that causes deeply emotional feelings; a
   feeling of deep emotion
     Synonyms: poignancy; suffering, sadness, passion
FOREBODING (fohr <u>bohd</u> ihng) *n.*
   a feeling or presentiment of upcoming evil
     Synonyms: prediction, omen, portent
TRANSITORY (<u>traan</u> sih tohr ee) *adj.*
   short-lived, existing only briefly
     Synonyms: transient, ephemeral, fleeting, fugitive,
   momentary
EPOCH (<u>eh</u> pihk) *n.(See page 460.)*
EMINENCE (<u>ehm</u> uh nuhnts) *n.*
   1. a position of distinction or superiority
     Synonyms: prominence, importance
   2. a prominent place, something which projects outward
     Synonyms: elevation, summit, peak
PREVAILING (prih <u>vayl</u> ihng) *adj.*
   lasting; predominant
     Synonyms: persisting, enduring; principle, main
ELOQUENCE (<u>eh</u> luh kwuhns) *n. (See page 284.)*
SANCTITY (<u>saank</u> tih tee) *n.*
   holiness, saintliness
     Synonyms: devoutness, divinity, piety
EXALT (ihg <u>zahlt</u>) *v.* **-ing,-ed.**
   praise, elevate
     Synonyms: important, high-ranking, superior

relation between the Deity and the communities of mankind, with a special reference to the New England which they were here planting in the wilderness. And, as he drew towards the close, a spirit as of prophecy had come upon him, **constraining** him to its purpose as mightily as the old **prophets** of Israel were **constrained**; only with this difference, that, whereas the Jewish seers had **denounced** judgments and ruin on their country, it was his mission to foretell a high and glorious destiny for the newly gathered people of the Lord. But, throughout it all, and through the whole **discourse**, there had been a certain deep, sad undertone of **pathos**, which could not be interpreted otherwise than as the natural regret of one soon to pass away. Yes; their minister whom they so loved—and who so loved them all, that he could not depart heavenward without a sigh—had the **foreboding** of untimely death upon him, and would soon leave them in their tears! This idea of his **transitory** stay on earth gave the last emphasis to the effect which the preacher had produced; it was as if an angel, in his passage to the skies, had shaken his bright wings over the people for an instant—at once a shadow and a splendor—and had shed down a shower of golden truths upon them.

Thus, there had come to the Reverend Mr. Dimmesdale—as to most men, in their various spheres, though seldom recognized until they see it far behind them—an **epoch** of life more brilliant and full of triumph than any previous one, or than any which could hereafter be. He stood, at this moment, on the very proudest **eminence** of superiority, to which the gifts of intellect, rich lore, **prevailing eloquence**, and a reputation of whitest **sanctity**, could **exalt** a clergyman in New England's earliest days, when the professional character was of itself a lofty pedestal. Such was the position which the minister occupied, as he bowed his head

SOLEMN (<u>sah</u> luhm) *adj.*
somberly impressive, deeply serious
Synonyms: dignified, earnest, ceremonial

VENERABLE (<u>veh</u> nehr uh buhl) *adj.*
respected because of age
Synonyms: distinguished, elderly

REVERENTLY (<u>rehv</u> uhr ehn lee) *adv.*
with great awe and respect
Synonyms: devotedly, faithfully, adoringly, admiringly

MAGISTRATE (<u>maa</u> juh strayt) *n.*
an official who can administrate laws
Synonyms: judge, arbiter, authority, marshal

EMINENT (<u>ehm</u> uh nuhnt) *adj.*
celebrated, distinguished, outstanding, towering
Synonyms: noted, famous, prominent, important, illustrious

RENOWNED (rih <u>nownd</u>) *adj.*
famed, having widespread acclaim
Synonyms: eminent, distinguished, prestigious

KINDLE (<u>kihn</u> duhl) *v.* **-ing,-ed.**
to excite or inspire; to set fire to or ignite
Synonyms: arouse, awaken; light, spark

AUDITOR (<u>aw</u> dih tuhr) *n.*
a listener; one who formally examines financial records
Synonyms: hearer, attendee; reviewer, corrector

ELOQUENCE (<u>eh</u> luh kwuhns) *n.*
persuasive and effective speech
Synonyms: expressiveness, fluency

IMPULSE (<u>ihm</u> puhls) *n.*
sudden tendency, inclination
Synonyms: urge, whim

ZENITH (<u>zee</u> nihth) *n.*
highest point, summit
Synonyms: acme, apex, climax, crown, pinnacle

forward on the cushions of the pulpit, at the close of his Election Sermon. Meanwhile Hester Prynne was standing beside the scaffold of the <u>pillory</u>, with the scarlet letter still burning her breast!

Now was heard again the clangor of the music, and the measured tramp of the military escort, issuing from the church-door. The procession was to be marshalled thence to the town-hall, where a **solemn** banquet would complete the ceremonies of the day.

Once more, therefore, the train of **venerable** and majestic fathers was seen moving through a broad pathway of the people, who drew back **reverently** on either side as the Governor and **magistrates**, the old and wise men, the holy ministers, and all that were **eminent** and **renowned**, advanced into the midst of them. When they were fairly in the market-place, their presence was greeted by a shout. This—though doubtless it might acquire additional force and volume from the childlike loyalty which the age awarded to its rulers—was felt to be an irrepressible outburst of enthusiasm **kindled** in the **auditors** by that high strain of **eloquence** which was yet reverberating in their ears. Each felt the **impulse** in himself, and, in the same breath, caught it from his neighbor. Within the church, it had hardly been kept down; beneath the sky, it pealed upward to the **zenith**. There were human beings enough, and enough of highly wrought and symphonious feeling, to produce that more impressive sound than the organ tones of the blast, or the thunder, or the roar of the sea; even that mighty swell of many voices, blended into one great voice by the universal **impulse** which makes likewise one vast heart of the many. Never, from the soil of New England, had gone up such a shout! Never, on New England soil, had stood the man so honored by his mortal brethren as the preacher!

How fared it with him then? Were there not the

ETHEREALIZE (ih <u>theer</u> ee uh liez) *v.* **-ing,-ed.**
to become or make heavenly
Synonym: spiritualize

CIVIL (<u>sih</u> vuhl) *adj.*
involving the public or government; polite
Synonyms: communal; courteous

TOTTER (<u>tah</u> tuhr) *v.* **-ing,-ed.**
to stand with much unsteadiness
Synonyms: wobble, sway, reel, stagger

VENERABLE (<u>veh</u> nehr uh buhl) *adj.*
respected because of age
Synonyms: distinguished, elderly

TREMULOUSLY (<u>treh</u> myoo luhs lee) *adv.*
in a trembling, quivering manner; fearfully, timidly
Synonyms: unsteadily, weakly; timorously,
anxiously

REPEL (rih <u>pehl</u>) *v.* **-ling,-led.**
to rebuff, repulse; to disgust, offend
Synonyms: reject, spurn, parry; nauseate, revolt

IMPERCEPTIBLE (ihn puhr <u>sehp</u> tih buhl) *adj.*
unable to be seen or perceived
Synonyms: unnoticeable, insignificant, invisible,
faint

IGNOMINIOUS (ihg nuh <u>mih</u> nee uhs) *adj.*
disgraceful and dishonorable
Synonyms: despicable, degrading, debasing

brilliant particles of a halo in the air about his head? So **etherealized** by spirit as he was, and so <u>apotheosized</u> by worshipping admirers, did his footsteps, in the procession, really tread upon the dust of earth?

As the ranks of military men and **civil** fathers moved onward, all eyes were turned towards the point where the minister was seen to approach among them. The shout died into a murmur, as one portion of the crowd after another obtained a glimpse of him. How feeble and pale he looked, amid all his triumph! The energy—or say, rather, the inspiration which had held him up until he should have delivered the sacred message that brought its own strength along with it from Heaven—was withdrawn, now that it had so faithfully performed its office. The glow, which they had just before beheld burning on his cheek, was extinguished, like a flame that sinks down hopelessly among the late-decaying embers. It seemed hardly the face of a man alive, with such a deathlike hue; it was hardly a man with life in him that **tottered** on his path so nervelessly, yet **tottered**, and did not fall!

One of his clerical brethren—it was the **venerable** John Wilson—observing the state in which Mr. Dimmesdale was left by the retiring wave of intellect and sensibility, stepped forward hastily to offer his support. The minister **tremulously**, but decidedly, **repelled** the old man's arm. He still walked onward, if that movement could be so described, which rather resembled the wavering effort of an infant with its mother's arms in view, outstretched to tempt him forward. And now, almost **imperceptible** as were the latter steps of his progress, he had come opposite the well-remembered and weather-darkened scaffold, where, long since, with all that dreary lapse of time between, Hester Prynne had encountered the world's **ignominious** stare. There stood Hester, holding little Pearl by the hand! And there

INEVITABLY (ihn <u>ehv</u> ih tuh blee) *adv.*
  certainly, unavoidably
    Synonyms: inescapably, surely, predictably

MAGISTRATE (<u>maa</u> juh strayt) *n.*
  an official who can administrate laws
    Synonyms: judge, arbiter, authority, marshal

INTIMATION (ihn tuh <u>may</u> shuhn) *n.*
  suggestion, clue
    Synonyms: implication, allusion, insinuation

ASCEND (uh <u>sehnd</u>) *v.* **-ing,-ed.**
  to rise to another level or climb; to move upward
    Synonyms: elevate, escalate, mount; hoist, lift

WAX (waaks) *v.* **-ing,-ed.**
  to begin to be; to increase gradually
    Synonyms: become, grow; enlarge, expand, swell

IMPEL (ihm <u>pehl</u>) *v.* **-ling,-led.**
  to urge forward as if driven by a strong moral pressure
    Synonyms: push, prompt, incite, instigate

INEVITABLE (ihn <u>ehv</u> ih tuh buhl) *adj.*
  certain, unavoidable
    Synonyms: inescapable, sure, predictable

was the scarlet letter on her breast! The minister here made a pause, although the music still played the stately and rejoicing march to which the procession moved. It summoned him onward—onward to the festival—but here he made a pause.

Bellingham, for the last few moments, had kept an anxious eye upon him. He now left his own place in the procession, and advanced to give assistance, judging, from Mr. Dimmesdale's aspect, that he must otherwise **inevitably** fall. But there was something in the latter's expression that warned back the **magistrate**, although a man not readily obeying the vague **intimations** that pass from one spirit to another. The crowd, meanwhile, looked on with awe and wonder. This earthly faintness was, in their view, only another phase of the minister's celestial strength; nor would it have seemed a miracle too high to be wrought for one so holy, had he **ascended** before their eyes, **waxing** dimmer and brighter, and fading at last into the light of Heaven.

He turned towards the scaffold, and stretched forth his arms.

"Hester," said he, "come hither! Come, my little Pearl!"

It was a ghastly look with which he regarded them; but there was something at once tender and strangely triumphant in it. The child, with the bird-like motion which was one of her characteristics, flew to him, and clasped her arms about his knees. Hester Prynne—slowly, as if **impelled** by **inevitable** fate, and against her strongest will—likewise drew near, but paused before she reached him. At this instant, old Roger Chillingworth thrust himself through the crowd—or, perhaps so dark, disturbed and evil, was his look, he rose up out of some nether region—to snatch back his victim from what he sought to do! Be that as it might, the old man rushed forward, and caught the minister by the arm.

INFAMY (<u>ihn</u> fuh mee) *n.*
reputation for bad deeds
Synonyms: disgrace, dishonor, shame

TUMULT (<u>tuh</u> muhlt) *n.*
state of confusion, agitation
Synonyms: disturbance, turmoil, din, commotion

PERPLEXED (puhr <u>plekst</u>) *adj.*
puzzled or confused
Synonyms: bewildered, distracted, disoriented

PURPORT (puhr <u>pohrt</u>) *n.*
intention, purpose
Synonyms: importance, meaning

PROVIDENCE (<u>prah</u> vih dehnts) *n.*
divine control and direction by God; preparation
and foresight
Synonyms: fate, destiny, good luck; prudence,
precaution

ASCEND (uh <u>sehnd</u>) *v.* **-ing,-ed.**
to rise to another level or climb; to move upward
Synonyms: elevate, escalate, mount; hoist, lift

"Madman, hold! What is your purpose?" whispered he. "Wave back that woman! Cast off this child! All shall be well! Do not blacken your fame and perish in dishonor! I can yet save you! Would you bring **infamy** on your sacred profession?"

"Ha, tempter! Methinks thou art too late!" answered the minister, encountering his eye, fearfully but firmly. "Thy power is not what it was! With God's help, I shall escape thee now!"

He again extended his hand to the woman of the scarlet letter.

"Hester Prynne," cried he, with a piercing earnestness, "in the name of Him, so terrible and so merciful, who gives me grace, at this last moment, to do what—for my own heavy sin and miserable agony—I withheld myself from doing seven years ago, come hither now, and twine thy strength about me! Thy strength, Hester; but let it be guided by the will which God hath granted me! This wretched and wronged old man is opposing it with all his might, with all his own might, and the fiend's! Come, Hester, come! Support me up yonder scaffold!"

The crowd was in a **tumult**. The men of rank and dignity, who stood more immediately around the clergyman, were so taken by surprise and so **perplexed** as to the **purport** of what they saw—unable to receive the explanation which most readily presented itself, or to imagine any other—that they remained silent and inactive spectators of the judgment which **Providence** seemed about to work. They beheld the minister, leaning on Hester's shoulder and supported by her arm around him, approach the scaffold, and **ascend** its steps; while still the little hand of the sin-born child was clasped in his. Old Roger Chillingworth followed, as one intimately connected with the drama of guilt and sorrow in which they had all been actors, and well entitled, therefore, to be present, at its closing scene.

VENERABLE (<u>veh</u> nehr uh buhl) *adj.*
respected because of age
Synonyms: distinguished, elderly

APPALLED (uh <u>pahld</u>) *adj.*
overcome with shock or dismay
Synonyms: horrified, astounded, petrified

REPENTANCE (rih <u>pehn</u> tehnts) *n.*
sorrow expressed for sins or offenses, penitence
Synonyms: remorse, contrition, apology

SOLEMN (<u>sah</u> luhm) *adj.*
somberly impressive, deeply serious
Synonyms: dignified, earnest, ceremonial

FATHOMLESS (<u>faath</u> uhm lihs) *adj.*
unmeasurable, extremely deep; very difficult to
understand
Synonyms: infinite, unending; incomprehensible

REMORSE (rih <u>mohrs</u>) *n.*
a gnawing distress arising from a sense of guilt
Synonyms: anguish, ruefulness, shame, penitence

"Hadst thou sought the whole earth over," said he, looking darkly at the clergyman, "there was no one place so secret—no high place nor lowly place where thou couldst have escaped me—save on this very scaffold!"

"Thanks be to Him who hath led me hither!" answered the minister.

Yet he trembled, and turned to Hester with an expression of doubt and anxiety in his eyes, not the less evidently betrayed, that there was a feeble smile upon his lips.

"Is not this better," murmured he, "than what we dreamed of in the forest?"

"I know not! I know not!" she hurriedly replied. "Better? Yea; so we may both die, and little Pearl die with us!"

"For thee and Pearl, be it as God shall order," said the minister; "and God is merciful! Let me now do the will which He hath made plain before my sight. For, Hester, I am a dying man. So let me make haste to take my shame upon me!"

Partly supported by Hester Prynne and holding one hand of little Pearl's, the Reverend Mr. Dimmesdale turned to the dignified and **venerable** rulers; to the holy ministers, who were his brethren; to the people, whose great heart was thoroughly **appalled**, yet overflowing with tearful sympathy, as knowing that some deep life-matter—which, if full of sin, was full of anguish and **repentance** likewise—was now to be laid open to them. The sun, but little past its meridian, shone down upon the clergyman, and gave a distinctness to his figure, as he stood out from all the earth to put in his plea of guilty at the bar of Eternal Justice.

"People of New England!" cried he, with a voice that rose over them, high, **solemn**, and majestic—yet had always a tremor through it, and sometimes a shriek, struggling up out of a **fathomless** depth of **remorse** and

SUSTAIN (suh <u>stayn</u>) *v.* **-ing,-ed.**
  to support, uphold; to endure, undergo
    Synonyms: maintain, prop, encourage; withstand

GROVEL (<u>grah</u> vuhl) *v.* **-ling,-led.**
  to humble oneself in a demeaning way
    Synonyms: cringe, fawn, kowtow, bootlick

REPOSE (rih <u>pohz</u>) *n.*
  a state of peace or tranquility; sleep, rest, ease
    Synonyms: calmness, serenity; relaxation, leisure,
    idleness

LURID (<u>loor</u> ihd) *adj.*
  harshly shocking, revolting; glowing
    Synonyms: ghastly, garish, gruesome, grisly,
    macabre; fiery

REPUGNANCE (rih <u>puhg</u> nehnts) *n.*
  strong dislike, distaste, or antagonism; an instance of
  contradiction or inconsistency
    Synonyms: repulsion, aversion; incompatibility

INFAMY (<u>ihn</u> fuh mee) *n.*
  reputation for bad deeds
    Synonyms: disgrace, dishonor, shame

UNDISCLOSED (uhn dihs <u>klohzd</u>) *adj.*
  unknown, hidden
    Synonyms: concealed, secret

MIEN (meen) *n.*
  characteristics expressive of attitude or personality
    Synonyms: manner, demeanor, expression, style

STIGMA (<u>stihg</u> mah) *n.*
  a mark of disgrace or inferiority
    Synonyms: stain, blot, brand, taint

woe. "Ye, that have loved me, ye, that have deemed me holy! Behold me here, the one sinner of the world! At last—at last—I stand upon the spot where, seven years since, I should have stood; here, with this woman, whose arm, more than the little strength wherewith I have crept hitherward, **sustains** me, at this dreadful moment, from **grovelling** down upon my face! Lo, the scarlet letter which Hester wears! Ye have all shuddered at it! Wherever her walk hath been—wherever, so miserably burdened, she may have hoped to find **repose**—it hath cast a **lurid** gleam of awe and horrible **repugnance** round about her. But there stood one in the midst of you, at whose brand of sin and **infamy** ye have not shuddered!"

It seemed, at this point, as if the minister must leave the remainder of his secret **undisclosed**. But he fought back the bodily weakness—and, still more, the faintness of heart—that was striving for the mastery with him. He threw off all assistance, and stepped passionately forward a pace before the woman and the child.

"It was on him!" he continued, with a kind of fierceness, so determined was he to speak out the whole. "God's eye beheld it! The angels were forever pointing at it! The Devil knew it well, and fretted it continually with the touch of his burning finger! But he hid it cunningly from men, and walked among you with the **mien** of a spirit, mournful, because so pure in a sinful world—and sad, because he missed his heavenly kindred! Now, at the death-hour, he stands up before you! He bids you look again at Hester's scarlet letter! He tells you that, with all its mysterious horror, it is but the shadow of what he bears on his own breast, and that even this, his own red **stigma**, is no more than the type of what has seared his inmost heart! Stand any here that question God's judgment on a sinner? Behold! Behold a dreadful witness of it!"

IRREVERENT (ih <u>rehv</u> uhr uhnt) *adj.*
disrespectful, gently or humorously mocking
Synonyms: insulting, impious, iconoclastic, satirical

MULTITUDE (<u>muhl</u> tuh tood) *n.*
a crowd; the state of being many, a great number
Synonyms: throng; mass, myriad

ACUTE (uh <u>kyoot</u>) *adj.*
sharp, pointed, severe; clever, shrewd
Synonyms: intense, fierce; ingenious, keen

COUNTENANCE (<u>kown</u> tuh nuhns) *n.*
appearance, facial expression
Synonyms: face, features, visage

REPOSE (rih <u>pohz</u>) *n.*
a state of peace or tranquility; sleep, rest, ease
Synonyms: calmness, serenity; relaxation, leisure,
idleness

SPORTIVE (<u>spohr</u> tihv) *adj.*
frolicsome, playful
Synonyms: frisky, merry, lively

With a convulsive motion, he tore away the ministerial band from before his breast. It was revealed! But it were **irreverent** to describe that revelation. For an instant, the gaze of the horror-stricken **multitude** was concentred on the ghastly miracle; while the minister stood, with a flush of triumph in his face, as one who, in the crisis of **acutest** pain, had won a victory. Then, down he sank upon the scaffold! Hester partly raised him, and supported his head against her bosom. Old Roger Chillingworth knelt down beside him, with a blank, dull **countenance**, out of which the life seemed to have departed.

"Thou hast escaped me!" he repeated more than once. "Thou hast escaped me!"

"May God forgive thee!" said the minister. "Thou, too, hast deeply sinned!"

He withdrew his dying eyes from the old man, and fixed them on the woman and the child.

"My little Pearl," said he, feebly—and there was a sweet and gentle smile over his face, as of a spirit sinking into deep **repose**; nay, now that the burden was removed, it seemed almost as if he would be **sportive** with the child—"dear little Pearl, wilt thou kiss me now? Thou wouldst not, yonder, in the forest! But now thou wilt?"

Pearl kissed his lips. A spell was broken. The great scene of grief, in which the wild infant bore a part, had developed all her sympathies; and as her tears fell upon her father's cheek, they were the pledge that she would grow up amid human joy and sorrow, nor forever do battle with the world, but be a woman in it. Towards her mother, too, Pearl's errand as a messenger of anguish was all fulfilled.

"Hester," said the clergyman, "farewell!"

"Shall we not meet again?" whispered she, bending her face down close to his. "Shall we not spend our

TREMULOUS (<u>treh</u> myoo luhs) *adj.*
  fearful, timid; trembling, quivering
    Synonyms: timorous, anxious; shaking, palsied

SOLEMNITY (suh <u>lehm</u> nih tee) *n.*
  dignified seriousness
    Synonyms: ceremoniousness, formality

REVERENCE (<u>reh</u> vuhr ehnts) *n.*
  deep respect, awe
    Synonyms: veneration, adoration, admiration

AFFLICTION (uh <u>flihk</u> shuhn) *n.*
  severe distress, persistent anguish
    Synonyms: hurt, calamity, suffering, pain

IGNOMINY (<u>ihg</u> nuh mih nee) *n.*
  disgrace and dishonor
    Synonyms: degradation, debasement

EXPIRING (ehk <u>spier</u> ihng) *adj.*
  dying; come to an end; breathing out
    Synonyms: perishing; terminating; exhaling

MULTITUDE (<u>muhl</u> tuh tood) *n.*
  a crowd; the state of being many, a great number
    Synonyms: throng; mass, myriad

immortal life together? Surely, surely, we have ransomed one another, with all this woe! Thou lookest far into eternity, with those bright dying eyes! Then tell me what thou seest?"

"Hush, Hester, hush!" said he, with **tremulous solemnity**. "The law we broke! The sin here so awfully revealed! Let these alone be in thy thoughts! I fear! I fear! It may be that, when we forgot our God—when we violated our **reverence** each for the other's soul—it was thenceforth vain to hope that we could meet here-after, in an everlasting and pure reunion. God knows; and He is merciful! He hath proved his mercy, most of all, in my **afflictions**. By giving me this burning torture to bear upon my breast! By sending yonder dark and terrible old man to keep the torture always at red-heat! By bringing me hither, to die this death of triumphant **ignominy** before the people! Had either of these agonies been wanting, I had been lost forever! Praised be His name! His will be done! Farewell!"

That final word came forth with the minister's **expiring** breath. The **multitude**, silent till then, broke out in a strange, deep voice of awe and wonder, which could not as yet find utterance, save in this murmur that rolled so heavily after the departed spirit.

CONJECTURAL (kuhn <u>jehk</u> shuhr uhl) *adj.*
speculative, doubtful
Synonyms: supposed, tentative, surmised

AFFIRM (uh <u>fihrm</u>) *v.* **-ing,-ed.**
to assert as valid or confirmed, to state positively
Synonyms: declare, avow, maintain

IGNOMINIOUS (ihg nuh <u>mih</u> nee uhs) *adj.*
disgraceful and dishonorable
Synonyms: despicable, degrading, debasing

PENANCE (<u>peh</u> nihns) *n.*
voluntary suffering to repent for a wrong
Synonyms: atonement, reparation, chastening,
reconciliation

FUTILE (<u>fyoo</u> tuhl) (fyoo <u>tiel</u>) *adj.*
hopeless, useless; serving no useful purpose
Synonyms: ineffective, worthless; unimportant

STIGMA (<u>stihg</u> mah) *n.*
a mark of disgrace or inferiority
Synonyms: stain, blot, brand, taint

SUBSEQUENT (<u>suhb</u> suh kwehnt) *adj.*
following in time or order
Synonyms: succeeding, next, after

REMORSE (rih <u>mohrs</u>) *n.*
a gnawing distress arising from a sense of guilt
Synonyms: anguish, ruefulness, shame, penitence

MANIFEST (<u>maan</u> uh fehst) *v.* **-ing,-ed.**
to make evident or certain by display
Synonyms: exhibit, showcase, expose

PORTENT (<u>pohr</u> tehnt) *n.*
an omen, a sign of what is to come
Synonyms: token, prodigy

Conclusion
Chapter 24

After many days, when time sufficed for the people to arrange their thoughts in reference to the foregoing scene, there was more than one account of what had been witnessed on the scaffold.

Most of the spectators testified to having seen, on the breast of the unhappy minister, a SCARLET LETTER—the very semblance of that worn by Hester Prynne—imprinted in the flesh. As regarded its origin, there were various explanations, all of which must necessarily have been **conjectural**. Some **affirmed** that the Reverend Mr. Dimmesdale, on the very day when Hester Prynne first wore her **ignominious** badge, had begun a course of **penance**—which he afterwards, in so many **futile** methods, followed out—by inflicting a hideous torture on himself. Others contended that the **stigma** had not been produced until a long time **subsequent**, when old Roger Chillingworth, being a potent <u>necromancer</u>, had caused it to appear, through the agency of magic and poisonous drugs. Others, again—and those best able to appreciate the minister's peculiar sensibility, and the wonderful operation of his spirit upon the body—whispered their belief that the awful symbol was the effect of the ever-active tooth of **remorse**, gnawing from the inmost heart outwardly, and at last **manifesting** Heaven's dreadful judgment by the visible presence of the letter. The reader may choose among these theories. We have thrown all the light we could acquire upon the **portent**, and would gladly, now that it has done its office, erase its deep print out of our own brain, where long meditation has fixed it in very undesirable distinctness.

SINGULAR (<u>sihn</u> gyuh luhr) *adj.*
peculiar, uncommon
Synonyms: odd, unique, individual, unusual, rare

REVERENCE (<u>reh</u> vuhr ehnts) *n.*
deep respect, awe
Synonyms: veneration, adoration, admiration

MULTITUDE (<u>muhl</u> tuh tood) *n.*
a crowd; the state of being many, a great number
Synonyms: throng; mass, myriad

DISCERN (dihs <u>uhrn</u>) *v.* **-ing,-ed.**
to perceive or recognize something
Synonyms: descry, observe, glimpse, distinguish

REPUDIATE (rih <u>pyoo</u> dee ayt) *v.* **-ing,-ed.**
to reject as having no authority
Synonyms: disown, abjure, forswear, renounce,
disclaim

MERIT (<u>mehr</u> iht) *n.*
a high quality or excellence; an admirable ability or
attribute
Synonyms: credit, perfection; virtue, capacity,
strength

ASPIRINGLY (uh <u>spier</u> ihng lee) *adv.*
with hopes and goals
Synonyms: eagerly, purposefully, ambitiously

FIDELITY (fih <u>dehl</u> ih tee) (fie <u>dehl</u> ih tee) *n.*
loyalty
Synonyms: allegiance, faithfulness

It is **singular**, nevertheless, that certain persons, who were spectators of the whole scene, and professed never once to have removed their eyes from the Reverend Mr. Dimmesdale, denied that there was any mark whatever on his breast, more than on a new-born infant's. Neither, by their report, had his dying words acknowledged, nor even remotely implied, any, the slightest connection, on his part, with the guilt for which Hester Prynne had so long worn the scarlet letter. According to these highly respectable witnesses, the minister, conscious that he was dying—conscious, also, that the **reverence** of the **multitude** placed him already among saints and angels—had desired, by yielding up his breath in the arms of that fallen woman, to express to the world how utterly <u>nugatory</u> is the choicest of man's own righteousness. After exhausting life in his efforts for mankind's spiritual good, he had made the manner of his death a <u>parable</u>, in order to impress on his admirers the mighty and mournful lesson that, in the view of Infinite Purity, we are sinners all alike. It was to teach them, that the holiest among us has but attained so far above his fellows as to **discern** more clearly the Mercy which looks down, and **repudiate** more utterly the phantom of human **merit**, which would look **aspiringly** upward. Without disputing a truth so momentous, we must be allowed to consider this version of Mr. Dimmesdale's story as only an instance of that stubborn **fidelity** with which a man's friends—and especially a clergyman's—will sometimes uphold his character, when proofs, clear as the mid-day sunshine, on the scarlet letter, establish him a false and sin-stained creature of the dust.

The authority which we have chiefly followed—a manuscript of old date, drawn up from the verbal testimony of individuals, some of whom had known Hester Prynne, while others had heard the tale from

DEMEANOR (dih <u>meen</u> uhr) *n.*
one's behavior or conduct
Synonyms: attitude, disposition, manner, presence

CONSUMMATION (kahn suh <u>may</u> shuhn) *n.*
fulfillment, an ultimate goal
Synonyms: accomplishment, completion, end

FORLORN (fohr <u>lohrn</u>) *adj.*
hopeless, despairing; dreary, deserted; unhappy
Synonyms: dejected, despondent; desolate;
downcast, depressed

DESOLATE (<u>deh</u> soh liht) *adj.*
showing the effects of abandonment or neglect;
devoid of warmth or comfort
Synonyms: barren, bleak, forsaken, vacant;
cheerless, somber, wretched

contemporary witnesses—fully confirms the view taken in the foregoing pages. Among many morals which press upon us from the poor minister's miserable experience, we put only this into a sentence: "Be true! Be true! Be true! Show freely to the world, if not your worst, yet some trait whereby the worst may be inferred!"

Nothing was more remarkable than the change which took place, almost immediately after Mr. Dimmesdale's death, in the appearance and **demeanor** of the old man known as Roger Chillingworth. All his strength and energy—all his vital and intellectual force—seemed at once to desert him; insomuch that he positively withered up, shrivelled away, and almost vanished from mortal sight, like an uprooted weed that lies wilting in the sun. This unhappy man had made the very principle of his life to consist in the pursuit and systematic exercise of revenge; and when, by its completest triumph and **consummation**, that evil principle was left with no further material to support it, when, in short, there was no more Devil's work on earth for him to do, it only remained for the unhumanized mortal to betake himself whither his Master would find him tasks enough, and pay him his wages duly. But to all these shadowy beings, so long our near acquaintances—as well Roger Chillingworth as his companions—we would <u>fain</u> be merciful. It is a curious subject of observation and inquiry, whether hatred and love be not the same thing at bottom. Each, in its utmost development, supposes a high degree of intimacy and heart-knowledge; each renders one individual dependent for the food of his affections and spiritual life upon another; each leaves the passionate lover, or the no less passionate hater, **forlorn** and **desolate** by the withdrawal of his subject. Philosophically considered, therefore, the two passions seem essentially the same, except that one happens to be seen in a celestial radiance, and the other in a dusky and

LURID (<u>loor</u> ihd) *adj.*
    harshly shocking, revolting; glowing
        Synonyms: ghastly, garish, gruesome, grisly,
        macabre; fiery

ANTIPATHY (aan <u>tih</u> puh thee) *n.*
    dislike, hostility, extreme opposition or aversion
        Synonyms: antagonism, enmity, malice

TRANSMUTE (traans <u>myoot</u>) *v.* **-ing,-ed.**
    to change in appearance or shape
        Synonyms: transform, convert, metamorphose

EXECUTOR (ehk <u>sehk</u> yoo tuhr) *n.*
    one who is appointed to carry out the terms of a will
        Synonyms: representative, mediary, advocate

BEQUEATH (bih <u>kweeth</u>) *v.* **-ing.-ed.**
    to give, as in a will; to hand down
        Synonyms: bestow; pass on, transmit

EPOCH (<u>eh</u> pihk) *n.*
    a particular day or time; a specific time in history
        Synonyms: date; period, era, generation

DEVOUT (dih <u>vowt</u>) *adj.*
    devoted, as to religion
        Synonyms: pious, observant, sincere, earnest

lurid glow. In the spiritual world, the old physician and the minister—mutual victims as they have been—may, unawares, have found their earthly stock of hatred and **antipathy transmuted** into golden love.

Leaving this discussion apart, we have a matter of business to communicate to the reader. At old Roger Chillingworth's decease (which took place within the year), and by his last will and testament, of which Governor Bellingham and the Reverend Mr. Wilson were **executors**, he **bequeathed** a very considerable amount of property, both here and in England, to little Pearl, the daughter of Hester Prynne.

So Pearl—the elf-child—the demon offspring, as some people, up to that **epoch**, persisted in considering her—became the richest heiress of her day, in the New World. Not improbably, this circumstance wrought a very material change in the public estimation; and, had the mother and child remained here, little Pearl, at a marriageable period of life, might have mingled her wild blood with the lineage of the **devoutest** <u>Puritan</u> among them all. But, in no time after the physician's death, the wearer of the scarlet letter disappeared, and Pearl along with her. For many years, though a vague report would now and then find its way across the sea—like a shapeless piece of driftwood tossed ashore, with the initials of a name upon it—yet no tidings of them unquestionably authentic were received. The story of the scarlet letter grew into a legend. Its spell, however, was still potent, and kept the scaffold awful where the poor minister had died, and likewise the cottage by the seashore, where Hester Prynne had dwelt. Near this latter spot, one afternoon, some children were at play, when they beheld a tall woman, in a gray robe, approach the cottage-door. In all those years it had never once been opened; but either she unlocked it, or the decaying wood and iron

IMPEDIMENT (ihm <u>pehd</u> uh muhnt) *n.*
barrier, obstacle; speech disorder
Synonyms: obstruction, hindrance, hurdle; lisp

DESOLATE (<u>deh</u> soh liht) *adj.*
devoid of warmth or comfort; showing the effects of
abandonment or neglect
Synonyms: cheerless, somber, wretched; barren,
bleak, forsaken, vacant

FORSAKEN (fohr <u>say</u> kehn) *adj.*
given up, left behind
Synonyms: renounced, abandoned, deserted

RECLUSE (<u>rehk</u> kloos) (rih <u>kloos</u>) *n.*
a person who is shut off from the world
Synonyms: solitaire, hermit

LUXURY (<u>luhg</u> zhoor ee) *n.*
something done or had purely for enjoyment
Synonyms: comfort, indulgence, splendor, frill

TRIFLE (<u>trie</u> fuhl) *n.*
something of slight worth or little importance; a
slight degree or small amount
Synonyms: triviality, novelty, trinket, bit; speck,
fraction, trace, dash

IMPULSE (<u>ihm</u> puhls) *n.*
sudden tendency, inclination
Synonyms: urge, whim

LAVISH (<u>laa</u> vihsh) *adj.*
extravagant; abundant and excessive
Synonyms: luxuriant, sumptuous; overgenerous,
plentiful

TUMULT (<u>tuh</u> muhlt) *n.*
state of confusion, agitation
Synonyms: disturbance, turmoil, din, commotion

SOBER (<u>soh</u> buhr) *adj.*
serious; simple and self-controlled; not intoxicated
Synonyms: subdued; sedate; dry, not drunk

yielded to her hand, or she glided shadowlike through these **impediments**—and, at all events, went in.

On the threshold she paused—turned partly round—for, perchance, the idea of entering all alone, and all so changed, the home of so intense a former life, was more dreary and **desolate** than even she could bear. But her hesitation was only for an instant, though long enough to display a scarlet letter on her breast.

And Hester Prynne had returned, and taken up her long-**forsaken** shame! But where was little Pearl? If still alive, she must now have been in the flush and bloom of early womanhood. None knew—nor ever learned, with the fulness of perfect certainty—whether the elf-child had gone thus untimely to a maiden grave, or whether her wild, rich nature had been softened and subdued, and made capable of a woman's gentle happiness. But, through the remainder of Hester's life, there were indications that the **recluse** of the scarlet letter was the object of love and interest with some inhabitant of another land. Letters came, with armorial seals upon them, though of bearing unknown to English heraldry. In the cottage there were articles of comfort and **luxury** such as Hester never cared to use, but which only wealth could have purchased, and affection have imagined for her. There were **trifles**, too, little ornaments, beautiful tokens of a continual remembrance, that must have been wrought by delicate fingers, at the **impulse** of a fond heart. And, once, Hester was seen embroidering a baby-garment, with such a **lavish** richness of golden fancy as would have raised a public **tumult**, had any infant, thus apparelled, been shown to our **sober**-hued community.

In fine, the gossips of that day believed—and Mr. Surveyor Pue, who made investigations a century later, believed—and one of his recent successors in office, moreover faithfully believes—that Pearl was not only

PENITENCE (<u>peh</u> nih tehnts) *n.*
sorrow expressed for sins or offenses, repentance
Synonyms: remorse, contrition, apology

MAGISTRATE (<u>maa</u> juh strayt) *n.*
an official who can administrate laws
Synonyms: judge, arbiter, authority, marshal

IMPOSE (ihm <u>pohz</u>) *v.* **-ing,-ed.**
to inflict, force upon
Synonyms: dictate, decree, demand, ordain

STIGMA (<u>stihg</u> mah) *n.*
a mark of disgrace or inferiority
Synonyms: stain, blot, brand, taint

REVERENCE (<u>reh</u> vuhr ehnts) *n.*
deep respect, awe
Synonyms: veneration, adoration, admiration

PERPLEXITY (puhr <u>plek</u> sih tee) *n.*
the state of being puzzled or confused
Synonyms: bewilderment, distraction, disorientation

PROPHETESS (<u>prah</u> feh tihs) *n.*
a woman who has the ability to foretell events
Synonyms: clairvoyant, predictor, seer, oracle

alive, but married, and happy, and mindful of her mother, and that she would most joyfully have entertained that sad and lonely mother at her fireside.

But there was a more real life for Hester Prynne here, in New England than in that unknown region where Pearl had found a home. Here had been her sin; here, her sorrow; and here was yet to be her **penitence**. She had returned, therefore, and resumed—of her own free will, for not the sternest **magistrate** of that iron period would have **imposed** it—resumed the symbol of which we have related so dark a tale. Never afterwards did it quit her bosom. But, in the lapse of the toilsome, thoughtful, and self-devoted years that made up Hester's life, the scarlet letter ceased to be a **stigma** which attracted the world's scorn and bitterness, and became a type of something to be sorrowed over, and looked upon with awe, yet with **reverence**, too. And, as Hester Prynne had no selfish ends, nor lived in any measure for her own profit and enjoyment, people brought all their sorrows and **perplexities**, and besought her counsel, as one who had herself gone through a mighty trouble. Women, more especially—in the continually recurring trials of wounded, wasted, wronged, misplaced, or erring and sinful passion—or with the dreary burden of a heart unyielded, because unvalued and unsought—came to Hester's cottage, demanding why they were so wretched, and what the remedy! Hester comforted and counselled them, as best she might. She assured them, too, of her firm belief that, at some brighter period, when the world should have grown ripe for it, in Heaven's own time, a new truth would be revealed, in order to establish the whole relation between man and woman on a surer ground of mutual happiness. Earlier in life, Hester had vainly imagined that she herself might be the destined **prophetess**, but had long since recognized the

ETHEREAL (ih <u>theer</u> ee uhl) *adj.*
  not earthly, spiritual; intangible
    Synonyms: heavenly; diaphanous, airy, gossamer,
    sheer

MEDIUM (<u>mee</u> dee uhm) *n.*
  a substance or object that is used to transmit or
  accomplish something
    Synonyms: means, instrument, vehicle, mechanism

DELVE (dehlv) *v.* **-ing,-ed.**
  to dig; to search or explore intensely
    Synonyms: shovel, excavate; probe, examine,
    research

DISCERN (dihs <u>uhrn</u>) *v.* **-ing,-ed.**
  to perceive or recognize something
    Synonyms: descry, observe, glimpse, distinguish

PERPLEX (puhr <u>pleks</u>) *v.* **-ing,-ed.**
  to puzzle or confuse
    Synonyms: bewilder, distract, disorient

PURPORT (puhr <u>pohrt</u>) *n.*
  intention, purpose
    Synonyms: importance, meaning

SOMBRE or SOMBER (<u>sahm</u> buhr) *adj.*
  melancholy, dismal, dark and gloomy
    Synonyms: serious, grave, mournful, lugubrious,
    funereal

impossibility that any mission of divine and mysterious truth should be confided to a woman stained with sin, bowed down with shame, or even burdened with a life-long sorrow. The angel and apostle of the coming revelation must be a woman indeed, but lofty, pure, and beautiful; and wise, moreover, not through dusky grief, but the **ethereal medium** of joy; and showing how sacred love should make us happy, by the truest test of a life successful to such an end!

So said Hester Prynne, and glanced her sad eyes downward at the scarlet letter. And, after many, many years a new grave was **delved**, near an old and sunken one, in that burial-ground beside which King's Chapel has since been built. It was near that old and sunken grave, yet with a space between, as if the dust of the two sleepers had no right to mingle. Yet one tombstone served for both. All around, there were monuments carved with armorial bearings; and on this simple slab of slate—as the curious investigator may still **discern**, and **perplex** himself with the **purport**—there appeared the semblance of an engraved <u>escutcheon</u>. It bore a device, a herald's wording of which might serve for a motto and brief description of our now concluded legend; so **sombre** is it, and relieved only by one ever-glowing point of light gloomier than the shadow:

"ON A FIELD, SABLE, THE LETTER A, <u>GULES</u>."

Glossary

The following words appear <u>underlined</u> throughout the text:

abstruse (aab <u>stroos</u>) *adj.* difficult to understand

alloy (uh <u>loy</u>) *v.* **-ing,-ed.** to mix or combine

animadversion (aan ihm aad <u>vuhr</u> zhihn) *n.*
 harsh disapproval or opposition

annals (<u>aa</u> nuhls) *n.* a record of historic events

Antinomian (aan tih <u>noh</u> mee ihn) *n.*
 a person who believes that the only virtue needed for
 salvation is one's faith in God

apostolic (aa puh <u>stahl</u> ihk) *adj.*
 relating to or like a religious apostle, ecclesiastic

apotheosize (uh <u>pah</u> thee oh siez) *v.* **-ing,-ed.**
 to treat like a god, to glorify or worship

aqua-vitae (<u>ah</u> kwah veet) *n.* a clear, Scandinavian
liquor

askance (uh <u>skaans</u>) *adv.* with doubt or disapproval

Assabeth (<u>aas</u> uh behth) a river in Massachusetts

bandy (<u>baan</u> dee) *v.* **-ing,-ied.**
 to toss back and forth, to exchange

bedizen (bih <u>die</u> zehn) *v.* **-ing,-ed.**
 to dress in a showy or garish manner

behest (bih <u>hehst</u>) *n.* a command with authority

besom (<u>bee</u> zuhm) *n.* a broom, something which sweeps

betimes (bih <u>tiemz</u>) *adv.* early or quickly; sometimes

betoken (bih <u>toh</u> kehn) *v.* **-ing,-ed.** to signal or indicate

betwixt (bih <u>twihkst</u>) *adv.* between

The Black Man the devil who is believed to live in the
 forest with the witches

black-a-visaged (<u>blaak</u> uh vihz ihjd) *adj.*
 having a dark face or complexion

531

Glossary

blackguard (<u>blaa</u> guhrd) *n.*
a person without morals, a scoundrel

Boreas (<u>bohr</u> ee uhs) *n.* the Greek god of the north wind

buckramed (<u>buhk</u> ruhmd) *adj.* rigid and stiff

Burns, Robert a Scottish poet of the late 1700s

cabalistic (kaa buh <u>lihs</u> tihk) *adj.*
cryptic, having secret meaning

career (kuh <u>reer</u>) *v.* **-ing,-ed.** to move with extreme speed

catechism (<u>kaa</u> tih kih zuhm) *n.* a book or selection of
basic principles on a subject, such as Christianity

chirography (kie <u>rahg</u> ruh fee) *n.* handwriting

chirurgical (kie <u>ruhr</u> jih kuhl) *adj.* surgical

clarion (<u>klaar</u> ee uhn) *n.*
a medieval trumpet-like instrument

coadjutor (koh <u>aa</u> jih tuhr) *n.* a coworker or partner

colloquy (<u>kahl</u> uh kwee) *n.* a formal conversation

compeer (kuhm <u>peer</u>) *n.* a companion or peer

contiguity (kahn tih <u>gyoo</u> ih tee) *n.* closeness, proximity

contumaciously (kahn too <u>may</u> shuhs lee) *adv.*
disobediently, rebelliously

cuirass (kwih <u>raas</u>) *n.* armor for the back and breast plate

cumbrous (<u>kuhm</u> bruhs) *adj.* bulky and cumbersome

depredation (deh prih <u>day</u> shuhn) *n.*
damaging action, destruction

Derby, Elias Hasket He was the "king" shipping pioneer
who opened up trade with the Orient in the late 1700s.

disport (dih <u>spohrt</u>) *v.* **-ing,-ed.**
to entertain oneself in a playful manner

Glossary

dotage (<u>doh</u> tihj) *n.* senility, mental deterioration

dryad (<u>drie</u> ihd) *n.* a nymph that watches over the woods and trees

eldritch (<u>ehl</u> drihch) *adj.* strange, weird, eerie

Emerson, Ralph Waldo an American writer of the 1800s, and leader of transcendentalism

emissary (<u>eh</u> mih sayr ee) *n.* one who acts on someone else's behalf, an agent

emolument (ih <u>mahl</u> yoo mehnt) *n.* payment for a service or employment

encumbrance (ehn <u>kuhm</u> brihnts) *n.* a burden

endue (ehn <u>doo</u>) *v.* **-ing,-ed.** to wear a piece of clothing

Enoch a highly respected man in the bible who was said to "walk with God three hundred years"

escutcheon (ih <u>skuhch</u> ihn) *n.* a shield-like emblem

expatiate (ihk <u>spay</u> shee ayt) *v.* **-ing,-ed.** to give many details in speech or in writing

fain (fayn) *adv.* gladly, rather

festoon (fehs <u>toon</u>) *v.* **-ing,-ed.** to drape something in a decorative manner

firmament (<u>fuhr</u> muh mehnt) *n.* the sky, the heavens

foolscap (<u>fools</u> kaap) *n. British.* a large piece of paper

forenoon (<u>fohr</u> noon) *n.* morning

frontispiece (<u>fruhn</u> tihs pees) *n.* a decorative structure on top of a door or window

galliard (<u>gaal</u> yuhrd) *adj.* lively and happy

gorget (<u>gohr</u> jiht) *n.* armor for the neck and throat

gourmandism (<u>gohr</u> mahn dihz uhm) *n.* excessive eating and drinking, gluttony

Glossary

gouty (<u>gow</u> tee) *adj.* having a bodily condition in which one's joints are painfully inflamed, arthritic

greaves (greevs) *n. pl.* armor for the lower legs

gules (gyoolz) *n.* the color red, represented with lines when on a stone or metal surface

halberd (<u>haal</u> buhrd) *n.*
an axlike weapon with a steel spike on the end

hermitage (<u>huhr</u> mih tihj) *n.* a secluded place, a retreat

heterodox (<u>heht</u> uhr uh dahks) *adj.*
having opinions that oppose those of the church or accepted doctrine

hew (hyoo) *v.* **-ing,-ed, hewn.**
to cut or shape, as if with an ax

hieroglyphic (hie ruh <u>glih</u> fihk) *n.* an undecipherable symbol or piece of illegible writing

imbecility (ihm bih <u>sihl</u> ih tee) *n.* stupidity, idiocy

imbibe (ihm <u>bieb</u>) *v.* **-ing,-ed.**
1. to absorb into one's mind 2. to drink

impost (<u>ihm</u> pohst) *n.* a tax or tariff

inalienable (ihn <u>ayl</u> ee ehn uh buhl) *adj.*
unable to be transferred or taken away

incantation (ihn kaan <u>tay</u> shuhn) *n.*
recitation of a charm or spell for a magical result

inclement (<u>ihn</u> kluh mehnt) *adj.* stormy; severe, harsh

inditing (ihn <u>die</u> tihng) *n.* writing, dictation

insubordination (ihn suh bohr dihn <u>ay</u> shuhn) *n.*
defiance or rebelliousness against authority

intercourse (<u>ihn</u> tuhr kohrs) *n.*
communication between people

Glossary

intervolution (ihn tuhr vuh <u>loo</u> shuhn) *n.*
a coil or spring-like form

inviolable (ihn <u>vie</u> uh luh buhl) *adj.*
unable to be violated or harmed, invincible

irrefragable (ih <u>reh</u> fruh guh buhl) *adj.*
definite, indisputable, proven

Lethe (<u>lee</u> thee) *n.* a river in Greek mythology thought to bring about forgetfulness

Locofoco Surveyor
a slang term for a radical democratic inspector

Longfellow, Henry Wadsworth
a popular American writer of the 1800s

lucubration (loo kyuh <u>bray</u> shuhn) *n.*
a written work produced through laborious efforts

lumber (<u>luhm</u> buhr) *v.* **-ing,-ed.** *British.* to clutter

maw *n.* the mouth of something vicious (i.e. animal, hell)

meed *n.* a repayment or reward

morion (<u>mohr</u> ee ahn) *n.* a soldier's metal helmet

mountebank (<u>mown</u> tuh bangk) *n.* a person who attracts onlookers with flamboyance and trickery

necromancy (<u>neh</u> kruh maan see) *n.* communication with the dead in order to foretell future events

Nepenthe (nih <u>pehn</u> thee) *n.*
an Egyptian drug used to ease pain

nigh (nie) *adv.; adj.* near in location, time, or relation

nugatory (<u>noo</u> guh tohr ee) *adj.* having little or no value

obeisance (oh <u>bay</u> sihnts) *n.* a bow or curtsy, done in order to show reverence or submission

panoply (<u>paan</u> uh plee) *n.* a complete set of armor

Glossary

Papist and Papistry (<u>pay</u> pihst, -stree) *n.* offensive terms
   for a Roman Catholic and the Roman Catholic Church

parable (<u>paa</u> ruh buhl) *n.*
   a short story with a moral lesson, a fable

Paracelsus a Swiss physician of the 1500s who
   arrogantly dubbed himself this name, after Celsus,
   one of the first great medicinal masters

paramour (<u>paa</u> ruh mohr) *n.* a woman's lover

penal (<u>pee</u> nuhl) *adj.* relating to punishment

peradventure (puhr ehd <u>vehn</u> chuhr) *adv.*
   by chance, perhaps

phantasmagoric (faan taaz muh <u>gohr</u> ihk) *adj.*
   surreal, imaginary

pharmacopaeia (fahr muh kuh <u>pee</u> uh) *n.*
   a collection of medicines, a book of medicines

phosphorescent (fahs fuh <u>reh</u> sehnt) *adj.*
   emitting light through the oxidation of phosphorus

pillory (<u>pih</u> luh ree) *n.; v.* **-ing,-ied.**
   a wooden instrument used for public punishment,
   with holes to hold one's head and hands in place;
   to punish in a pillory, to abuse or scorn

pitch (pihch) *v.* **-ing,-ed.** to discard by throwing

pomp (pahmp) *n.* a display of magnificence, splendor

portico (<u>pohr</u> tih koh) *n.*
   an entry porch with a roof supported by columns

posthumous (<u>pahs</u> chuh muhs) *adj.*
   happening after a person's death

prolix and prolixity (pruh <u>lihks</u>, -ih tee) *adj.; n.*
   prolonged, wordy; wordiness, great length

Glossary

propinquity (proh <u>pihng</u> kwih tee) *n.* nearness, proximity

propound (pruh <u>pownd</u>) *v.* **-ing,-ed.**
to suggest for consideration

Protectorate England's government under Lord
Protectorate, Oliver Cromwell and his son, Richard

Puritanism (<u>pyuhr</u> ih tih nihz uhm) *n.*
a sect of English Protestantism which simplified the
cermonial aspects of the Church of England and
enforced a strict lifestyle with few pleasures

quaff (kwahf) *v.* **-ing,-ed.** to drink greedily, to gulp

Quaker (<u>kway</u> kuhr) *n.* a member of the Religious
Society of Friends, a religious sect which the Puritans
opposed

rankle (<u>raang</u> kuhl) *v.* **-ing,-ed.**
to irritate or inflame; to fester

reproof (rih <u>proof</u>) *n.* an act of criticism, a scolding

ruff (ruhf) *n.* a tight, frilly, circular collar

sagamore (<u>saa</u> guh mohr) *n.* an Algonquian Indian chief

schooner (<u>skoo</u> nuhr) *n.*
a sailing vessel with at least two masts

scrofula (<u>skrahf</u> yuh luh) *n.* a strain of tuberculosis that
affects the neck and lymph nodes

scythe (sieth) *n.*
a long, single-edged blade used to cut grass

sepulchre (<u>seh</u> puhl kuhr) *n.* a burial chamber

sere (seer) *adj.* dry and shrivelled

somnambulism (sahm <u>naam</u> byuh lihz uhm) *n.*
sleepwalking

somniferous (sahm <u>nih</u> fuhr uhs) *adj.*
hypnotic, sleep-inducing, tranquilizing

Glossary

spectral (<u>spehk</u> truhl) *adj.* ghostlike, spiritual, hazy

sprite (spriet) *n.* a fairy or pixie-like being

supposition (suh puh <u>zih</u> shuhn) *n.*
an assumption, a hypothesis based on little evidence

tarry (<u>tahr</u> ee) *adj.* resembling tar, blackened or dirty

tarry (<u>taa</u> ree) *v.* **-ing,-ied.** to wait, to loiter or linger

temporal (<u>tehm</u> puhr uhl) *adj.* worldly, real-life

Thoreau, Henry David an American writer of the 1800s known for his transcendental period on Walden Pond

The Town Pump This is a reference to Hawthorne's monologue, told from the point of view of the town pump, in "A Rill from the Town Pump," a story about old Salem.

transfiguration (traanz fih gyuh <u>ray</u> shuhn) *n.*
a conversion, alteration

transfigure (traanz <u>fih</u> gyuhr) *v.* **-ing,-ed.**
to change the appearance or nature of

unbreeched (uhn <u>breechd</u>) *adj.* unclothed

unction (<u>uhnk</u> shuhn) *n.* earnest devotion

vitiate (<u>vihsh</u> ee ayt) *v.* **-ing,-ed.**
to lessen the value of something, to corrupt

vivify (<u>vih</u> vih fie) *v.* **-ing,-ied.**
to give life (to an inanimate object)

vixenly (<u>vihk</u> zehn lee) *adj.* maliciously tempered, often used to describe a female

Wapping a low-class, run-down docking yard in London

Whig (wihg) *n.* a member of a political party that opposed the democratic party in the 1800s

whit (wiht) *n.* a tiny amount, a bit, an iota

wit (wiht) *v.* **wist, witting, wot.** to know or be aware of

❧ Index ❦

N-O

Q-R